OXFORD ENGLISH MEMOIRS AND TRAVELS

General Editor: James Kinsley

A Voyage round the World

RICHARD WALTER
and
BENJAMIN ROBINS

A Voyage round the World

in the Years MDCCXL, I, II, III, IV

by George Anson

Edited with an Introduction by
Glyndwr Williams

LONDON
OXFORD UNIVERSITY PRESS
NEW YORK   TORONTO
1974

Oxford University Press, Ely House, London W1

GLASGOW NEW YORK TORONTO MELBOURNE WELLINGTON
CAPE TOWN IBADAN NAIROBI DAR ES SALAAM LUSAKA ADDIS ABABA
DELHI BOMBAY CALCUTTA MADRAS KARACHI LAHORE DACCA
KUALA LUMPUR SINGAPORE HONG KONG TOKYO

ISBN 0 19 255402 6

Introduction, Bibliography, Notes, and Index
© Oxford University Press 1974

Printed in Great Britain
by W & J Mackay Limited, Chatham

Contents

	Page
Introduction	ix
Note on the Text	xvii
Select Bibliography	xix
The Problem of Authorship	xxi
A VOYAGE ROUND THE WORLD	1
Explanatory Notes	373
Index	396

Illustrations

between pages

George Anson, *c.* 1747

Anson's squadron approaching the Le Maire Straits } 84–5

The Commodore's tent on Juan Fernandes Island

Sea lions

The burning of Paita } 180–1

The watering place at Tinian

A 'flying proa'

The engagement between the *Centurion* and the *Covadonga* } 340–1

Chinese junks

Maps (at end of book)

The track of the *Centurion* round the world

The track of the *Centurion* round Cape Horn

All illustrations are from the 1748 edition of Anson's *Voyage*, with the exception of the portrait of Anson, which is reproduced here by kind permission of the National Maritime Museum, and the chart of the track of the *Centurion* round the world which is taken from the 1780 edition of the *Voyage*.

Introduction

In Hanoverian Britain Anson's voyage round the world was one of the few memorable episodes of the European hostilities of 1739–48. In a drab and wearisome war it stood out as a dramatic highlight. With the final triumph of the seizure of the celebrated Acapulco treasure galleon it captured public attention in a way few of the inconclusive continental campaigns had done. On his return Anson found himself compared with Drake, and his exploits with the half-forgotten feats of arms against the Spain of Philip II. Descriptions of the voyage appeared in newspapers and periodicals; doggerel verses and popular ballads were composed in Anson's honour; unofficial narratives of the voyage were published soon after the expedition's return; and in 1748 the long-awaited authorized account appeared under the name of Richard Walter, chaplain of Anson's flagship the *Centurion*.

If the true authorship of the book has long remained in dispute, of its popularity there can be no doubt. *A Voyage round the World* was by eighteenth-century standards a best-seller. Its first edition in May 1748 attracted more than 1,800 advance subscribers, who included some of the greatest names in the land, and it went through four further editions before the end of the year. It was a classic story of adventure at sea, and a reasoned plea for the expansion of British power and commerce inside the closed world of Spanish America and the Pacific; and in both capacities it retained the interest of the British reading public for the rest of the century. To the modern reader the literary style may seem to veer uneasily between the pedestrian and the turgid, but the narrative has unmistakable power as it unfolds its terrible story of catastrophe and death. And there are some passages of striking quality, notably when the author sketches the demoralizing contrast between carefree expectation and sombre reality which occurred as the expedition struggled to round Cape Horn.*

As an official account the *Voyage* has some expected defects; it is decorous in tone, and eulogistic whenever it refers to Anson. The less inhibited journals of other members of the expedition serve as a corrective to these tendencies, and they have been drawn upon heavily in the present edition. Compared with the slipshod literary efforts of most of Anson's privateering predecessors in the South Seas, the book was a detailed, unsensational work which strove for factual accuracy; and although the expedition was bent on war, not exploration, the number of maps and views in the first edition showed Anson's concern to provide a guide to future voyagers in a region which was still largely uncharted and unknown to British navigators. In this sense it anticipated the monumental works of Cook, Vancouver, and the other Pacific explorers of the second half of the century, for the *Voyage* was above all else a work of information, often downright pedagogic in tone, whose intent was summed up in the Introduction as the encouragement of 'the more important purposes of navigation, commerce, and national interest. . . .'

These considerations were present from the beginning, for the expedition was in origin far more than a predatory raid on Spain's overseas territories. It contains, it is true, an echo of Elizabethan concepts of privateering warfare, of Drake and a long line of semi-piratical ventures. But the significant links were with later developments: the capture of Manila by the British in 1762, the expanding China trade, the opening of the Pacific by Cook and other explorers searching for new markets and bases, and the repeated attempts during the French Revolutionary and Napoleonic wars to force open the shuttered markets of Spanish America. Many of the motives which sent British explorers into the Pacific later in the century are visible in the government discussions of 1739 which led to a decision to fit out a squadron under Anson; and the voyage itself, with its disasters and triumphs vividly narrated in the account of 1748, was to play a prominent part in reawakening British interest in the Pacific.

Anson's instructions were ambitious, allowing as they did for attacks along the Pacific coastline of Spanish America from Chile to Panama, the encouraging of rebellion in Peru, and the capture of the great galleon from Manila off Acapulco. To achieve these objectives

* See pp. 83–90.

Anson was given a squadron consisting of the *Centurion* (60 guns), *Gloucester* and *Severn* (50), *Pearl* (40), *Wager* (28), *Tryal* (8), and two supply vessels. On paper this was a well-balanced fighting force, but to get the vessels to sea, manned and in a fit condition for a voyage to the other side of the world, proved an arduous and depressing task. In competition with fleets fitting out for the Caribbean and home waters, Anson's expedition at Spithead was low on the list of Admiralty priorities. Major repairs were delayed or ignored, while Anson's requests for more sailors were met with an order to make up his complement with men discharged from hospital, drafts brought in by the press gang, and marines quartered near by. Fleets fitting out for sea in the eighteenth century expected to receive their share of human flotsam and jetsam, gaolbirds, and men with neither aptitude nor enthusiasm for life at sea. Only a few years later Dr. Johnson was to write: 'No man will be a sailor who has contrivance enough to get himself into a jail; for being in a ship is being in a jail, with the chance of being drowned.'* It was one of the grim achievements of the Georgian navy that the unpromising material it received was beaten into a disciplined fighting force; but with the pathetic procession of pensioners from Chelsea Hospital which straggled on board Anson's ships in place of the regiment of regular soldiers he had expected nothing could be done. The passionate tones of the 1748 account on this subject clearly reflect Anson's own indignation, for not a single pensioner survived the voyage, and their ill-health in the first months probably contributed to the rapid spread of disease among the crews. To help these veteran invalids storm the bastions of Spanish America 210 marines arrived, so raw that few of them had fired a musket or set foot on board a ship before.

Even when the ships were ready for sea further delays resulted from unfavourable winds and an order to escort a convoy sailing to the West Indies on the first part of its crossing. The expedition did not sail until mid-September 1740, by which time it had lost its most effective weapon—surprise. In October a force of five powerful Spanish ships commanded by Don José Pizarro left Santander to intercept Anson, and the two squadrons missed each other only by the narrowest margin (the *Pearl* was actually sighted and chased by Pizarro's ships). Good

* Samuel Johnson, 16 March 1759. *The Oxford Dictionary of Quotations* (2nd edn., 1953), p. 270.

fortune had helped Anson to evade this superior force, but he soon faced other dangers. Another result of his late start was that he approached Cape Horn in the autumn, when the westerlies were at their fiercest. He met this ordeal with crews already weakened by the ravages of scurvy. This dreadful scourge had swept through the ships, aided by the poor condition of many of the men, overcrowding (with several hundred 'soldiers' on board hammocks were spaced even closer together than the regulation fourteen inches), exposure to wet and cold, and inferior provisions. In the weeks of tremendous gales which buffeted the squadron as it tried to pass into the Pacific men died in their hundreds, the *Wager* was wrecked, and the *Severn* and *Pearl* turned back.

When Anson's remaining warships, the *Centurion*, the *Gloucester*, and the little *Tryal*, limped into the old privateering base of Juan Fernández they had lost two-thirds of their crews. Scurvy had wreaked more havoc than Pizarro's squadron could ever have hoped to do. The *Severn* and *Pearl* were two of Anson's most powerful ships; the *Wager* carried the field-guns, mortars, and ammunition indispensable for land operations. This weakening of the squadron made the full execution of Anson's orders impossible, and wrecked any hopes of aggressive operations against the great cities of Spanish America. The best that could now be expected were hit-and-run raids on Spanish shipping and some of the smaller coastal towns.

As Anson set sail from Juan Fernández with his thinly-manned ships in September 1741 he at least had no thought of returning home. After long, complacent years of security in the Pacific the Spaniards were unprepared for war, and Anson was able to take several prizes and sack the little town of Paita before heading north towards Acapulco. There he intended to lie in wait for the Manila galleon, 'the Prize of all the Oceans'. Each year one or more galleons made the voyage between Manila and Acapulco, at 8,000 miles the longest regular oceanic crossing in the world. From Manila the galleons carried silks, spices, tea, and other oriental luxuries; on the return voyage an even more valuable cargo of silver coin and plate. It was characteristic of the ill-luck which seemed to dog Anson that he arrived off Acapulco three weeks too late to intercept the eastbound galleon as she entered port; and after a long vigil outside the harbour he decided to sail westward across the vast stretches of the north

Pacific to China. On this long run scurvy once more broke out, the *Gloucester* was scuttled, and when Anson arrived at Macao in November 1742 he had only 210 men and one ship left.

Even now Anson's troubles were far from over. The difficulties he encountered in his efforts to refit his ship during the five-month stay at Macao are tartly described in the 1748 account. The East India Company records for their part reveal something of the predicament the Company traders were placed in by the unexpected arrival of a British warship. The Company's trade at Canton depended upon a precarious relationship with the local merchants and the watchful, suspicious Chinese authorities. Subject to stringent restrictions and sometimes under threat of suspension, it would have suffered irreparable damage if Anson had been tempted to use force against the unforthcoming local officials. Notions of total war were still largely unfamiliar in the mid-eighteenth century, and nowhere more so than in a trading centre as remote from Europe and its conflicts as Canton, where ships from nations officially at war ignored each other's presence and concentrated on their lucrative trading activities. Despite Anson's reluctance to accept the painful fact there can be no doubt that his appearance at Macao was an unwelcome embarrassment to all concerned.

In April 1743 the *Centurion*, refitted but manned by less than half her normal complement, left Macao. Ostensibly she was bound for England, after a voyage in which catastrophe had become commonplace, success rare and fleeting. In a bitter letter home from Macao Anson told an acquaintance, 'I am certainly unfortunate, and a fatality attends me.'* He could not bring himself to write at all to his patron, Lord Hardwicke. As he explained later, 'I ought to have wrote to your Lordship on my arrival at Canton . . . but . . . these misfortunes gave me an uneasiness I could not express to your Lordship'.† One exploit alone could redeem the story of repeated disaster—the capture of the treasure galleon from Acapulco on its way into Manila. As the *Centurion* sailed south from Macao, Anson assembled the crew on deck to tell them he was making, not for home, but for Cape Espíritu Santo, the normal landfall of the westbound

* Anson [to James Naish], Canton [December 1742]. Letter in the possession of the late Commander C. G. Pitcairn Jones.

† Anson to Lord Hardwicke, 14 June 1744. B. M. Add. MSS. 35,359, fo. 360.

galleon. After a month's tense wait off the Cape, Anson's look-outs sighted the galleon at daybreak on 20 June 1743. Slowly the two ships closed with each other, soon after noon they opened fire, and after a ninety-minute action at close range the galleon, the *Nuestra Señora de Covadonga*, struck her flag.

The official account gives the accepted English version of the action—of a triumphant battle against odds by a smaller vessel with well under half the complement of the Spaniard. Peircy Brett's sketch of the action which was published in the book gives the same impression as it shows the tall masts and high hull of the galleon looming over the *Centurion*. In reality the odds were weighted heavily against the Spaniard. The *Centurion's* first lieutenant, Philip Saumarez, later went on board the *Covadonga* and wrote that he was 'amazed to think what he could propose against our weight of metal and a ship of our appearance.'* The *Centurion* was a specialist fighting ship mounting sixty guns, twenty-four of them heavy 24-pounders firing a ball which would smash through a ship's side and send a hail of splinters ricochetting across the decks. The *Covadonga* was smaller than the *Centurion*, the heaviest of her cannon were only 12-pounders, and she was essentially a trading vessel, with low bulwarks which gave little protection to the men on deck, and narrow gun-ports which made it impossible to traverse the cannon. Anson's achievement lay, not in defeating the poorly-armed galleon, but in keeping his ship and enough of his crew intact to be able to offer battle in the third year of one of the most arduous voyages in naval history.

Even the Spaniards' numerical superiority, on which the official account laid such stress, was more apparent than real. A statement made by the galleon's commander, Don Gerónimo Montero, after the action showed that of the 530 men on board only 266 were crew-members; most of the rest were servants, passengers, and convicts.†️ The fact that Montero made no attempt to board the *Centurion* does not suggest that he had much confidence in the fighting spirit of his crew. Certainly they did not have the incentive to fight of Anson's men. Of the 227 on board the *Centurion* during the engagement about two-thirds had sailed from England with Anson; the remainder were

* Philip Saumarez MSS., Guernsey, Log IV, 20 June 1743.

†️ Deposition of Don Gerónimo Montero, 21 July 1743. P.R.O. High Court of Admiralty 32/135, Bundle A.

Lascars, Negroes, and Peruvian Indians picked up at various stages of the voyage, and some European seamen who had joined at Macao. Of the original crews of the *Centurion, Gloucester,* and *Tryal* only the hardiest had survived, and confronted with the alternatives of a fortune in prize-money or the inside of a Spanish prison they fought with grim determination. Their temper was noted by an observer on the *Centurion* who wrote that hours before there was any possibility of action, 'the ship was cleared and the guns unlashed in an instant, anything standing in the way, let it belong to who, or be of what value it would, the sailors immediately threw it overboard!'*

From the Philippines the *Centurion* returned with her prize to the Canton River, where once more Anson became involved in protracted disputes with agitated East India Company factors and obstructive Chinese officials. No part of the official account aroused more comment in England than the sections on the expedition's two visits to the Chinese coast, where some forthright comments on the behaviour of the local inhabitants were expressed. In the prevailing climate of thought in Europe these remarks fell little short of lese-majesty. To Voltaire, Diderot and their disciples China was a blessed land free from the superstition, bigotry, and corruption of Europe; but the critical comments of Anson's men were among the first of a series of disillusioning reports which reached home about aspects of Chinese society less admirable than those praised by the ecstatic *philosophes* of western Europe.

The rest of the voyage was a welcome anti-climax as the *Centurion* slipped quietly home by way of the Sunda Strait and the Cape of Good Hope. She arrived in England in June 1744, with 145 out of the original members of the expedition left alive on her. On the six vessels of Anson's squadron which had sailed from Spithead almost four years earlier, only four men had died from enemy action, but more than 1,300 had perished from disease. In England these melancholy figures were swept from sight by the news that on board the *Centurion* was treasure worth 'not much short of £400,000', a colossal sum whose modern equivalent might be about £3,000,000. After the Mediterranean fleet's failure off Toulon in February the navy stood in need of a popular triumph, and the capture of a treasure galleon was in the

* Journal of Lawrence Millechamp, National Maritime Museum, MS. 9354/JOD 36.

public mind the next best thing to a fleet victory. Day after day the newspapers carried reports of the homecoming: the procession of 32 treasure-laden waggons from Portsmouth to London; the feting of Anson and his men; details of the prize-money and the legal dispute over its allocation.

To Anson, himself came fame, fortune, and promotion. As one of the few national heroes to emerge from the war he found the most important posts in the navy open to him. He was a commander who had lost all his ships except one, whose men had died in their hundreds 'like rotten sheep'* while he watched helplessly; but who never wavered in his determination to carry out as much of his task as was humanly possible. On a voyage fraught with appalling stresses he had shown himself to be a just and humane commander who in time of danger worked alongside his men, kept their respect, and was never confronted with a serious threat of mutiny. After his return he was promoted to Rear-Admiral, and appointed to the Board of Admiralty. From 1751 until his death in 1762 he was (with one brief interlude) First Lord of the Admiralty. As he moved into the highest circles of politics and administration Anson did not forget the talented young officers who had sailed with him on the expedition. Under his patronage Brett, Campbell, Denis, Keppel, Parker, and Saunders played prominent parts as captains in the remaining years of the war and in the Seven Years War, and went on to become admirals. To a large extent the navy of the middle decades of the eighteenth century was shaped by Anson and the officers who had accompanied him on his voyage round the world.

* The phrase occurs in a newspaper 'interview' with one of Anson's officers in *The Universal Spectator*, 25 August 1744.

Note on the Text

THE text is printed from a copy in the British Museum of the first edition (671 i. 12), published at London in 1748 by John and Paul Knapton of Ludgate Street; a quarto volume on royal paper, pp. [xxx] + 417. The table of 1,823 subscribers in the preliminaries, and the directives at the end of the volume for placing the plates, have been omitted from the present edition. The errata listed on the last 'Contents' page have been incorporated into the text. Many minor variations of wording, punctuation, and capitalization crept into later editions; none of these are of substance, and they appear to be printer's errors rather than author's revisions.

Select Bibliography

THE first edition of *A Voyage round the World . . . by George Anson* was published in May 1748. The forty-two plates were available separately at 7/- a set. It was followed before the end of the year by four further editions, and by 1776 no fewer than fifteen editions, mostly in the cheaper octavo or duodecimo format, had appeared. Translations into French, Dutch, and German were published in 1749, and an Italian edition in 1756. In London extracts from the book were given in serial form in the newspapers and periodicals of the day, most fully in *The Gentleman's Magazine*, xix (1749), 393–8, 441–6, 543–7; xx (1750), 64–8, 113–16; and abridged versions were included in most of the collections of voyages and travels published in the second half of the century. More recently, the *Voyage* has been reprinted with an introduction by John Masefield (Everyman's Library, 1911), another edition has an introduction and valuable annotations by G. S. Laird Clowes (1928), and an abridged version was published by Penguin Books in 1947 with an introduction and notes by S. W. C. Pack. All these are now out of print.

Among other contemporary narratives of the voyage the earliest general account was published under a *nom de plume*, 'John Philips, Midshipman of the Centurion', *An Authentic Journal of the late Expedition under the command of Commodore Anson . . .* (1744), a book quickly followed by several pirated editions. In 1745 appeared the much superior account by Pascoe Thomas, 'Teacher of the Mathematicks on board the Centurion', *A True and Impartial Journal of a Voyage to the South Seas and Round the Globe in His Majesty's Ship the Centurion . . .* (1745). The events which followed the wreck of the *Wager* gave rise to a whole spate of books by the survivors: John

Bulkeley and John Cummins, *A Voyage to the South-Seas by His Majesty's Ship Wager* (1743); Alexander Campbell, *The Sequel to Bulkeley and Cummins's Voyage to the South-Seas* . . . (1747); Isaac Morris, *A Narrative of the Dangers and Distresses which befell Isaac Morris and seven more of the crew belonging to the Wager* (1750?); [*John Young*], *An affecting narrative of the unfortunate voyage and catastrophe of His Majesty's Ship Wager* . . . (1751); John Byron, *The narrative of . . . the Honourable John Byron . . . containing an account of the great distresses suffered by himself and his companions on the coast of Patagonia* (1768).

There are biographies of Anson, all containing sections on the famous voyage, by Sir John Barrow, *The Life of George Lord Anson* (1839); Walter Vernon Anson, *The Life of Admiral Lord Anson, the Father of the British Navy, 1697–1762* (1912); and S. W. C. Pack, *Admiral Lord Anson* (1960). A full-length study of the expedition based on published sources has been produced by Boyle Somerville, *Commodore Anson's Voyage into the South Seas and around the World* (1934); and there is a good account of the *Wager* episode by S. W. C. Pack, *The Wager Mutiny* (1964). The present editor collected material on the expedition from British, French, and Spanish archives in *Documents relating to Anson's Voyage round the World 1740–1744* (The Navy Records Society, 1967), and first produced his reassessment of the engagement between the *Centurion* and the *Covadonga* in 'Commodore Anson and the Acapulco Galleon' in *History Today*, xvii (1967), 525–32. The standard work on the Pacific galleons remains W. L. Schurz, *The Manila Galleon* (1939). Among more recent books on the voyage, Leo Heaps, *Log of the Centurion* (1973), contains lengthy extracts from the journals of one of the *Centurion*'s officers, Philip Saumarez.

The Problem of Authorship

THE importance and popularity of *A Voyage round the World . . . by George Anson* make it the more puzzling that the question of its authorship has long remained in doubt. The title-page of the first edition is specific enough: the book was 'Compiled From Papers and other Materials of the Right Honourable George Lord Anson, and published under his Direction, By Richard Walter, M.A. Chaplain of his Majesty's Ship the Centurion . . .' Nor does the fact that Walter left the *Centurion* at Canton in December 1742 necessarily invalidate this statement. On p. *365* (p. *326 infra*) the author notes that several officers returned to England in East India Company ships, and that 'I, having obtained the Commodore's leave to return home, embarked with them'. At this point the narrative changes from first to third person, and becomes much more summary—precisely what one would expect in the circumstances. On publication in May 1748 the book was accepted by newspapers and reviews as Walter's work, and no mention was made in print of any other possible author.

Not until 1761 did any published statement appear challenging Walter's position. In that year a volume of *Mathematical Tracts of the late Benjamin Robins, Esq.; Fellow of the Royal Society and Engineer-General to the Honourable the East India Company*, edited by James Wilson, was published in London. In the preface Wilson asserted that Robins, a talented and versatile mathematician, engineer, and pamphleteer,* who had died at Madras in the service of the East India Company in 1751, had written a major part of the *Voyage*:

* Among Robins's scientific publications were several mathematical discourses, numerous papers read to the Royal Society (which awarded him its Copley Medal in 1747) and then printed in the *Philosophical Transactions* and, perhaps his best-known work, *New Principles of Gunnery* (1742). His interest in

. . . what Mr. Walter had done being, as Mr. Robins informed me, almost all taken verbatim from the journals, was to serve as materials only. And upon a strict perusal of both the performances, I find Mr. Robins's to contain about as much matter again as that of Mr. Walter; indeed the introduction entire, with many dissertations in the body of the work, were composed by Mr. Robins, without having the least hint from Mr. Walter's manuscript; and what he had thence transcribed regarded chiefly the wind and weather, the currents, courses, bearings, distances, offings, soundings, moorings, and the qualities of the ground they anchored on, with such particulars, as generally fill up a sailor's account.

Wilson's claims on behalf of his dead friend were accepted by some contemporary reference works, including Andrew Kippis's *Biographia Britannica*, which in its second edition (1778) mentioned the Anson voyage and the 'excellent account that has been written of it by the late Mr. Robins'. Walter was still alive (though seriously ill), but made no attempt to refute these statements, and it was left to his widow Jane, four years after his death in 1785, to write to a relative, John Walter the Charing Cross bookseller, recalling that

During the time of Mr. Walter's writing that voyage, he visited me almost daily previous to our marriage, and I have frequently heard him say how closely he had been engaged in writing for some hours to prepare for his constant attendance upon Lord Anson at six every morning for his approbation, as his Lordship overlooked every sheet that was written. At some of these meetings Mr. Robins assisted, as he was consulted in the disposition of the drawings; and I also know that Mr. Robins left England (for he was sent to Bergen-op-zoom) some months before the publication of the book, and I have frequently seen Mr. Walter correct the proof sheets for the printer.*

A spasmodic correspondence in *Notes and Queries* between 1875 and 1892 brought to light Mrs. Walter's letter and some other documents, including an interesting memoir on Walter by the Cambridge antiquarian William Cole, who had met him

---

gunnery, and his association with Anson, led him in 1747 to publish his *Proposal for increasing the strength of the British Navy by changing all the guns from the eighteen-pounders downwards into others of equal weight but of a greater bore.* As early as 1739 he was writing (anonymously) political pamphlets, often with a strong anti-Spanish tinge, as shown in his *Observations on the Present Convention with Spain* of that year. Robins was appointed engineer-general to the East India Company in 1749, arrived at Madras in July 1750, and died there in July 1751.

* *Notes and Queries*, 8th Series, ii, pp. 86–7.

at Cambridge, where he was Fellow of Sidney College, and was always esteemed as very worthy and sober man. His father was a silk mercer in London. He was rather a puny, weakly, and sickly man, pale and of a low stature, and suffered great hardships on board, being often forced to do the most laborious duty, for want of sufficient hands to work the ship, when at times it was so deplorably overrun with the scurvy. . . . After he got home he married, and settled at Portsmouth, where I think he had one of the churches; and coming sometime afterwards to Cambridge I met him several times. . . .*

But these recollections did little to clear the confused situation left by the contradictory statements made by Wilson and Mrs. Walter. This uncertainty is reflected in the relevant entries in the *Dictionary of National Biography*. In the entry on Robins, Colonel R. H. Vetch confined himself to stating that 'it seems probable that Robins revised and edited the work', and that he was entrusted with a second volume which never appeared. In the entry on Walter, Sir John Knox Laughton was more assertive, pointing out that 'the book is unquestionably the work of a man familiar with the daily life on board a ship of war, and that Robins was not'; and in the entry on Anson contended that 'in any case whether edited by Walter or Robins, the book was virtually written by Anson himself'. One problem is that the evidence found hitherto mostly dates from a period some considerable time after the book's publication; but some intriguing contemporary comments on the book's authorship exist in the correspondence between the Rev. Thomas Birch, F.R.S., F.S.A., and the Hon. Philip Yorke, eldest son of the Lord Chancellor, the Earl of Hardwicke, and from 1748 Anson's brother-in-law. Birch and Yorke collaborated on several literary projects, and each year Birch left his London rectory to spend some time at Yorke's country house at Wrest in Bedfordshire. When living in London Birch wrote to Yorke each week, recounting the political and literary news of the day. From the time of Anson's return to England in 1744 Birch frequently mentioned the celebrated voyage (a subject in which Yorke was naturally interested), and the progress of the account being written of it. Birch was well acquainted with Robins, whom he seems to have met often in London, and the information he gleaned from him he repeated in his letters to Yorke. On 2 September 1746 he wrote:

* *Ibid.*, 7th Series, viii, p. 517.

. . . Mr. Anson has now put his papers into the hands of Mr. Robins, Mr. Walter, the first undertaker, having made scarce any progress in the work, and having little occasion for the emoluments of it since his preferment to the chaplainship of the docks at Portsmouth. Mr. Robins attended the Admiral thither lately, in order to consult the officers engaged in his expedition, and to collect further materials for the history of it. . .*

Independent confirmation of Anson's dissatisfaction with Walter's literary capabilities is contained in the *Anecdotes and Characters* of the Revd. Dr. Alexander Carlyle (written in 1800–4), who was a young man in his early twenties at the time of Anson's return. Among his friends was Captain David Cheap of the *Wager*, who had arrived back in England in April 1746, and, remembered Carlyle, 'Being a Man of Sense and Knowledge, he was employ'd by L⁴ Anson to look out for a Proper Person to write his voyage, the Chaplain whose Journal furnish'd the Chief Materials being unequal to the work'.†

Despite the fact that Robins was not on the voyage it is in some ways easier to accept that a writer of his repute was responsible for an account which is one of the most compelling of sea narratives, than that it was the work of a man who apparently never published another word after the success of 1748. But difficulties remain: in particular the appearance of Walter's name, linked with Anson's, on the title-page; the change from first to third person narration after Walter's departure at Canton; and the testimony of Mrs. Walter's letter. A possible explanation of the first two is that Walter agreed to hand over the material he had collected only on condition that his name was still used; or it may have been that the publishers considered that the book would sell better if ostensibly written by someone who had sailed with Anson. The problem presented by Mrs. Walter's letter cannot be lightly dismissed. Her assertion that Robins was at Bergen-op-zoom before the publication of the book is confirmed by Birch's letters. Robins left England for the Low Countries in August or September 1747, and though the date of his return is not certain he must have been away for much of the time that the book, published the following May, was in the press. It seems fea-

---

* B.M. Add. MSS. 35,397, fo. 20.

† *Anecdotes and Characters of the Times*, ed. James Kinsley, Oxford English Memoirs and Travels, 1973, p. 99. I am indebted to Professor Kinsley for this reference.

sible that it fell to Walter to see the book through the press in Robins's absence, and that proof-reading and correcting formed the main burdens of those labours remembered by his widow more than forty years later.

The weight of evidence strongly suggests that the literary idio-syncrasies of the book derived from Robins's contribution to it in 1746–7. Given Anson's preoccupation with war and politics at this time, and his known aversion to writing, Laughton's assertion that 'the book was virtually written by Anson himself' is unacceptable. But the establishment as co-author (at least) of a man who was not on the voyage, the evidence in Birch's correspondence of Anson's initial determination 'to give the world an account himself',* and Mrs. Walter's recollection of close supervision by Anson of the final stages of the book, point to the *Voyage* as being in every respect an official history. The material for the book clearly came from the journals of several officers, the style would seem to be that of Robins, but there can be no doubt that the perspective was Anson's. The work is valu-able not so much as an impartial account—for that was never its primary purpose—but as a narrative which reflects the views and in places the private thoughts† of the expedition's commanding officer.

* B.M. Add. MSS. 35,396, fo. 258.   † See, e.g., pp. 196, 233, 292, 332-3.

A Voyage round the World

In the Years MDCCXL, I, II, III, IV.

by George Anson

TO HIS GRACE

JOHN

DUKE OF BEDFORD,

MARQUIS OF TAVISTOCK,

EARL OF BEDFORD,

BARON RUSSEL,

BARON RUSSEL OF THORNHAUGH,

AND

BARON HOWLAND *of Streatham;*

One of His Majesty's Principal Secretaries of State; and Lord-Lieutenant, and Custos Rotulorum of the County of Bedford.

My Lord, The following Narrative of a very singular naval achievement is addressed to Your GRACE, both on account of the infinite obligations which the Commander in Chief at all times professes to have received from your Friendship; and also, as the Subject itself naturally claims the patronage of One, under whose direction, the *British* Navy has resumed its ancient Spirit and Lustre, and has in one summer ennobled itself by two victories,[1] the most decisive, and (if the strength and number of the captures be considered) the most important, that are to be met with in our Annals. Indeed, an uninterrupted series of success, and a manifest superiority gained universally over the enemy, both in commerce and glory, seem to be the necessary effects of a revival of strict discipline, and of an unbiassed regard to merit and service. These are marks that must distinguish the happy period of time in which Your GRACE presided, and afford a fitter subject for history, than for an address of this nature. Very signal advantages of rank and distinction, obtained and secured to the naval profession by Your GRACE's auspicious influence, will remain a lasting monument of Your unwearied zeal and attachment to it, and be for ever remembered with the highest gratitude, by all who shall be employed in it. As these were the generous rewards of past exploits, they will be likewise the noblest incentives, and surest pledges of the

3

future. That Your GRACE's eminent talents, magnanimity, and disinterested zeal, whence the Public has already reaped such signal benefits, may in all times prove equally successful in advancing the prosperity of *Great-Britain*, is the ardent wish of,

    My LORD,

        Your GRACE's

           Most obedient,

             Most devoted,

              and

                Most humble Servant,

                  RICHARD WALTER.

CONTENTS

BOOK I.

CHAP. I.
Of the equipment of the squadron: The incidents relating thereto, from its first appointment to its setting sail from St. Helens   19

CHAP. II.
The passage from St. Helens *to the Island of* Madera, *with a short account of that Island, and of our stay there*   30

CHAP. III.
The history of the squadron commanded by Don Joseph Pizarro   35

CHAP. IV.
From Madera *to St.* Catherine's   47

CHAP. V.
Proceedings at St. Catherine's, *and a description of the place, with a short account of* Brazil   54

CHAP. VI.
The run from St. Catherine's *to port St.* Julian, *with some account of that port, and of the country to the southward of the river of* Plate   67

CHAP. VII.
Departure from the bay of St. Julian, *and the passage from thence to Streights* Le Maire   79

CHAP. VIII.
From Streights Le Maire *to Cape* Noir   84

Contents

CHAP. IX.
Observations and directions for facilitating the passage of our future Cruisers round Cape Horn   91

CHAP. X.
From Cape Noir *to the Island of* Juan Fernandes   103

BOOK II.

CHAP. I.
The arrival of the Centurion *at the Island of* Juan Fernandes, *with a description of that Island*   111

CHAP. II.
The arrival of the Gloucester *and the* Anna Pink *at the Island of* Juan Fernandes, *and the transactions at that place during this interval*   126

CHAP. III.
A short narrative of what befel the Anna Pink *before she joined us, with an account of the loss of the* Wager, *and of the putting back of the* Severn *and* Pearl, *the two remaining ships of the squadron*   135

CHAP. IV.
Conclusion of our proceedings at Juan Fernandes, *from the arrival of the* Anna Pink, *to our final departure from thence*   150

CHAP. V.
Our cruise from the time of our leaving Juan Fernandes, *to the taking the town of* Paita   162

CHAP. VI.
The taking of Paita, *and our proceedings till we left the coast of* Peru   178

CHAP. VII.
From our departure from Paita, *to our arrival at* Quibo   193

CHAP. VIII.
Our proceedings at Quibo, *with an account of the place*   201

CHAP. IX.
From Quibo *to the coast of* Mexico   208

Contents

CHAP. X.
An account of the commerce carried on between the city of Manila *on the Island of* Luconia, *and the port of* Acapulco *on the coast of* Mexico   215
CHAP. XI.
Our cruise off the port of Acapulco *for the* Manila *ship*   229
CHAP. XII.
Description of the harbour of Chequetan, *and of the adjacent coast and country*   237
CHAP. XIII.
Our proceedings at Chequetan *and on the adjacent coast, till our setting sail for* Asia   246
CHAP. XIV.
A brief account of what might have been expected from our squadron, had it arrived in the South-Seas *in good time*   255

BOOK III.

CHAP. I.
The run from the coast of Mexico *to the* Ladrones *or* Marian *Islands* 265
CHAP. II.
Our arrival at Tinian, *and an account of the Island, and of our proceedings there, till the* Centurion *drove out to sea*   276
CHAP. III.
Transactions at Tinian *after the departure of the* Centurion   290
CHAP. IV.
Proceedings on board the Centurion, *when driven out to sea*   298
CHAP. V.
Employment at Tinian, *till the final departure of the* Centurion *from thence; with a description of the* Ladrones   301
CHAP. VI.
From Tinian *to* Macao   310
CHAP. VII.
Proceedings at Macao   317

Contents

CHAP. VIII.

From Macao *to Cape* Espiritu Santo: *The taking of the* Manila *galeon, and returning back again*   332

CHAP. IX.

Transactions in the river of Canton   346

CHAP. X.

Proceedings at the city of Canton, *and the return of the* Centurion *to* England   359

Introduction

NOTWITHSTANDING the great improvement of navigation within the last two Centuries, a Voyage round the World is still considered as an enterprize of a very singular nature; and the Public have never failed to be extremely inquisitive about the various accidents and turns of fortune, with which this uncommon attempt is generally attended: And though the amusement expected in a narration of this kind, is doubtless one great source of this curiosity, and a strong incitement with the bulk of readers, yet the more intelligent part of mankind have always agreed, that from these relations, if faithfully executed, the more important purposes of navigation, commerce, and national interest may be greatly promoted: For every authentic account of foreign coasts and countries will contribute to one or more of these great ends, in proportion to the wealth, wants, or commodities of those countries, and our ignorance of those coasts; and therefore a Voyage round the World promises a species of information, of all others the most desirable and interesting; since great part of it is performed in seas, and on coasts, with which we are as yet but very imperfectly acquainted, and in the neighbourhood of a country renowned for the abundance of its wealth, though it is at the same time, stigmatized for its poverty, in the necessaries and conveniences of a civilized life.

These considerations have occasioned the publication of the ensuing work; which, in gratifying the inquisitive turn of mankind, and contributing to the safety and success of future navigators, and to the extension of our commerce and power, may doubtless vie with any narration of this kind hitherto made public: Since the circumstances of this undertaking already known to the world, may be supposed to have strongly excited the general curiosity; for whether we consider the force of the squadron sent on this service, or the diversified distresses that each single ship was separately involved in, or the uncommon instances of varying fortune, which attended the whole enterprize, each part, I conceive, must, from its rude well-known outlines, appear worthy of a compleater and more finished delineation: And if this be allowed with respect to the narrative part of the work, there can be no doubt about the more useful and instructive parts, which are almost every where interwoven with it; for I can venture to affirm, without fear of being contradicted on a comparison, that no voyage I have yet seen, furnishes such a number of views of land, soundings, draughts of roads and ports, charts, and other materials, for the improvement of geography and navigation, as are contained in the ensuing volume;[1] which are of the more importance too, as the greatest part of them relate to such Islands or Coasts, as have been hitherto not at all or erroneously described, and where the want of sufficient and authentic information might occasion future enterprizes to prove abortive, perhaps with the destruction of the men and vessels employed therein.

And besides the number and choice of these marine drawings and descriptions, there is another very essential circumstance belonging to them, which much enhances their value; and that is, the great accuracy they were drawn with. I shall express my opinion of them in this particular very imperfectly, when I say, that they are not exceeded, and perhaps not equalled by any thing of this nature hitherto made public: For they were not copied from the works of others, or composed at home from imperfect accounts, given by incurious and unskilful observers, as hath been frequently the case in these matters; but the greatest part of them were drawn on the spot with the utmost exactness, by the direction, and under the eye of Mr. *Anson* himself; and where (as is the case in three or four of them) they have been done by less skilful hands, or were found in possession of the enemy, and consequently their justness could be less relied on, I have always taken care to apprize the reader of it, and to put him on his guard against giving entire credit to them; although I doubt not, but these less authentic draughts, thus cautiously inserted, are to the full as correct as those, which are usually published on these occasions. For as actual surveys of roads and harbours, and nice and critical delineations of views of land, take up much time and attention, and require a good degree of skill both in planning and drawing, those who are defective in industry and ability, supply these wants by bold conjectures, and fictitious descriptions; and as they can be no otherwise confuted than by going on the spot, and running the risque of suffering by their misinformation, they have no apprehensions of being detected; and therefore, when they intrude their suppositious productions on the Public, they make no conscience of boasting at the same time, with how much skill and care they are performed. And let not those who are unacquainted with naval affairs imagine, that impositions of this kind are of an innocent nature; for as exact views of land are the surest guide to a seaman, on a coast where he has never been before, all fictions in so interesting a matter must be attended with numerous dangers, and sometimes with the destruction of those who are thus unhappily deceived.

Besides these draughts of such places as Mr. *Anson* or the ships under his command have touched at in the course of this expedition, and the descriptions and directions relating thereto, there is inserted, in the ensuing work, an ample description, with a chart annexed to it, of a particular navigation, of which hitherto little more than the name has been known, except to those immediately employed in it: I mean the track described by the *Manila* ship, in her passage to *Acapulco*, through the northern part of the *Pacific* Ocean. This material part is collected from the draughts and journals met with on board the *Manila* galeon, founded on the experience of more than a hundred and fifty years practice, and corroborated in its principal circumstances by the concurrent evidence of all the *Spanish* prisoners taken in that vessel. And as many of their journals, which I have examined, appear to have been not ill kept, I presume, the chart of that northern Ocean, and the particulars of their route through it, may be very safely relied on by future Navigators. The advantages, which may be drawn from an exact knowledge of this navigation, and the beneficial projects that may be formed thereon, both in war and peace, are by no means proper to be discussed in this place: But they will easily offer themselves to the skilful in maritime affairs. However, as the *Manila* ships are the only ones which have ever traversed this vast ocean, except a *French* straggler or two, which have been afterwards seized on the coast of *Mexico*, and as during near two ages, in which this trade has been carried on, the *Spaniards* have, with the greatest care, secreted all accounts of their voyages from the rest of the world; these reasons alone would authorize the insertion of those papers, and would recommend them to the inquisitive, as a very great improvement in geography, and worthy of attention from the singularity of many circumstances recited therein. I must add too, (what in my opinion is far from being the least recommendation of these materials) that the observations of the variation of the compass in that Ocean, which are inserted in the chart from these *Spanish* journals, tend greatly to compleat the general system of the magnetic variation, of infinite import to the commercial and seafaring part of mankind. These observations were, though in vain, often publickly called for by our learned countryman the late Dr. *Halley*, and to his immortal reputation they confirm, as far as they extend, the wonderful hypothesis he had entertained on this head, and very nearly correspond in their quantity, to the predictions he published above fifty years since, long before he was acquainted with any one observation made in those seas.[1] The ascertaining the variation in that part of the world is just now too of more than ordinary consequence, as the Editors of a new variation-chart lately published, have, for want of observations in those parts, been misled by an erroneous analogy, and have mistaken the very species of variation in those northern seas; for they make it westerly where it is easterly, and have laid it down 12° or 13° short of its real quantity.

Thus much it has been thought necessary to premise with regard to the hydrographical and geographical part of the ensuing work; which it is hoped the reader will, on perusal, find much ampler and more important than this slight sketch can well indicate. But as there are hereafter occasionally interspersed some accounts of *Spanish* transactions, and many observations on the disposition of the *American Spaniards*, and on the condition of the countries bordering on the *South-Seas*, and as herein I may appear to differ greatly from the opinions generally established, I think it incumbent on me particularly to recite the authorities I have been guided by on this occasion, that I may not be censured, as having given way either to a thoughtless credulity on one hand, or, what would be a much more criminal imputation, to a wilful and deliberate misrepresentation on the other.

Mr. *Anson*, before he set sail upon this expedition, besides the printed journals to those parts, took care to furnish himself with the best manuscript accounts he could procure of all the *Spanish* settlements upon the coasts of *Chili, Peru* and *Mexico*: These he carefully compared with the examinations of his prisoners, and the informations of several intelligent persons, who fell into his hands in the *South-Seas*. He had likewise the good fortune, in some of his captures, to possess himself of a great number of letters and papers of a public nature, many of them written by the Viceroy of *Peru*, to the Viceroy of *Santa Fee*, to the Presidents of *Panama* and *Chili*, to Don *Blass de Lezo*, Admiral of the galeons, and to divers other persons in public employments; and in these letters there was usually inserted a recital of those they were intended to answer; so that they contained a considerable Part of the correspondence between these officers for some time previous to our arrival on that coast: We took besides many letters sent from persons employed by the Government to their friends and correspondents, which were frequently filled with narrations of public business, and sometimes contained undisguised animadversions on the views and conduct of their superiors. From these materials those accounts of the *Spanish* affairs are taken, which may at first sight appear the most exceptionable. In particular, the history of the various casualties which befel *Pizarro*'s squadron, is for the most part composed from intercepted letters: Though indeed the relation of the insurrection of *Orellana* and his followers, is founded on rather a less disputable authority: For it was taken from the mouth of an *English* Gentleman then on board *Pizarro*, who often conversed with *Orellana*; and it was, on enquiry, confirmed in its principal circumstances by others who were in the ship at the same time.[1] So that the fact, however extraordinary, is, I conceive, not to be contested.

And on this occasion I cannot but mention, that though I have endeavoured, with my utmost care, to adhere strictly to truth in every article of the ensuing narration; yet I am apprehensive, that in so complicated a work, some oversights must have been committed, by the inattention to which at times all mankind are liable. However, I know of none but literal mistakes, some of which are corrected in the table of Errata.[2] And if there are other errors which have escaped me, I flatter myself they are not of moment enough to affect any material transaction, and therefore I hope they may justly claim the readers indulgence.

After this general account of the contents of the ensuing work, it might be expected, perhaps, that I should proceed to the work itself, but I cannot finish this Introduction, without adding a few reflexions on a matter very nearly connected with the present subject; and, as I conceive, neither destitute of utility, nor unworthy the attention of the Public; I mean, the animating my countrymen both in their public and private stations, to the encouragement and pursuit of all kinds of geographical and nautical observations, and of every species of mechanical and commercial information.[1] It is by a settled attachment to these seemingly minute particulars, that our ambitious neighbours have established some part of that power, with which we are now struggling: And as we have the means in our hands of pursuing these subjects more effectually, than they can, it would be a dishonour to us long to neglect so easy and beneficial a practice: For, as we have a Navy much more numerous than theirs, great part of which is always employed in very distant stations, either in the protection of our colonies and commerce, or in assisting our allies against the common enemy, this gives us frequent opportunities of furnishing ourselves with such kind of materials, as are here recommended, and such as might turn greatly to our advantage either in war or peace: For, not to mention what might be expected from the officers of the Navy, if their application to these subjects was properly encouraged, it would create no new expence to the Government to establish a particular regulation for this purpose; since all that would be requisite, would be constantly to embark on board some of our men of war, which are sent on these distant cruises, a person, who with the character of an engineer, and the skill and talents necessary to that profession, should be employed in drawing such coasts, and planning such harbours, as the ship should touch at, and in making such other observations of all kinds, as might either prove of advantage to future Navigators, or might any ways tend to promote the Public service. Besides, persons habituated to this employment (which could not fail at the same time of improving them in their proper business) would be extremely useful in many other lights, and might serve to secure our Fleets from those disgraces, with which their attempts against places on shore have been often attended: And, in a Nation like ours, where all sciences are more eagerly and universally pursued, and better understood than in any other part of the world, proper subjects for such employments could not long be wanting, if due incouragement were given to them. This method here recommended is known to have been frequently practised by the *French*, particularly in the instance of Monsieur *Frezier*, an Engineer, who has published a celebrated voyage to the *South-Seas*:[1] For this person in the year 1711, was purposely sent by the *French* King into that country on board a merchantman, that he might examine and describe the coast, and take plans of all the fortified places, the better to enable the *French* to prosecute their illicit trade, or, in case of a rupture with the court of *Spain*, to form their enterprizes in those seas with more readiness and certainty. Should we pursue this method, we might hope, that the emulation amongst those who were thus employed, and the experience, which even in time of peace, they would hereby acquire, might at length procure us a proper number of able Engineers, and might efface the national scandal, which our deficiency in that species of men has some times exposed us to: And surely, every step to encourage and improve this profession is of great moment to the Public; as no persons, when they are properly instructed, make better returns in war, for the encouragement and emoluments bestowed on them in time of peace. Of which the advantages the *French* have reaped from their dexterity (too numerous and recent to be soon forgot) are an ample confirmation.

And having mentioned Engineers, or such as are skilled in drawing, and the other usual practices of that profession, as the properest persons to be employed in these foreign enquires, I cannot (as it offers itself so naturally to the subject in hand) but lament, how very imperfect many of our accounts of distant countries are rendered by the relators being unskilled in drawing, and in the general principles of surveying; even where other abilities have not been wanting. Had more of our travellers been initiated in these acquirements, and had there been added thereto some little skill in the common astronomical observations, (all which a person of ordinary talents might attain, with a very moderate share of application) we should by this time have seen the geography of the globe much correcter, than we now find it; the dangers of navigation would have been considerably lessened, and the manners, arts and produce of foreign countries would have been much better known to us, than they are. Indeed, when I consider, the strong incitements that all travellers have to acquire some part at least of these qualifications, especially drawing; when I consider how much it would facilitate their observations, assist and strengthen their memories, and of how tedious, and often un-intelligible, a load of description it would rid them, I cannot but wonder that any person, that intends to visit distant countries, with a view of informing either himself or others, should be unfurnished with so useful a piece of skill. And to inforce this argument still further, I must add, that besides the uses of drawing, which are already mentioned, there is one, which, though not so obvious, is yet perhaps of more consequence than all that has been hitherto urged; and that is, that those who are accustomed to draw objects, observe them with more distinctness, than others who are not habituated to this practice. For we may easily find, by a little experience, that in viewing any object however simple, our attention or memory is scarcely at any time so strong, as to enable us, when we have turned our eyes away from it, to recollect exactly every part it consisted of, and to recal all the circumstances of its appearance; since, on examination, it will be discovered, that in some we were mistaken, and others we had totally overlooked: But he that is employed in drawing what he sees, is at the same time employed in rectifying this inattention; for by confronting his ideas copied on the paper, with the object he intends to represent, he finds in what manner he has been deceived in its appearance, and hence he in time acquires the habit of observing much more at one view, and retains what he sees with more correctness than he could ever have done, without his practice and proficiency in drawing.

If what has been said merits the attention of Travellers of all sorts, it is, I think, more particularly applicable to the Gentlemen of the Navy; since, without drawing and planning, neither charts nor views of land can be taken; and without these it is sufficiently evident, that navigation is at a full stand. It is doubtless from a persuasion of the utility of these qualifications, that his Majesty has established a drawing Master at *Portsmouth*, for the instruction of those, who are presumed to be hereafter intrusted with the command of his Royal Navy: And though some have been so far misled, as to suppose that the perfection of Sea-officers consisted in a turn of mind and temper resembling the boisterous element they had to deal with, and have condemned all literature and science as effeminate, and derogatory to that ferocity, which, they would falsely persuade us, was the most unerring characteristic of courage: Yet it is to be hoped, that such absurdities as these have at no time been authorised by the Public

16

opinion, and that the belief of them daily diminishes. If those who adhere to these mischievous positions were capable of being influenced by reason, or swayed by example, I should think it sufficient for their conviction to observe, that the most valuable drawings inserted in the following work, though done with such a degree of skill, that even professed artists can with difficulty imitate them, were taken by Mr. *Peircy Brett*, one of Mr. *Anson's* Lieutenants, and since Captain of the *Lion* man of war; who, in his memorable engagement with the *Elizabeth* (for the importance of the service, or the resolution with which it was conducted, inferiour to none this age has seen) has given ample proof, that a proficiency in the arts I have been here recommending is extremely consistent with the most exemplary bravery, and the most distinguished skill in every function belonging to the duty of a Sea-officer. Indeed, when the many branches of science are considered, of which even the common practice of navigation is composed, and the many improvements, which men of skill have added to this practice within these few years, it would induce one to believe, that the advantages of reflection and speculative knowledge were in no profession more eminent than in that of a sea-officer: For, not to mention some expertness in geography, geometry and astronomy, which it would be dishonourable for him to be without, (as his journal and his estimate of the daily position of the ship are no more than the practice of particular branches of these arts) it may be well supposed, that the management and working of a ship, the discovery of her most eligible position in the water, (usually stiled her Trim) and the disposition of her sails in the most advantageous manner, are articles, wherein the knowledge of mechanics cannot but be greatly assistant: And perhaps the application of this kind of knowledge to naval subjects may produce as great improvements in sailing and working a ship, as it has already done in many other matters conducive to the ease and convenience of human life: For when the fabric of a ship, and the variety of her sails are considered, together with the artificial contrivances of adapting them to her different motions, as it cannot be doubted, but these things have been brought about by more than ordinary sagacity and invention, so neither can it be doubted but that a speculative and scientific turn of mind may find out the means of directing and disposing this complicated mechanism much more advantageously than can be done by mere habit, or by a servile copying

17

of what others may perhaps have erroneously practised in the like emergency: But it is time to finish this digression and to leave the reader to the perusal of the ensuing work; which, with how little art soever it may be executed, will yet, from the importance of the subject, and the utility and excellence of the materials, merit some share of the Public attention.

BOOK I.

CHAP. I.

Of the equipment of the squadron: The incidents
relating thereto, from its first appointment to its
setting sail from St. *Helens*.

THE squadron under the Command of Mr. *Anson* (of which I here
propose to recite the most material proceedings) having undergone
many changes in its destination, its force, and its equipment, in the
ten months between its first appointment and its final sailing from St.
Helens; I conceive the history of these alterations is a detail necessary
to be made public, both for the honour of those who first planned and
promoted this enterprize, and for the justification of those who have
been entrusted with its execution. Since it will from hence appear, that
the accidents the expedition was afterwards exposed to, and which
prevented it from producing all the national advantages the strength
of the squadron, and the expectation of the public, seemed to presage,
were principally owing to a series of interruptions, which delayed the
Commander in the course of his preparations, and which it exceeded
his utmost industry either to avoid or to get removed.

When in the latter end of the summer of the year 1739, it was
foreseen that a war with *Spain* was inevitable, it was the opinion of
several considerable persons then trusted with the Administration of
affairs, that the most prudent step the Nation could take, on the
breaking out of the war, was attacking that Crown in her distant
settlements; for by this means (as at that time there was the greatest
probability of success) it was supposed that we should cut off the
principal resources of the enemy, and reduce them to the necessity of
sincerely desiring a peace, as they would hereby be deprived of the
returns of that treasure by which alone they could be enabled to carry
on a war.

In pursuance of these sentiments, several projects were examined,
and several resolutions taken in Council. And in all these deliberations

19

it was from the first determined, that *George Anson*, Esq; then Captain of the *Centurion*, should be employed as Commander in Chief of an expedition of this kind: And he then being absent on a cruize, a vessel was dispatched to his station so early as the beginning of *September*, to order him to return with his ship to *Portsmouth*. And soon after he came there, that is, on the 10th of *November* following, he received a letter from Sir *Charles Wager*,[1] ordering him to repair to *London*, and to attend the board of Admiralty: Where, when he arrived, he was informed by Sir *Charles*, that two Squadrons would be immediately fitted out for two secret expeditions, which however would have some connexion with each other: That he, Mr. *Anson*, was intended to command one of them, and Mr. *Cornwall* (who hath since lost his life gloriously in the defence of his Country's honour) the other: That the squadron under Mr. *Anson* was to take on board three Independent Companies of a hundred men each, and *Bland's* regiment of Foot: That Colonel *Bland* was likewise to imbark with his regiment, and to command the land-forces: And that, as soon as this squadron could be fitted for the sea, they were to set sail, with express orders to touch at no place till they came to *Java-Head* in the *East-Indies*: That there they were only to stop to take in water, and thence to proceed directly to the city of *Manila*, situated on *Luconia*, one of the *Philippine* Islands: That the other squadron was to be of equal force with this commanded by Mr. *Anson*, and was intended to pass round Cape *Horn* into the *South-Seas*, and there to range along that coast; and after cruizing upon the enemy in those parts, and attempting their settlements, this squadron in its return was to rendezvous at *Manila*, and there to join the squadron under Mr. *Anson*, where they were to refresh their men, and refit their ships, and perhaps receive further orders.

This scheme was doubtless extremely well projected, and could not but greatly advance the Public Service, and at the same time the reputation and fortune of those concerned in its execution; for had Mr. *Anson* proceeded for *Manila* at the time and in the manner proposed by Sir *Charles Wager*, he would, in all probability, have arrived there before they had received any advice of the war between us and *Spain*, and consequently before they had been in the least prepared for the reception of an enemy, or had any apprehensions of their danger. The city of *Manila* might be well supposed to have been at that time in the same defenceless condition with all the other *Spanish* settlements, just at the breaking out of the war: That is to say, their fortifications neglected, and in many places decayed; their cannon dismounted, or useless by the mouldring of their carriages; their magazines, whether of military stores or provision, all empty; their garrisons unpaid, and consequently thin, ill-affected, and dispirited; and the royal chests in *Peru*, whence alone all these disorders could receive their redress, drained to the very bottom: This, from the intercepted letters of their Viceroys and Governors, is well known to have been the defenceless state of *Panama*, and the other *Spanish* places on the coast of the *South-Sea*, for near a twelvemonth after our declaration of war. And it cannot be supposed that the city of *Manila*, removed still farther by almost half the circumference of the globe, should have experienced from the *Spanish* Government, a greater share of attention and concern for its security, than *Panama*, and the other important ports in *Peru* and *Chili*, on which their possession of that immense Empire depends. Indeed, it is well known, that *Manila* was at that time incapable of making any considerable defence, and in all probability would have surrendered only on the appearance of our squadron before it. The consequence of this city, and the island it stands on, may be in some measure estimated, from the healthiness of its air, the excellency of its port and bay, the number and wealth of its inhabitants, and the very extensive and beneficial commerce which it carries on to the principal Ports in the *East-Indies*, and *China*, and its exclusive trade to *Acapulco*, the returns for which, being made in silver, are, upon the lowest valuation, not less than three millions of Dollars *per annum*.

And on this Scheme Sir *Charles Wager* was so intent, that in a few days after this first conference, that is, on *November* 18, Mr. *Anson* received an order to take under his command the *Argyle*, *Severn*, *Pearl*, *Wager*, and *Tryal Sloop*; and other orders were issued to him in the same month, and in the *December* following, relating to the victualling of this squadron. But Mr. *Anson* attending the Admiralty the beginning of *January*, he was informed by Sir *Charles Wager*, that for reasons with which he, Sir *Charles*, was not acquainted, the expedition to *Manila* was laid aside.[1] It may be conceived, that Mr. *Anson* was extremely chagrined at the losing the command of so infallible, so honourable, and in every respect, so desirable an enterprize, especially too as he had already, at a very great expence, made the necessary provision for his own accommodation in this voyage, which he had reason to expect would prove a very long one. However, Sir *Charles*, to render this disappointment in some degree more tolerable, informed him that the expedition to the *South-Seas* was still intended, and that he, Mr. *Anson*, and his squadron, as their first destination was now countermanded, should be employed in that service. And on the 10th of *January* he received his commission, appointing him Commander in Chief of the forementioned squadron, which (the *Argyle* being in the course of their preparation changed for the *Gloucester*) was the same he sailed with above eight months after from St. *Helens*. On this change of destination, the equipment of the squadron was still prosecuted with as much vigour as ever, and the victualling, and what ever depended on the Commodore, was so far advanced, that he conceived the ships might be capable of putting to sea the instant he should receive his final orders, of which he was in daily expectation. And at last, on the 28th of *June* 1740, the Duke of *Newcastle*, Principal Secretary of State, delivered to him his Majesty's instructions, dated *January* 31, 1739,[1] with an additional instruction from the Lords Justices, dated *June* 19, 1740. On the receipt of these, Mr. *Anson* immediately repaired to *Spithead*, with a resolution to sail with the first fair wind, flattering himself that all his delays were now at an end. For though he knew by the musters that his squadron wanted three hundred seamen of their complement, (a deficiency which, with all his assiduity, he had not been able to get supplied) yet, as Sir *Charles Wager* informed him, that an order from the board of Admiralty was dispatched to Sir *John Norris* to spare him the numbers which he wanted, he doubted not of his complying therewith. But on his arrival at *Portsmouth*, he found himself greatly mistaken, and disappointed in this persuasion: for on his application, Sir *John Norris* told him, he could spare him none, for he wanted men for his own fleet. This occasioned an inevitable and a very considerable delay; for it was the end of *July* before this deficiency was by any means supplied, and all that was then done was extremely short of his necessities and expectation. For Admiral *Balchen*, who succeeded to the command at *Spithead*, after Sir *John Norris* had sailed to the westward, instead of three hundred able sailors, which Mr. *Anson* wanted of his complement, ordered on board the squadron a hundred and seventy men only;

of which thirty-two were from the hospital and sick quarters, thirty-seven from the *Salisbury*, with three officers of Colonel *Lowther's* regiment, and ninety-eight marines, and these were all that were ever granted to make up the forementioned deficiency.

But the Commodore's mortification did not end here. It has been already observed, that it was at first intended that Colonel *Bland's* regiment, and three independent companies of a hundred men each, should embark as land-forces on board the squadron. But this disposition was now changed, and all the land-forces that were to be allowed, were five hundred invalids to be collected from the out-pensioners of *Chelsea* college. As these out-pensioners consist of soldiers, who from their age, wounds, or other infirmities, are incapable of service in marching regiments, Mr. *Anson* was greatly chagrined at having such a decrepid detachment allotted him; for he was fully persuaded that the greatest part of them would perish long before they arrived at the scene of action, since the delays he had already encountered, necessarily confined his passage round Cape *Horn* to the most rigorous season of the year. Sir *Charles Wager* too joined in opinion with the Commodore, that invalids were no ways proper for this service, and sollicited strenuously to have them exchanged;[1] but he was told that persons, who were supposed to be better judges of soldiers than he or Mr. *Anson*, thought them the properest men that could be employed on this occasion. And upon this determination they were ordered on board the squadron on the 5th of *August*: But instead of five hundred, there came on board no more than two hundred and fifty-nine; for all those who had limbs and strength to walk out of *Portsmouth* deserted, leaving behind them only such as were literally invalids, most of them being sixty years of age, and some of them upwards of seventy. Indeed it is difficult to conceive a more moving scene than the imbarkation of these unhappy veterans: They were themselves extremely averse to the service they were engaged in, and fully apprized of all the disasters they were afterwards exposed to; the apprehensions of which were strongly mark'd by the concern that appeared in their countenances, which was mixed with no small degree of indignation, to be thus hurried from their repose into a fatiguing employ, to which neither the strength of their bodies, nor the vigour of their minds, were any ways proportioned, and where, without seeing the face of an enemy, or in the least promoting the success of the enterprize they were engaged in, they would in all probability uselessly perish by lingring and painful diseases; and this too, after they had spent the activity and strength of their youth in their Country's service.

And I cannot but observe, on this melancholy incident, how extremely unfortunate it was, both to this aged and diseased detachment, and to the expedition they were employed in; that amongst all the outpensioners of *Chelsea* Hospital, which were supposed to amount to two thousand men, the most crazy and infirm only should be culled out for so fatiguing and perilous an undertaking. For it was well known, that however unfit, invalids in general might be for this service, yet by a prudent choice, there might have been found amongst them five hundred men who had some remains of vigour left: And Mr. *Anson* fully expected, that the best of them would have been allotted him; whereas the whole detachment that was sent to him, seemed to be made up of the most decrepid and miserable objects, that could be collected out of the whole body; and by the desertion above-mentioned, these were a second time cleared of that little health and strength which were to be found amongst them, and he was to take up with such as were much fitter for an infirmary, than for any military duty.

And here it is necessary to mention another material particular in the equipment of this squadron. It was proposed to Mr. *Anson*, after it was resolved that he should be sent to the *South-Seas*, to take with him two persons under the denomination of Agent Victuallers. Those who were mentioned for this employment had formerly been in the *Spanish West-Indies*, in the *South-Sea* Company's service, and it was supposed that by their knowledge and intelligence on that coast, they might often procure provisions for him by compact with the inhabitants, when it was not to be got by force of arms: These Agent Victuallers were, for this purpose, to be allowed to carry to the value of 15,000 *l.* in merchandize on board the squadron; for they had represented, that it would be much easier for them to procure provisions with goods, than with the value of the same goods in money. Whatever colours were given to this scheme, it was difficult to persuade the generality of mankind, that it was not principally intended for the enrichment of the Agents, by the beneficial commerce they proposed to carry on upon that coast. Mr. *Anson*, from the beginning, objected both to the appointment of Agent Victuallers, and the allowing them to carry a cargo on board the squadron: For he conceived, that in those few amicable ports where the squadron might touch, he needed not their assistance to contract for any provisions the place afforded; and on the enemy's coast, he did not imagine that they could ever procure him the necessaries he should want, unless (which he was resolved not to comply with) the military operations of his squadron were to be regulated by the ridiculous views of their trading projects. All that he thought the Government ought to have done on this occasion, was to put on board to the value of 2 or 3000 *l.* only of such goods, as the *Indians,* or the *Spanish* Planters in the less culti-vated parts of the coast, might be tempted with; since it was in such places only that he imagined it would be worth while to truck with the enemy for provisions: And in these places it was sufficiently evident, a very small cargo would suffice.

But though the Commodore objected both to the appointment of these officers, and to their project; yet, as they had insinuated that their scheme, besides victualling the squadron, might contribute to settling a trade upon that coast, which might be afterwards carried on without difficulty, and might thereby prove a very considerable national advantage, they were much listened to by some considerable persons: And of the 15,000 *l.* which was to be the amount of their cargo, the Government agreed to advance them 10,000 upon imprest, and the remaining 5000 they raised on bottomry bonds; and the goods pur-chased with this sum, were all that were taken to sea by the squadron, how much soever the amount of them might be afterwards magnified by common report.[1]

This cargo was at first shipped on board the *Wager* Store Ship, and one of the Victuallers; no part of it being admitted on board the men of war. But when the Commodore was at St. *Catherine's,* he considered, that in case the squadron should be separated, it might be pretended that some of the ships were disappointed of provisions for want of a cargo to truck with, and therefore he distributed some of the least bulky commodities on board the men of war, leaving the remainder principally on board the *Wager,* where it was lost: And more of the goods perishing by various accidents to be recited hereafter, and no part of them being disposed of upon the coast, the few that came home to *England,* did not produce, when sold, above a fourth part of the original price. So true was the Commodore's prediction about the event of this project, which had been by many considered as infallibly productive of immense gains. But to return to the transactions at *Portsmouth*.

To supply the place of the two hundred and forty invalids which had deserted, as is mentioned above, there were ordered on board two hundred and ten marines detached from different regiments: These were raw and undisciplined men, for they were just raised, and had scarcely any thing more of the soldier than their regimentals, none of them having been so far trained, as to be permitted to fire.[1] The last detachment of these marines came on board the 8th of *August*, and on the 10th the squadron sailed from *Spithead* to St. *Helens*, there to wait for a wind to proceed on the expedition.

But the delays we had already suffered had not yet spent all their influence, for we were now advanced into a season of the year, when the westerly winds are usually very constant, and very violent; and it was thought proper that we should put to sea in company with the fleet commanded by Admiral *Balchen*, and the expedition under Lord *Cathcart*. And as we made up in all twenty-one men of war, and a hundred and twenty-four sail of merchantmen and transports, we had no hopes of getting out of the Channel with so large a number of ships, without the continuance of a fair wind, for some considerable time. This was what we had every day less and less reason to expect, as the time of the equinox drew near; so that our golden dreams, and our ideal possession of the *Peruvian* treasures, grew each day more faint, and the difficulties and dangers of the passage round Cape *Horn* in the winter season filled our imaginations in their room.[2] For it was forty days from our arrival at St. *Helens*, to our final departure from thence: And even then (having orders to proceed without Lord *Cathcart*) we tided it down the Channel with a contrary wind. But this interval of forty days was not free from the displeasing fatigue of often setting sail, and being as often obliged to return; nor exempt from dangers, greater than have been sometimes experienced in surrounding the globe. For the wind coming fair for the first time, on the 23rd of *August*, we got under sail, and Mr. *Balchen* shewed himself truly solicitous to have proceeded to sea, but the wind soon returning to its old quarter, obliged us to put back to St. *Helens*, not without considerable hazard, and some damage received by two of the transports, who, in tacking, ran foul of each other: Besides this, we made two or three more attempts to sail, but without any better success. And, on the 6th of *September*, being returned to an anchor at St. *Helens*, after one of these fruitless efforts, the wind blew so fresh, that the whole fleet struck their yards and topmasts to prevent their driving: And, notwithstanding this precaution, the *Centurion* drove the next evening, and brought both cables a-head, and we were in no small danger of driving foul of the Prince *Frederick*, a seventy-gun ship, moored at a small distance under our stern; which we happily escaped, by her driving at the same time, and so preserving her distance: nor did we think ourselves secure, till we at last let go the sheet anchor, which fortunately brought us up.

However, on the 9th *September*, we were in some degree relieved from this lingring vexatious situation, by an Order which Mr. *Anson* received from the Lords Justices, to put to sea the first opportunity with his own squadron only, if Lord *Cathcart* should not be ready. Being thus free from the troublesome company of so large a fleet, our Commodore resolved to weigh and tide it down Channel, as soon as the weather should become sufficiently moderate; and this might easily have been done with our own squadron alone full two months sooner, had the orders of the Admiralty, for supplying us with seamen, been punctually complied with, and had we met with none of those other delays mentioned in this narration. It is true, our hopes of a speedy departure were even now somewhat damped, by a subsequent order which Mr. *Anson* received on the 12th of *September*; for by that he was required to take under his convoy the St. *Albans* with the *Turkey* fleet, and to join the *Dragon*, and the *Winchester*, with the *Streights* and the *American* trade at *Torbay* or *Plymouth*, and to proceed with them to sea as far as their way and ours lay together: This incumbrance of a convoy gave us some uneasiness, as we feared it might prove the means of lengthening our passage to the *Maderas*. However, Mr. *Anson*, now having the command himself, resolved to adhere to his former determination, and to tide it down the Channel with the first moderate weather; and that the junction of his Convoy might occasion as little a loss of time as possible, he immediately sent directions to *Torbay*, that the fleets he was there to take under his care, might be in a readiness to join him instantly on his approach. And at last, on the 18th of *September*, he weighed from St. *Helens*; and though the wind was at first contrary, had the good fortune to get clear of the Channel in four days, as will be more particularly related in the ensuing chapter.

Having thus gone through the respective steps taken in the equipment of this squadron, it is sufficiently obvious how different an aspect this expedition bore at its first appointment in the beginning of *January*, from what it had in the latter end of *September*, when it left the Channel; and how much its numbers, its strength, and the probability of its success were diminished, by the various incidents which took place in that interval. For instead of having all our old and ordinary seamen exchanged for such as were young and able, (which the Commodore was at first promised) and having our numbers compleated to their full complement, we were obliged to retain our first crews, which were very indifferent; and a deficiency of three hundred men in our numbers was no otherwise made up to us, than by sending us on board a hundred and seventy men, the greatest part composed of such as were discharged from hospitals, or new-raised marines who had never been at sea before. And in the land-forces allotted us, the change was still more disadvantageous; for there, instead of three independent companies of a hundred men each, and *Bland*'s regiment of foot, which was an old one, we had only four hundred and seventy invalids and marines, one part of them incapable for action by age and infirmities, and the other part useless by their ignorance of their duty. But the diminishing the strength of the squadron was not the greatest inconveniency which attended these alterations; for the contests, representations, and difficulties which they continually produced, (as we have above seen, that in these cases the authority of the Admiralty was not always submitted to) occasioned a delay and waste of time, which in its consequences was the source of all the disasters to which this enterprize was afterwards exposed: for by this means we were obliged to make our passage round Cape *Horn* in the most tempestuous season of the year; whence proceeded the separation of our squadron, the loss of numbers of our men, and the imminent hazard of our total destruction: And by this delay too, the enemy had been so well informed of our designs, that a person who had been employed in the *South-Sea* Company's service, and arrived from *Panama* three or four days before we left *Portsmouth*, was able to relate to Mr. *Anson* most of the particulars of the destination and strength of our squadron, from what he had learnt amongst the *Spaniards* before he left them.[1] And this was afterwards confirmed by a more extraordinary circumstance: For we shall find, that when the *Spaniards* (fully satisfied that our expedition was intended for the *South-Seas*) had fitted out a squadron to oppose us, which had so far got the start of us, as to arrive before us off the island of *Madera*, the Commander of this squadron was so well instructed in the form and make of Mr. *Anson's* broad pennant, and had imitated it so exactly, that he thereby decoyed the *Pearl*, one of our squadron, within gun-shot of him, before the Captain of the *Pearl* was able to discover his mistake.

CHAP. II.

The passage from St. *Helens* to the Island of *Madera*; with a short account of that Island, and of our stay there.

ON the 18th of *September*, 1740, the squadron, as we have observed in the preceding chapter, weighed from St. *Helens* with a contrary wind, the Commodore proposing to tide it down the Channel, as he dreaded less the inconveniencies he should thereby have to struggle with, than the risk he should run of ruining the enterprize, by an uncertain, and, in all probability, a tedious attendance for a fair wind.

The squadron allotted to this service consisted of five men of war, a sloop of war, and two victualling ships. They were the *Centurion* of sixty guns, four hundred men, *George Anson*, Esq; Commander; the *Gloucester* of fifty guns, three hundred men, *Richard Norris* Commander; the *Severn* of fifty guns, three hundred men, the Honourable *Edward Legg* Commander; the *Pearl* of forty guns, two hundred and fifty men, *Matthew Mitchel* Commander; the *Wager* of twenty-eight guns, one hundred and sixty men, *Dandy Kidd* Commander; and the *Tryal* Sloop of eight guns, one hundred men, the Honourable *John Murray*[1] Commander; the two Victuallers were Pinks,[2] the largest of about four hundred, and the other of about two hundred tons burthen, these were to attend us, till the provisions we had taken on board were so far consumed, as to make room for the additional quantity they carried with them, which, when we had taken into our ships, they were to be discharged. Besides the complement of men born by the above-mentioned ships as their crews, there were embarked on board the squadron about four hundred and seventy invalids and marines, under the denomination of land-forces, as has been particularly mentioned in the preceding chapter, which were commanded by Lieutenant Colonel *Cracherode*. With this squadron, together with the St. *Albans* and the *Lark*, and the trade under their convoy, Mr. *Anson*, after weighing from St. *Helens*, tided it down the Channel for the first forty-eight hours; and, on the 20th, in the morning, we discovered off the *Ram-*

Head the *Dragon, Winchester, South-Sea Castle,* and *Rye,* with a number of merchantmen under their Convoy: These we joined about noon the same day, our Commodore having orders to see them (together with the St. *Albans* and *Lark*) as far into the sea as their course and ours lay together.When we came in sight of this last mentioned fleet, Mr. *Anson* first hoisted his broad pennant, and was saluted by all the men of war in company.

When we had joined this last Convoy, we made up eleven men of war, and about one hundred and fifty sail of merchantmen, consisting of the *Turky,* the *Streights,* and the *American* trade. Mr. *Anson,* the same day, made a signal for all the Captains of the men of war to come on board him, where he delivered them their fighting and sailing instructions, and then, with a fair wind, we all stood towards the South-West; and the next day at noon, being the 21st, we had run forty leagues from the *Ram-Head*; and being now clear of the land, our Commodore, to render our view more extensive, ordered Captain *Mitchel,* in the *Pearl,* to make sail two leagues a-head of the fleet every morning, and to repair to his station every evening. Thus we proceeded till the 25th, when the *Winchester* and the *American* Convoy made the concerted signal for leave to separate, which being answered by the Commodore, they left us: As the St. *Albans* and the *Dragon,* with the *Turky* and *Streights* Convoy, did on the 29th. After which separation, there remained in company only our own squadron and our two victuallers, with which we kept on our course for the Island of *Madera.* But the winds were so contrary, that we had the mortification to be forty days in our passage thither from St. *Helens,* though it is known to be often done in ten or twelve. This delay was a most unpleasing circumstance, productive of much discontent and ill-humour amongst our people, of which those only can have a tolerable idea, who have had the experience of a like situation. And besides the peevishness and despondency which foul and contrary winds, and a lingring voyage never fail to create on all occasions, we, in particular, had very substantial reasons to be greatly alarmed at this unexpected impediment. For as we had departed from *England* much later than we ought to have done, we had placed almost all our hopes of success in the chance of retrieving in some measure at sea, the time we had so unhappily wasted at *Spithead* and St. *Helens.* However, at last, on *Monday, October* the 25th, at five in the morning, we, to our great joy,

31

made the land, and in the afternoon came to an anchor in *Madera Road*, in forty fathom water; the *Brazen-head* bearing from us E by S, the *Loo* N N W, and the great Church N N E. We had hardly let go our anchor, when an *English* privateer sloop ran under our stern, and saluted the Commodore with nine guns, which we returned with five. And, the next day, the Consul of the Island coming to visit the Commodore, we saluted him with nine guns on his coming on board.

This Island of *Madera*, where we are now arrived, is famous through all our *American* settlements for its excellent wines, which seem to be designed by Providence for the refreshment of the inhabitants of the Torrid Zone. It is situated in a fine climate, in the latitude of 32:27 North; and in the longitude from *London* of, by our different reckonings from 18°½ to 19°½ West, though laid down in the charts in 17°.[1] It is composed of one continued hill, of a considerable height, extending itself from East to West: The declivity of which, on the South-side, is cultivated and interspersed with vineyards; and in the midst of this slope the Merchants have fixed their country seats, which help to form an agreeable prospect. There is but one considerable town in the whole Island, it is named *Fonchiale*, and is seated on the South part of the Island, at the bottom of a large bay. This is the only place of trade, and indeed the only one where it is possible for a boat to land. *Fonchiale*, towards the sea, is defended by a high wall, with a battery of cannon, besides a castle on the *Loo*, which is a rock standing in the water at a small distance from the shore. Even here the beach is covered with large stones, and a violent surf continually beats upon it; so that the Commodore did not care to venture the ships long boats to fetch the water off, as there was so much danger of their being lost; and therefore ordered the Captains of the squadron to employ *Portuguese* boats on that service.

We continued about a week at this Island, watering our ships, and providing the squadron with wine and other refreshments. And, on the 3d of *November*, Captain *Richard Norris* having signified by a letter to the Commodore, his desire to quit his command on board the *Gloucester*, in order to return to *England* for the recovery of his health, the Commodore complied with his request; and thereupon was pleased to appoint Captain *Matthew Mitchel* to command the *Gloucester* in his room, and to remove Captain *Kidd* from the *Wager* to the *Pearl*, and Captain *Murray* from the *Tryal* Sloop to the *Wager*, giving the com-

mand of the *Tryal* to Lieutenant *Cheap*. These promotions being
settled, with other changes in the Lieutenancies, the Commodore, on
the following day, gave to the Captains their orders, appointing St.
Jago, one of the *Cape de Verd* Islands, to be the first place of rendezvous in case of separation; and directing them, if they did not meet
the *Centurion* there, to make the best of their way to the Island of St.
Catherine's, on the coast of *Brazil*. The water for the squadron being
the same day compleated, and each ship supplied with as much wine
and other refreshments as they could take in, we weighed anchor in
the afternoon, and took our leave of the Island of *Madera*. But before
I go on with the narration of our own transactions, I think it necessary
to give some account of the proceedings of the enemy and of the
measures they had taken to render all our designs abortive.

When Mr. *Anson* visited the Governor of *Madera*, he received
information from him, that for three or four days, in the latter end of
October, there had appeared, to the westward of that Island, seven or
eight ships of the line, and a Patache,[1] which last was sent every day
close in to make the land. The Governor assured the Commodore,
upon his honour, that none upon the Island had either given them
intelligence, or had in any sort communicated with them, but that he
believed them to be either *French* or *Spanish*, but was rather inclined
to think them *Spanish*. On this intelligence, Mr. *Anson* sent an Officer
in a clean sloop, eight leagues to the westward, to reconnoitre them,
and, if possible, to discover what they were: But the Officer returned
without being able to get a sight of them, so that we still remained in
uncertainty. However, we could not but conjecture, that this fleet was
intended to put a stop to our expedition, which, had they cruised to
the eastward of the Island instead of the westward, they could not
but have executed with great facility. For as, in that case, they must
have certainly fallen in with us, we should have been obliged to throw
overboard vast quantities of provision to clear our ships for an engagement, and this alone, without any regard to the event of the
action, would have effectually prevented our progress. This was so
obvious a measure, that we could not help imagining reasons which
might have prevented them from pursuing it. And we therefore supposed, that this *French* or *Spanish* squadron was sent out, upon advice
of our sailing in company with Admiral *Balchen* and Lord *Cathcart's*
expedition: And thence, from an apprehension of being over-matched,

they might not think it adviseable to meet with us, till we had parted company, which they might judge would not happen, before our arrival at this Island. These were our speculations at that time; and from hence we had reason to suppose, that we might still fall in with them, in our way to the *Cape de Verd* Islands. And afterwards, in the course of our expedition, we were many of us persuaded, that this was the *Spanish* squadron commanded by *Don Joseph Pizarro,* which was sent out purposely to traverse the views and enterprizes of our squadron, to which, in strength, they were greatly superior. As this *Spanish* armament then was so nearly connected with our expedition, and as the catastrophe it underwent, though not effected by our force, was yet a considerable advantage to this Nation, produced in consequence of our equipment, I have, in the following chapter, given a summary account of their proceedings, from their first setting out from *Spain* in the year 1740, till the *Asia,* the only ship which returned to *Europe* of the whole squadron, arrived at the *Groyne* in the beginning of the year 1746.

CHAP. III.

The history of the squadron commanded by Don *Joseph Pizarro*.

THE squadron fitted out by the Court of *Spain* to attend our motions, and traverse our projects, we supposed to have been the ships seen off *Madera*, as mentioned in the preceding chapter. And as this force was sent out particularly against our expedition, I cannot but imagine, that the following history of the casualties it met with, as far as by intercepted letters and other information the same has come to my knowledge, is a very essential part of the present work: For by this it will appear we were the occasion, that a considerable part of the naval power of *Spain* was diverted from the prosecution of the ambitious Views of that Court in *Europe*; and the men and ships, lost by the enemy in this undertaking, were lost in consequence of the precautions they took to secure themselves against our enterprizes. This squadron (besides two ships intended for the *West-Indies*, which did not part company till after they had left the *Maderas*) was composed of the following men of war, commanded by Don *Joseph Pizarro*:

The *Asia* of sixty-six guns, and seven hundred men; this was the
    Admiral's ship.
The *Guipuscoa* of seventy-four guns, and seven hundred men.
The *Hermiona* of fifty-four guns, and five hundred men.
The *Esperanza* of fifty guns, and four hundred and fifty men.
The St. *Estevan* of forty guns, and three hundred and fifty men.
And a Patache of twenty guns.

These ships, over and above their complement of sailors and marines, had on board an old *Spanish* regiment of foot, intended to reinforce the garrisons on the coast of the *South-Seas*. When this fleet had cruised for some days to the leeward of the *Maderas*, as is mentioned in the preceding chapter, they left that station in the beginning of *November*, and steered for the river of *Plate*, where they arrived the 5th of *January*, O.S. and coming to an anchor in the bay of *Maldonado*, at the mouth of that river, their Admiral *Pizarro* sent immediately to

35

Buenos Ayres for a supply of provisions; for they had departed from *Spain* with only four months provisions on board. While they lay here expecting this supply, they received intelligence, by the Treachery of the *Portuguese* Governor of St. *Catherine's*, of Mr. *Anson's* having arrived at that Island on the 21st of *December* preceding, and of his preparing to put to sea again with the utmost expedition. *Pizarro*, notwithstanding his superior force, had his reasons (and as some say his orders likewise) for avoiding our squadron any where short of the *South-Seas*. He was besides extremely desirous of getting round Cape *Horn* before us, as he imagined that step alone would effectually baffle all our designs; and therefore, on hearing that we were in his neighbourhood, and that we should soon be ready to proceed for Cape *Horn*, he weighed anchor with the five large ships, (the Patache being disabled and condemned, and the men taken out of her) after a stay of seventeen days only, and got under sail without his provisions, which arrived at *Maldonado* within a day or two after his departure. But notwithstanding the precipitation, with which he departed, we put to sea from St. *Catherine's* four days before him, and in some part of our passage to Cape *Horn*, the two squadrons were so near together, that the *Pearl*, one of our ships, being departed from the rest, fell in with the *Spanish* Fleet, and mistaking the *Asia* for the *Centurion*, had got within gun-shot of *Pizarro*, before she discovered her error, and narrowly escaped being taken.

It being the 22nd of *January* when the *Spaniards* weighed from *Maldonado*, (as has been already mentioned) they could not expect to get into the latitude of Cape *Horn* before the equinox; and as they had reason to apprehend very tempestuous weather in doubling it at that season, and as the *Spanish* sailors, being for the most part accustomed to a fair weather country, might be expected to be very averse to so dangerous and fatiguing a navigation, the better to encourage them, some part of their pay was advanced to them in *European* goods, which they were to be permitted to dispose of in the *South-Seas*, that so the hopes of the great profit, each man was to make on his small venture, might animate him in his duty, and render him less disposed to repine at the labour, the hardships and the perils he would in all probability meet with before his arrival on the coast of *Peru*.

Pizarro with his squadron having, towards the latter end of

February, run the length of Cape *Horn*, he then stood to the westward in order to double it; but in the night, of the last day of *February*, *O. S.* while with this view they were turning to windward, the *Guipuscoa*, the *Hermiona*, and the *Esperanza*, were separated from the Admiral; and, on the 6th of *March* following, the *Guipuscoa* was separated from the other two; and, on the 7th (being the day after we had passed *Streights le Maire*) there came on a most furious storm at N W, which, in despight of all their efforts, drove the whole squadron to the eastward, and obliged them, after several fruitless attempts, to bear away for the river of *Plate*, where *Pizarro* in the *Asia* arrived about the middle of *May*, and a few days after him the *Esperanza* and the *Estevan*. The *Hermiona* was supposed to founder at sea, for she was never heard of more; and the *Guipuscoa* was run a-shore, and sunk on the coast of *Brazil*. The calamities of all kinds, which this squadron underwent in this unsuccessful navigation, can only be paralleled by what we ourselves experienced in the same climate, when buffeted by the same storms. There was indeed some diversity in our distresses, which rendered it difficult to decide, whose situation was most worthy of commiseration. For to all the misfortunes we had in common with each other, as shattered rigging, leaky ships, and the fatigues and despondency, which necessarily attend these disasters, there was superadded on board our squadron the ravage of a most destructive and incurable disease, and on board the *Spanish* squadron the devastation of famine.

For this squadron, either from the hurry of their outset, their presumption of a supply at *Buenos Ayres*, or from other less obvious motives, departed from *Spain*, as has been already observed, with no more than four months provision, and even that, as it is said, at short allowance only; so that, when by the storms they met with off Cape *Horn*, their continuance at sea was prolonged a month or more beyond their expectation, they were thereby reduced to such infinite distress, that rats, when they could be caught, were sold for four dollars a-piece; and a sailor, who died on board, had his death concealed for some days by his brother, who, during that time, lay in the same hammock with the corpse, only to receive the dead man's allowance of provisions. In this dreadful situation they were alarmed (if their horrors were capable of augmentation) by the discovery of a conspiracy among the marines, on board the *Asia*, the Admiral's ship.

This had taken its rise chiefly from the miseries they endured: For though no less was proposed by the conspirators than the massacring the officers and the whole crew, yet their motive for this bloody resolution seemed to be no more than their desire of relieving their hunger, by appropriating the whole ships provisions to themselves. But their designs were prevented, when just upon the point of execution, by means of one of their confessors, and three of their ringleaders were immediately put to death. However, though the conspiracy was suppressed, their other calamities admitted of no alleviation, but grew each day more and more destructive. So that by the complicated distress of fatigue, sickness and hunger, the three ships which escaped lost the greatest part of their men: The *Asia*, their Admiral's ship, arrived at *Monte Vedio* in the river of *Plate*, with half her crew only; the St. *Estevan* had lost in like manner half her hands, when she anchored in the bay of *Barragan*; the *Esperanza*, a fifty gun ship, was still more unfortunate, for of four hundred and fifty hands which she brought from *Spain*, only fifty-eight remained alive, and the whole regiment of foot perished except sixty men. But to give the reader a more distinct and particular idea of what they underwent upon this occasion, I shall lay before him a short account of the fate of the *Guipuscoa*, from a letter written by Don *Joseph Mendinuetta* her Captain, to a person of distinction at *Lima*; a copy of which fell into our hands afterwards in the *South-Seas*.

He mentions, that he separated from the *Hermiona* and the *Esperanza* in a fog, on the 6th of *March*, being then, as I suppose, to the S.E. of *Staten-Land*, and plying to the westward; that in the night after, it blew a furious storm at N.W, which, at half an hour after ten, split his mainsail, and obliged him to bear away with his foresail; that the ship went ten knots an hour with a prodigious sea, and often ran her gangway under water; that he likewise sprung his main-mast; and the ship made so much water, that with four pumps and bailing he could not free her. That on the 19th it was calm, but the sea continued so high, that the ship in rolling opened all her upper works and seams, and started the butt ends of her planking and the greatest part of her top timbers, the bolts being drawn by the violence of her roll: That in this condition, with other additional disasters to the hull and rigging, they continued beating to the westward till the 12th: That they were then in sixty degrees of south latitude, in great want of provisions, numbers every day perishing by the fatigue of pumping, and those who survived, being quite dispirited by labour, hunger, and the severity of the weather, they having two spans of snow upon the decks: That then finding the wind fixed in the western quarter, and blowing strong, and consequently their passage to the westward impossible, they resolved to bear away for the river of *Plate*: That on the 22d, they were obliged to throw overboard all the upper-deck guns, and an anchor, and to take six turns of the cable round the ship to prevent her opening: That on the 4th of *April*, it being calm but a very high sea, the ship rolled so much, that the mainmast came by the board, and in a few hours after she lost, in like manner, her fore-mast and her mizen-mast; and that, to accumulate their misfortunes, they were soon obliged to cut away their bowsprit, to diminish, if possible, the leakage at her head: That by this time he had lost two hundred and fifty men by hunger and fatigues; for those who were capable of working at the pumps, (at which every Officer without exception took his turn) were allowed only an ounce and half of biscuit *per diem*; and those who were so sick or so weak, that they could not assist in this necessary labour, had no more than an ounce of wheat; so that it was common for the men to fall down dead at the pumps: That, including the Officers, they could only muster from eighty to a hundred persons capable of duty: That the South West winds blew so fresh, after they had lost their masts, that they could not immediately set up jury masts, but were obliged to drive like a wreck, between the latitudes of 32 and 28, till the 24th of *April*, when they made the coast of *Brazil* at *Rio de Patas*, ten leagues to the southward of the Island of St. *Catherine*'s; that here they came to an anchor, and that the Captain was very desirous of proceeding to St. *Catherine*'s if possible, in order to save the hull of the ship, and the guns and stores on board her; but the crew instantly left off pumping, and being enraged at the hardships they had suffered, and the numbers they had lost, (there being at that time no less than thirty dead bodies lying on the deck) they all with one voice cried out *on shore, on shore*, and obliged the Captain to run the ship in directly for the land, where, the 5th day after, she sunk with her stores, and all her furniture on board her, but the remainder of the crew, whom hunger and fatigue had spared, to the number of four hundred, got safe on shore.

From this account of the adventures and catastrophe of the

Guipuscoa, we may form some conjecture of the manner, in which the *Hermiona* was lost, and of the distresses endured by the three remaining ships of the squadron, which got into the river of *Plate.* These last being in great want of masts, yards, rigging, and all kind of naval stores, and having no supply at *Buenos Ayres,* nor in any other of their settlements, *Pizarro* dispatched an advice boat with a letter of credit to *Rio Janeiro,* to purchase what was wanting from the *Portuguese.* He, at the same time, sent an express across the continent to *San Jago* in *Chili,* to be thence forwarded to the Viceroy of *Peru,* informing him of the disasters that had befallen his squadron, and desiring a remittance of 200,000 dollars from the royal chests at *Lima,* to enable him to victual and refit his remaining ships, that he might be again in a condition to attempt the passage to the *South-Seas,* as soon as the season of the year should be more favourable. It is mentioned by the *Spaniards* as a most extraordinary circumstance, that the *Indian* charged with this express (though it was then the depth of winter, when the *Cordilleras* are esteemed impassable on account of the snow) was only thirteen days in his journey from *Buenos Ayres* to *St. Jago* in *Chili*; though these places are distant three hundred *Spanish* leagues, near forty of which are amongst the snows and precipices of the *Cordilleras.*

The return to this dispatch of *Pizarro's* from the Viceroy of *Peru* was no ways favourable; instead of 200,000 dollars, the sum demanded, the Viceroy remitted him only 100,000 telling him, that it was with great difficulty he was able to procure him even that: Though the inhabitants at *Lima,* who considered the presence of *Pizarro* as absolutely necessary to their security, were much discontented at this procedure, and did not fail to assert, that it was not the want of money, but the interested views of some of the Viceroy's confidents, that prevented *Pizarro* from having the whole sum he had asked for.

The advice-boat sent to *Rio Janeiro* also executed her commission, but imperfectly; for though she brought back a considerable quantity of pitch, tar and cordage, yet she could not procure either masts or yards: and as an additional misfortune, *Pizarro* was disappointed of some masts he expected from *Paraguay*; for a carpenter, whom he entrusted with a large sum of money, and had sent there to cut masts, instead of prosecuting the business he was employed in, had married in the country, and refused to return. However, by removing the masts of the *Esperanza* into the *Asia*, and making use of what spare masts and yards they had on board, they made a shift to refit the *Asia* and the St. *Estevan*. And in the *October* following, *Pizarro* was preparing to put to sea with these two ships, in order to attempt the passage round Cape *Horn* a second time; but the St. *Estevan*, in coming down the river *Plate*, ran on a shoal, and beat off her rudder, on which, and other damages she received, she was condemned and broke up, and *Pizarro* in the *Asia* proceeded to sea without her. Having now the summer before him, and the winds favourable, no doubt was made of his having a fortunate and speedy passage; but being off Cape *Horn*, and going right before the wind in very moderate weather, though in a swelling sea, by some misconduct of the officer of the watch the ship rolled away her masts, and was a second time obliged to put back to the river of *Plate* in great distress.

The *Asia* having considerably suffered in this second unfortunate expedition, the *Esperanza*, which had been left behind at *Monte Vedio*, was ordered to be refitted, the command of her being given to *Mindinuetta*, who was Captain of the *Guipuscoa*, when she was lost. He, in the *November* of the succeeding year, that is, in *November* 1742, sailed from the river of *Plate* for the *South-Seas*, and arrived safe on the coast of *Chili*; where his Commodore *Pizarro* passing over land from *Buenos Ayres* met him. There were great animosities and contests between these two Gentlemen at their meeting, occasioned principally by the claim of *Pizarro* to command the *Esperanza*, which *Mindinuetta* had brought round: For *Mindinuetta* refused to deliver her up to him; insisting, that as he came into the *South-Seas* alone, and under no superior, it was not now in the power of *Pizarro* to resume that authority, which he had once parted with. However, the President of *Chili* interposing, and declaring for *Pizarro*, *Mindinuetta*, after a long and obstinate struggle, was obliged to submit.

But *Pizarro* had not yet compleated the series of his adventures; for when he and *Mindinuetta* came back by land from *Chili* to *Buenos Ayres*, in the year 1745, they found at *Monte Vedio* the *Asia*, which near three years before they had left there. This ship they resolved, if possible, to carry to *Europe*, and with this view they refitted her in the best manner they could: But their great difficulty was to procure a sufficient number of hands to navigate her, for all the remaining sailors of the squadron to be met with in the neighbourhood of *Buenos Ayres*, did not amount to a hundred men. They endeavoured to supply this defect by pressing many of the inhabitants of *Buenos Ayres*, and putting on board besides all the *English* prisoners then in their custody, together with a number of *Portuguese* smugglers, which they had taken at different times, and some of the *Indians* of the country. Among these last there was a Chief and ten of his followers, which had been surprized by a party of *Spanish* soldiers about three months before. The name of this Chief was *Orellana*, he belonged to a very powerful Tribe, which had committed great ravages in the neighbourhood of *Buenos Ayres*. With this motly crew (all of them, except the *European Spaniards*, extremely averse to the voyage) *Pizarro* set sail from *Monte Vedio* in the river of *Plate*, about the beginning of *November* 1745, and the native *Spaniards* being no strangers to the dissatisfaction of their forced men, treated both those, the *English* prisoners and the *Indians*, with great insolence and barbarity; but more particularly the *Indians*, for it was common for the meanest officers in the ship to beat them most cruelly on the slightest pretences, and oftentimes only to exert their superiority. *Orellana* and his followers, though in appearance sufficiently patient and submissive, meditated a severe revenge for all these inhumanities. As he conversed very well in *Spanish*, (these *Indians* having in time of peace a great intercourse with *Buenos Ayres*) he affected to talk with such of the *English* as understood that language, and seemed very desirous of being informed how many *Englishmen* there were on board, and which they were. As he knew that the *English* were as much enemies to the *Spaniards* as himself, he had doubtless an intention of disclosing his purposes to them, and making them partners in the scheme he had projected for revenging his wrongs, and recovering his liberty; but having sounded them at a distance, and not finding them so precipitate and vindictive as he expected, he proceeded no further with them, but resolved to trust alone to the resolution of his ten faithful followers. These, it should seem, readily engaged to observe his directions, and to execute whatever commands he gave them; and having agreed on the measures necessary to be taken, they first furnished themselves with *Dutch* knives sharp at the point, which being the common knives used in the ship, they found no difficulty in procuring: Besides this, they employed their leisure in secretly cutting out thongs from raw hides, of which there were great numbers on board, and in fixing to each end of these thongs the double-headed shot of the small quarter-deck guns; this, when swung round their heads, according to the practice of their country, was a most mischievous weapon, in the use of which the *Indians* about *Buenos Ayres* are trained from their infancy, and consequently are extremely expert. These particulars being in good forwardness, the execution of their scheme was perhaps precipitated by a particular outrage committed on *Orellana* himself. For one of the Officers, who was a very brutal fellow, ordered *Orellana* aloft, which being what he was incapable of performing, the Officer, under pretence of his disobedience, beat him with such violence, that he left him bleeding on the deck, and stupified for some time with his bruises and wounds. This usage undoubtedly heightened his thirst for revenge, and made him eager and impatient, till the means of executing it were in his power; so that within a day or two after this incident, he and his followers opened their desperate resolves in the ensuing manner.

It was about nine in the evening, when many of the principal Officers were on quarter-deck, indulging in the freshness of the night air; the waste of the ship was filled with live cattle, and the forecastle was manned with its customary watch. *Orellana* and his companions, under cover of the night, having prepared their weapons, and thrown off their trouzers and the more cumbrous part of their dress, came all together on the quarter-deck, and drew towards the door of the great cabbin. The Boatswain immediately reprimanded them, and ordered them to be gone. On this *Orellana* spoke to his followers in his native language, when four of them drew off, two towards each gangway, and the Chief and the six remaining *Indians* seemed to be slowly quitting the quarter-deck. When the detached *Indians* had taken possession of the gangway, *Orellana* placed his hands hollow to his mouth, and bellowed out the war-cry used by those savages, which is said to be the harshest and most terrifying sound known in nature. This hideous yell was the signal for beginning the massacre: For on this they all drew their knives, and brandished their prepared double-headed shot, and the six with their Chief, which remained on the quarter-deck, immediately fell on the *Spaniards*, who were intermingled with them, and laid near forty of them at their feet, of which about twenty were killed on the spot, and the rest disabled. Many of the Officers, in the beginning of the tumult, pushed into the great cabbin, where they put out the lights, and barricadoed the door. And of the others, who had avoided the first fury of the *Indians*, some endeavoured to escape along the gangways into the forecastle, but the *Indians*, placed there on purpose, stabbed the greatest part of them, as they attempted to pass by, or forced them off the gangways into the waste. Others threw themselves voluntarily over the barricadoes into the waste, and thought themselves happy to lie concealed amongst the cattle; but the greatest part escaped up the main shrouds, and sheltered themselves either in the tops or rigging. And though the *Indians* attacked only the quarter-deck, yet the watch in the forecastle finding their communication cut off, and being terrified by the wounds of the few, who not being killed on the spot, had strength sufficient to force their passage along the gangways, and not knowing either who their enemies were, or what were their numbers, they likewise gave all over for lost, and in great confusion ran up into the rigging of the foremast and bowsprit.

Thus these eleven *Indians*, with a resolution perhaps without example, possessed themselves almost in an instant of the quarter-deck of a ship mounting sixty-six guns, with a crew of near five hundred men, and continued in peaceable possession of this post a considerable time. For the Officers in the great cabbin, (amongst whom were *Pizarro* and *Mindinuetta*) the crew between decks, and those who had escaped into the tops and rigging, were only anxious for their own safety, and were for a long time incapable of forming any project for suppressing the insurrection, and recovering the possession of the ship. It is true, the yells of the *Indians*, the groans of the wounded, and the confused clamours of the crew, all heightened by the obscurity of the night, had at first greatly magnified their danger, and had filled them with the imaginary terrors, which darkness, disorder, and an ignorance of the real strength of an enemy never fail to produce. For as the *Spaniards* were sensible of the disaffection of their prest hands, and were also conscious of their barbarity to their prisoners, they imagined, the conspiracy was general, and considered their own destruction as infallible; so that, it is said, some of them had once taken the resolution of leaping into the sea, but were prevented by their companions.

However, when the *Indians* had entirely cleared the quarter-deck, the tumult in a great measure subsided; for those, who had escaped, were kept silent by their fears, and the *Indians* were incapable of pursuing them to renew the disorder. *Orellana*, when he saw himself master of the quarter-deck, broke open the arm-chest, which, on a slight suspicion of mutiny, had been ordered there a few days before, as to a place of the greatest security. Here he took it for granted, he should find cutlasses sufficient for himself and his companions, in the use of which weapon they were all extremely skilful, and with these, it was imagined, they proposed to have forced the great cabbin: But on opening the chest, there appeared nothing but fire-arms, which to them were of no use. There were indeed cutlasses in the chest, but they were hid by the fire-arms being laid over them. This was a sensible disappointment to them, and by this time *Pizarro* and his companions in the great cabbin were capable of conversing aloud, through the cabbin windows and port-holes, with those in the gun-room and between decks, and from hence they learnt, that the *English* (whom they principally suspected) were all safe below, and had not intermedled in this mutiny; and by other particulars they at last discovered, that none were concerned in it but *Orellana* and his people. On this *Pizarro* and the Officers resolved to attack them on the quarter-deck, before any of the discontented on board should so far recover their first surprize, as to reflect on the facility and certainty of seizing the ship by a junction with the *Indians* in the present emergency. With this view *Pizarro* got together what arms were in the cabbin, and distributed them to those who were with him: But there were no other fire-arms to be met with but pistols, and for these they had neither powder nor ball. However, having now settled a correspondence with the gun-room, they lowered down a bucket out of the cabbin-window, into which the gunner, out of one of the gun-room ports, put a quantity of pistol cartridges. When they had thus procured ammunition, and had loaded their pistols, they set the cabbin-door partly open, and fired some shot amongst the *Indians* on the quarter-deck, at first without effect. But at last *Mindinuetta*, whom we have often mentioned, had the good fortune to shoot *Orellana* dead on the spot; on which his faithful companions abandoning all thoughts of farther resistance, instantly leaped into the sea, where they every man perished. Thus was this insurrection quelled, and the possession of the quarter-deck regained, after it had been full two hours in the power of this great and daring Chief, and his gallant and unhappy countrymen.

Pizarro having escaped this imminent peril steered for *Europe*, and arrived safe on the coast of *Galicia* in the beginning of the year 1746, after having been absent between four and five years, and having, by his attendance on our expedition, diminished the naval power of *Spain* by above three thousand hands, (the flower of their sailors) and by four considerable ships of war and a Patache. For we have seen, that the *Hermiona* foundered at sea; the *Guipuscoa* was stranded, and sunk on the coast of *Brazil*; the St. *Estevan* was condemned, and broke up in the river of *Plate*; and the *Esperanza* being left in the *South-Seas*, is doubtless by this time incapable of returning to *Spain*. So that the *Asia* only, with less than one hundred hands, may be considered as all the remains of that squadron, with which *Pizarro* first put to sea. And whoever attends to the very large proportion, which this squadron bore to the whole navy of *Spain*, will, I believe, confess, that had our undertaking been attended with no other advantages than that of ruining so great a part of the sea-force of so dangerous an enemy, this alone would be a sufficient equivalent for our equipment, and an incontestible proof of the service, which the Nation has thence received. Having thus concluded this summary of *Pizarro*'s adventure, I shall now return again to the narration of our own transactions.

CHAP. IV.

From *Madera* to St. *Catherine's*

I HAVE already mentioned, that on the 3d of *November* we weighed from *Madera*, after orders had been given to the Captains to rendezvous at St. *Jago*, one of the *Cape de Verd* Islands, in case the squadron was separated. But the next day, when we were got to sea, the Commodore considering that the season was far advanced, and that touching at St. *Jago* would create a new delay, he for this reason thought proper to alter his rendezvous, and to appoint the Island of St. *Catherine's*, on the coast of *Brazil*, to be the first place to which the ships of the squadron were to repair in case of separation.

In our passage to the Island of St. *Catherine's*, we found the direction of the trade-winds to differ considerably from what we had reason to expect, both from the general histories given of these winds, and the experience of former Navigators. For the learned Dr. *Halley*, in his account of the trade winds,[1] which take place in the *Ethiopic* and *Atlantic* Ocean, tells us, that from the latitude of 28° N, to the latitude of 10° N, there is generally a fresh gale of N. E. wind, which towards the *African* side rarely comes to the eastward of E. N. E, or passes to the northward of N. N. E: But on the *American* side, the wind is somewhat more easterly, though most commonly even there it is a point or two to the northward of the East: That from 10° N. to 4° N, the calms and tornadoes take place; and from 4° N. to 30° S, the winds are generally and perpetually between the South and the East. This account we expected to have verified by our own experience; but we found considerable variations from it, both in respect to the steadiness of the winds, and the quarter from whence they blew. For though we met with a N. E. wind about the latitude of 28° N, yet from the latitude of 25° to the latitude of 18° N, the wind was never once to the northward of the East, but on the contrary, almost constantly to the southward of it. However, from thence to the latitude of 6° : 20' N, we had it usually to the northward of the East, though not entirely, it having for a short time changed to E. S. E. From hence, to about 4° : 46' N, the weather was very unsettled; sometimes the wind was N. E. then changed to S. E, and sometimes we had a dead calm, attended with small rain and lightning. After this, the wind continued almost invariably between the S. and E, to the latitude of 7° : 30′ S; and then again as invariably between the N. and E, to the latitude of 15° : 30′ S; then E. and S. E, to 21° : 37′ S. But after this, even to the latitude of 27° : 44′ S, the wind was never once between the S. and the E, though we had it at times in all the other quarters of the compass. But this last circumstance may be in some measure accounted for, from our approach to the main continent of the *Brazils*. I mention not these particulars with a view of cavilling at the received accounts of these trade-winds, which I doubt not are in general sufficiently accurate; but I thought it a matter worthy of public notice, that such deviations from the established rules do sometimes take place. This observation may not only be of service to Navigators, by putting them on their guard against these hitherto unexpected irregularities, but may perhaps contribute to the solution of that great question about the causes of trade-winds, and monsoons, a question, which, in my opinion, has not been hitherto discussed with that clearness and accuracy, which its importance (whether it be considered as a naval or philosophical inquiry) seems to demand.

On the 16th of *November*, one of our Victuallers made a signal to speak with the Commodore, and we shortened sail for her to come up with us. The Master came on board, and acquainted Mr. *Anson*, that he had complied with the terms of his charter-party, and desired to be unloaded and dismissed. Mr. *Anson*, on consulting the Captains of the squadron, found all the ships had still such quantities of provision between their decks, and were withal so deep, that they could not without great difficulty take in their several proportions of brandy from the *Industry Pink*, one of the Victuallers only: And consequently he was obliged to continue the other of them, the *Anna Pink*, in the service of attending the squadron. And the next day the Commodore made a signal for the ships to bring to, and to take on board their shares of the brandy from the *Industry Pink*; and in this, the long boats of the squadron were employed the three following days, that is, till the 19th in the evening, when the *Pink* being unloaded, she parted company with us, being bound for *Barbadoes*, there to take in a freight for *England*. Most of the Officers of the squadron took the opportunity of writing to their friends at home by this ship; but she was afterwards, as I have been since informed, unhappily taken by the *Spaniards*.

On the 20th of *November*, the Captains of the squadron represented to the Commodore, that their ships companies were very sickly, and that it was their own opinion as well as their surgeons, that it would tend to the preservation of the men to let in more air between decks; but that their ships were so deep, they could not possibly open their lower ports. On this representation, the Commodore ordered six air scuttles to be cut in each ship, in such places where they would least weaken it.

And on this occasion I cannot but observe, how much it is the duty of all those, who either by office or authority, have any influence in the direction of our naval affairs, to attend to this important article, the preservation of the lives and health of our seamen. If it could be supposed, that the motives of humanity were insufficient for this purpose, yet policy, and a regard to the success of our arms, and the interest and honour of each particular Commander, should naturally lead us to a careful and impartial examination of every probable method proposed for maintaining a ship's crew in health and vigour. But hath this been always done? Have the late invented plain and obvious methods of keeping our ships sweet and clean, by a constant supply of fresh air, been considered with that candour and temper, which the great benefits promised hereby ought naturally to have inspired![1] On the contrary, have not these salutary schemes been often treated with neglect and contempt? And have not some of those who have been entrusted with experimenting their effects, been guilty of the most indefensible partiality, in the accounts they have given of these trials? Indeed, it must be confessed, that many distinguished persons, both in the direction and command of our fleets, have exerted themselves on these occasions with a judicious and dispassionate examination, becoming the interesting nature of the inquiry; but the wonder is, that any could be found irrational enough to act a contrary part, in despight of the strongest dictates of prudence and humanity. I must however own, that I do not believe this conduct to have arisen from motives so savage, as the first reflection thereon does naturally suggest: But I rather impute it to an obstinate, and in some degree, superstitious attachment to such practices as have been long established, and to a settled contempt and hatred of all kinds of innovations, especially such as are projected by landmen and persons residing on shore. But let us return from this, I hope not, impertinent digression.

We crossed the equinoctial[1] with a fine fresh gale at S. E., on *Friday* the 28th of *November*, at four in the morning, being then in the longitude of 27° : 59' W. from *London*. And on the 2d of *December*, in the morning, we saw a sail in the N. W. quarter, and made the *Gloucester*'s and *Tryal*'s signals to chase; and half an hour after, we let out our reefs and chased with the squadron; and about noon a signal was made for the *Wager* to take our remaining Victualler, the *Anna Pink*, in tow. But at seven in the evening, finding we did not near the chace, and that the *Wager* was very far a-stern, we shortened sail, and made a signal for the cruizers to join the squadron. The next day but one we again discovered a sail, which, on a nearer approach, we judged to be the same vessel. We chased her the whole day, and though we rather gained upon her, yet night came on before we could overtake her, and obliged us to give over the chace, to collect our scattered squadron. We were much chagrined at the escape of this vessel, as we then apprehended her to be an advice-boat sent from *Old Spain* to *Buenos Ayres*, with notice of our expedition. But we have since learnt, that we were deceived in this conjecture, and that it was our *East-India* Company's Packet bound to St. *Helena*.

On the 10th of *December*, being by our accounts in the latitude of 20° S, and 36° : 30' longitude West from *London*, the *Tryal* fired a gun to denote soundings. We immediately sounded, and found sixty fathom water, the bottom coarse ground with broken shells. The *Tryal* being a-head of us, had at one time thirty-seven fathom, which afterwards increased to 90: And then she found no bottom, which happened to us too at our second trial, though we sounded with a hundred and fifty fathom of line. This is the shoal which is laid down in most charts by the name of the *Abrollos*; and it appeared we were upon the very edge of it; perhaps farther in, it may be extremely dangerous. We were then, by our different accounts, from ninety to sixty leagues East of the coast of *Brazil*. The next day but one we spoke with a *Portuguese* Brigantine from *Rio Janeiro*, bound to *Bahia del todos Santos*, who informed us, that we were thirty four leagues from Cape St. *Thomas*, and forty leagues from Cape *Frio*, which last bore from us W. S. W. By our accounts we were near eighty leagues from

Cape *Frio*; and though, on the information of this Brigantine, we altered our course, and stood more to the southward, yet by our coming in with the land afterwards, we were fully convinced that our reckoning was much correcter than our *Portuguese* intelligence. We found a considerable current setting to the southward, after we had passed the latitude of 16° S. And the same took place all along the coast of *Brazil*, and even to the southward of the river of *Plate*, it amounting sometimes to thirty miles in twenty-four hours, and once to above forty miles.

If this current is occasioned (as it is most probable) by the running off of the water, accumulated on the coast of *Brazil* by the constant sweeping of the eastern trade-wind over the *Ethiopic* Ocean, then it is most natural to suppose, that its general course is determined by the bearings of the adjacent shore. Perhaps too, in almost every other instance of currents, the same may hold true, as I believe no examples occur of considerable currents being observed at any great distance from land. If this then could be laid down for a general principle, it would be always easy to correct the reckoning by the observed latitude. But it were much to be wished, for the general interests of navigation, that the actual settings of the different currents which are known to take place in various parts of the world, were examined more frequently and accurately than hitherto appears to have been done.

We now began to grow impatient for a sight of land, both for the recovery of our sick, and for the refreshment and security of those who as yet continued healthier. When we departed from St. *Helens*, we were in so good a condition, that we lost but two men on board the *Centurion*, in our long passage to *Madera*. But in this present run between *Madera* and St. *Catherine's* we have been very sickly, so that many died, and great numbers were confined to their hammocks, both in our own ship and in the rest of the squadron, and several of these past all hopes of recovery. The disorders they in general labour under are such as are common to the hot climates, and what most ships bound to the southward experience in a greater or less degree. These are those kind of fevers, which they usually call Calentures: A disease, which was not only terrible in its first instance, but even the remains of it often proved fatal to those who considered themselves as recovered from it. For it always left them in a very weak and helpless condition, and usually afflicted with fluxes and tenasmus's. And by our continuance at sea all our complaints were every day increasing, so that it was with great joy that we discovered the coast of *Brazil* on the 18th of *December*, at seven in the morning.

The coast of *Brazil* appeared high and mountainous land, extending from the W. to W. S. W, and when we first saw it, it was about seventeen leagues distant. At noon we perceived a low double land, bearing W. S. W. about ten leagues distant, which we took to be the Island of St. *Catherine's*. That afternoon and the next morning, the wind being N. N. W, we gained very little to windward, and were apprehensive of being driven to the leeward of the Island; but a little before noon, the next day, the wind came about to the southward, and enabled us to steer in between the North point of St. *Catherine's*, and the neighbouring Island of *Alvoredo*. As we stood in for the land, we had regular soundings gradually decreasing, from thirty-six to twelve fathom, all muddy ground. In this last depth of water we let go our anchor at five o'clock in the evening of the 18th, the North West point of the Island of St. *Catherine's* bearing S.S.W., distant three miles; and the Island *Alvoredo* N. N. E, distant two leagues. Here we found the tide to set S. S. E. and N. N. W, at the rate of two knots, the tide of flood coming from the southward. We could from our ships observe two fortifications at a considerable distance within us, which seemed designed to prevent the passage of an enemy between the Island of St. *Catherine's* and the main. And we could soon perceive that our squadron had alarmed the coast, for we saw the two forts hoist their colours, and fire several guns, which we supposed to be intended for assembling the inhabitants. To prevent any confusion, the Commodore immediately sent a boat with an Officer on shore, to compliment the Governor, and to desire a Pilot to carry us into the road. The Governor returned a very civil answer, and ordered us a Pilot. On the morning of the 20th we weighed and stood in, and towards noon the Pilot came on board us, who, the same afternoon, brought us to an anchor in five fathom and an half, in a large commodious bay on the continent side, called by the *French, Bon Port*. In standing from our last anchorage to this place, we every where found an ouzy bottom, with a depth of water first regularly decreasing to five fathom, and then increasing to seven, after which we had six and five fathom alternately. The next morning we weighed again with the squadron, in order to run above the two fortifications we have mentioned, which are called the castles of *Santa Cruiz* and St. *Juan*. And now the soundings between the Island and the Main were four, five and six fathom, with muddy ground. As we passed by the castle of *Santa Cruiz* we saluted it with eleven guns, and were answered by an equal number; and at one in the afternoon, the squadron came to an anchor in five fathom and a half, the Governor's Island bearing N. N. W, St. *Juan's* Castle N. E. $\frac{1}{2}$ E, and the Island of St. *Antonio* South. In this position we moored at the Island of St. *Catherine's* on *Sunday* the 21st of *December*, the whole squadron being, as I have already mentioned, sickly, and in great want of refreshments: Both which inconveniencies we hoped to have soon removed at this settlement, celebrated by former Navigators for its healthiness and its provisions, and for the freedom, indulgence, and friendly assistance there given to the ships of all *European* Nations, in amity with the Crown of *Portugal*.

CHAP. V.

Proceedings at St. *Catherine's*, and a description of the place, with a short account of *Brazil*.

OUR first care, after having moored our ships, was to send our sick men on shore, each ship being ordered by the Commodore to erect two tents for that purpose: One of them for the reception of the diseased, and the other for the accommodation of the surgeon and his assistants. We sent about eighty sick from the *Centurion*, and the other ships I believe sent nearly as many, in proportion to the number of their hands. As soon as we had performed this necessary duty, we scraped our decks, and gave our ship a thorough cleansing; then smoked it between decks, and after all washed every part well with vinegar. These operations were extremely necessary for correcting the noisome stench on board, and destroying the vermin; for from the number of our men, and the heat of the climate, both these nuisances had increased upon us to a very loathsome degree, and besides being most intolerably offensive, they were doubtless in some sort productive of the sickness we had laboured under for a considerable time, before our arrival at this Island.

Our next employment was wooding and watering our squadron, caulking our ships sides and decks, overhaling our rigging, and securing our masts against the tempestuous weather we were, in all probability, to meet with in our passage round Cape *Horn*, in so advanced and inconvenient a season. But before I engage in the particulars of these transactions, it will not be improper to give some account of the present state of this Island of St. *Catherine's*, and of the neighbouring country; both as the circumstances of this place are now greatly changed from what they were in the time of former writers, and as these changes laid us under many more difficulties and perplexities than we had reason to expect, or than other *British* ships, hereafter bound to the *South-Seas*, may perhaps think it prudent to struggle with.

This Island is esteemed by the natives to be no where above two leagues in breadth, though about nine in length; it lies in 49° : 45' of

west longitude from *London,* and extends from the South latitude of
27° *35',* to that of 28°. Although it be of a considerable height, yet it
is scarce discernible at the distance of ten leagues, being then obscured
under the continent of *Brazil,* whose mountains are exceeding high;
but on a nearer approach it is easy to be distinguished, and may be
readily known by a number of small Islands lying at each end, and
scattered along the East side of it. In the annexed plate there is
exhibited a very exact view of the N. E. end of the Island, where (*a*)
is its N. E. point, as it appears when it bears N. W. And (*b*) is the
small Island of *Alvoredo,* bearing N. N. W, at the distance of 7 leagues.
The best entrance to the harbour is between the point (*a*) and the
Island of *Alvoredo,* where ships may pass under the guidance of their
lead, without the least apprehensions of danger. The view of this
North entrance of the harbour is represented in the second plate,
where (*a*) is the N. W. end of St. *Catherine's* Island, (*b*) *Parrot* Island,
(*c*) a battery on St. *Catherine's,* and (*d*) a battery on a small Island
near the continent. *Frezier* has given a draught of this Island of St.
Catherine's, and of the neighbouring coast, and the minuter isles
adjacent; but he has by mistake called the Island of *Alvoredo* the Isle
de Gal, whereas the true Isle *de Gal* lies seven or eight miles to the
North-westward of it, and is much smaller. He has also called an
Island, to the southward of St. *Catherine's, Alvoredo,* and has omitted
the Island *Masaqura;* in other respects his plan is sufficiently exact.

The North entrance of the harbour is in breadth about five miles,
and the distance from thence to the Island of St. *Antonio* is eight miles,
and the course from the entrance to St. *Antonio* is S. S. W. ½ W.
About the middle of the Island the harbour is contracted by two points
of land to a narrow channel, no more than a quarter of a mile broad;
and to defend this passage, a battery was erecting on the point of land
on the Island side. But this seems to be a very useless work, as the
channel has no more than two fathom water, and consequently is
navigable only for barks and boats, and therefore seems to be a passage
that an enemy could have no inducement to attempt, especially as the
common passage at the North end of the Island is so broad and safe,
that no squadron can be prevented from coming in by any of their
fortifications, when the sea-breeze is made. However, the Brigadier
Don *Jose Sylva de Paz,* the Governor of this settlement, is esteemed
an expert Engineer, and he doubtless understands one branch of his

business very well, which is the advantages which new works bring to those who are entrusted with the care of erecting them: For besides the battery mentioned above, there are three other forts carrying on for the defence of the harbour, none of which are yet compleated. The first of these, called St. *Juan,* is built on a point of St. *Catherine's* near *Parrot* Island; the second, in form of a half moon, is on the Island of St. *Antonio*; and the third, which seems to be the chief, and has some appearance of a regular fortification, is on an Island near the continent, where the Governor resides.

The soil of the Island is truly luxuriant, producing fruits of most kinds spontaneously; and the ground is covered over with one continued forest of trees of a perpetual verdure, which from the exuberance of the soil, are so entangled with briars, thorns, and underwood, as to form a thicket absolutely impenetrable, except by some narrow pathways which the inhabitants have made for their own convenience. These, with a few spots cleared for plantations along the shore facing the continent, are the only uncovered parts of the Island. The woods are extremely fragrant, from the many aromatick trees and shrubs with which they abound; and the fruits and vegetables of all climates thrive here, almost without culture, and are to be procured in great plenty; so that here is no want of pine-apples, peaches, grapes, oranges, lemons, citrons, melons, apricots, nor plantains. There are besides great abundance of two other productions of no small consideration for a sea-store, I mean onions and potatoes.[1] The provisions of other kinds are however inferior to their vegetables: There are small wild cattle to be purchased, somewhat like buffaloes, but these are very indifferent food, their flesh being of a loose contexture, and generally of a disagreable flavour, which is probably owing to the wild calabash on which they feed. There are likewise great plenty of pheasants, but they are much inferiour in taste to those we have in *England.* The other provisions of the place are monkeys, parrots, and fish of various sorts, which abound in the harbour, and are all exceeding good, and are easily catched, for there are a great number of small sandy bays very convenient for haling the *Seyne.*

The water both on the Island and the opposite continent is excellent, and preserves at sea as well as that of the *Thames.* For after it has been in the cask a day or two it begins to purge itself, and stinks most intolerably, and is soon covered over with a green scum: But this, in a few days, subsides to the bottom, and leaves the water as clear as chrystal, and perfectly sweet. The *French* (who, during their *South-Sea* trade in Queen *Anne's* reign first brought this place into repute) usually wooded and watered in *Bon Port*, on the continent side, where they likewise anchored with great safety in six fathom water; and this is doubtless the most commodious road for such ships as intend to make only a short stay. But we watered on the St. *Catherine's* side, at a plantation opposite to the Island of St. *Antonio*.

These are the advantages of this Island of St. *Catherine's*; but there are many inconveniences attending it, partly from its climate, but more from its new regulations, and the late form of government established there. With regard to the climate, it must be remembred, that the woods and hills which surround the harbour, prevent a free circulation of the air. And the vigorous vegetation which constantly takes place there, furnishes such a prodigious quantity of vapour, that all the night and a great part of the morning a thick fog covers the whole country, and continues till either the sun gathers strength to dissipate it, or it is dispersed by a brisk sea-breeze. This renders the place close and humid, and probably occasioned the many fevers and fluxes we were there afflicted with. To these exceptions I must not omit to add, that all the day we were pestered with great numbers of muscatos, which are not much unlike the gnats in *England*, but more venemous in their stings. And at sun-set, when the muscatos retired, they were succeeded by an infinity of sand-flies, which, though scarce discernible to the naked eye, make a mighty buzzing, and wherever they bite raise a small bump in the flesh, which is soon attended with a painful itching, like that arising from the bite of an *English* harvest bug.

But as the only light in which this place deserves our consideration, is its favourable situation for supplying and refreshing our cruizers intended for the *South-Seas*: In this view its greatest inconveniences remain still to be related; and to do this more distinctly, it will not be amiss to consider the changes which it has lately undergone, both in its inhabitants, its police, and its governor.

In the time of *Frezier* and *Shelvocke*,[1] this place served only as a retreat to vagabonds and outlaws, who fled thither from all parts of *Brazil*. They did indeed acknowledge a subjection to the Crown of *Portugal*, and had a person among them whom they called their

Captain, who was considered in some sort as their Governor: But both their allegiance to their King, and their obedience to their Captain, seemed to be little more than verbal. For as they had plenty of provisions but no money, they were in a condition to support themselves without the assistance of any neighbouring settlements, and had not amongst them the means of tempting any adjacent Governor to busy his authority about them. In this situation they were extremely hospitable and friendly to such foreign ships as came amongst them. For these ships wanting only provisions, of which the natives had great store; and the natives wanting clothes, (for they often despised money, and refused to take it) which the ships furnished them with in exchange for their provisions, both sides found their account in this traffic, and their Captain or Governor had neither power nor interest to restrain it or to tax it. But of late (for reasons which shall be hereafter mentioned) these honest vagabonds have been obliged to receive amongst them a new colony, and to submit to new laws and government. Instead of their former ragged bare legged Captain (whom however they took care to keep innocent) they have now the honour to be governed by Don *Jose Sylva de Paz*, a Brigadier of the armies of *Portugal*. This Gentleman has with him a garrison of soldiers, and has consequently a more extensive and a better supported power than any of his predecessors, and as he wears better clothes, and lives more splendidly, and has besides a much better knowledge of the importance of money than they could ever pretend to: So he puts in practice certain methods of procuring it, with which they were utterly unacquainted. But it may be much doubted, if the inhabitants consider these methods as tending to promote either their interests, or that of their Sovereign the King of *Portugal*. This is certain, that his behaviour cannot but be extremely embarrassing to such *British* ships as touch there in their way to the *South-Seas*. For one of his practices was placing centinels at all the avenues, to prevent the people from selling us any refreshments, except at such exorbitant rates as we could not afford to give. His pretence for this extraordinary stretch of power was, that he was obliged to preserve their provisions for upwards of an hundred families, which they daily expected to reinforce their colony. Hence he appears to be no novice in his profession, by his readiness at inventing a plausible pretence for his interested management. However, this, though sufficiently provoking, was far from being the most exceptionable part of his conduct. For by the neighbourhood of the river *Plate*, a considerable smuggling traffic is carried on between the *Portuguese* and the *Spaniards*, especially in the exchanging gold for silver, by which both Princes are defrauded of their fifths, and in this prohibited commerce *Don Jose* was so deeply engaged, that in order to ingratiate himself with his *Spanish* correspondents (for no other reason can be given for his procedure) he treacherously dispatched an express to *Buenos Ayres* in the river of *Plate*, where *Pizarro* then lay, with an account of our arrival, and of the strength of our squadron; particularly the number of ships, guns and men, and every circumstance which he could suppose our enemy desirous of being acquainted with. And the same perfidy every *British* cruizer may expect, who touches at St. *Catherine's*, while it is under the Government of Don *Jose Sylva de Paz*.[1]

Thus much, with what we shall be necessitated to relate in the course of our own proceedings, may suffice as to the present state of St. *Catherine's*, and the character of its Governor. But as the reader may be desirous of knowing to what causes the late new modelling of this settlement is owing; to satisfy him in this particular, it will be necessary to give a short account of the adjacent continent of *Brazil*, and of the wonderful discoveries which have been made there within this last forty years, which, from a country of but mean estimation, has rendered it now perhaps the most considerable colony on the face of the globe.

This country was first discovered by *Americus Vesputio* a *Florentine*, who had the good fortune to be honoured with giving his name to the immense continent, some time before found out by *Columbus*: He being in the service of the *Portuguese*, it was settled and planted by that Nation, and with the other dominions of *Portugal*, devolved to the Crown of *Spain*, when that Kingdom became subject to it. During the long war between *Spain* and the State of *Holland*, the *Dutch* possessed themselves of the northermost part of *Brazil*, and were masters of it for some years. But when the *Portuguese* revolted from the *Spanish* Government, this country took part in the revolt, and soon repossessed themselves of the places the *Dutch* had taken; since which time it has continued without interruption under the Crown of *Portugal*, being, till the beginning of the present century, only productive of sugar, and tobacco, and a few other commodities of very little account.

But this country, which for many years was only considered for the produce of its plantations, has been lately discovered to abound with the two minerals, which mankind hold in the greatest esteem, and which they exert their utmost art and industry in acquiring, I mean, gold and diamonds. Gold was first found in the mountains, which lie adjacent to the city of *Rio Janeiro*. The occasion of its discovery is variously related, but the most common account is, that the *Indians*, lying on the back of the *Portuguese* settlements, were observed by the soldiers employed in an expedition against them to make use of this metal for their fish hooks; and their manner of procuring it being enquired into, it appeared that great quantities of it were annually washed from the hills, and left amongst the sand and gravel, which remained in the vallies after the running off, or evaporation of the water. It is now little more than forty years since any quantities of gold worth notice have been imported to *Europe* from *Brazil*; but since that time the annual imports from thence have been continually augmented by the discovery of places in other provinces, where it is to be met with as plentifully as at first about *Rio Janeiro*. And it is now said, that there is a small slender vein of it spread through all the country, at about twenty-four feet from the surface, but that this vein is too thin and poor to answer the expence of digging; however where the rivers or rains have had any course for a considerable time, there gold is always to be collected, the water having separated the metal from the earth, and deposited it in the sands, thereby saving the expences of digging: So that it is esteemed an infallible gain to be able to divert a stream from its channel, and to ransack its bed. From this account of gathering this metal, it should follow, that there are properly no gold mines in *Brazil*; and this the Governor of *Rio Grande* (who being at St. *Catherine's*, frequently visited Mr. *Anson*) did most confidently affirm, assuring us, that the gold was all collected either from rivers, or from the beds of torrents after floods. It is indeed asserted, that in the mountains, large rocks are found abounding with this metal; and I myself have seen the fragment of one of these rocks with a considerable lump of gold intangled in it; but even in this case, the workmen break off the rocks, and do not properly mine into them; and the great expence in subsisting among these mountains, and afterwards in separating the metal from the stone, makes this method of procuring gold to be but rarely put in practice.

The examining the bottoms of rivers, and the gullies of torrents, and the washing the gold found therein from the sand and dirt, with which it is always mixed, are works performed by slaves, who are principally Negroes, kept in great numbers by the *Portuguese* for these purposes. The regulation of the duty of these slaves is singular: For they are each of them obliged to furnish their master with the eighth part of an ounce of gold *per diem*; and if they are either so fortunate or industrious as to collect a greater quantity, the surplus is considered as their own property, and they have the liberty of disposing of it as they think fit. So that it is said some Negroes who have accidentally fallen upon rich washing places have themselves purchased slaves, and have lived afterwards in great splendor, their original master having no other demand on them than the daily supply of the forementioned eighth; which as the *Portuguese* ounce is somewhat lighter than our troy ounce, may amount to about nine shillings sterling.

The quantity of gold thus collected in the *Brazils*, and returned annually to *Lisbon*, may be in some degree estimated from the amount of the King's fifth. This hath of late been esteemed one year with another to be one hundred and fifty arroves of 32 *l.* *Portuguese* weight, each of which, at 4 *l.* the troy ounce, makes very near 300,000 *l.* sterling; and consequently the capital, of which this is the fifth, is about a million and a half sterling. And the annual return of gold to *Lisbon* cannot be less than this, though it be difficult to determine how much it exceeds it; perhaps we may not be very much mistaken in our conjecture, if we suppose the gold exchanged for silver with the *Spaniards* at *Buenos Ayres*, and what is brought privily to *Europe*, and escapes the duty, amounts to near half a million more, which will make the whole annual produce of the *Brasilian* gold near two millions sterling; a prodigious sum to be found in a country, which a few years since was not known to furnish a single grain.

I have already mentioned, that besides gold, this country does likewise produce diamonds. The discovery of these valuable stones is much more recent than that of gold, it being as yet scarce twenty years since the first were brought to *Europe*. They are found in the same manner as the gold, in the gullies of torrents and beds of rivers, but only in particular places, and not so universally spread through the country. They were often found in washing the gold before they were known to be diamonds, and were consequently thrown away with the sand and gravel separated from it. And it is very well remembered, that numbers of very large stones, which would have made the fortunes of the possessors, have passed unregarded through the hands of those, who now with impatience support the mortifying reflection. However, about twenty years since, a person acquainted with the appearance of rough diamonds, conceived that these pebbles, as they were then esteemed, were of the same kind: But it is said, that there was a considerable interval between the first starting of this opinion, and the confirmation of it by proper trials and examination, it proving difficult to persuade the inhabitants, that what they had been long accustomed to despise, could be of the importance represented by the discovery; and I have been informed, that in this interval, a Governor of one of their places procured a good number of these stones, which he pretended to make use of at cards to mark with, instead of counters. But to proceed: It was at last confirmed by skilful Jewellers in *Europe*, consulted on this occcasion, that the stones thus found in *Brazil* were truly diamonds, many of which were not inferiour either in lustre, or any other quality to those of the *East-Indies*. On this determination the *Portuguese*, in the neighbourhood of those places where they had first been observed, set themselves to search for them with great assiduity. And they were not without great hopes of discovering considerable masses of them, as they found large rocks of christal in many of the mountains, from whence the streams came which washed down the diamonds.

But it was soon represented to the King of *Portugal*, that if such plenty of diamonds should be met with as their sanguine conjectures seemed to indicate, this would so debase their value, and diminish their estimation, that besides ruining all the *Europeans* who had any quantity of *Indian* diamonds in their possession, it would render the discovery itself of no importance, and would prevent his Majesty from receiving any advantages from it. And on these considerations his Majesty has thought proper to restrain the general search of diamonds, and has erected a Diamond Company for that purpose, with an exclusive charter. This Company, in consideration of a sum paid by them to the King, have the property of all diamonds found in *Brazil*: But to hinder their collecting too large quantities, and thereby debasing their value, they are prohibited from employing above eight hundred slaves in searching after them. And to prevent any of his other subjects from acting the same part, and likewise to secure the Company from being defrauded by the interfering of interlopers in their trade, he has depopulated a large town, and a considerable district round it, and has obliged the inhabitants, who are said to amount to six thousand, to remove to another part of the country; for this town being in the neighbourhood of the diamonds, it was thought impossible to prevent such a number of people, who were on the spot, from frequently smuggling.

In consequence of these important discoveries in *Brazil*, new laws, new governments, and new regulations have been established in many parts of the country. For not long since, a considerable tract, possessed by a set of inhabitants, who from their principal settlement were called *Paulists*, was almost independent of the Crown of *Portugal*, to which they scarcely acknowledged more than a nominal allegiance. These are said to be descendants of those *Portuguese*, who retired from the northern part of *Brazil*, when it was invaded and possessed by the *Dutch*. And being for a long time neglected and obliged to provide for their own security and defence, the necessity of their affairs produced a kind of government amongst them, which they found sufficient for the confined manner of life to which they were inured. And therefore rejecting and despising the authority and mandate of the Court of *Lisbon*, they were often engaged in a state of downright rebellion: And the mountains surrounding their country, and the difficulty of clearing the few passages that open into it, generally put it in their power to make their own terms before they submitted. But as gold was found to abound in this country of the *Paulists*, the present King of *Portugal*[1] (during whose reign almost the whole discoveries I have mentioned were begun and compleated) thought it incumbent on him to reduce this province, which now became of great consequence, to the same dependency and obedience with the rest of the country, which, I am told, he has at last, though with great difficulty, happily effected. And the same motives which induced his Majesty to undertake the reduction of the *Paulists*, has also occasioned the changes I have mentioned, to have taken place at the Island of St. *Catherine's*. For the Governor of *Rio Grande*, of whom I have already spoken, assured us, that in the neighbourhood of this Island there were considerable rivers which were found to be extremely rich, and that this was the reason that a garrison, a military Governor, and a new colony was settled there. And as the harbour at this Island is by much the securest and the most capacious of any on the coast, it is not improbable, if the riches of the neighbourhood answer their expectation, but it may become in time the principal settlement in *Brazil*, and the most considerable port in all South *America*.

Thus much I have thought necessary to insert, in relation to the present state of *Brazil*, and of the Island of St. *Catherine's*. For as this last place has been generally recommended as the most eligible port for our cruisers to refresh at, which are bound to the *South-Seas*, I believed it to be my duty to instruct my countrymen, in the hitherto unsuspected inconveniences which attend that place. And as the *Brazilian* gold and diamonds are subjects, about which, from their novelty, very few particulars have been hitherto published, I conceived this account I had collected of them, would appear to the reader to be neither a trifling nor a useless digression. These subjects being thus dispatched, I shall now return to the series of our own proceedings.

When we first arrived at St. *Catherine's*, we were employed in refreshing our sick on shore, in wooding and watering the squadron, cleaning our ships, and examining and securing our masts and rigging, as I have already observed in the foregoing chapter. At the same time Mr. *Anson* gave directions, that the ships companies should be supplied with fresh meat, and that they should be victualled with whole allowance of all the kinds of provision. In consequence of these orders, we had fresh beef sent on board us continually for our daily expence, and what was wanting to make up our allowance we received from our Victualler the *Anna Pink*, in order to preserve the provisions on board our squadron entire for our future service. The season of the year growing each day less favourable for our passage round Cape *Horn*, Mr. *Anson* was very desirous of leaving this place as soon as possible; and we were at first in hopes that our whole business would be done, and we should be in a readiness to sail in about a fortnight from our arrival: But, on examining the *Tryal's* masts, we, to our no small vexation, found inevitable employment for twice that time. For, on a survey, it was found that the main-mast was sprung at the upper woulding,[1] though it was thought capable of being secured by a couple of fishes;[2] but the fore-mast was reported to be unfit for service, and thereupon the Carpenters were sent into the woods, to endeavour to find a stick proper for a fore-mast. But after a search of four days, they returned without having been able to meet with any tree fit for the purpose. This obliged them to come to a second consultation about the old fore-mast, when it was agreed to endeavour to secure it by casing it with three fishes: And in this work the carpenters were employed, till within a day or two of our sailing. In the mean time, the Commodore thinking it necessary to have a clean vessel on our arrival in the *South-Seas*, ordered the *Tryal* to be hove down, as this would not occasion any loss of time, but might be compleated while the Carpenters were refitting her masts, which was done on shore.

On the 27th of *December* we discovered a sail in the offing, and not knowing but she might be a *Spaniard*, the eighteen oared-boat was manned and armed, and sent under the command of our second Lieutenant, to examine her, before she arrived within the protection of the forts. She proved to be a *Portuguese* Brigantine from *Rio Grande*. And though our Officer, as it appeared on inquiry, had behaved with the utmost civility to the Master, and had refused to accept a calf, which the Master would have forced on him as a present: Yet the Governor took great offence at our sending our boat; and talked of it in a high strain, as a violation of the peace subsisting between the Crowns of *Great-Britain* and *Portugal*. We at first imputed this ridiculous blustering to no deeper a cause, than Don *Jose*'s insolence; but as we found he proceeded so far as to charge our Officer with behaving rudely, and opening letters, and particularly with an attempt to take out of the vessel, by violence, the very calf which we knew he had refused to receive as a present, (a circumstance which we were satisfied the Governor was well acquainted with) we had hence reason to suspect, that he purposely sought this quarrel, and had more important motives for engaging in it, than the mere captious biass of his temper. What these motives were it was not so easy for us to determine at that time; but as we afterwards found by letters, which fell into our hands in the *South-Seas*, that he had dispatched an express to *Buenos Ayres*, where *Pizarro* then lay, with an account of our squadron's arrival at St. *Catherine's*, together with the most ample and circumstantial intelligence of our force and condition, we thence conjectured that Don *Jose* had raised this groundless clamour, only to prevent our visiting the Brigantine when she should put to sea again, least we might there find proofs of his perfidious behaviour, and

perhaps at the same time discover the secret of his smuggling correspondence with his neighbouring Governors, and the *Spaniards* at
Buenos Ayres. But to proceed,

It was near a month before the *Tryal* was refitted; for not only
her lower masts were defective, as hath been already mentioned, but
her main top-mast and fore-yard were likewise decayed and rotten.
While this work was carrying on, the other ships of the squadron fixed
new standing rigging, and set up a sufficient number of preventer
shrouds[1] to each mast, to secure them in the most effectual manner.
And in order to render the ships stiffer, and to enable them to carry
more sail abroad, and to prevent their labouring in hard gales of
wind, each Captain had orders given him to strike down some of their
great guns into the hold. These precautions being complied with, and
each ship having taken in as much wood and water as there was room
for, the *Tryal* was at last compleated, and the whole squadron was
ready for the sea: On which the tents on shore were struck, and all the
sick were received on board. And here we had a melancholy proof how
much the healthiness of this place had been over-rated by former
writers, for we found that though the *Centurion* alone had buried no
less than twenty-eight men since our arrival, yet the number of her
sick was in the same interval increased from eighty to ninety-six. And
now our crews being embarked, and every thing prepared for our
departure, the Commodore made a signal for all Captains, and
delivered them their orders, containing the successive places of rendezvous from hence to the coast of *China*. And then, on the next day,
being the 18th of *January*, the signal was made for weighing, and the
squadron put to sea, leaving without regret this Island of St. *Catherine's*; where we had been so extremely disappointed in our refreshments, in our accommodations, and in the humane and friendly
offices which we had been taught to expect in a place, which hath
been so much celebrated for its hospitality, freedom, and conveniency.

CHAP. VI.

The run from St. *Catherine's* to port St. *Julian*, with some account of that port, and of the country to the southward of the river of *Plate*.

IN leaving St. *Catherine's*, we left the last amicable port we proposed to touch at, and were now proceeding to an hostile, or at best, a desart and inhospitable coast. And as we were to expect a more boisterous climate to the southward than any we had yet experienced, not only our danger of separation would by this means be much greater than it had been hitherto, but other accidents of a more pernicious nature were likewise to be apprehended, and as much as possible to be provided against. And therefore Mr. *Anson*, in appointing the various stations at which the ships of the squadron were to rendezvous, had considered, that it was possible his own ship might be disabled from getting round Cape *Horn*, or might be lost, and had given proper directions, that even in that case the expedition should not be abandoned. For the orders delivered to the Captains, the day before we sailed from St. *Catherine's*, were, that in case of separation, which they were with the utmost care to endeavour to avoid, the first place of rendezvous should be the bay of port St. *Julian*; describing the place from Sir *John Narborough's* account of it:[1] There they were to supply themselves with as much salt as they could take in, both for their own use, and for the use of the squadron; and if, after a stay there of ten days, they were not joined by the Commodore, they were then to proceed through *Streights le Maire* round Cape *Horn*, into the *South-Seas*, where the next place of rendezvous was to be the Island of *Nostra Senora del Socoro*, in the latitude of 45° South, and longitude from the *Lizard* 71°:12' West. They were to bring this Island to bear E. N. E, and to cruize from five to twelve leagues distance from it, as long as their store of wood and water would permit, both which they were to expend with the utmost frugality. And when they were under an absolute necessity of a fresh supply, they were to stand in, and endeavour to find out an anchoring place; and in case they could not, and the weather made it dangerous to supply their ships by standing off and on, they were then to make the best of their way to the Island of *Juan Fernandes*, in the latitude of 33°:37′ South. And as soon as they had there recruited their wood and water, they were to continue cruizing off the anchoring place of that Island for fifty-six days; in which time, if they were not joined by the Commodore, they might conclude that some accident had befallen him, and they were forthwith to put themselves under the command of the senior Officer, who was to use his utmost endeavours to annoy the enemy both by sea and land. That with these views their new Commodore was to continue in those seas as long as his provisions lasted, or as long as they were recruited by what he should take from the enemy, reserving only a sufficient quantity to carry him and the ships under his command to *Macao*, at the entrance of the river *Tigris* near *Canton* on the coast of *China*, where having supplied himself with a new stock of provisions, he was thence, without delay, to make the best of his way to *England*. And as it was found impossible as yet to unload our Victualler the *Ann Pink*, the Commodore gave the Master of her the same rendezvous, and the same orders to put himself under the command of the remaining senior Officer.

Under these orders the squadron sailed from St. *Catherine's* on *Sunday* the 18th of *January*, as hath been already mentioned in the preceding chapter. The next day we had very squally weather, attended with rain, lightning and thunder, but it soon became fair again with light breezes, and continued thus till *Wednesday* evening, when it blew fresh again; and encreasing all night, by eight the next morning it became a most violent storm, and we had with it so thick a fog, that it was impossible to see at the distance of two ships length, so that the whole squadron disappeared. On this, a signal was made, by firing guns, to bring to with the larboard tacks, the wind being then due East. We ourselves immediately handed[1] the top sails, bunted[2] the main-sail, and lay to under a reefed mizen till noon, when the fog dispersed, and we soon discovered all the ships of the squadron except the *Pearl*, who did not join us till near a month afterwards. The *Tryal* Sloop was a great way to leeward, having lost her main-mast in this squall, and having been obliged, for fear of bilging,[3] to cut away the raft. We bore down with the squadron to her relief, and the *Gloucester* was ordered to take her in tow, for the weather did not entirely abate till the day after, and even then, a great swell continued from the eastward, in consequence of the preceding storm.

After this accident we stood to the southward with little interruption, and here we experienced the same setting of the current, which we had observed before our arrival at St. *Catherine's*; that is, we generally found ourselves to the southward of our reckoning, by about twenty miles each day. This error continued, with a little variation, till we had passed the latitude of the river of *Plate*; and even then, we found that the same current, however difficult to be accounted for, did yet undoubtedly take place; for we were not satisfied in deducing it from the error in our reckoning, but we actually tried it more than once, when a calm made it practicable.

When we had passed the latitude of the river of *Plate*, we had soundings all along the coast of *Patagonia*. These soundings, when well ascertained, being of great use in determining the position of the ship, and we having tried them more frequently, in greater depths, and with more attention, than I believe had been done before us, I shall recite our observations as succinctly as I can, referring to the chart hereafter inserted in the ninth chapter of this book, for a general view of the whole. In the latitude of 36°:52' we had sixty fathom of water, with a bottom of fine black and grey sand; from thence, to 39°:55', we varied our depths from fifty to eighty fathom, though we had constantly the same bottom as before; between the last mentioned latitude, and 43°:16', we had only fine grey sand, with the same variation of depths, except that we once or twice lessened our water to forty fathom. After this, we continued in forty fathom for about half a degree, having a bottom of coarse sand and broken shells, at which time we were in sight of land, and not above seven leagues from it: As we edged from the land we met with variety of soundings; first black sand, then muddy, and soon after rough ground with stones; but then encreasing our water to forty-eight fathom, we had a muddy bottom to the latitude of 46°:10'. We then returned again into thirty-six fathom, and kept shoaling our water, till at length we came into twelve fathom, having constantly small stones and pebbles at the bottom. Part of this time we had a view of Cape *Blanco*, which lies in about the latitude of 46°:52', and longitude West from *London* 66°:43'. This is the most remarkable land upon the coast: Two very exact views of it are exhibited in the annexed plate, where (*b*) represents the Cape itself; these draughts will fully enable future Voyagers to distinguish it. Steering from hence S. by E. nearly, we, in a run of about thirty leagues, deepned our water to fifty fathom, without once altering the bottom; and then drawing towards the shore with a S. W. course, varying rather to the westward, we had every where a sandy bottom, till our coming into thirty fathom, where we had again a sight of land distant from us, about eight leagues, lying in the latitude of 48°:31′. We made this land on the 17th of *February*, and at five in the afternoon we came to an anchor upon the same bottom, in the latitude of 48°:58′, the southermost land then in view bearing S. S. W, the northermost N. N. $\frac{1}{2}$ E, a small Island N. W. and the westermost hummock W. S. W. In this station we found the tide to set S. by W; and weighing again at five the next morning, we, an hour afterwards, discovered a sail, upon which the *Severn* and *Gloucester* were both directed to give chace; but we soon perceived it to be the *Pearl*, which separated from us a few days after we left St. *Catherine's*, and on this we made a signal for the *Severn* to rejoin the squadron, leaving the *Gloucester* alone in the pursuit. And now we were surprized to see, that on the *Gloucester*'s approach, the people on board the *Pearl* increased their sail, and stood from her. However, the *Gloucester* came up with them, but found them with their hammocks in their nettings, and every thing ready for an engagement. At two in the afternoon the *Pearl* joined us, and running up under our stern, Lieutenant *Salt* hailed the Commodore, and acquainted him that Captain *Kidd* died on the 31st of *January*. He likewise informed him, that he had seen five large ships the 10th instant, which he for some time imagined to be our squadron: That he suffered the commanding ship, which wore a red broad pennant, exactly resembling that of the Commodore, at the main top-mast head, to come within gun-shot of him before he discovered his mistake; but then finding it not to be the *Centurion*, he haled close upon the wind, and crowded from them with all his sail, and standing cross a ripling, where they hesitated to follow him, he happily escaped. He made them to be five *Spanish* men of war, one of them exceedingly like the *Gloucester*, which was the occasion of his apprehensions when the *Gloucester* chased him. By their appearance he thought they consisted of two ships of seventy guns, two of fifty, and one of forty guns. The whole squadron continued in chace of him all that day, but at night finding they could not get near him, they gave over the chace, and directed their course to the southward.[1]

And now had it not been for the necessity we were under of refitting the *Tryal*, this piece of intelligence would have prevented our making any stay at St. *Julian's*; but as it was impossible for that sloop to proceed round the Cape in her present condition, some stay there was inevitable, and therefore the same evening we came to an anchor again in twenty-five fathom water, the bottom a mixture of mud and sand, and the high hummock bearing S. W. by W. And weighing at nine in the morning, we soon after sent the two Cutters belonging to the *Centurion* and *Severn* in shore, to discover the harbour of St. *Julian*, while the ships kept standing along the coast, at about the distance of a league from the land. At six o'clock we anchored in the bay of St. *Julian*, in nineteen fathom, the bottom muddy ground with sand, the northermost land in sight bearing N. and by E, the southermost S. $\frac{1}{2}$ E, and the high hummock, to which Sir *John Narborough* formerly gave the name of *Wood's Mount*, W. S. W. Soon after, the Cutter returned on board having discovered the harbour, which did not appear to us in our situation, the northermost point shutting in upon the southermost, and in appearance closing the entrance. To facilitate the knowledge of this coast to future Navigators, there are two views annexed; the first of the land of *Patagonia*, to the northward of port St. *Julian*, where (*w*) is *Wood's Mount*, and the bay of St. *Julian* lies round the point (*c*). The second view is of the bay itself; and here again (*w*) is *Wood's Mount*, (*a*) is cape St. *Julian*, and (*b*) the port or river's mouth.

Being come to an anchor in this bay of St. *Julian*, principally with a view of refitting the *Tryal*, the Carpenters were immediately employed in that business, and continued so during our whole stay at the place. The *Tryal*'s main mast having been carried away about twelve feet below the cap, they contrived to make the remaining part of the mast serve again; and the *Wager* was ordered to supply her with a spare main top-mast, which the Carpenters converted into a new foremast. And I cannot help observing, that this accident to the *Tryal*'s mast, which gave us so much uneasiness at that time, on account of the delay it occasioned, was, in all probability, the means of preserving the sloop, and all her crew. For before this, her masts, how well soever proportioned to a better climate, were much too lofty for these

71

high southern latitudes: So that had they weathered the preceding storm, it would have been impossible for them to have stood against those seas and tempests we afterwards encountered in passing round Cape *Horn*, and the loss of masts in that boisterous climate, would scarcely have been attended with less than the loss of the vessel, and of every man on board her; since it would have been impracticable for the other ships to have given them any relief, during the continuance of those impetuous storms.

Whilst we stayed at this place, the Commodore appointed the Honourable Captain *Murray* to succeed to the *Pearl*, and Captain *Cheap* to the *Wager*, and he promoted Mr. *Charles Saunders*, his first Lieutenant, to the command of the *Tryal* Sloop. But Capt. *Saunders* lying dangerously ill of a fever on board the *Centurion*, and it being the opinion of the surgeons, that the removing him on board his own ship, in his present condition, might tend to the hazard of his life; Mr. *Anson* gave an order to Mr. *Saumarez*, first Lieutenant of the *Centurion*, to act as Master and Commander of the *Tryal*, during the illness of Captain *Saunders*.

Here the Commodore too, in order to ease the expedition of all unnecessary expence, held a farther consultation with his Captains about unloading and discharging the *Anna Pink*; but they represented to him, that they were so far from being in a condition of taking any part of her loading on board, that they had still great quantities of provisions in the way of their guns between decks, and that their ships were withal so very deep, that they were not fit for action without being cleared. This put the Commodore under a necessity of retaining the *Pink* in the service; and as it was apprehended we should certainly meet with the *Spanish* squadron, in passing the Cape, Mr. *Anson* thought it adviseable to give orders to the Captains, to put all their provisions, which were in the way of their guns, on board the *Anna Pink*, and to remount such of their guns as had formerly, for the ease of their ships, been ordered into the hold.

This bay of St. *Julian*, where we are now at anchor, being a convenient rendezvous, in case of separation, for all cruisers bound to the southward, and the whole coast of *Patagonia*, from the river of *Plate* to the Streights of *Magellan*, lying nearly parallel to their usual route, a short account of the singularity of this country, with a particular description of port St. *Julian*, may perhaps be neither unacceptable to the curious, nor unworthy the attention of future Navigators, as some of them, by unforeseen accidents, may be obliged to run in with the land, and to make some stay on this coast, in which case the knowledge of the country, its produce and inhabitants, cannot but be of the utmost consequence to them.

To begin then with the tract of country usually stiled *Patagonia*. This is the name often given to the southermost part of South *America*, which is unpossessed by the *Spaniards*, extending from their settlements to the Streights of *Magellan*. On the east side, this country is extremely remarkable, for a peculiarity not to be paralleled in any other known part of the globe; for though the whole territory to the northward of the river of *Plate* is full of wood, and stored with immense quantities of large timber trees, yet to the southward of the river no trees of any kind are to be met with, except a few peach-trees, first planted and cultivated by the *Spaniards* in the neighbourhood of *Buenos Ayres*: So that on the whole eastern coast of *Patagonia*, extending near four hundred leagues in length, and reaching as far back as any discoveries have yet been made, no other wood has been found than a few insignificant shrubs. Sir *John Narborough* in particular, who was sent out, by King *Charles* the second, expressly to examine this country, and the Streights of *Magellan*, and who, in pursuance of his orders, wintered upon this coast in port St. *Julian* and port *Desire*, in the year 1670; Sir *John Narborough*, I say, tells us, that he never saw a stick of wood in the country, large enough to make the handle of an hatchet.

But though this country be so destitute of wood, it abounds with pasture. For the land appears in general to be made up of downs of a light dry gravelly soil, and produces great quantities of long coarse grass, which grows in tufts interspersed with large barren spots of gravel between them. This grass, in many places, feeds immense herds of cattle: For the *Spaniards* at *Buenos Ayres*, having brought over a few black cattle from *Europe* at their first settlement, they have thriven prodigiously by the plenty of herbage which they found here, and are now encreased to that degree, and are extended so far into the country, that they are not considered as private property; but many thousands at a time are slaughtered every year by the Hunters, only for their hides and tallow. The manner of killing these cattle, being a practice peculiar to that part of the world, merits a more circumstantial description. The Hunters employed on this occasion being all of them mounted on horseback, (and both the *Spaniards* and *Indians* in that part of the world are usually most excellent horsemen) they arm themselves with a kind of a spear, which, at its end, instead of a blade fixed in the same line with the wood in the usual manner, has its blade fixed across; with this instrument they ride at a beast, and surround him. The Hunter that comes behind him hamstrings him; and as after this operation the beast soon tumbles, without being able to raise himself again, they leave him on the ground, and pursue others, whom they serve in the same manner. Sometimes there is a second party, who attend the Hunters, to skin the cattle as they fall: But it is said, that at other times the Hunters chuse to let them languish in torment till the next day, from an opinion that the anguish, which the animal in the mean time endures, may burst the lymphaticks, and thereby facilitate the separation of the skin from the carcass: And though their Priests have loudly condemned this most barbarous practice, and have gone so far, if my memory does not fail me, as to excommunicate those who follow it, yet all their efforts to put an entire stop to it have hitherto proved ineffectual.

Besides the numbers of cattle which are every year slaughtered for their hides and tallow, in the manner already described, it is often necessary for the purposes of agriculture, and likewise with other views, to take them alive, and without wounding them: This is performed with a most wonderful and almost incredible dexterity, and principally by the use of a machine, which the *English*, who have resided at *Buenos Ayres*, generally denominate a lash. It is made of a thong of several fathoms in length, and very strong, with a running noose at one end of it: This the Hunters (who in this case are also mounted on horseback) take in their right hands, it being first properly coiled up, and having its end opposite to the noose fastened to the saddle; and thus prepared they ride at a herd of cattle. When they arrive within a certain distance of a beast, they throw their thong at him with such exactness, that they never fail of fixing the noose about his horns. The beast, when he finds himself entangled, generally runs, but the horse, being swifter, attends him, and prevents the thong from being too much strained, till a second Hunter, who follows the game, throws another noose about one of its hind legs; and this being done, both horses (they being trained for the purpose) instantly turn different ways, in order to strain the two thongs in contrary directions, on which the beast, by their opposite pulls, is presently overthrown, and then the horses stop, keeping the thongs still upon the stretch: Being thus on the ground, and incapable of resistance, (for he is extended between the two horses) the Hunters alight, and secure him in such a manner, that they afterwards easily convey him to whatever place they please. In the same manner they noose horses, and, as it is said, even tygers; and however strange this last circumstance may appear, there are not wanting persons of credit who assert it. Indeed, it must be owned, that the address both of the *Spaniards* and *Indians* in that part of the world, in the use of this lash or noose, and the certainty with which they throw it, and fix it on any intended part of the beast at a considerable distance, are matters only to be believed, from the repeated and concurrent testimony of all who have frequented that country, and might reasonably be questioned, did it rely on a single report, or had it been ever contradicted or denied by any one who had resided at *Buenos Ayres*.

The cattle which are killed in the manner I have already observed, are slaughtered only for their hides and tallow, to which sometimes are added their tongues, and the rest of their flesh is left to putrify, or to be devoured by the birds and wild beasts; but the greatest part of this carion falls to the share of the wild dogs, of which there are immense numbers to be found in that country. They are supposed to have been originally produced by *Spanish* dogs from *Buenos Ayres*, who, allured by the great quantity of carion, and the facility they had by that means of subsisting, left their Masters, and ran wild amongst the cattle; for they are plainly of the breed of the *European* dogs, an animal not originally found in *America*. But though these dogs are said to be some thousands in a company, they hitherto neither diminish nor prevent the increase of the cattle, not daring to attack them, by reason of the numbers which constantly feed together; but contenting themselves with the carion left them by the Hunters, and perhaps now and then with a few stragglers, who, by accidents, are separated from the herd they belong to.

Besides the wild cattle which have spread themselves in such vast herds from *Buenos Ayres* towards the southward, the same country is in like manner furnished with horses. These too were first brought from *Spain*, and are also prodigiously encreased, and run wild to a much greater distance than the black cattle: And though many of them are excellent, yet their number makes them of very little value; the best of them being often sold, in a country where money is plenty and commodities very dear, for not more than a dollar a-piece. It is not as yet certain how far to the southward these herds of wild cattle and horses have extended themselves; but there is some reason to conjecture, that stragglers of both kinds are to be met with very near the Streights of *Magellan*; and they will in time doubtless fill the southern part of this Continent with their breed, which cannot fail of proving of considerable advantage to such ships as may touch upon the coast; for the horses themselves are said to be very good eating, and as such, to be preferred by some of the *Indians* even before the black cattle. But whatever plenty of this kind may be hereafter found here, there is one material refreshment which this eastern side of *Patagonia* seems to be very defective in, and that is fresh water; for the land being generally of a nitrous and saline nature, the ponds and streams are frequently brackish. However, as good water has been found there, though in small quantities, it is not improbable, but on a further search, this inconvenience may be removed.

Besides the cattle and horses which I have mentioned, there are in all parts of this country a good number of *Vicunnas* or *Peruvian* sheep; but these, by reason of their shyness and swiftness, are killed with difficulty. On the eastern coast too, there abounds immense quantities of seals, and a vast variety of sea-fowl, amongst which the most remarkable are the *Penguins*; they are in size and shape like a goose, but instead of wings they have short stumps like fins, which are of no use to them except in the water; their bills are narrow, like that of an *Albitross*, and they stand and walk in an erect posture. From this, and their white bellies, Sir *John Narborough* has whimsically likened them to little children standing up in white aprons.

The inhabitants of this eastern coast (to which I have all along hitherto confined my relation) appear to be but few, and have rarely been seen more than two or three at a time, by any ships that have touched here. We, during our stay at the port of St. *Julian*, saw none. However, towards *Buenos Ayres* they are sufficiently numerous, and oftentimes very troublesome to the *Spaniards*; but there the greater breadth and variety of the country, and a milder climate, yield them a better protection; for in that place the Continent is between three and four hundred leagues in breadth, whereas at port St. *Julian* it is little more than a hundred: So that I conceive the same *Indians*, that frequent the western coast of *Patagonia* and the Streights of *Magellan*, often ramble to this side. As the *Indians* near *Buenos Ayres* exceed these southern *Indians* in number, so they greatly surpass them in activity and spirit, and seem in their manners to be nearly allied to those gallant *Chilian Indians*, who have long set the whole *Spanish* power at defiance, have often ravaged their country, and remain to this hour independent. For the *Indians* about *Buenos Ayres* have learnt to be excellent horsemen, and are extreamly expert in the management of all cutting weapons, though ignorant of the use of fire-arms, which the *Spaniards* are very solicitous to keep out of their hands. And of the vigour and resolution of these *Indians*, the behaviour of *Orellana* and his followers, whom we have formerly mentioned, is a memorable instance. Indeed were we disposed to aim at the utter subversion of the *Spanish* power in *America*, no means seem more probable to effect it, than due encouragement and assistance given to these *Indians* and those of *Chili*.[1]

Thus much may suffice in relation to the eastern coast of *Patagonia*. The western coast is of less extent; and by reason of the *Andes* which skirt it, and stretch quite down to the water, is a very rocky and dangerous shore. However, I shall be hereafter necessitated to make further mention of it, and therefore shall not enlarge thereon at this time, but shall conclude this account with a short description of the harbour of St. *Julian*, the general form of which may be conceived from the annexed sketch. But it must be remembered, that the bar, which is there marked at the entrance, is often shifting and has many holes in it. The tide flows here N. and S, and at full and change, rises four fathom.

We, on our first arrival here, sent an Officer on shore to the salt-pond, marked (D) in the plan, in order to procure a quantity of salt for the use of the Squadron, Sir *John Narborough* having observed, when he was here, that the salt produced in that place was very white and good, and that in *February* there was enough of it to fill a thousand ships; but our Officer returned with a sample which was very bad, and he told us, that even of this there was but little to be got; I suppose the weather had been more rainy than ordinary, and had destroyed it. To give the reader a better idea of this port, and of the adjacent country, to which the whole coast I have described bears a great resemblance, I have inserted two very accurate views, one of them representing the appearance of the country, when looking up the river; the other, being a view taken from the same spot, but the observer is now supposed to turn round opposite to his former situation, and consequently this is a representation of the appearance of the country down the river, betwixt the station of the observer, and the river's mouth.

CHAP. VII.

Departure from the bay of St. *Julian*, and the passage from there to Streights *Le Maire*.

THE *Tryal* being nearly refitted, which was our principal occupation at this bay of St. *Julian*, and the sole occasion of our stay, the Commodore thought it necessary, as we were now directly bound for the *South-Seas* and the enemy's coasts, to regulate the plan of his future operations: And therefore, on the 24th of *February*, a signal was made for all Captains, and a Council of war was held on board the *Centurion*, at which were present the Honourable *Edward Legg*, Captain *Matthew Mitchel*, the Honourable *George Murray*, Captain *David Cheap*, together with Colonel *Mordaunt Cracherode*, Commander of the land-forces. At this Council Mr. *Anson* proposed, that their first attempt, after their arrival in the *South-Seas*, should be the attack of the town and harbour of *Baldivia*, the principal frontier of the district of *Chili*; Mr. *Anson* informing them, at the same time, that it was an article contained in his Majesty's instructions to him, to endeavour to secure some port in the *South-Seas*, where the ships of the squadron might be careened and refitted. To this proposition made by the Commodore, the Council unanimously and readily agreed; and in consequence of this resolution, new instructions were given to the Captains of the squadron, by which, though they were still directed, in case of separation, to make the best of their way to the Island of *Nuestra Senora del Socoro*, yet (notwithstanding the orders they had formerly given them at St. *Catherine's*) they were to cruize off that Island only ten days; from whence, if not joined by the Commodore, they were to proceed, and cruize off the harbour of *Baldivia*, making the land between the latitudes of 40°, and 40°:30, and taking care to keep to the southward of the port; and, if in fourteen days they were not joined by the rest of the squadron, they were then to quit this station, and to direct their course to the Island of *Juan Fernandes*, after which they were to regulate their further proceedings by their former orders. The same directions were also given to the Master of the *Anna Pink*, and he was particularly instructed to be very careful in

79

answering the signals made by any ship of the squadron, and likewise to destroy his papers and orders, if he should be so unfortunate, as to fall into the hands of the enemy. And as the separation of the squadron might prove of the utmost prejudice to his Majesty's service each Captain was ordered to give it in charge to the respective Officers of the watch, not to keep their ship at a greater distance from the *Centurion* than two miles, as they would answer it at their peril; and if any Captain should find his ship beyond the distance specified, he was to acquaint the Commodore with the name of the Officer, who had thus neglected his duty.

These necessary regulations being established, and the *Tryal* Sloop compleated, the squadron weighed on *Friday* the 27th of *February*, at seven in the morning, and stood to the sea; the *Gloucester* indeed found a difficulty in purchasing[1] her anchor, and was left a considerable way a-stern, so that in the night we fired several guns as a signal to her Captain to make sail, but he did not come up to us till the next morning, when we found that they had been obliged to cut their cable, and leave their best bower[2] behind them. At ten in the morning, the day after our departure, *Wood's Mount*, the highland over St. *Julian*, bore from us N. by W. distant ten leagues, and we had fifty-two fathom of water. And now standing to the southward, we had great expectation of falling in with *Pizarro's* squadron; for, during our stay at port St. *Julian*, there had generally been hard gales between the W. N. W. and S. W, so that we had reason to conclude the *Spaniards* had gained no ground upon us in that interval. And it was the prospect of meeting with them, that had occasioned our Commodore to be so very solicitous to prevent the separation of our ships: For had we been solely intent on getting round Cape *Horn* in the shortest time, the properest method for this purpose would have been, to have ordered each ship to have made the best of her way to the rendezvous, without waiting for the rest.

From our departure from St. *Julian* to the 4th of *March*, we had little wind, with thick hazy weather, and some rain; and our soundings were generally from forty to fifty fathom, with a bottom of black and grey sand, sometimes intermixed with pebble stones. On the 4th of *March* we were in sight of cape *Virgin Mary*, and not more than six or seven leagues distant from it: This is the northern cape of the Streights of *Magellan*, it lies in the latitude of 52° : 21′ South, and longitude from *London* 71° : 44′ West, and seems to be a low flat land, ending in a point. And for a direction to such ships as may, by particular reasons, be induced hereafter to pass through those Streights into the *South-Seas*, I have annexed a very accurate draught of its appearance, where (*a*) represents the Cape itself. Off this Cape our depth of water was from thirty-five to forty-eight fathom. The afternoon of this day was very bright and clear, with small breezes of wind, inclinable to a calm, and most of the Captains took the opportunity of this favourable weather to pay a visit to the Commodore; but while they were in company together, they were all greatly alarmed by a sudden flame, which burst out on board the *Gloucester*, and which was succeeded by a cloud of smoak. However, they were soon relieved from their apprehensions, by receiving information, that the blast was occasioned by a spark of fire from the forge, lighting on some gunpowder and other combustibles, which an Officer on board was preparing for use, in case we should fall in with the *Spanish* fleet; and that it had been extinguished, without any damage to the ship.

We here found what was constantly verified by all our observations in these high latitudes, that fair weather was always of an exceeding short duration, and that when it was remarkably fine, it was a certain presage of a succeeding storm, for the calm and sunshine of our afternoon ended in a most turbulent night, the wind freshning from the S. W. as the night came on, and encreasing its violence continually till nine in the morning the next day, when it blew so hard, that we were obliged to bring to with the squadron, and to continue under a reefed mizen till eleven at night, having in that time from forty-three to fifty-seven fathom water, with black sand and gravel; and by an observation we had at noon, we concluded a current had set us twelve miles to the southward of our reckoning. Towards midnight, the wind abating, we made sail again; and steering South, we discovered in the morning for the first time the land, called *Terra del Fuego*, stretching from the S. by W, to the S. E. $\frac{1}{2}$ E. This indeed afforded us but a very uncomfortable prospect, it appearing of a stupendous height, covered every where with snow. And though the dreariness of this scene can be but imperfectly represented by any Drawing, yet the annexed plate contains so exact a delineation of the form of the country, that it may greatly assist the reader in framing some idea of this uncouth and rugged coast. In this Drawing (*a*) is the opening of Streights *Le Maire*, (*b*) Cape St. *Diego*, (1) (2) (3) the three hills, called the three

81

brothers, and (4) *Montegorda,* an highland which lies up in the country, and appears over the three brothers. We steered along this shore all day, having soundings from forty to fifty fathom, with stones and gravel. And as we intended to pass through Streights *Le Maire* next day, we lay to at night, that we might not overshoot them, and took this opportunity to prepare ourselves for the tempestuous climate we were soon to be engaged in; with which view, we employed our-selves good part of the night in bending an entire new suit of sails to the yards. At four the next morning, being the 7th of *March,* we made sail, and at eight saw the land; and soon after we began to open the Streights, at which time Cape St. *James* bore from us E. S. E, Cape St. *Vincent* S. E. $\frac{1}{2}$ E, the middlemost of the three brothers S. and by W, *Montegorda* South, and Cape St. *Bartholomew,* which is the souther-most point of *Staten-land,* E. S. E. The appearance of the Streights in this situation, is represented in the annexed plate,[1] where (*a*) is part of *Staten-land,* (*b*) Cape St. *Bartholomew,* (*c*) part of *Terra del Fuego,* (*d*) port *Maurice,* and (*e*) supposed to be *Valentine's* bay, or the bay of good success. And here I must observe, that *Frezier* has given us a very correct prospect of the part of *Terra del Fuego,* which borders on the Streights, but has omitted that of *Staten-land,* which forms the opposite shore: Hence we found it difficult to determine exactly where the Streights lay, till they began to open to our view; and for want of this, if we had not happened to have coasted a considerable way along shore, we might have missed the Streights, and have got to the east-ward of *Staten-land* before we knew it. This is an accident that has happened to many ships, particularly, as *Frezier* mentions, to the *Incarnation* and *Concord*; who intending to pass through Streights *Le Maire,* were deceived by three hills on *Staten-land* like the three brothers, and some creeks resembling those of *Terra del Fuego,* and thereby over-shot the Streights. To prevent these accidents for the future, there is inserted the West prospect of *Staten-land,* where (*a*) is Cape St. *Diego,* on *Terra del Fuego,* (*b*) Cape St. *Bartholomew,* on *Staten-land.* This Drawing will hereafter render it impossible for any ships to be deceived in the manner abovementioned, or to find any difficulty in distinguishing the points of land by which the Streights are formed.

And on occasion of this prospect of *Staten-land* here inserted, I cannot but remark, that though *Terra del Fuego* had an aspect extremely barren and desolate, yet this Island of *Staten-land* far surpasses it, in the wildness and horror of its appearance: It seeming to be entirely composed of inaccessible rocks, without the least mixture of earth or mold between them. These rocks terminate in a vast number of ragged points, which spire up to a prodigious height, and are all of them covered with everlasting snow; the points themselves are on every side surrounded with frightful precipices, and often overhang in a most astonishing manner; and the hills which bear them, are generally separated from each other by narrow clefts, which appear as if the country had been rent by earthquakes; for these chasms are nearly perpendicular, and extend through the substance of the main rocks, almost to their very bottoms: So that nothing can be imagined more savage and gloomy, than the whole aspect of this coast. But to proceed,

I have above-mentioned, that on the 7th of *March*, in the morning, we opened Streights *Le Maire*, and soon after, or about ten o'clock, the *Pearl* and the *Tryal* being ordered to keep a-head of the squadron, we entered them with fair weather and a brisk gale, and were hurried through by the rapidity of the tide in about two hours, though they are between seven and eight leagues in length. As these Streights are often considered as the boundary between the *Atlantick* and *Pacifick* Oceans, and as we presumed we had nothing now before us but an open sea, till we arrived on those opulent coasts where all our hopes and wishes centered, we could not help flattering ourselves, that the greatest difficulty of our passage was now at an end, and that our most sanguine dreams were upon the point of being realized; and hence we indulged our imaginations in those romantick schemes, which the fancied possession of the *Chilian* gold and *Peruvian* silver might be conceived to inspire. These joyous ideas were heightened by the brightness of the sky, and the serenity of the weather, which was indeed most remarkably pleasing; for tho' the winter was now advancing apace, yet the morning of this day, in its brilliancy and mildness, gave place to none we had seen since our departure from *England.* Thus animated by these delusions, we travers'd these memorable Streights, ignorant of the dreadful calamities that were then impending, and just ready to break upon us; ignorant that the time drew near, when the squadron would be separated never to unite again, and that this day of our passage was the last chearful day that the greatest part of us would ever live to enjoy.

CHAP. VIII.

From Streights *Le Maire* to Cape *Noir*.

WE had scarcely reached the southern extremity of the Streights of *Le Maire*, when our flattering hopes were instantly lost in the apprehensions of immediate destruction: For before the sternmost ships of the squadron were clear of the Streights, the serenity of the sky was suddenly changed, and gave us all the presages of an impending storm; and immediately that wind shifted to the southward, and blew in such violent squalls, that we were obliged to hand our top-sails, and reef our main-sail: The tide too, which had hitherto favoured us, now turned against us, and drove us to the eastward with prodigious rapidity, so that we were in great anxiety for the *Wager* and the *Anna Pink*, the two sternmost vessels, fearing they would be dashed to pieces against the shore of *Staten-land*; nor were our apprehensions without foundation, for it was with the utmost difficulty they escaped. And now the whole squadron, instead of pursuing their intended course to the S. W, were driven to the eastward by the united force of the storm, and of the currents; so that next day in the morning we found ourselves near seven leagues to the eastward of *Staten-land*, which then bore from us N. W. The violence of the current, which had set us with so much precipitation to the eastward, together with the force and constancy of the westerly winds, soon taught us to consider the doubling of Cape *Horn* as an enterprize, that might prove too mighty for our efforts, though some amongst us had lately treated the difficulties which former voyagers were said to have met with in this undertaking, as little better than chimerical, and had supposed them to arise rather from timidity and unskilfulness, than from the real embarrassments of the winds and seas; but we were now severely convinced, that these censures were rash and ill-grounded. For the distresses with which we struggled, during the three succeeding months, will not easily be paralleled in the relation of any former naval expedition. This will, I doubt not, be readily allowed by those who shall carefully peruse the ensuing narration.

From the storm which came on before we had well got clear of

Lord Anson, c. 1747, by an unknown French artist

A view of Streights Le Maire be

a del Fuego and Staten Land

A View of the Commodore's Tent at the Island of Juan Fernandes

Streights *Le Maire*, we had a continual succession of such tempestuous weather, as surprized the oldest and most experienced Mariners on board, and obliged them to confess, that what they had hitherto called storms were inconsiderable gales, compared with the violence of these winds, which raised such short, and at the same time such mountainous waves, as greatly surpassed in danger all seas known in any other part of the globe: And it was not without great reason, that this unusual appearance filled us with continual terror; for had any one of these waves broke fairly over us, it must, in all probability, have sent us to the bottom. Nor did we escape with terror only; for the ship rolling incessantly gunwale to, gave us such quick and violent motions, that the men were in perpetual danger of being dashed to pieces against the decks, or sides of the ship. And though we were extremely careful to secure ourselves from these shocks, by grasping some fixed body, yet many of our people were forced from their hold, some of whom were killed, and others greatly injured; in particular, one of our best seamen was canted over-board and drowned, another dislocated his neck, a third was thrown into the main-hold and broke his thigh, and one of our Boatswain's Mates broke his collar-bone twice; not to mention many other accidents of the same kind. These tempests, so dreadful in themselves, though unattended by any other unfavourable circumstance, were yet rendered more mischievous to us by their inequality, and the deceitful intervals which they at sometimes afforded; for though we were oftentimes obliged to lie to for days together under a reefed mizen, and were sometimes reduced to lie at the mercy of the waves under our bare poles, yet now and then we ventured to make sail with our courses double reefed; and the weather proving more tolerable, would perhaps encourage us to set our top-sails; after which, the wind, without any previous notice, would return upon us with redoubled force, and would in an instant tear our sails from the yards. And that no circumstance might be wanting which could aggrandize our distress, these blasts generally brought with them a great quantity of snow and sleet, which cased our rigging, and froze our sails, thereby rendring them and our cordage brittle, and apt to snap upon the slightest strain, adding great difficulty and labour to the working of the ship, benumbing the limbs of our people, and making them incapable of exerting themselves with their usual activity, and even disabling many of them, by mortifying their toes and fingers. It were indeed endless to enumerate the various disasters of different kinds which befel us; and I shall only mention the most material, which will sufficiently evince the calamitous condition of the whole squadron, during the course of this navigation.

It was on the 7th of *March*, as hath been already observed, that we passed Streights *Le Maire*, and were immediately afterwards driven to the eastward by a violent storm, and the force of the current which set that way. For the four or five succeeding days we had hard gales of wind from the same quarter, with a most prodigious swell; so that though we stood, during all that time, towards the S. W, yet we had no reason to imagine, we had made any way to the westward. In this interval we had frequent squalls of rain and snow, and shipped great quantities of water; after which, for three or four days, though the seas ran mountains high, yet the weather was rather more moderate: But, on the 18th, we had again strong gales of wind with extreme cold, and at midnight the main top-sail split, and one of the straps of the main dead eyes[1] broke. From hence, to the 23d, the weather was more favourable, though often intermixed with rain and sleet, and some hard gales; but as the waves did not subside, the ship, by labouring in this lofty sea, was now grown so loose in her upper works, that she let in the water at every seam, so that every part within board was constantly exposed to the sea-water, and scarcely any of the Officers ever lay in dry beds. Indeed it was very rare, that two nights ever passed without many of them being driven from their beds, by the deluge of water that came upon them.

On the 23d, we had a most violent storm of wind, hail, and rain, with a very great sea; and though we handed the main top-sail before the height of the squall, yet we found the yard sprung; and soon after the foot-rope of the main-sail breaking, the main-sail itself split instantly to rags, and, in spite of our endeavours to save it, much the greater part of it was blown over-board. On this, the Commodore made the signal for the squadron to bring to; and the storm at length flattening to a calm, we had an opportunity of getting down our main top-sail yard to put the Carpenters at work upon it, and of repairing our rigging; after which, having bent a new mainsail, we got under sail again with a moderate breeze; but in less than twenty-four hours we were attacked by another storm still more furious than the former; for it proved a perfect hurricane, and reduced us to the necessity of lying to under our bare poles. As our ship kept the wind better than any of the rest, we were obliged, in the afternoon, to wear ship, in order to join the squadron to the leeward, which otherwise we should have been in danger of losing in the night: And as we dared not venture any sail abroad, we were obliged to make use of an expedient, which answered our purpose; this was putting the helm a weather, and manning the fore-shrouds:[1] But though this method proved successful for the end intended, yet in the execution of it, one of our ablest seaman was canted over-board; and notwithstanding the prodigious agitation of the waves, we perceived that he swam very strong, and it was with the utmost concern that we found ourselves incapable of assisting him; and we were the more grieved at his unhappy fate, since we lost sight of him struggling with the waves, and conceived from the manner in which he swam, that he might continue sensible for a considerable time longer, of the horror attending his irretrievable situation.[2]

Before this last mentioned storm was quite abated, we found two of our main-shrouds and one mizen-shroud broke, all which we knotted, and set up immediately; and from hence we had an interval of three or four days less tempestuous than usual, but accompanied with a thick fog, in which we were obliged to fire guns almost every half hour, to keep our squadron together. On the 31st, we were alarmed by a gun fired from the *Gloucester*, and a signal made by her to speak with the Commodore; we immediately bore down to her, and were prepared to hear of some terrible disaster; but we were apprized of it before we joined her, for we saw that her main-yard was broke in the slings. This was a grievous misfortune to us all at this juncture; as it was obvious it would prove an hindrance to our sailing, and would detain us the longer in these inhospitable latitudes. But our future success and safety was not to be promoted by repining, but by resolution and activity; and therefore, that this unlucky incident might delay us as little as possible, the Commodore ordered several Carpenters to be put on board the *Gloucester* from the other ships of the squadron, in order to repair her damage with the utmost expedition. And the Captain of the *Tryal* complaining at the same time, that his pumps were so bad, and the sloop made so great a quantity of water, that he was scarcely able to keep her free, the Commodore ordered him a pump ready fitted from his own ship. It was very fortunate for the *Gloucester* and the *Tryal*, that the weather proved more favourable this day than for many days, both before and after; since by this means they were enabled to receive the assistance which seemed essential to their preservation, and which they could scarcely have had at any other time, as it would have been extremely hazardous to have ventured a boat on board.

The next day, that is, on the 1st of *April*, the weather returned again to its customary bias, the sky looked dark and gloomy, and the wind began to freshen and to blow in squalls; however, it was not yet so boisterous, as to prevent our carrying our top-sails close reefed; but its appearance was such, as plainly prognosticated that a still severer tempest was at hand: And accordingly, on the 3d of *April*, there came on a storm, which both in its violence and continuation (for it lasted three days) exceeded all that we had hitherto encountered. In its first onset we received a furious shock from a sea which broke upon our larboard quarter, where it stove in the quarter gallery, and rushed into the ship like a deluge; our rigging too suffered extremely, for one of the straps of the main dead-eyes was broke, as was also a main-shroud and puttock-shroud,[1] so that to ease the stress upon the masts and shrouds, we lowered both our main and fore-yards, and furled all our sails, and in this posture we lay to for three days, when the storm somewhat abating, we ventured to make sail under our courses only; but even this we could not do long, for, the next day, which was the 7th, we had another hard gale of wind, with lightning and rain, which obliged us to lie to again till night. It was wonderful, that notwithstanding the hard weather we had endured, no extraordinary accident had happened to any of the squadron since the breaking of the *Gloucester*'s main-yard: But this wonder soon ceased; for at three the next morning, several guns were fired to leeward as signals of distress. And the Commodore making a signal for the squadron to bring to, we, at day-break, saw the *Wager* a considerable way to leeward of any of the other ships; and we soon perceived that she had lost her mizen-mast, and main top-sail yard. We immediately bore down to her, and found this disaster had arisen from the badness of her iron work; for all the chain-plates to windward had given way, upon the ship's fetching a deep roll. This proved the more unfortunate to the *Wager*, as her Carpenter had been on board the *Gloucester* ever since the 31st of *March*, and the weather was now too severe to permit him to return: Nor was the *Wager* the only ship of the squadron that had suffered in the late tempest; for, the next day, a signal of distress was made by the *Anna Pink*, and, upon speaking with the Master, we learnt that they had broke their fore-stay and the gammon[1] of the bowsprit, and were in no small danger of having all the masts come by the board; so that we were obliged to bear away until they had made all fast, after which we haled upon a wind again.[2]

And now, after all our solicitude, and the numerous ills of every kind, to which we had been incessantly exposed for near forty days, we had great consolation in the flattering hopes we entertained, that our fatigues were drawing to a period, and that we should soon arrive in a more hospitable climate, where we should be amply repayed for all our past sufferings. For, towards the latter end of *March*, we were advanced, by our reckoning, near 10° to the westward of the westermost point of *Terra del Fuego*, and this allowance being double what former Navigators have thought necessary to be taken, in order to compensate the drift of the eastern current, we esteemed ourselves to be well advanced within the limits of the southern Ocean, and had therefore been ever since standing to the northward with as much expedition, as the turbulence of the weather, and our frequent disasters permitted. And, on the 13th of *April*, we were but a degree in latitude to the southward of the West entrance of the Streights of *Magellan*; so that we fully expected, in a very few days, to have experienced the celebrated tranquility of the *Pacifick* Ocean.

But these were delusions which only served to render our disappointment more terrible; for the next morning, between one and two, as we were standing to the northward, and the weather, which had till then been hazy, accidentally cleared up, the *Pink* made a signal for seeing land right a-head; and it being but two miles distant, we were all under the most dreadful apprehensions of running on shore; which, had either the wind blown from its usual quarter with its wonted vigour, or had not the moon suddenly shone out, not a ship amongst us could possibly have avoided: But the wind, which some few hours before blew in squalls from the S. W, having fortunately shifted to W. N. W, we were enabled to stand to the southward, and to clear ourselves of this unexpected danger; so that by noon we had gained an offing of near twenty leagues.

By the latitude of this land we fell in with, it was agreed to be a part of *Terra del Fuego*, near the southern outlet described in *Frezier*'s Chart of the Streights of *Magellan*, and was supposed to be that point called by him Cape *Noir*. It was indeed most wonderful, that the currents should have driven us to the eastward with such strength; for the whole squadron esteemed themselves upwards of ten degrees more westerly than this land, so that in running down, by our account, about nineteen degrees of longitude, we had not really advanced above half that distance.[1] And now, instead of having our labours and anxieties relieved by approaching a warmer climate and more tranquil seas, we were to steer again to the southward, and were again to combat those western blasts, which had so often terrified us; and this too, when we were weakned by our men falling sick, and dying apace, and when our spirits, dejected by a long continuance at sea, and by our late disappointment, were much less capable of supporting us in the various difficulties, which we could not but expect in this new undertaking. Add to all this too, the discouragement we received by the diminution of the strength of the squadron; for three days before this, we lost sight of the *Severn* and the *Pearl* in the morning; and though we spread our ships, and beat about for them some time, yet we never saw them more; whence we had apprehensions that they too might have fallen in with this land in the night, and by being less favoured by the wind and the moon than we were, might have run on shore and have perished.[2] Full of these dejected thoughts and gloomy presages, we stood away to the S. W, prepared by our late disaster to suspect, that how large soever an allowance we made in our westing for the drift of the eastern current, we might still, upon a second trial, perhaps find it insufficient.

CHAP. IX.

Observations and directions for facilitating the passage of our future Cruisers round Cape *Horn*.

THE improper season of the year in which we attempted to double Cape *Horn*, and to which is to be imputed the disappointment (recited in the foregoing chapter) in falling in with *Terra del Fuego*, when we reckoned ourselves at least a hundred leagues to the westward of that whole coast, and consequently well advanced into the *Pacifick* Ocean; this unseasonable navigation, I say, to which we were necessitated by our too late departure from *England*, was the fatal source of all the misfortunes we afterwards encountered. For from hence proceeded the separation of our ships, the destruction of our people, the ruin of our project on *Baldivia*, and of all our other views on the *Spanish* places, and the reduction of our squadron from the formidable condition in which it passed Streights *Le Maire*, to a couple of shattered half manned cruisers and a sloop, so far disabled, that in many climates they scarcely durst have put to sea. To prevent therefore, as much as in me lies, all ships hereafter bound to the *South-Seas* from suffering the same calamities, I think it my duty to insert in this place, such directions and observations, as either my own experience and reflection, or the converse of the most skilful Navigators on board the squadron could furnish me with, in relation to the most eligible manner of doubling Cape *Horn*, whether in regard to the season of the year, the course proper to be steered, or the places of refreshment both on the East and West-side of *South America*.

And first with regard to the proper place for refreshment on the East-side of *South America*. For this purpose the Island of St. *Catherine's* has been usually recommended by former writers, and on their faith we put in there, as has been formerly mentioned: But the treatment we met with, and the small store of refreshments we could procure there, are sufficient reasons to render all ships for the future cautious, how they trust themselves in the government of *Don Jose Silva de Paz*; for they may certainly depend on having their strength, condition and designs betrayed to the *Spaniards*, as far as the knowledge, the Governor can procure of these particulars, will give leave. And as this treacherous conduct is inspired by the views of private gain, in the illicit commerce carried on to the river of *Plate*, rather than by any national affection which the *Portuguese* bear the *Spaniards*, the same perfidy may perhaps be expected from most of the Governors of the *Brazil* coast; since these smuggling engagements are doubtless very extensive and general. And though the Governors should themselves detest so faithless a procedure, yet as ships are perpetually passing from some or other of the *Brazil* ports to the river of *Plate*, the *Spaniards* could scarcely fail of receiving, by this means, casual intelligence of any *British* ships upon the coast; which, however imperfect such intelligence might be, would prove of dangerous import to the views and interests of those cruisers who were thus discovered.

For the *Spanish* trade in the *South-Seas* running all in one track from North to South, with very little deviation to the eastward or westward, it is in the power of two or three cruisers, properly stationed in different parts of this track, to possess themselves of every ship that puts to sea: But this is only so long as they can continue concealed from the neighbouring coast; for the instant an enemy is known to be in those seas, all navigation is stopped, and consequently all captures are at an end; since the *Spaniards*, well apprized of these advantages of the enemy, send expresses along the coast, and lay a general embargo on all their trade; a measure, which they prudentially foresee, will not only prevent their vessels being taken, but will soon lay any cruisers, who have not strength sufficient to attempt their places, under a necessity of returning home. Hence then appears the great importance of concealing all expeditions of this kind; and hence too it follows, how extremely prejudicial that intelligence may prove, which is given by the *Portuguese* Governors to the *Spaniards*, in relation to the designs of ships touching at the ports of *Brazil*.

However, notwithstanding the inconveniences we have mentioned of touching on the coast of *Brazil*, it will oftentimes happen, that ships bound round Cape *Horn* will be obliged to call there for a supply of wood and water, and other refreshments. In this case St. *Catherine's* is the last place I would recommend, both as the proper animals for a live stock at sea, as hogs, sheep and fowls cannot be procured there, (for want of which we found ourselves greatly distressed, by being reduced to live almost entirely on salt provisions) but also because

from its being nearer the river of *Plate* than many of their other settlements, the inducements and conveniences of betraying us are much
stronger. The place I would recommend is *Rio Janeiro*, where two of
our squadron put in after they were separated from us in passing Cape
Horn, for here, as I have been informed by one of the Gentlemen on
board those ships, any quantity of hogs and poultry may be procured,
and this place being more distant from the river of *Plate*, the difficulty
of intelligence is somewhat inhanced, and consequently the chance of
continuing there undiscovered, in some degree augmented. Other
measures, which may effectually obviate all these embarrassments,
will be considered more at large hereafter.

And now I proced to the consideration of the proper course to be
steered for doubling Cape *Horn*. And here, I think, I am sufficiently
authorized by our own fatal experience, and by a careful comparison
and examination of the journals of former Navigators, to give this
piece of advice, which in prudence I think ought never to be departed
from: That is, that all ships bound to the *South-Seas*, instead of passing
through Streights *le Maire*, should constantly pass to the eastward of
Staten-land, and should be invariably bent on running to the southward, as far as the latitude of 61 or 62 degrees, before they endeavour to stand to the westward; and that when they are got into that
latitude, they should then make sure of sufficient westing, before they
once think of steering to the northward.

But as directions diametrically opposite to these have been formerly given by other writers, it is incumbent on me to produce my
reasons for each part of this maxim. And first, as to the passing to the
eastward of *Staten-land*. Those who have attended to the risque we
ran in passing Streights *Le Maire*, the danger we were in of being
driven upon *Staten-land* by the current, when, though we happily
escaped being put on shore, we were yet carried to the eastward of
that Island: Those who reflect on this, and on the like accidents which
have happened to other ships, will surely not esteem it prudent to pass
through Streights *Le Maire*, and run the risque of shipwreck, and after
all find themselves no farther to the westward (the only reason
hitherto given for this practice) than they might have been in the
same time, by a secure navigation in an open sea.

And next, as to the directions I have given for running into the
latitude of 61 or 62 South, before any endeavour is made to stand to

the westward. The reasons for this precept are, that in all probability
the violence of the currents will be hereby avoided, and the weather
will prove less tempestuous and uncertain. This last circumstance we
ourselves experienced most remarkably; for after we had unexpectedly
fallen in with the land, as has been mentioned in the preceding chapter,
we stood away to the southward to run clear of it, and were no sooner
advanced into sixty degrees or upwards, but we met with much better
weather, and smoother water than in any other part of the whole
passage: The air indeed was very cold and sharp, and we had strong
gales, but they were steady and uniform, and we had at the same time
sunshine and a clear sky; whereas in the lower latitudes, the winds
every now and then intermitted, as it were, to recover new strength,
and then returned suddenly in the most violent gusts, threatening at
each blast the loss of our masts, which must have ended in our certain
destruction. And that the currents in this high latitude would be of
much less efficacy than nearer the land, seems to be evinced from these
considerations, that all currents run with greater violence near the
shore than at sea, and that at greater distances from shore they are
scarcely perceptible: Indeed the reason of this seems sufficiently
obvious, if we consider, that constant currents are, in all probability,
produced by constant winds, the wind driving before it, though with a
flow and imperceptible motion, a large body of water, which being
accumulated upon any coast that it meets with, this superfluous water
must escape along the shore by the endeavours of its surface, to reduce itself to the same level with the rest of the Ocean. And it is
reasonable to suppose, that those violent gusts of wind which we experienced near the shore, so very different from what we found in the
latitude of sixty degrees and upwards, may be owing to a similar
cause; for a westerly wind almost perpetually prevails in the southern
part of the *Pacifick* Ocean: And this current of air being interrupted by
those immense hills called the *Andes*, and by the mountains on *Terra
del Fuego*, which together bar up the whole country to the southward
as far as Cape *Horn*, a part of it only can escape over the tops of those
prodigious precipices, and the rest must naturally follow the direction
of the coast, and must range down the land to the southward, and
sweep with an impetuous and irregular blast round Cape *Horn*, and
the southermost part of *Terra del Fuego*. However, not to rely on these
speculations, we may, I believe, establish, as incontestable, these

matters of fact, that both the rapidity of the currents, and the violence of the western gales, are less sensible in the latitude of 61 or 62 degrees, than nearer the shore of *Terra del Fuego*.

But though I am satisfied both from our own experience, and the relations of other Navigators, of the importance of the precept I here insist on, that of running into the latitude of 61 or 62 degrees, before any endeavours are made to stand to the westward; yet I would advise no ships hereafter to trust so far to this management, as to neglect another most essential maxim, which is the making this passage in the height of summer, that is, in the months of *December* and *January*; and the more distant the time of passing is taken from this season, the more disastrous it may be reasonably expected to prove. Indeed, if the mere violence of the western winds be considered, the time of our passage, which was about the Equinox, was perhaps the most unfavourable season; but then it must be considered, that in the depth of winter there are many other inconveniences to be apprehended in this navigation, which are almost insuperable: For the severity of the cold, and the shortness of the days, would render it impracticable at that season to run so far to the southward as is here recommended; and the same reasons would greatly augment the alarms of sailing in the neighbourhood of an unknown shore, dreadful in its appearance in the midst of summer, and would make a winter navigation on this coast to be, of all others, the most dismaying and terrible. As I would therefore advise all ships to make their passage in *December* and *January*, if possible, so I would warn them never to attempt the seas to the southward of Cape *Horn*, after the month of *March*.[1]

And now as to the remaining consideration, that is, the properest port for cruisers to refresh at on their first arrival in the *South-Seas*. On this head there is scarcely any choice, the Island of *Juan Fernandes* being the only place that can be prudently recommended for this purpose. For though there are many ports on the western side of *Patagonia*, between the Streights of *Magellan* and the *Spanish* settlements (a plan of one of which I shall insert in the course of this work) where ships might ride in great safety, might recruit their wood and water, and might procure some few refreshments; yet that coast is in itself so terrible, from the rocks and breakers it abounds with, and from the violence of the western winds, which blow constantly full upon it, that it is by no means adviseable to fall in with that land, at least till the roads, channels and anchorage in each part of it are accurately surveyed, and both the dangers and shelter it abounds with are more distinctly known.

Thus having given the best directions in my power for the success of future cruisers bound to the *South-Seas*, it might be expected that I should again resume the thread of my narration. But as both in the preceding and subsequent parts of this work, I have thought it my duty not only to recite all such facts, and to inculcate such maxims as had the least appearance of proving beneficial to future Navigators, but also occasionally to recommend such measures to the Public, as I conceive are adapted to promote the same laudable purpose, I cannot desist from the present subject, without beseeching those to whom the conduct of our naval affairs is committed, to endeavour to remove the many perplexities and embarrassments with which the navigation to the *South-Seas* is, at present, necessarily encumbered. An effort of this kind could not fail of proving highly honourable to themselves, and extremely beneficial to their country. For it is to me sufficiently evident, that whatever advantages navigation shall receive, either by the invention of methods that shall render its practice less hazardous, or by the more accurate delineation of the coasts, roads and ports already known, or by the discovery of new nations, or new species of commerce; it is evident, I say, to me, that by whatever means navigation is promoted, the conveniences hence arising must ultimately redound to the emolument of *Great-Britain*. Since as our fleets are at present superior to those of the whole world united, it must be a matchless degree of supineness or mean-spiritedness, if we permitted any of the advantages which new discoveries, or a more extended navigation may produce to mankind, to be ravished from us.

As therefore it appears that all our future expeditions to the *South-Seas* must run a considerable risque of proving abortive, whilst we are under the necessity of touching at *Brazil* in our passage thither, an expedient that might relieve us from this difficulty, would surely be a subject worthy of the attention of the Public; and this seems capable of being effected, by the discovery of some place more to the southward, where ships might refresh and supply themselves with the necessary sea-stock for their voyage round Cape *Horn*. And we have in reality the imperfect knowledge of two places, which might perhaps, on examination, prove extremely convenient for this purpose; the first of them is *Pepys*'s Island, in the latitude of 47° South, and laid down by Dr. *Halley*, about eighty leagues to the eastward of Cape *Blanco*, on the coast of *Patagonia*; the second, is *Falkland*'s Isles, in the latitude of 51°½ nearly South of *Pepys*'s Island. The first of these was discovered by Captain *Cowley*, in his Voyage round the World in the year 1696; who represents it as a commodious place for ships to wood and water at, and says, it is provided with a very good and capacious harbour, where a thousand sail of ships might ride at anchor, in great safety; that it abounds with fowls, and as the shore is either rocks or sands, it seems to promise great plenty of fish.[1] The second place, or *Falkland*'s Isles, have been seen by many ships both *French* and *English*, being the land laid down by *Frezier*, in his Chart of the extremity of South *America*, under the title of the *New Islands*. *Woods Rogers*, who run along the N. E. coast of these Isles in the year 1708,[2] tells us, that they extended about two degrees in length, and appeared with gentle descents from hill to hill, and seemed to be good ground, with woods and harbours. Either of these places, as they are Islands at a considerable distance from the Continent, may be supposed, from their latitude, to lie in a climate sufficiently temperate. It is true, they are too little known to be at present recommended for proper places of refreshment for ships bound to the southward: But if the Admiralty should think it adviseable to order them to be surveyed, which may be done at a very small expence, by a vessel fitted out on purpose; and if, on this examination, one or both of these places should appear proper for the purpose intended, it is scarcely to be conceived, of what prodigious import a convenient station might prove, situated so far to the south-ward, and so near Cape *Horn*.[3] The Duke and Duchess of *Bristol* were but thirty-five days from their losing sight of *Falkland*'s Isles to their arrival at *Juan Fernandes* in the *South-Seas*; And as the returning back is much facilitated by the western winds, I doubt not but a voyage might be made from *Falkland*'s Isles to *Juan Fernandes* and back again, in little more than two months. This, even in time of peace, might be of great consequence to this Nation; and, in time of war, would make us masters of those seas.

And as all discoveries of this kind, though extremely honourable to those who direct and promote them, may yet be carried on at an inconsiderable expence, since small vessels are much the properest to be employed in this service, it were to be wished, that the whole coast of

Patagonia, *Terra del Fuego*, and *Staten-land*, were carefully surveyed, and the numerous channels, roads and harbours with which they abound, accurately examined; this might open to us facilities of passing into the *Pacifick* Ocean, which as yet we may be unacquainted with, and would render all that southern navigation infinitely securer than at present; and particularly, an exact draught of the West coast of *Patagonia*, from the Streights of *Magellan* to the *Spanish* settlements, might perhaps furnish us with better and more convenient ports for refreshment, and better situated for the purposes either of war or commerce, and above a fortnight's sail nearer to *Falkland*'s Islands, than the Island of *Juan Fernandes*. The discovery of this coast hath formerly been thought of such consequence, by reason of its neighbourhood to the *Araucos* and other *Chilian Indians*, who are generally at war, or at least on ill terms with their *Spanish* neighbours, that Sir *John Narborough* was purposely fitted out in the reign of King *Charles* II, to survey the Streights of *Magellan*, the neighbouring coast of *Patagonia*, and the *Spanish* ports on that frontier, with directions, if possible, to procure some intercourse with the *Chilian Indians*, and to establish a commerce and a lasting correspondence with them. His Majesty's views in employing Sir *John Narborough* in this expedition, were not solely the advantage he might hope to receive from the alliance of those savages, in restraining and intimidating the Crown of *Spain*, but he conceived, that, independent of those motives, the immediate traffick with these *Indians* might prove extremely advantagious to the *English* Nation. For it is well known, that at the first discovery of *Chili* by the *Spaniards*, it abounded with vast quantities of gold, much beyond what it has at any time produced, since it has been in their possession. And hence it has been generally believed, that the richest mines are prudently concealed by the *Indians*, as well knowing that the discovery of them to the *Spaniards* would only excite in them a greater thirst for conquest and tyranny, and render their own independence precarious. But with respect to their commerce with the *English*, these reasons would no longer influence them; since it would be in our power to furnish them with arms and ammunition of all kinds, of which they are extremely desirous, together with many other conveniences which their intercourse with the *Spaniards* has taught them to relish. They would then, in all probability, open their mines, and gladly embrace a traffick of such mutual convenience to both Nations; for then their gold, instead of proving the means of enslaving them, would procure them weapons to assert their liberty, to chastise their tyrants, and to secure themselves for ever from the *Spanish* yoke; whilst with our assistance, and under our protection, they might become a considerable people, and might secure to us that wealth, which formerly by the House of *Austria*, and lately by the House of *Bourbon*, has been most mischievously lavished in the pursuit of universal Monarchy.

It is true, that Sir *John Narborough* did not succeed in opening this commerce, which in appearance promised so many advantages to this Nation. However, his disappointment was merely accidental, and his transactions upon that coast (besides the many valuable improvements he furnished to geography and navigation) are rather an encouragement for future trials of this kind, than any objection against them; his principal misfortune being the losing company of a small bark which attended him, and having some of his people trapanned at *Baldivia*. However, it appeared, by the precautions and fears of the *Spaniards*, that they were fully convinced of the practicability of the scheme he was sent to execute, and extremely alarmed with the apprehension of its consequences.

It is said, that his Majesty King *Charles* the Second was so far prepossessed with the hopes of the advantages redounding from this expedition, and so eager to be informed of the event of it, that having intelligence of Sir *John Narborough*'s passing through the *Downs* on his return, he had not patience to attend his arrival at Court, but went himself in his barge to *Gravesend* to meet him.

To facilitate as much as possible any attempts of this kind, which may be hereafter undertaken, I have, in the annexed plate[1], given a chart of that part of the world, as far as it is hitherto known, which I flatter myself is in some respects much correcter than any hitherto published. To evince which, it may be necessary to mention what materials I have principally made use of, and what changes I have introduced different from other authors.

The two most celebrated charts hitherto published of the southermost part of South *America*, are those of Dr. *Halley*, in his general chart of the magnetic variations, and of *Frezier* in his voyage to the *South-Seas*. But besides these, there is a chart of the Streights of *Magellan*, and of some part of the adjacent coast, by Sir *John*

Narborough abovementioned, which is doubtless infinitely exacter in that part than *Frezier*, and in some respects superior to *Halley*, particularly in what relates to the longitudes of the different parts of those Streights. The coast from Cape *Blanco* to *Terra del Fuego*, and thence to Streights *Le Maire*, we were in some measure capable of correcting by our own observations, as we ranged that shore generally in sight of land. The position of the land, to the northward of the Streights of *Magellan*, on the West side, is doubtless laid down in our chart but very imperfectly; and yet I believe it to be much nearer the truth than what has hitherto been done: As it is drawn from the information of some of the *Wager's* crew, who were shipwrecked on that shore, and afterwards coasted it down; and as it agrees pretty nearly with the description of some *Spanish* manuscripts I have seen.

The Channel dividing *Terra del Fuego* is drawn from *Frezier*; but in the *Spanish* manuscripts there are several Channels delineated, and I have reason to suppose, that whenever this country is thoroughly examined, this circumstance will prove true, and *Terra del Fuego* will be found to consist of several Islands.

And having mentioned *Frezier* so often, I must not omit warning all future Navigators, against relying on the longitude of Streights *Le Maire*, or of any part of that coast, laid down in his chart; the whole being from 8 to 10 degrees too far to the eastward, if any faith can be given to the concurrent evidences of a great number of journals, verified in some particulars by astronomical observation. For instance, Sir *John Narborough* lays down Cape *Virgin Mary* in 65° : 42′ of West longitude from the *Lizard*, that is in 71° : 20′ from *London*. And the ships of our squadron, who took their departure from St. *Catherine's* (where the longitude was rectified by an observation of the eclipse of the moon) found Cape *Virgin Mary* to be from 70° : 46′, to 71° : 30′ from *London*, according to their different reckonings: And there were no circumstances in our run that could render it considerably erroneous, so that it cannot be esteemed in less than 71 degrees of West longitude; whereas *Frezier* lays it down in less than 66 degrees from *Paris*, that is little more than 63 degrees from *London*, which is doubtless 8 degrees short of its true quantity[1]. Again, our squadron found Cape *Virgin Mary* and Cape St. *Bartholomew* on the eastern side of Streights *Le Maire* to be only 2° : 8′ different in longitude, which in *Frezier* are distant near 4 degrees; so that not only the longitude of

Cape St. *Bartholomew* is laid down in him near 10 degrees too little, but the whole coast, from the Streights of *Magellan* to Streights *Le Maire*, is enlarged to near double its real extent.

But to have done with *Frezier*, whose errors, the importance of the subject and not a fondness for cavilling, has obliged me to remark, (though his treatment of Dr. *Halley* might, on the present occasion, authorize much severer usage)[1] I must, in the next place, particularize wherein the chart I have here inserted differs from that of our learned countryman.

It is well known that this Gentleman was sent abroad by the Public, to make such geographical and astronomical observations, as might facilitate the future practice of navigation, and particularly to determine the variation of the compass in such places as he should touch at, and if possible, to ascertain its general laws and affections.

These things Dr. *Halley*, to his immortal reputation and the honour of our Nation, in good measure accomplished, particularly with regard to the variation of the compass, a subject, of all others, the most interesting to those employed in the art of navigation. He likewise corrected the position of the coast of *Brazil*, which had been very erroneously laid down by all former Hydrographers; and by a judicious comparison of the observations of others, has happily succeeded in settling the geography of many parts of the globe, where he had not himself been. So that the chart he published, with the variation of the needle marked thereon, being the result of his labours on this subject, was allowed by all *Europe* to be far compleater in its geography than any that had then appeared, and at the same time most surprizingly exact in the quantity of variation assigned to the different parts of the globe; a subject so very intricate and perplexing, that all general determinations about it had till then appeared impossible.

But as the only means he had of correcting those coasts where he did not touch himself was the observations of others; where those observations were wanting, or were inaccurate, it was no imputation on his skill, that his determinations were defective. And this, upon the best comparison I have been able to make, is the case with regard to that part of his chart, which contains the South part of South *America*. For though the coast of *Brazil*, and the opposite coast of *Peru* on the *South-Seas* are laid down, I presume, with the greatest accuracy, yet from about the river of *Plate* on the East side, and its opposite point on the West, the coast gradually declines too much to the westward, so as at the Streights of *Magellan* to be as I conceive, about fifty leagues removed from its true position.[1] At least, this is the result of the observations of our squadron, which agree extremely well with those of Sir *John Narborough*. I must add, that Dr. *Halley* has, in the Philosophical Transactions, given the foundation on which he has proceeded, in fixing Port St. *Julian* in $76°\frac{1}{2}$ of West longitude: (which the concurrent journals of our squadron place from $70°\frac{3}{4}$ to $71°\frac{1}{2}$) This, he tells us, was an observation of an eclipse of the moon, made at that place by Mr. *Wood*, then Sir *John Narborough*'s Lieutenant, and which is said to have happened there at eight in the evening, on the 18th of *September*, 1670. But Capt. *Wood*'s journal of this whole voyage under Sir *John Narborough* is since published, together with this observation, in which he determines the longitude of Port St. *Julian* to be 73 degrees from *London*, and the time of the eclipse to have been different from Dr. *Halley*'s account. But the numbers he has given are so faultily printed, that nothing can be determined from them.

To what I have already mentioned with regard to the chart hereunto annexed,[2] I shall only add, that to render it more compleat, I have inserted therein the route of our squadron, and have delineated, in the passage round Cape *Horn*, both the real track which we described, and the imaginary track exhibited by our reckoning; whence the violence of the currents in that part of the world, and the enormous deviations which they produce, will appear by inspection. And that no material article might be omitted in this important affair, the soundings on the coast of *Patagonia*, and the variation of the magnetic needle, are annexed to those parts of this track, where, by our observations, we found them to be of the quantity there specified.

CHAP. X.

From Cape *Noir* to the Island of *Juan Fernandes*.

AFTER the mortifying disappointment of falling in with the coast of *Terra del Fuego*, when we esteemed ourselves ten degrees to the westward of it; after this disappointment, I say, recited in the eighth chapter, we stood away to the S. W. till the 22d of *April*, when we were in upwards of 60° of South latitude, and by our account near 6° to the westward of Cape *Noir*; and in this run, we had a series of as favourable weather, as could well be expected in that part of the world, even in a better season: So that this interval, setting the inquietude of our thoughts aside, was by far the most eligible of any we enjoyed from Streights *Le Maire* to the West coast of *America*. This moderate weather continued, with little variation, till the 24th; but on the 24th, in the evening, the wind began to blow fresh, and soon encreased to a prodigious storm; and the weather being extremely thick, about midnight we lost sight of the other four ships of the squadron, which, notwithstanding the violence of the preceding storms, had hitherto kept in company with us. Nor was this our sole misfortune; for, the next morning, endeavouring to hand the top-sails, the clew-lines and bunt-lines broke, and the sheets being half flown, every seam in the top-sails was soon split from top to bottom, and the main top-sail shook so strongly in the wind, that it carried away the top lanthorn, and endangered the head of the mast; however, at length some of the most daring of our men ventured upon the yard, and cut the sail away close to the reefs, though with the utmost hazard of their lives. At the same time, the foretop-sail beat about the yard with so much fury, that it was soon blown to pieces; and that we might have full employment, the main-sail blew loose, which obliged us to lower down the yard to secure the sail, and the foreyard being likewise lowered, we lay to under a mizen: And besides the loss of our top-sails, we had much of our other rigging broke, and lost a main studding-sail-boom out of the chains.

On the 25th, about noon, the weather became more moderate, which enabled us to sway up our yards, and to repair, in the best

manner we could, our shattered rigging; but still we had no sight
of the rest of our squadron, nor indeed were we joined by any of
them again, till after our arrival at *Juan Fernandes*; nor did any two
of them, as we have since learned, continue in company together:
And this total separation was the more wonderful, as we had hitherto
kept together for seven weeks, through all the reiterated tempests of
this turbulent climate. It must indeed be owned, that this separation
gave us room to expect, that we might make our passage in a shorter
time, than if we had continued together, because we could now make
the best of our way without being retarded by the misfortunes of the
other ships; but then we had the melancholy reflection, that we ourselves were hereby deprived of the assistance of others, and our safety
would depend upon our single ship; so that if a plank started, or any
other accident of the same nature should take place, we must all
irrecoverably perish; or should we be driven on shore, we had the
uncomfortable prospect of ending our days on some desolate coast,
without any reasonable hope of ever getting away; whereas with
another ship in company, all these calamities are much less formidable,
since in every kind of danger, there would be some probability that
one ship at least might escape, and might be capable of preserving or
relieving the crew of the other.

The remaining part of this month of *April* we had generally hard
gales, although we had been every day, since the 22d, edging to the
northward; however, on the last day of the month, we flattered ourselves with the hopes of soon terminating all our sufferings, for we
that day found ourselves in the latitude of 52°:13′, which being to the
northward of the Streights of *Magellan*, we were assured that we had
compleated our passage, and had arrived in the confines of the southern
Ocean; and this Ocean being nominated *Pacifick*, from the equability
of the seasons which are said to prevail there, and the facility and
security with which navigation is there carried on, we doubted not
but we should be speedily cheared with the moderate gales, the
smooth water, and the temperate air, for which that tract of the globe
has been so renowned. And under the influence of these pleasing
circumstances, we hoped to experience some kind of compensation;
for the complicated miseries which had so constantly attended us for
the last eight weeks. But here we were again disappointed; for in the
succeeding month of *May*, our sufferings rose to a much higher pitch

than they had ever yet done, whether we consider the violence of the storms, the shattering of our sails and rigging, or the diminishing and weakening of our crew by deaths and sickness, and the probable prospect of our total destruction. All this will be sufficiently evident, from the following circumstantial account of our diversified misfortunes.

Soon after our passing Streights *Le Maire*, the scurvy began to make its appearance amongst us; and our long continuance at sea, the fatigue we underwent, and the various disappointments we met with, had occasioned its spreading of such a degree, that at the latter end of *April* there were but few on board, who were not in some degree afflicted with it, and in that month no less than forty-three died of it on board the *Centurion*. But though we thought that the distemper had then risen to an extraordinary height, and were willing to hope, that as we advanced to the northward its maliginity would abate, yet we found, on the contrary, that in the month of *May* we lost near double that number: And as we did not get to land till the middle of *June*, the mortality went on increasing, and the disease extended itself so prodigiously, that after the loss of above two hundred men, we could not at last muster more than six fore-mast men in a watch capable of duty.

This disease so frequently attending all long voyages, and so particularly destructive to us, is surely the most singular and unaccountable of any that affects the human body.[1] For its symptoms are inconstant and innumerable, and its progress and effects extremely irregular; for scarcely any two persons have the same complaints, and where there hath been found some conformity in the symptoms, the order of their appearance has been totally different. However, though it frequently puts on the form of many other diseases, and is therefore not to be described by any exclusive and infallible criterions; yet there are some symptoms which are more general than the rest, and therefore, occurring the oftnest, deserve a more particular enumeration. These common appearances are large discoloured spots dispersed over the whole surface of the body, swelled legs, putrid gums, and above all, an extraordinary lassitude of the whole body, especially after any exercise, however inconsiderable; and this lassitude at last degenerates into a proneness of swoon on the least exertion of strength, or even on the least motion.

This disease is likewise usually attended with a strange dejection of the spirits, and with shiverings, tremblings, and a disposition to be seized with the most dreadful terrors on the slightest accident. Indeed, it was most remarkable, in all our reiterated experience of this malady, that whatever discouraged our people, or at any time damped their hopes, never failed to add new vigour to the distemper; for it usually killed those who were in the last stages of it, and confined those to their hammocks, who were before capable of some kind of duty, so that it seemed as if alacrity of mind, and sanguine thoughts, were no contemptible preservatives from its fatal malignity.

But it is not easy to compleat the long roll of the various concomitants of this disease; for it often produced putrid fevers, pleurisies, the jaundice, and violent rheumatick pains, and sometimes it occasioned an obstinate costiveness, which was generally attended with a difficulty of breathing; and this was esteemed the most deadly of all the scorbutick symptoms: At other times the whole body, but more especially the legs, were subject to ulcers of the worst kind, attended with rotten bones, and such a luxuriancy of funguous flesh, as yielded to no remedy. But a most extraordinary circumstance, and what would be scarcely credible upon any single evidence, is, that the scars of wounds which had been for many years healed, were forced open again by this virulent distemper: Of this, there was a remarkable instance in one of the invalids on board the *Centurion*, who had been wounded above fifty years before at the battle of the *Boyne*; for though he was cured soon after, and had continued well for a great number of years past, yet on his being attacked by the scurvy, his wounds, in the progress of his disease, broke out afresh, and appeared as if they had never been healed: Nay, what is still more astonishing, the callous of a broken bone, which had been compleatly formed for a long time, was found to be hereby dissolved, and the fracture seemed as if it had never been consolidated. Indeed, the effects of this disease were in almost every instance wonderful; for many of our people, though confined to their hammocks, appeared to have no inconsiderable share of health, for they eat and drank heartily, were chearful, and talked with much seeming vigour, and with a loud strong tone of voice; and yet on their being the least moved, though it was only from one part of the ship to the other, and that in their hammocks, they have immediately expired; and others, who have confided in their seeming strength, and have resolved to get out of their hammocks, have died before they could well

106

reach the deck; and it was no uncommon thing for those who were able to walk the deck, and to do some kind of duty, to drop down dead in an instant, on any endeavours to act with their utmost vigour, many of our people having perished in this manner during the course of this voyage.

With this terrible disease we struggled the greatest part of the time of our beating round Cape *Horn*; and though it did not then rage with its utmost violence, yet we buried no less than forty-three men on board the *Centurion*, in the month of *April*, as hath been already observed, but we still entertained hopes, that when we should have once secured our passage round the Cape, we should put a period to this, and all the other evils which had so constantly pursued us. But it was our misfortune to find, that the *Pacifick* Ocean was to us less hospitable than the turbulent neighbourhood of *Terra del Fuego* and Cape *Horn*: For being arrived, on the 8th of *May*, off the Island of *Socoro*, which was the first rendezvous appointed for the squadron, and where we hoped to have met with some of our companions, we cruized for them in that station several days. And here we were not only disappointed in our hopes of being joined by our friends, and were thereby induced to favour the gloomy suggestions of their having all perished; but we were likewise perpetually alarmed with the fears of being driven on shore upon this coast, which appeared too craggy and irregular to give us the least hopes, that in such a case any of us could possibly escape immediate destruction. For the land had indeed a most tremendous aspect: The most distant part of it, and which appeared far within the country, being the mountains usually called the *Andes* or *Cordilleras*, was extremely high, and covered with snow; and the coast itself seemed quite rocky and barren, and the water's edge skirted with precipices. In some places indeed there appeared several deep bays running into the land, but the entrance into them was generally blocked up by numbers of little Islands; and though it was not improbable but there might be convenient shelter in some of those bays, and proper channels leading thereto; yet as we were utterly ignorant of the coast, had we been driven ashore by the western winds which blew almost constantly there, we did not expect to have avoided the loss of our ships and of our lives.

And this continued peril, which lasted for above a fortnight, was greatly aggravated by the difficulties we found in working the ship;

as the scurvy had by this time destroyed so great a part of our hands, and had in some degree affected almost the whole crew. Nor did we, as we hoped, find the winds less violent, as we advanced to the north-ward; for we had often prodigious squalls which split our sails, greatly damaged our rigging, and endangered our masts. Indeed, during the greatest part of the time we were upon this coast, the wind blew so hard, that in another situation, where we had sufficient sea-room, we should certainly have lain to; but in the present exigency we were necessitated to carry both our courses and top-sails, in order to keep clear of this lee-shore. In one of these squalls, which was attended by several violent claps of thunder, a sudden flash of fire darted along our decks, which, dividing, exploded with a report like that of several pistols, and wounded many of our men and officers as it passed, mark-ing them in different parts of the body: This flame was attended with a strong sulphurous stench, and was doubtless of the same nature with the larger and more violent blasts of lightning which then filled the air.

It were endless to recite minutely the various disasters, fatigues and terrors which we encountered on this coast; all these went on encreasing till the 22d of *May*, at which time, the fury of all the storms which we had hitherto encountered, seemed to be combined, and to have conspired our destruction. In this hurricane almost all our sails were split, and great part of our standing rigging broken; and, about eight in the evening, a mountainous overgrown-sea took us upon our starboard-quarter, and gave us so prodigious a shock, that several of our shrouds broke with the jerk, by which our masts were greatly endangered; our ballast and stores too were so strangely shifted, that the ship heeled afterwards two streaks to port.[1] Indeed it was a most tremendous blow, and we were thrown into the utmost consternation from the apprehension of instantly foundering; and though the wind abated in a few hours, yet, as we had no more sails left in a condition to bend to our yards, the ship laboured very much in a hollow sea, rolling gunwale to, for want of sail to steady her: So that we expected our masts, which were now very slenderly supported, to come by the board every moment. However, we exerted ourselves the best we could to stirrup our shrouds,[2] to reeve new lanyards,[3] and to mend our sails; but while these necessary operations were carrying on, we ran great risque of being driven on shore on the Island of *Chiloe*, which was not far distant from us; but in the midst of our peril the wind happily shifted to the southward, and we steered off the land with the main-sail only, the Master and myself undertaking the management of the helm, while every one else on board was busied in securing the masts, and bending the sails as fast as they could be repaired. This was the last effort of that stormy climate; for in a day or two after, we got clear of the land, and found the weather more moderate than we had yet experienced since our passing Streights *Le Maire*. And now having cruized in vain for more than a fortnight in quest of the other ships of the squadron, it was resolved to take the advantage of the present favourable season and the offing we had made from this terrible coast, and to make the best of our way for the Island of *Juan Fernandes*. For though our next rendezvous was appointed off the harbour of *Baldivia*, yet as we had hitherto seen none of our companions at this first rendezvous, it was not to be supposed that any of them would be found at the second: Indeed we had the greatest reason to suspect, that all but ourselves had perished. Besides, we were by this time reduced to so low a condition, that instead of attempting to attack the places of the enemy, our utmost hopes could only suggest to us the possibility of saving the ship, and some part of the remaining enfeebled crew, by our speedy arrival at *Juan Fernandes*; for this was the only road in that part of the world where there was any probability of our recovering our sick, or refitting our vessel, and consequently our getting thither was the only chance we had left to avoid perishing at sea.

Our deplorable situation then allowing no room for deliberation, we stood for the Island of *Juan Fernandes*; and to save time, which was now extremely precious, (our men dying four, five and six in a day) and likewise to avoid being engaged again with a lee-shore, we resolved, if possible, to hit the Island upon a meridian.[1] And, on the 28th of *May*, being nearly in the parallel upon which it is laid down, we had great expectations of seeing it: But not finding it in the position in which the charts had taught us to expect it, we began to fear that we had got too far to the westward; and therefore, though the Commodore himself was strongly persuaded, that he saw it on the morning of the 28th, yet his Officers believing it to be only a cloud, to which opinion the haziness of the weather gave some kind of countenance, it was, on a consultation, resolved to stand to the eastward, in the parallel of the Island; as it was certain, that by this course we should either fall in with the Island, if we were already to the westward of it; or should at least make the main-land of *Chili*, from whence we might take a new departure, and assure ourselves, by running to the westward afterwards, of not missing the Island a second time.

On the 30th of *May* we had a view of the Continent of *Chili*, distant about twelve or thirteen leagues; the land made exceeding high and uneven, and appeared quite white; what we saw being doubtless a part of the *Cordilleras*, which are always covered with snow. Though by this view of the land we ascertained our position, yet it gave us great uneasiness to find that we had so needlessly altered our course, when we were, in all probability just upon the point of making the Island; for the mortality amongst us was now encreased to a most dreadful degree, and those who remained alive were utterly dispirited by this new disappointment, and the prospect of their longer continuance at sea: Our water too began to grow scarce; so that a general dejection prevailed amongst us, which added much to the virulence of the disease, and destroyed numbers of our best men; and to all these calamities there was added this vexatious circumstance, that when, after having got a sight of the Main, we tacked and stood to the westward in quest of the Island, we were so much delayed by calms and contrary winds, that it cost us nine days to regain the westing, which, when we stood to the eastward, we ran down in two. In this desponding condition, with a crazy ship, a great scarcity of fresh water, and a crew so universally diseased, that there were not above ten fore-mast men in a watch capable of doing duty, and even some of these lame, and unable to go aloft: Under these disheartning circumstances, I say, we stood to the westward; and, on the 9th of *June* at day-break, we at last discovered the long-wished for Island of *Juan Fernandes*. And with this discovery I shall close this chapter and the first book, after observing (which will furnish a very strong image of our unparalleled distresses) that by our suspecting ourselves to be to the westward of the Island on the 28th of *May*, and, in consequence of this, standing in for the Main, we lost between seventy and eighty of our men, whom we should doubtless have saved had we made the Island that day, which, had we kept on our course for a few hours longer, we could not have failed to have done.

END OF BOOK I.

110

BOOK II.

CHAP. I.

The arrival of the *Centurion* at the Island of *Juan Fernandes*, with a description of that Island.

ON the 9th of *June*, at day break, as is mentioned in the preceding chapter, we first descried the Island of *Juan Fernandes*; bearing N. by E. $\frac{1}{2}$ E, at eleven or twelve leagues distance. And though, on this first view, it appeared to be a very mountainous place, extremely ragged and irregular; yet as it was land, and the land we sought for, it was to us a most agreeable sight: For at this place only we could hope to put a period to those terrible calamities we had so long struggled with, which had already swept away above half our crew, and which, had we continued a few days longer at sea, would inevitably have compleated our destruction. For we were by this time reduced to so helpless a condition, that out of two hundred and odd men which remained alive, we could not, taking all our watches together, muster hands enough to work the ship on an emergency, though we included the officers, their servants, and the boys.

The wind being northerly when we first made the Island, we kept plying[1] all that day, and the next night, in order to get in with the land; and wearing the ship[2] in the middle watch, we had a melancholy instance of the almost incredible debility of our people; for the Lieutenant could muster no more than two Quarter-masters, and six Foremast men capable of working; so that without the assistance of the officers, servants and the boys, it might have proved impossible for us to have reached the Island, after we had got sight of it; and even with this assistance they were two hours in trimming the sails: To so wretched a condition was a sixty gun ship reduced, which had passed Streights *Le Maire* but three months before, with between four and five hundred men, almost all of them in health and vigour.

However, on the 10th in the afternoon, we got under the lee of the Island, and kept ranging along it, at about two miles distance, in order

111

to look out for the proper anchorage, which was described to be in a
bay on the North side. And now being nearer in with the shore, we
could discover that the broken craggy precipices, which had appeared
so unpromising at a distance, were far from barren, being in most
places covered with woods; and that between them there were every
where interspersed the finest vallies, clothed with a most beautiful
verdure, and watered with numerous streams and cascades, no valley,
of any extent, being unprovided of its proper rill. The water too, as
we afterwards found, was not inferiour to any we had ever tasted, and
was constantly clear: So that the aspect of this country would, at all
times, have been extremely delightful, but in our distressed situation,
languishing as we were for the land and its vegetable productions, (an
inclination constantly attending every stage of the sea-scurvy) it is
scarcely credible with what eagerness and transport we viewed the
shore, and with how much impatience we longed for the greens and
other refreshments which were then in sight, and particularly for the
water, for of this we had been confined to a very sparing allowance for
a considerable time, and had then but five ton remaining on board.
Those only who have endured a long series of thirst, and who can
readily recal the desire and agitation which the ideas alone of springs
and brooks have at that time raised in them, can judge of the emotion
with which we eyed a large cascade of the most transparent water,
which poured itself from a rock near a hundred feet high into the sea,
at a small distance from the ship. Even those amongst the diseased,
who were not in the very last stages of the distemper, though they
had been long confined to their hammocks, exerted the small remains
of strength that was left them, and crawled up to the deck to feast
themselves with this reviving prospect. Thus we coasted the shore,
fully employed in the contemplation of this diversified landskip, which
improved upon us the farther we advanced. But at last the night closed
upon us, before we had satisfied ourselves which was the proper bay
to anchor in; and therefore we resolved to keep in soundings all night,
(we having then from sixty-four to seventy fathom) and to send our
boat next morning to discover the road: However, the current shifted
in the night, and set us so near the land, that we were obliged to let go
the best bower in fifty-six fathom, not half a mile from the shore. At
four in the morning, the Cutter was dispatched with our third Lieutenant to find out the bay we were in search of, who returned again at

noon with the boat laden with seals and grass; for though the Island abounded with better vegetables, yet the boats-crew, in their short stay, had not met with them; and they well knew that even grass would prove a dainty, and indeed it was all soon and eagerly devoured. The seals too were considered as fresh provision; but as yet were not much admired, tho' they grew afterwards into more repute: For what rendered them less valuable at this juncture, was the prodigious quantity of excellent fish, which the people on board had taken, during the absence of the boat.

The Cutter, in this expedition, had discovered the bay where we intended to anchor, which we found was to the westward of our present station; and, the next morning, the weather proving favourable, we endeavoured to weigh, in order to proceed thither: But though, on this occasion, we mustered all the strength we could, obliging even the sick, who were scarce able to keep on their leggs, to assist us; yet the capstan was so weakly manned, that it was near four hours before we hove the cable right up and down: After which, with our utmost efforts, and with many surges and some purchases we made use of to encrease our power, we found ourselves incapable of starting the anchor from the ground. However, at noon, as a fresh gale blew towards the bay, we were induced to set the sails, which fortunately tripped the anchor; on which we steered along shore, till we came a-breast of the point that forms the eastern part of the bay. On the opening of the bay, the wind, that had befriended us thus far, shifted and blew from thence in squalls; but by means of the head-way we had got, we loofed close in, till the anchor brought us up in fifty-six fathom. Soon after we had thus got to our new birth, we discovered a sail, which we made no doubt was one of our squadron; and on its nearer approach, we found it to be the *Tryal* Sloop. We immediately sent some of our hands on board her, by whose assistance she was brought to an anchor between us and the land. We soon found that the Sloop had not been exempted from those calamities which we had so severely felt; for her Commander, Captain *Saunders*, waiting on the Commodore, informed him, that out of his small complement, he had buried thirty-four of his men; and those that remained were so universally afflicted with the scurvy, that only himself, his Lieutenant, and three of his men, were able to stand by the sails. The *Tryal* came to an anchor within us, on the 12th, about noon, and we carried our hawsers on board her, in order to moor ourselves nearer in shore; but the wind coming off the land in violent gusts, prevented our mooring in the birth we intended, especially as our principal attention was now employed on business rather of more importance; for we were now extremely occupied in sending on shore materials to raise tents for the reception of the sick, who died apace on board, and doubtless the distemper was considerably augmented, by the stench and filthiness in which they lay; for the number of the diseased was so great, and so few could be spared from the necessary duty of the sails to look after them, that it was impossible to avoid a great relaxation in the article of cleanliness, which had rendered the ship extremely loathsome between decks. But notwithstanding our desire of freeing the sick from their hateful situation, and their own extreme impatience to get on shore, we had not hands enough to prepare the tents for their reception before the 16th; but on that and the two following days we sent them all on shore, amounting to a hundred and sixty-seven persons, besides at least a dozen who died in the boats, on their being exposed to the fresh air. The greatest part of our sick were so infirm, that we were obliged to carry them out of the ship in their hammocks, and to convey them afterwards in the same manner from the water-side to their tents, over a stony beach. This was a work of considerable fatigue to the few who were healthy, and therefore the Commodore, with his accustomed humanity, not only assisted herein with his own labour, but obliged his Officers, without distinction, to give their helping hand. The extreme weakness of our sick may in some measure be collected from the numbers who died after they had got on shore; for it had generally been found, that the land, and the refreshments it produces, very soon recover most stages of the sea-scurvy; and we flattered ourselves, that those who had not perished on this first exposure to the open air, but had lived to be placed in their tents, would have been speedily restored to their health and vigour: But, to our great mortification, it was near twenty days after their landing, before the mortality was tolerably ceased; and for the first ten or twelve days, we buried rarely less than six each day, and many of those, who survived, recovered by very slow and insensible degrees. Indeed, those who were well enough at their first getting on shore, to creep out of their tents, and crawl about, were soon relieved, and recovered their health and strength in a very short time; but in the rest, the disease seemed to have acquired a degree of inveteracy which was altogether without example.

Having proceeded thus far, and got our sick on shore, I think it necessary, before I enter into any longer detail of our transactions, to give a distinct account of this Island of *Juan Fernandes*, its situation, productions, and all its conveniences. These particulars we were well enabled to be minutely instructed in, during our three months stay there; and as it is the only commodious place in those seas, where *British* cruisers can refresh and recover their men after their passage round Cape *Horn*, and where they may remain for some time without alarming the *Spanish* coast, these its advantages well merit a circumstantial description. And indeed Mr. *Anson* was particularly industrious in directing the roads and coasts to be surveyed, and other observations to be made, knowing, from his own experience, of how great consequence these materials might prove to any *British* vessels hereafter employed in those seas. For the uncertainty we were in of its position, and our standing in for the Main on the 28th of *May*, in order to secure a sufficient easting, when we were indeed extremely near it, cost us the lives of between seventy and eighty of our men, by our longer continuance at sea: From which fatal accident we might have been exempted, had we been furnished with such an account of its situation, as we could fully have depended on.

The Island of *Juan Fernandes* lies in the latitude of 33°:40' South, and is a hundred and ten leagues distant from the Continent of *Chili*. It is said to have received its name from a *Spaniard*, who formerly procured a grant of it, and resided there some time with a view of settling it, but afterwards abandoned it. On approaching it on its east side, it appears, as represented in the annexed plate, where (a) is a small Island, called *Goat Island*, to the S. W. of it; (b) a rock, called *Monkey key*, almost contiguous to it; (c) is the East bay, (d) *Cumberland Bay*, where we moored, and which, as will be observed, is the best road for shipping, and (e) the East bay. The Island itself is of an irregular figure, as may be seen by the very exact plan of it here inserted; its greatest extent being between four and five leagues, and its greatest breadth somewhat short of two leagues. The only safe anchoring at this Island is on the North side, where are the three bays mentioned above, but the middlemost known by the name of *Cumberland Bay*, is the widest and deepest, and in all respects much the best;

the other two bays, denominated the East and West bays, are scarcely more than good landing places, where boats may conveniently put their cask on shore. A plan of the N. E. side of the Island, containing these three bays, drawn by a large scale, is here inserted, where it appears, that *Cumberland Bay* is pretty well secured to the southward, lying only exposed from the N. by W. to the E. by S; and as the northerly winds seldom blow in that climate, and never with any violence, the danger from that quarter is not worth attending to. To distinguish this bay the better at sea, I have added a very exact view of it, which will enable all future Navigators readily to find it.

As the bay last described, or *Cumberland Bay*, is by far the most commodious road in the Island, so it is adviseable for all ships to anchor on the western side of this bay, within little more than two cables length of the beach. Here they may ride in forty fathom of water, and be, in a great measure, sheltered from a large heavy sea, which comes rolling in whenever an eastern or a western wind blows. It is however expedient, in this case, to cackle[1] or arm the cables with an iron chain, or good rounding,[2] for five or six fathom from the anchor, to secure them from being rubbed by the foulness of the ground.

I have before observed, that a northerly wind, to which alone this bay is exposed, very rarely blew during our stay here; and as it was then winter, it may be supposed, in other seasons, to be less frequent. Indeed, in those few instances when it was in that quarter, it did not blow with any great force: But this perhaps might be owing to the highlands on the southward of the bay, which checked its current, and thereby abated its violence; for we had reason to suppose, that a few leagues off it blew with considerable force, since it sometimes drove before it a prodigious sea, in which we rode fore-castle in. But though the northern winds are never to be apprehended, yet the southern winds, which generally prevail here, frequently blow off the land in violent gusts and squalls, which however rarely last longer than two or three minutes. This seems to be owing to the obstruction of the southern gale, by the hills in the neighbourhood of the bay; for the wind being collected by this means, at last forces its passage through the narrow vallies, which, like so many funnels, both facilitate its escape, and increase its violence. These frequent and sudden gusts make it difficult for ships to work in with the wind off shore, or to keep a clear hawse[3] when anchored.

The northern part of this Island is composed of high craggy hills, many of them inaccessible, though generally covered with trees. The soil of this part is loose and shallow, so that very large trees on the hills soon perish for want of root, and are easily overturned; which occasioned the unfortunate death of one of our sailors, who being upon the hills in search of goats, caught hold of a tree upon a declivity to assist him in his ascent, and this giving way, he immediately rolled down the hill, and though in his fall he fastened on another tree of considerable bulk, yet that too gave way, and he fell amongst the rocks, and was dashed to pieces. Mr. *Brett* too met with an accident only by resting his back against a tree, near as large about as himself, which stood on a slope, for the tree giving way, he fell to a considerable distance, though without receiving any harm.

The southern, or rather the S. W. part of the Island, as distinguished in the plan, is widely different from the rest, being dry, stony, and destitute of trees, but very flat and low, compared with the hills on the northern part. This part of the Island is never frequented by ships, being surrounded by a steep shore, and having little or no fresh water; and besides, it is exposed to the southerly wind, which generally blows here the whole year round, and in the winter solstice very hard. The trees of which the woods on the northern side of the Island are composed, are most of them aromaticks, and of many different sorts: There are none of them of a size to yield any considerable timber, except the myrtle-trees, which are the largest on the Island, and supplied us with all the timber we made use of; but even these would not work to a greater length than forty feet. The top of the myrtle-tree is circular, and appears as uniform and regular, as if it had been clipped by art; it bears on its bark an excrescence like moss, which in taste and smell resembles garlick, and was used by our people instead of it. We found here too the piemento-tree and likewise the cabbage-tree, though in no great plenty.

Our prisoners[1] observed, that the appearance of the hills in some part of the Island resembled that of the mountains in *Chili*, where the gold is found: So that it is not impossible but mines might be discovered here. We observed, in some places, several hills of a peculiar sort of red earth, exceeding vermilion in colour, which perhaps, on examination, might prove useful for many purposes.

Besides a great number of plants of various kinds which are to be

met with upon the Island, but which we were not botanists enough
either to describe, or attend to, we found there almost all the vegetables, which are usually esteemed to be particularly adapted to the
cure of those scorbutick disorders, which are contracted by salt diet
and long voyages. For here we had great quantities of watercresses
and purslain, with excellent wild sorrel, and a vast profusion of turnips and *Sicilian* radishes: These two last, having some resemblance
to each other, were confounded by our people under the general name
of turnips. We usually preferred the tops of the turnips to the roots,
which were often stringy; though some of them were free from that
exception, and remarkably good. These vegetables, with the fish and
flesh we found here, and which I shall more particularly describe hereafter, were not only extremely grateful to our palates, after the long
course of salt diet which we had been confined to, but were likewise
of the most salutary consequence to our sick in recovering and invigorating them, and of no mean service to us who were well, in
destroying the lurking seeds of the scurvy, from which perhaps none
of us were totally exempt, and in refreshing and restoring us to our
wonted strength and activity.

Besides the vegetables I have mentioned, of which we made perpetual use, we found many acres of ground covered with oats and
clover. There were also some few cabbage-trees upon the Island, as
observed before; but as they generally grew on the precipices, and in
dangerous situations, and as it was necessary to cut down a large tree
for every single cabbage, this was a dainty that we were able but rarely
to indulge in.

The excellence of the climate and the looseness of the soil render
this place extremely proper for all kinds of vegetation; for if the
ground be any where accidentally turned up, it is immediately overgrown with turnips and *Sicilian* radishes; and therefore Mr. *Anson*
having with him garden seeds of all kinds, and stones of different
sorts of fruits, he, for the better accommodation of his countrymen
who should hereafter touch here, sowed both lettices, carrots, and
other garden plants, and sett in the woods a great variety of plumb,
apricock, and peach stones: And these last he has been informed have
since thriven to a very remarkable degree; for some Gentlemen, who
in their passage from *Lima* to *Old Spain* were taken and brought to
England, having procured leave to wait upon Mr. *Anson*, to thank him

for his generosity and humanity to his prisoners, some of whom were their relations, they, in casual discourse with him about his transactions in the *South-Seas*, particularly asked him, if he had not planted a great number of fruit-stones on the Island of *Juan Fernandes*, for they told him, their late Navigators had discovered there numbers of peach-trees and apricock-trees, which being fruits before unobserved in that place, they concluded them to be produced from kernels sett by him.

And this may in general suffice as to the soil and vegetable productions of this place: But the face of the country, at least of the North part of the Island, is so extremely singular, that I cannot avoid giving it a particular consideration. I have already taken notice of the wild, inhospitable air with which it first appeared to us, and the gradual improvement of this uncouth landskip as we drew nearer, till we were at last captivated by the numerous beauties we discovered on the shore. And I must now add, that we found, during the time of our residence there, that the inland parts of the Island did no ways fall short of the sanguine prepossessions which we first entertained in their favour.

For the woods which covered most of the steepest hills, were free from all bushes and underwood, and afforded an easy passage through every part of them; and the irregularities of the hills and precipices, in the northern part of the Island, necessarily traced out by their various combinations a great number of romantic vallies; most of which had a stream of the clearest water running through them, that tumbled in cascades from rock to rock, as the bottom of the valley, by the course of the neighbouring hills, was at any time broken into a sudden sharp descent: Some particular spots occurred in these vallies, where the shade and fragrance of the contiguous woods, the loftiness of the overhanging rocks, and the transparency and frequent falls of the neighbouring streams, presented scenes of such elegance and dignity, as would perhaps with difficulty be rivalled in any other part of the globe. It is in this place, perhaps, that the simple productions of unassisted nature may be said to excel all the fictitious descriptions of the most animated imagination. I shall finish this article with a short account of that spot where the Commodore pitched his tent, and which he made choice of for his own residence, though I despair of conveying an adequate idea of its beauty. This piece of ground which he chose was a small lawn, that lay on a little ascent, at the distance of about half a mile from the sea. In the front of his tent there was a large avenue cut through the woods to the sea-side, which sloping to the water with a gentle descent, opened a prospect of the bay and the ships at anchor. This lawn was screened behind by a tall wood of myrtle sweeping round it, in the form of a theatre, the ground on which the wood stood, rising with a much sharper ascent than the lawn itself, though not so much, but that the hills and precipices within land towered up considerably above the tops of the trees, and added to the grandeur of the view. There were, besides, two streams of chrystal water, which ran on the right and left of the tent, within an hundred yards distance, and were shaded by the trees which skirted the lawn on either side, and compleated the symmetry of the whole. Some faint conceptions of the elegance of this situation may perhaps be better deduced from the draught of it, inserted in the adjoining plate.[1]

It remains now only that we speak of the animals and provisions which we met with at this place. Former writers have related, that this Island abounded with vast numbers of goats, and their accounts are not to be questioned, this place being the usual haunt of the buc-caneers and privateers, who formerly frequented those seas. And there are two instances; one of a *Musquito Indian*, and the other of *Alex-ander Selkirk* a *Scotchman*, who were left by their respective ships, and lived alone upon this Island for some years, and consequently were no strangers to its produce. *Selkirk*, who was the last, after a stay of be-tween four and five years, was taken off the place by the Duke and Duchess Privateers of *Bristol*, as may be seen at large in the journal of their voyage:[2] His manner of life, during his solitude, was in most particulars very remarkable; but there is one circumstance he relates, which was so strangely verified by our own observation, that I cannot help reciting it. He tells us, amongst other things, as he often caught more goats than he wanted, he sometimes marked their ears and let them go. This was about thirty-two years before our arrival at the Island. Now it happened, that the first goat that was killed by our people at their landing had his ears slit, whence we concluded, that he had doubtless been formerly under the power of *Selkirk*. This was indeed an animal of a most venerable aspect, dignified with an exceed-ing majestic beard, and with many other symptoms of antiquity. During our stay on the Island, we met with others marked in the same manner, all the males being distinguished by an exuberance of beard, and every other characteristick of extreme age.

But the great numbers of goats, which former writers described to have been found upon this Island, are at present very much diminished: For the *Spaniards* being informed of the advantages which the buccaneers and privateers drew from the provisions which goats-flesh here furnished them with, they have endeavoured to extirpate the breed, thereby to deprive their enemies of this relief. For this purpose, they have put on shore great numbers of large dogs, who have encreased apace, and have destroyed all the goats in the accessible part of the country; so that there now remain only a few amongst the craggs and precipices, where the dogs cannot follow them. These are divided into separate herds of twenty or thirty each, which inhabit distinct fastnesses, and never mingle with each other: By this means we found it extremely difficult to kill them; and yet we were so desirous of their flesh, which we all agreed much resembled venison, that we got knowledge, I believe, of all their herds, and it was conceived, by comparing their numbers together, that they scarcely exceeded two hundred upon the whole Island. I remember we had once an opportunity of observing a remarkable dispute betwixt a herd of these animals and a number of dogs; for going in our boat into the eastern bay, we saw some dogs running very eagerly upon the foot, and being willing to discover what game they were after, we lay upon our oars some time to view them, and at last we saw them take to a hill, and looking a little further, we observed upon the ridge of it an herd of goats, which seemed drawn up for their reception; there was a very narrow path skirted on each side by precipices, on which the Master of the herd posted himself fronting the enemy, the rest of the goats being all behind him, where the ground was more open: As this spot was inaccessible by any other path, excepting where this champion had placed himself, the dogs, though they ran up-hill with great alacrity, yet when they came within about twenty yards of him, durst not encounter him, (for he would infallibly have driven them down the precipice) but gave over the chace, and quietly laid themselves down, panting at a great rate.

The dogs, who, as I have mentioned, are masters of all the accessible parts of the Island, are of various kinds, but some of them, very large, and are multiplied to a prodigious degree. They sometimes came down to our habitations at night, and stole our provision; and once or twice they set upon single persons, but assistance being at hand, they were driven off without doing any mischief. As at present it is rare for goats to fall in their way, we conceived that they lived principally upon young seals; and indeed some of our people had the curiosity to kill dogs sometimes and dress them, and they seemed to agree that they had a fishy taste.

Goats-flesh, as I have mentioned, being scarce, we rarely being able to kill above one a day; and our people growing tired of fish, (which, as I shall hereafter observe, abounds at this place) they at last condescended to eat seals, which by degrees they came to relish, and called it lamb. The seal, numbers of which haunt this Island, hath been so often described by former writers, that it is unnecessary to say any thing particular about them in this place. But there is another amphibious creature to be met with here, called a sea-lyon, that bears some resemblance to a seal, though it is much larger. This too we eat under the denomination of beef; and as it is so extraordinary an animal, I conceive, it well merits a particular annotation. They are in size, when arrived at their full growth, from twelve to twenty feet in length, and from eight to fifteen in circumference. They are extremely fat, so that after having cut thro' the skin, which is about an inch in thickness, there is at least a foot of fat before you can come at either lean or bones, and we experienced more than once, that the fat of some of the largest afforded us a butt of oil. They are likewise very full of blood, for if they are deeply wounded in a dozen places, there will instantly gush out as many fountains of blood, spouting to a considerable distance; and to try what quantity of blood they contained, we shot one first, and then cut its throat, and measuring the blood that came from him, we found, that besides what remained in the vessels, which to be sure was considerable, we got at least two hogsheads. Their skins are covered with short hair of a light dun colour, but their tails, and their fins, which serve them for feet on shore, are almost black; their fins or feet are divided at the ends like fingers, the web which joins them not reaching to the extremities, and each of these extremities is furnished with a nail. They have a distant resemblance to an overgrown seal, though in some particulars there is a manifest difference, especially in the males, who have a large snout or trunk hanging down five or six inches below the end of the upper jaw; this particular the females have not, and this renders the countenance of the male and female easy to be distinguished from each other, and besides, the males are of a much larger size. The form and appearance both of the male and female are very exactly represented in the annexed plate[1], only the disproportion of their size is not usually so great as is there exhibited, for the male was drawn from the life, after the largest of these animals, which was found upon the Island: He was the master of the flock, and from his driving off the other males, and keeping a great number of females to himself, he was by the seamen ludicrously stiled the Bashaw. These animals divide their time equally between the land and sea, continuing at sea all the summer, and coming on shore at the setting in of the winter, where they reside during that whole season. In this interval they engender and bring forth their young, and have generally two at a birth; these they suckle with their milk, they being at first about the size of a full-grown seal. During the time of these animals continuance on shore, they feed on the grass and verdure which grows near the bank of the fresh-water streams; and, when not employed in feeding, sleep in herds in the most miry places they can find out. As they seem to be of a very lethargic disposition, and not easily awakened, each herd was observed to place some of their males at a distance in the nature of sentinels, who never failed to alarm them, whenever our men attempted to molest, or even to approach them; and they were very capable of alarming even at a considerable distance, for the noise they make is very loud and of different kinds, sometimes grunting like hogs, and at other times snorting like horses in full vigour. They often, especially the males, have furious battles with each other, principally about their females; and we were one day extremely surprized by the sight of two animals, which at first appeared different from all we had ever observed, but, on a nearer approach, they proved to be two sea-lions, who had been goring each other with their teeth, and were covered over with blood: And the Bashaw before-mentioned, who generally lay surrounded with a seraglio of females, which no other male dared to approach, had not acquired that envied pre-eminence without many bloody contests, of which the marks still remained in the numerous scars which were visible in every part of his body. We killed many of them for food, particularly for their hearts and tongues, which we esteemed exceeding good eating, and preferable even to those of bullocks: And in general there was no difficulty in killing them, for they were incapable either of escaping or resisting, their motion being the most unweildy that can be conceived, their blubber, all the time they are moving, being agitated in large waves under their skins. However, a sailor one day being carelessly employed in skinning a young sea-lion, the female, from whence he had taken it, came upon him unperceived, and getting his head in her mouth, she with her teeth scored his skull in notches in many places, and thereby wounded him so desperately, that though all possible care was taken of him, he died in a few days.

These are the principal animals which we found upon the Island: For we saw but few birds, and those chiefly hawks, blackbirds, owls, and humming birds. We saw not the Pardela, which burrows in the ground, and which former writers have mentioned to be found here; but as we often met with their holes, we supposed that the dogs had destroyed them, as they have almost done the cats, which were very numerous in *Selkirk*'s time, but we saw not above one or two during our whole stay. However, the rats still keep their ground, and continue here in great numbers, and were very troublesome to us, by infesting our tents nightly.

But that which furnished us with the most delicious repasts at this Island, remains still to be described. This was the fish, with which the whole bay was most plentifully stored, and with the greatest variety: For we found here cod of a prodigious size; and by the report of some of our crew, who had been formerly employed in the *Newfoundland* fishery, not in less plenty than is to be met with on the banks of that Island. We caught also cavallies, gropers, large breams, maids, silver fish, congers of a peculiar kind, and above all, a black fish which we most esteemed, called by some a Chimney sweeper, in shape resembling a carp. Indeed the beach is every where so full of rocks and loose stones, that there is no possibility of haling the Seyne; but with hooks and lines we caught what numbers we pleased, so that a boat with two or three lines would return loaded with fish in about two or three hours time. The only interruption we ever met with, arose from great quantities of dog-fish and large sharks, which sometimes attended our boats and prevented our sport. Besides the fish we have already mentioned, we found here one delicacy in greater perfection, both as to size, flavour and quantity, than is perhaps to be met with in any other part of the world: This was sea cra-fish; they generally weighed eight or nine pounds apiece, were of a most excellent taste, and lay in such abundance near the water's edge, that the boat-hooks often struck into them, in putting the boat to and from the shore.

These are the most material articles relating to the accommodations, soil, vegetables, animals, and other productions of the Island of *Juan Fernandes*: By which it must appear, how properly that place was adapted for recovering us from the deplorable situation to which our tedious and unfortunate navigation round Cape *Horn* had reduced us. And having thus given the reader some idea of the site and circumstances of this place, which was to be our residence for three months, I shall now proceed, in the next chapter, to relate all that occurred to us in that interval, resuming my narration from the 18th day of *June*, being the day in which the *Tryal* Sloop, having by a squall been driven out to sea three days before, came again to her moorings, the day in which we finished the sending our sick on shore, and about eight days after our first anchoring at this Island.

CHAP. II.

The arrival of the *Gloucester* and the *Anna Pink* at the Island of *Juan Fernandes,* and the transactions at the place during this interval.

THE arrival of the *Tryal* Sloop at this Island, so soon after we came there ourselves, gave us great hopes of being speedily joined by the rest of the squadron; and we were for some days continually looking out, in expectation of their coming in sight. But near a fortnight being elapsed, without any of them having appeared, we began to despair of ever meeting them again; as we knew that had our ship continued so much longer at sea, we should every man of us have perished, and the vessel, occupied by dead bodies only, would have been left to the caprice of the winds and waves: And this we had great reason to fear was the fate of our consorts, as each hour added to the probability of these desponding suggestions.

But on the 21st of *June,* some of our people, from an eminence on shore, discerned a ship to leeward, with her courses even with the horizon; and they, at the same time, particularly observed, that she had no sail abroad except her courses and her main top sail. This circumstance made them conclude that it was one of our squadron, which had probably suffered in her sails and rigging as severely as we had done: But they were prevented from forming more definite conjectures about her; for, after viewing her for a short time, the weather grew thick and hazy, and they lost sight of her. On this report, and no ship appearing for some days, we were all under the greatest concern, suspecting that her people were in the utmost distress for want of water, and so diminished and weakened by sickness, as not to be able to ply up to windward; so that we feared that, after having been in sight of the Island, her whole crew would notwithstanding perish at sea. However, on the 26th, towards noon, we discerned a sail in the North East quarter, which we conceived to be the very same ship that had been seen before, and our conjectures proved true; and about one o'clock she approached so near, that we could distinguish her to be the

Gloucester. As we had no doubt of her being in great distress, the Commodore immediately ordered his boat to her assistance, laden with fresh water, fish and vegetables, which was a very seasonable relief to them; for our apprehensions of their calamities appeared to be but too well grounded, as perhaps there never was a crew in a more distressed situation. They had already thrown over-board two thirds of their complement, and of those that remained alive, scarcely any were capable of doing duty, except the officers and their servants. They had been a considerable time at the small allowance of a pint of fresh water to each man for twenty-four hours, and yet they had so little left, that, had it not been for the supply we sent them, they must soon have died of thirst. The ship plied in within three miles of the bay; but, the winds and currents being contrary, she could not reach the road. However, she continued in the offing the next day, but had no chance of coming to an anchor, unless the wind and currents shifted; and therefore the Commodore repeated his assistance, sending to her the *Tryal's* boat manned with the *Centurion's* people, and a farther supply of water and other refreshments. Captain *Mitchel*, the Captain of the *Gloucester*, was under a necessity of detaining both this boat and that sent the preceding day; for without the help of their crews he had no longer strength enough to navigate the ship. In this tantalizing situation the *Gloucester* continued for near a fortnight, without being able to fetch the road, though frequently attempting it, and at some times bidding very fair for it. On the 9th of *July*, we observed her stretching away to the eastward at a considerable distance, which we supposed was with a design to get to the southward of the Island; but as soon lost sight of her, and she did not appear for near a week, we were prodigiously concerned, knowing that she must be again in extreme distress for want of water. After great impatience about her, we discovered her again on the 16th, endeavouring to come round the eastern point of the Island; but the wind, still blowing directly from the bay, prevented her getting nearer than within four leagues of the land. On this, Captain *Mitchel* made signals of distress, and our long boat was sent to him with a store of water, and plenty of fish, and other refreshments. And the long-boat being not to be spared, the Cockswain had positive orders from the Commodore to return again immediately; but the weather proving stormy the next day, and the boat not appearing, we much feared she was lost, which would have proved an irretrievable misfortune to us all: But, the 3d day after, we were relieved from this anxiety, by the joyful sight of the long-boat's sails upon the water; and we sent the Cutter immediately to her assistance, who towed her along side in a few hours. The crew of our long boat had taken in six of the *Gloucester*'s sick men to bring them on shore, two of which had died in the boat. And now we learnt that the *Gloucester* was in a most dreadful condition, having scarcely a man in health on board, except those they received from us; and, numbers of their sick dying daily, we found that, had it not been for the last supply sent by our long-boat, both the healthy and diseased must have all perished together for want of water. And these calamities were the more terrifying, as they appeared to be without remedy: For the *Gloucester* had already spent a month in her endeavours to fetch the bay, and she was now no farther advanced than at the first moment she made the Island; on the contrary, the people on board her had worn out all their hopes of ever succeeding in it, by the many experiments they had made of its difficulty. Indeed, the same day her situation grew more desperate than ever, for after she had received our last supply of refreshments, we again lost sight of her; so that we in general despaired of her ever coming to an anchor.[1]

Thus was this unhappy vessel bandied about within a few leagues of her intended harbour, whilst the neighbourhood of that place and of those circumstances, which could alone put an end to the calamities they laboured under, served only to aggravate their distress, by torturing them with a view of the relief it was not in their power to reach. But she was at last delivered from this dreadful situation, at a time when we least expected it; for after having lost sight of her for several days, we were pleasingly surprized, on the morning of the 23d of *July,* to see her open the N. W. point of the bay with a flowing sail; when we immediately dispatched what boats we had to her assistance, and in an hour's time from our first perceiving her, she anchored safe within us in the bay. And now we were more particularly convinced of the importance of the assistance and refreshments we so often sent them, and how impossible it would have been for a man of them to have survived, had we given less attention to their wants; for notwithstanding the water, the greens, and fresh provisions which we supplied them with, and the hands we sent them to navigate the ship, by which the fatigue of their own people was diminished, their sick relieved, and the mortality abated; notwithstanding this indulgent care of the Commodore, they yet buried three fourths of their crew, and a very small proportion of the remainder were capable of assisting in the duty of the ship. On their coming to an anchor, our first care was to assist them in mooring, and our next to send the sick on shore: These were now reduced by deaths to less than fourscore, of which we expected to lose the greatest part; but whether it was, that those farthest advanced in the distemper were all dead, or that the greens and fresh provisions we had sent on board had prepared those which remained for a more speedy recovery, it happened contrary to our expectations, that their sick were in general relieved and restored to their strength, in a much shorter time than our own had been when we first came to the Island, and very few of them died on shore.

I have thus given an account of the principal events, relating to the arrival of the *Gloucester*, in one continued narration: I shall only add, that we never were joined by any other of our ships, except our Victualler, the *Anna Pink*, who came in about the middle of *August*, and whose history I shall more particularly relate hereafter. And I shall now return to the account of our own transactions on board and on shore, during the interval of the *Gloucester's* frequent and ineffectual attempts to reach the Island.

Our next employment, after sending our sick on shore from the *Centurion*, was cleansing our ship and filling our water. The first of these measures was indispensibly necessary to our future health, as the numbers of sick, and the unavoidable negligence arising from our deplorable situation at sea, had rendered the decks most intolerably loathsome. And the filling our water was a caution that appeared not less essential to our future security, as we had reason to apprehend that accidents might oblige us to quit the Island at a very short warning; for some Appearances, which we had discovered on shore upon our first landing, gave us grounds to believe, that there were *Spanish* cruisers in these seas, which had left the Island but a short time before our arrival, and might possibly return there again, either for a recruit of water, or in search of us; for as we could not doubt, but that the sole business they had at sea was to intercept us, and we knew that this Island was the likeliest place, in their own opinion, to meet with us. The circumstances, which gave rise to these reflections (in part of which we were not mistaken, as shall be observed more at large hereafter) were our finding on shore several pieces of earthen jars, made use of in those seas for water and other liquids, which appeared to be fresh broken: We saw too many heaps of ashes, and near them fish-bones and pieces of fish, besides whole fish scattered here and there, which plainly appeared to have been but a short time out of the water, as they were but just beginning to decay. These appearances were certain indications that there had been ships at this place but a short time before we came there; and as all *Spanish* Merchant-men are instructed to avoid the Island, on account of its being the common rendezvous of their enemies, we concluded those who had touched here to be ships of force; and not knowing that *Pizarro* was returned to *Buenos Ayres*, and ignorant what strength might have been fitted out at *Callao*, we were under some concern for our safety, being in so wretched and enfeebled a condition, that notwithstanding the rank of our ship, and the sixty guns she carried on board, which would only have aggravated our dishonour, there was scarcely a privateer sent to sea, that was not an over-match for us. However, our fears on this head proved imaginary, and we were not exposed to the disgrace, which might have been expected to have befallen us, had we been necessitated (as we must have been, had the enemy appeared) to fight our sixty-gun ship with no more than thirty hands.[1]

Whilst the cleaning our ship and the filling our water went on, we set up a large copper-oven on shore near the sick tents, in which we baked bread every day for the ship's company, being extremely desirous of recovering our sick as soon as possible, and conceiving that new bread added to their greens and fresh fish, might prove a powerful article in their relief. Indeed we had all imaginable reason to endeavour at the augmenting our present strength, as every little accident, which to a full crew would be insignificant, was extremely alarming in our present helpless situation: Of this, we had a troublesome instance on the 30th of *June*; for at five in the morning, we were astonished by a violent gust of wind directly off shore, which instantly parted our small bower cable about ten fathom from the ring of the anchor: The ship at once swung off to the best bower, which happily stood the violence of the jerk, and brought us up with two cables an end in eighty fathom. At this time we had not above a dozen seamen in the ship, and we were apprehensive, if the squall continued, that we should be driven to sea in this wretched condition. However, we sent the boat on shore, to bring off all that were capable of acting; and the wind, soon abating of its fury, gave us an opportunity of receiving the boat back again with a reinforcement. With this additional strength we immediately went to work, to heave in what remained of the cable, which we suspected had received some damage from the foulness of the ground before it parted; and agreeable to our conjecture, we found that seven fathom and a half of the outer end had been rubbed, and rendered unserviceable. In the afternoon, we bent the cable to the spare anchor, and got it over the ship's side; and the next morning, *July* 1, being favoured with the wind in gentle breezes, we warped the ship in again, and let go the anchor in forty-one fathom; the eastermost point now bearing from us E. $\frac{1}{2}$ S; the westermost N. W. by W; and the bay as before, S. S. W; a situation, in which we remained secure for the future. But we were much concerned for the loss of our anchor, and swept frequently for it, in hopes to have recovered it; but the buoy having sunk at the very instant that the cable parted, we were never able to find it.

And now as we advanced in *July*, some of our men being tolerably recovered, the strongest of them were employed in cutting down trees, and splitting them into billets; while others, who were too weak for this employ, undertook to carry the billets by one at a time to the water-side: This they performed, some of them with the help of crutches, and others supported by a single stick. We next sent the forge on shore, and employed our smiths, who were but just capable of working, in mending our chain-plates[1] and our other broken and decayed iron work. We began too the repairs of our rigging; but as we had not a sufficient quantity of junk[2] to make spun-yarn, we deferred the general over-hale, in hopes of the daily arrival of the *Gloucester*, who we knew had a great quantity of junk on board. However, that we might make as great dispatch as possible in our refitting, we set up a large tent on the beach for the sail-makers; and they were immediately employed in repairing our old sails, and making us new ones.

These occupations, with our cleansing and watering the ship, (which was by this time pretty well compleated) the attendance on our sick, and the frequent relief sent to the *Gloucester*, were the principal transactions of our infirm crew, till the arrival of the *Gloucester* at an anchor in the bay. And then Captain *Mitchel* waiting on the Commodore, informed him, that he had been forced by the winds, in his last absence, as far as the small Island called *Masa-Fuero*, lying about twenty-two leagues to the westward of *Juan Fernandes*; and that he endeavoured to send his boat on shore at this place for water, of which he could observe several streams, but the wind blew so strong upon the shore, and occasioned such a surf, that it was impossible for the boat to land; though the attempt was not altogether useless, as they returned with a boat-load of fish. This Island had been represented by former Navigators as a barren rock; but Captain *Mitchel* assured the Commodore, that it was almost every where covered with trees and verdure, and was near four miles in length; and added, that it appeared to him far from impossible, but some small bay might be found on it, which might afford sufficient shelter for any ship desirous of refreshing there.

As four ships of our squadron were missing, this description of the Island of *Masa-Fuero* gave rise to a conjecture, that some of them might possibly have fallen in with that Island, and have mistaken it for the true place of our rendezvous; and this suspicion was the more plausible, as we had no draught of either Island that could be relied on. In consequence of this reasoning, Mr. *Anson* determined to send the *Tryal* Sloop thither, as soon as she could be fitted for the sea, in order to examine all its bays and creeks, that we might be satisfied whether any of our missing ships were there or not. For this purpose, some of our best hands were sent on board the *Tryal* the next morning, to overhale and fix her rigging; and our long boat was employed in compleating her water; and whatever stores and necessaries she wanted, were immediately supplied, either from the *Centurion* or the *Gloucester*. But it was the 4th of *August* before the *Tryal* was in readiness to sail, when having weighed, it soon after fell calm, and the tide set her very near the eastern shore: Captain *Saunders* hung out lights, and fired several guns to acquaint us with his danger; upon which all the boats were sent to his relief, who towed the Sloop into the bay; where she anchored until the next morning, and then weighing again, proceeded on her cruize with a fair breeze.

And now after the *Gloucester's* arrival, we were employed in earnest in examining and repairing our rigging; but in the stripping our fore-mast, we were alarmed by discovering it was sprung just above the partners[1] of the upper deck. The spring was two inches in depth, and twelve in circumference; but the Carpenters inspecting it gave it as their opinion, that fishing it with two leaves of an anchor stock, would render it as secure as ever. But our greatest difficulty in refitting was the want of cordage and canvas; for tho' we had taken to sea much greater quantities of both, than had ever been done before, yet the continued bad weather we met with, had occasioned such a consumption of these stores, that we were driven to great straits: For after working up all our junk and old shrouds, to make twice-laid cordage, we were at last obliged to unlay a cable to work into running rigging. And with all the canvas, and remnants of old sails that could be mustered, we could only make up one compleat suit.

Towards the middle of *August* our men being indifferently recovered, they were permitted to quit their sick tents, and to build separate huts for themselves, as it was imagined, that by living apart, they would be much cleanlier, and consequently likely to recover their strength the sooner; but at the same time particular orders were given, that on the firing of a gun from the ship, they should instantly repair to the water-side. Their employment on shore was now either the procuring of refreshments, the cutting of wood, or the making of oil from the blubber of the sea-lions. This oil served us for several uses, as burning in lamps, or mixing with pitch to pay[2] the ships sides, or, when mixed with wood-ashes, to supply the use of tallow, of which we had none left, to give the ship boot-hose tops.[3] Some of the men too were occupied in salting of cod; for there being two *Newfoundland* fishermen in the *Centurion*, the Commodore made use of them in laying in a considerable quantity of salted cod for a sea-store; but very little of it was made use of, as it was afterwards thought to be as productive of the scurvy, as any other kind of salt provisions.

I have before-mentioned, that we had a copper-oven on shore to bake bread for the sick; but it happened that the greatest part of the flower, for the use of the squadron, was embarked on board our Victualler the *Anna Pink*: And I should have mentioned, that the *Tryal* Sloop, at her arrival, had informed us, that on the 9th of *May* she had fallen in with our Victualler, not far distant from the Continent of *Chili*; and had kept company with her for four days, when they were parted in a hard gale of wind. This gave us some room to hope that she was safe, and that she might join us; but all *June* and *July* being past without any news of her, we suspected she was lost; and at the end of *July* the Commodore ordered all the ships to a short allowance of bread. And it was not in our bread only, that we feared a deficiency; for since our arrival at this Island, we discovered that our former Purser had neglected to take on board large quantities of several kinds of provisions, which the Commodore had expressly ordered him to receive; so that the supposed loss of our Victualler, was on all accounts a mortifying consideration. However, on *Sunday*, the 16th of *August*, about noon, we espied a sail in the northern quarter, and a gun was immediately fired from the *Centurion*, to call off the people from shore; who readily obeyed the summons, and repaired to the beach, where the boats waited to carry them on board. And now being prepared for the reception of this ship in view, whether friend or enemy, we had various speculations about her; at first, many imagined it to be the *Tryal* Sloop returned from her cruize; but as she drew nearer this opinion was confuted, by observing she was a vessel with three masts; and then other conjectures were eagerly canvassed, some judging it to be the *Severn*, others the *Pearl*, and several affirming that it did not belong to our squadron: But about three in the afternoon our disputes were ended, by an unanimous persuasion that it was our Victualler the *Anna Pink*. This ship, though, like the *Gloucester*, she had fallen in to the northward of the Island, had yet the good fortune to come to an anchor in the bay, at five in the afternoon. Her arrival gave us all the sincerest joy; for each ship's company was now restored to their full allowance of bread, and we were now freed from the apprehensions of our provisions falling short, before we could reach some amicable port; a calamity, which in these seas is of all others the most irretrievable. This was the last ship that joined us; and the dangers she encountered, and the good fortune which she afterwards met with, being matters worthy of a separate narration, I shall refer them, together with a short account of the other ships of the squadron, to the ensuing chapter.

CHAP. III.

A short narrative of what befel the *Anna Pink* before she joined us, with an account of the loss of the *Wager*, and of the putting back of the *Severn* and *Pearl*, the two remaining ships of the squadron.

ON the first appearance of the *Anna Pink*, it seemed wonderful to us how the crew of a vessel, which came to this rendezvous two months after us, should be capable of working their ship in the manner they did, with so little appearance of debility and distress: But this difficulty was soon solved when she came to an anchor; for we then found that they had been in harbour since the middle of *May*, which was near a month before we arrived at *Juan Fernandes*: So that their sufferings (the risque they had run of shipwreck only excepted) were greatly short of what had been undergone by the rest of the squadron. It seems, on the 16th of *May*, they fell in with the land, which was then but four leagues distant, in the latitude of 45°: 15′ South. On the first sight of it they wore ship and stood to the southward, but their fore-topsail splitting, and the wind being W. S. W, they drove towards the shore; and the Captain at last, either unable to clear the land, or as others say, resolved to keep the sea no longer, steered for the coast, with a view of discovering some shelter amongst the many Islands which then appeared in sight: And about four hours after the first view of the land, the *Pink* had the good fortune to come to an anchor, to the eastward of the Island of *Inchin*; but as they did not run sufficiently near to the East-shore of that Island, and had not hands to veer away the cable briskly, they were soon driven to the eastward, deepening their water from twenty-five fathom to thirty-five, and still continuing to drive, they, the next day, the 17th of *May*, let go their sheet anchor; which though it brought them up for a short time, yet, on the 18th, they drove again, till they came into sixty-five fathom water, and were now within a mile of the land, and expected to be forced on shore every moment, in a place where the coast was very high and steep to, that there was not the least prospect of saving the ship or cargo; and their boats being very leaky, and there being no appearance of a landing-place, the whole crew, consisting of sixteen men and boys, gave themselves over for lost, for they apprehended, that if any of them by some extraordinary chance should get on shore, they would, in all probability, be massacred by the Savages on the coast: For these, knowing no other *Europeans* but *Spaniards*, it might be expected they would treat all strangers with the same cruelty which they had so often and so signally exerted against their *Spanish* neighbours. Under these terrifying circumstances the *Pink* drove nearer and nearer to the rocks which formed the shore; but at last, when the crew expected each instant to strike, they perceived a small opening in the land, which raised their hopes; and immediately cutting away their two anchors, they steered for it, and found it to be a small channel betwixt an Island and the Main, which led them into a most excellent harbour, which, for its security against all winds and swells, and the smoothness of its waters, may perhaps compare with any in the known world. And this place being scarcely two miles distant from the spot where they deemed their destruction inevitable, the horrors of shipwreck and of immediate death, which had so long, and so strongly possessed them, vanished almost instantaneously, and gave place to the more joyous ideas of security, repose, and refreshment.

In this harbour, discovered in this almost miraculous manner, the *Pink* came to an anchor in twenty-five fathom water, with only a hawser, and a small anchor of about three hundred weight: And here she continued for near two months, refreshing her people, who were many of them ill of the scurvy, but were soon restored to perfect health by the fresh provisions, of which they procured good store, and the excellent water with which the adjacent shore abounded. But as this place may prove of the greatest importance to future Navigators, who may be forced upon this coast by the westerly winds, which are almost perpetual in that part of the world, I shall, before I enter into any farther particulars of the adventures of the *Pink*, give the best account I could collect of this Port, its situation, conveniencies and productions.

To facilitate the knowledge of this place to those who may hereafter be desirous of making use of it, there is annexed a plan both of the harbour itself, and of the large bay[1] before it, thro' which the *Pink* drove. This plan is not perhaps in all respects so accurate as might be

wished, it being composed from the memorandums and rude sketches
of the Master and Surgeon, who were not, I presume, the ablest
draughts-men. But as the principal parts were laid down by their
estimated distances from each other, in which kind of estimations it is
well known the greatest part of sailors are very dextrous, I suppose
the errors are not very considerable. Its latitude, which is indeed an
important point, is not well ascertained, the *Pink* having no observation either the day before she came here, or within a day of her leaving
it: But it is supposed that it is not very distant from 45° 30′ South, and
the large extent of the bay before the harbour renders this uncertainty the less material. The Island of *Inchin* lying before the bay is
supposed to be one of the Islands of *Chonos*, which are mentioned in
the *Spanish* accounts, as spreading all along that coast; and are said
by them to be inhabited by a barbarous people, famous for their
hatred of the *Spaniards*, and for their cruelties to such of that Nation
as have fallen into their hands: And it is possible too that the land,
near which the harbour itself lies, may be another of those Islands, and
that the Continent may be considerably farther to the eastward. The
depths of water in the different parts of the Port, and the channels by
which it communicates with the bay, are sufficiently marked in the
plan. But it must be remembred, that there are two coves in it where
ships may conveniently heave down, the water being constantly
smooth: And there are several fine runs of excellent fresh water,
which fall into the harbour, and some of them so luckily situated, that
the casks may be filled in the long-boat with an hose: The most remarkable of these runs is the stream marked in the N. E. part of the
Port. This is a fresh water river, and here the *Pink*'s people got some
few mullets of an excellent flavour; and they were persuaded that, in
a proper season (it being winter when they were there) it abounded
with fish. The principal refreshments they met with in this port were
greens, as wild celery, nettle-tops, &c. (which after so long a continuance at sea they devoured with great eagerness) shelfish, as
cockles and muscles of an extraordinary size, and extremely delicious;
and good store of geese, shags, and penguins. The climate, though it
was the depth of winter, was not remarkably rigorous; nor the trees,
and the face of the country destitute of verdure; and doubtless in the
summer many other species of fresh provision, besides these here
enumerated, might be found there. And notwithstanding the tales of

the *Spanish* Historians, in relation to the violence and barbarity of the inhabitants, it doth not appear that their numbers are sufficient to give the least jealousy to any ship of ordinary force, or that their disposition is by any means so mischievous or merciless as hath hitherto been represented: And besides all these advantages, it is so far removed from the *Spanish* frontier, and so little known to the *Spaniards* themselves, that there is reason to suppose, that with proper precautions a ship might continue here undiscovered for a long time. It is also a place of great defence; for by possessing the Island that closes up the harbour, and which is accessible in very few places, a small force might defend this Port against all the strength the *Spaniards* could muster in that part of the world; for this Island towards the harbour is steep to, and has six fathom water close to the shore, so that the *Pink* anchored within forty yards of it: Whence it is obvious how impossible it would prove, either to board or to cut out any vessel protected by a force posted on shore within pistol-shot, and where those who were thus posted could not themselves be attacked. All these circumstances seem to render this place worthy of a more accurate examination; and it is to be hoped, that the important uses which this rude account of it seems to suggest, may hereafter recommend it to the consideration of the Public, and to the attention of those who are more immediately entrusted with the conduct of our naval affairs.

After this description of the place where the *Pink* lay for two months, it may be expected that I should relate the discoveries made by the crew on the adjacent coast, and the principal incidents during their stay there: But here I must observe, that, being only a few in number, they did not dare to detach any of their people on distant discoveries; for they were perpetually terrified with the apprehension that they should be attacked either by the *Spaniards* or the *Indians*; so that their excursions were generally confined to that tract of land which surrounded the Port, and where they were never out of view of the ship. But even had they at first known how little foundation there was for these fears, yet the country in the neighbourhood was so grown up with wood, and traversed with mountains, that it appeared impracticable to penetrate it: So that no account of the inland parts could be expected from them. Indeed they were able to disprove the relations given by *Spanish* writers, who had represented this coast as inhabited by a fierce and powerful people: For they were

certain that no such inhabitants were there to be found, at least during
the winter season; since all the time they continued there, they saw
no more than one *Indian* family, which came into the harbour in a
periagua, about a month after the arrival of the *Pink*, and consisted of
an *Indian* near forty years old, his wife, and two children, one three
years of age, and the other still at the breast. They seemed to have
with them all their property, which was a dog, and a cat, a fishing-net,
a hatchet, a knife, a cradle, some bark of trees intended for the covering of a hut, a reel, some worsted, a flint and steel, and a few roots of
a yellow hue and a very disagreeable taste, which served them for
bread. The Master of the *Pink*, as soon as he perceived them, sent his
yawl, who brought them on board; and fearing, least they might
discover him if they were permitted to go away, he took, as he conceived, proper precautions for securing them, but without any mixture
of ill usage or violence: For in the day-time they were permitted to
go where they pleased about the ship, but at night were locked up in
the fore-castle. As they were fed in the same manner with the rest of
the crew, and were often indulged with brandy which they seemed
greatly to relish, it did not at first appear that they were much dissatisfied with their situation, especially as the Master took the *Indian*
on shore when he went a shooting, (who always seemed extremely
delighted when the Master killed his game) and as all the crew treated
them with great humanity: But it was soon perceived, that though
the woman continued easy and chearful, yet the man grew pensive and
restless at his confinement. He seemed to be a person of good natural
parts, and tho' not capable of conversing with the *Pink*'s people,
otherwise than by signs, was yet very curious and inquisitive, and
showed great dexterity in the manner of making himself understood.
In particular, seeing so few people on board such a large ship, he let
them know, that he supposed they were once more numerous: And
to represent to them what he imagined was become of their companions, he laid himself down on the deck, closing his eyes, and
stretching himself out motionless, to imitate the appearance of a dead
body. But the strongest proof of his sagacity was the manner of his
getting away; for after being in custody on board the *Pink* eight days,
the scuttle of the fore-castle, where he and his family were locked up
every night, happened to be unnailed, and the following night being
extremely dark and stormy, he contrived to convey his wife and

139

children through the unnailed scuttle, and then over the ship's side into the yawl; and to prevent being pursued, he cut away the long-boat and his own periagua, which were towing a-stern, and immediately rowed ashore. All this he conducted with so much diligence and secrecy, that though there was a watch on the quarter-deck with loaded arms, yet he was not discovered by them, till the noise of his oars in the water, after he had put off from the ship, gave them notice of his escape; and then it was too late either to prevent him or to pursue him; for, their boats being all a drift, it was a considerable time before they could contrive the means of getting on shore themselves to search for their boats. The *Indian* too by this effort, besides the recovery of his liberty, was in some sort revenged on those who had confined him, both by the perplexity they were involved in from the loss of their boats, and by the terror he threw them into at his departure; for on the first alarm of the watch, who cried out, *the Indians,* the whole ship was in the utmost confusion, believing themselves to be boarded by a fleet of armed periagua's.

The resolution and sagacity with which the *Indian* behaved upon this occasion, had it been exerted on a more extensive object than the retrieving the freedom of a single family, might perhaps have immortalized the exploit, and have given him a rank amongst the illustrious names of antiquity. Indeed his late Masters did so much justice to his merit, as to own that it was a most gallant enterprize, and that they were grieved they had ever been necessitated, by their attention to their own safety, to abridge the liberty of a person, of whose prudence and courage they had now such a distinguished proof. And as it was supposed by some of them that he still continued in the woods in the neighbourhood of the port, where it was feared he might suffer for want of provisions, they easily prevailed upon the Master to leave a quantity of such food, as they thought would be most agreeable to him, in a particular part where they imagined he would be likely to find it: And there was reason to conjecture, that this piece of humanity was not altogether useless to him; for, on visiting the place sometime after, it was found that the provision was gone, and in a manner that made them conclude it had fallen into his hands.

But however, though many of them were satisfied that this *Indian* still continued near them; yet others would needs conclude, that he was gone to the Island of *Chiloe,* where they feared he would alarm the

Spaniards, and would soon return with a force sufficient to surprize the
Pink: And on this occasion the Master of the *Pink* was prevailed on
to omit firing the evening gun; for it must be remembered, (and there
is a particular reason hereafter for attending to this circumstance)
that the Master, from an ostentatious imitation of the practice of men
of war, had hitherto fired a gun every evening at the setting of the
watch. This he pretended was to awe the enemy, if there was any
within hearing, and to convince them that the *Pink* was always on her
guard; but it being now represented to him, that his great security
was his concealment, and that the evening gun might possibly discover him, and serve to guide the enemy to him, he was prevailed on,
as has been mentioned, to omit it for the future: And his crew being
now well refreshed, and their wood and water sufficiently replenished,
he, in a few days after the escape of the *Indian,* put to sea, and had a
fortunate passage to the rendezvous at the Island of *Juan Fernandes,*
where he arrived on the 16th of *August,* as hath been already mentioned in the preceding chapter.

This vessel, the *Anna Pink,* was, as I have observed, the last that
joined the Commodore at *Juan Fernandes.* The remaining ships of the
squadron were the *Severn,* the *Pearl,* and the *Wager* store-ship: The
Severn and *Pearl* parted company with the squadron off Cape *Noir,* and,
as we afterwards learnt, put back to the *Brazils:* So that of all the ships
which came into the *South-Seas,* the *Wager,* Captain *Cheap,* was the
only one that was missing. This ship had on board some field-pieces
mounted for land service, together with some coehorn mortars, and
several kinds of artillery, stores and tools, intended for the operations
on shore: And therefore, as the enterprize on *Baldivia* had been resolved on for the first undertaking of the squadron, Captain *Cheap* was
extremely solicitous that these materials, which were in his custody,
might be ready before *Baldivia*; that if the squadron should possibly
rendezvous there, (as he knew not the condition they were then reduced to) no delay nor disappointment might be imputed to him.

But whilst the *Wager,* with these views, was making the best of her
way to her first rendezvous off the Island of *Socoro,* whence (as there
was little probability of meeting any of the Squadron there) she
proposed to steer directly for *Baldivia,* she made the land on the
14th of *May,* about the latitude of 47° South; and, the Captain
exerting himself on this occasion, in order to get clear of it, he had

the misfortune to fall down the after-ladder, and thereby dislocated his shoulder, which rendered him incapable of acting. This accident, together with the crazy condition of the ship, which was little better than a wreck, prevented her from getting off to sea, and entangled her more and more with the land, so that the next morning, at day-break, she struck on a sunken rock, and soon after bilged, and grounded between two small Islands, at about a musquet shot from the shore.

In this situation the ship continued entire a long time, so that all the crew had it in their power to get safe on shore; but a general confusion taking place, numbers of them, instead of consulting their safety, or reflecting on their calamitous condition, fell to pillaging the ship, arming themselves with the first weapons that came to hand, and threatning to murder all who should oppose them. This frenzy was greatly heightned by the liquors they found on board, with which they got so extremely drunk, that some of them tumbling down between decks were drowned, as the water flowed in, being incapable of getting up and retreating to other places where the water had not yet entered: And the Captain, having done his utmost to get the whole crew on shore, was at last obliged to leave these mutineers behind him, and to follow his officers, and such as he had been able to prevail on; but he did not fail to send back the boats, to persuade those who remained, to have some regard to their preservation; tho' all his efforts were for some time without success. However, the weather next day proving stormy, and there being great danger of the ship's parting, they began to be alarmed with the fears of perishing, and were desirous of getting to land; but it seems their madness had not yet left them, for the boat not appearing to fetch them off so soon as they expected, they at last pointed a four pounder, which was on the quarter-deck, against the hut, where they knew the Captain resided on shore, and fired two shot which passed but just over it.

From this specimen of the behaviour of part of the crew, it will not be difficult to frame some conjecture of the disorder and anarchy which took place, when they at last got all on shore. For the men conceived, that by the loss of the ship, the authority of the officers was at an end; and, they being now on a desolate coast, where scarcely any other provisions could be got, except what should be saved out of the wreck, this was another insurmountable source of discord: For as the working upon the wreck, and the securing the provisions, so that they might be

preserved for future exigencies as much as possible, and the taking
care that what was necessary for immediate subsistance might be
sparingly and equally distributed, were matters not to be brought
about but by discipline and subordination; the mutinous disposition of
the people, stimulated by the impulses of immediate hunger, rendered every regulation made for this purpose ineffectual: So that there
were continual concealments, frauds and thefts, which animated each
man against his fellow, and produced infinite feuds and contests.
And hence there was constantly kept on foot a perverse and malevolent
turn of temper, which rendered them utterly ungovernable.

But besides these heart-burnings occasioned by petulance and
hunger, there was another important point, which set the greatest
part of the people at variance with the Captain. This was their differ-
ing with him in opinion, on the measures to be pursued in the present
exigency: For the Captain was determined, if possible, to fit up the
boats in the best manner he could, and to proceed with them to the
northward. For having with him above an hundred men in health, and
having gotten some fire-arms and ammunition from the wreck, he did
not doubt but they could master any *Spanish* vessel they should meet
with in those seas: And he thought he could not fail of meeting with
one in the neighbourhood of *Chiloe* or *Baldivia*, in which, when he had
taken her, he intended to proceed to the rendezvous at *Juan Fernandes*;
and he farther insisted, that should they meet with no prize by the way,
yet the boats alone would easily carry them there. But this was a
scheme that, however prudent, was no ways relished by the generality
of his people; for, being quite jaded with the distresses and dangers
they had already run through, they could not think of prosecuting an
enterprize farther, which had hitherto proved so disastrous: And
therefore the common resolution was to lengthen the long-boat, and
with that and the rest of the boats to steer to the southward, to pass
through the Streights of *Magellan*, and to range along the East side of
South America, till they should arrive at *Brazil*, where they doubted
not to be well received, and to procure a passage to *Great-Britain*.
This project was at first sight infinitely more hazardous and tedious
than what was proposed by the Captain; but as it had the air of returning home, and flattered them with the hopes of bringing them
once more to their native country, this circumstance alone rendered
them inattentive to all its inconveniencies, and made them adhere to it

with insurmountable obstinacy; so that the Captain himself, though he never changed his opinion, was yet obliged to give way to the torrent, and in appearance to acquiesce in this resolution, whilst he endeavoured under-hand to give it all the obstruction he could; particularly in the lengthning of the long-boat, which he contrived should be of such a size, that though it might serve to carry them to *Juan Fernandes*, would yet, he hoped, appear incapable of so long a navigation, as that to the coast of *Brazil*.

But the Captain, by his steady opposition at first to this favourite project, had much embittered the people against him; to which likewise the following unhappy accident greatly contributed. There was a Midshipman whose name was *Cozens*, who had appeared the foremost in all the refractory proceedings of the crew. He had involved himself in brawls with most of the officers who had adhered to the Captain's authority, and had even treated the Captain himself with great abuse and insolence. As his turbulence and brutality grew every day more and more intolerable, it was not in the least doubted, but there were some violent measures in agitation, in which *Cozens* was engaged as the ringleader: For which reason the Captain, and those about him, constantly kept themselves on their guard. But at last the Purser, having, by the Captain's order, stopped the allowance of a fellow who would not work, *Cozens*, though the man did not complain to him, intermedled in the affair with great eagerness; and grossly insulting the Purser, who was then delivering out provisions just by the Captain's tent, and was himself sufficiently violent, the Purser, enraged by his scurrility, and perhaps piqued by former quarrels, cried out a *mutiny*, adding, *that the dog had pistols*, and then himself fired a pistol at *Cozens*, which however mist him: But the Captain, on this outcry and the report of the pistol, rushed out of his tent; and, not doubting but it had been fired by *Cozens* as the commencement of a mutiny, he immediately shot him in the head without farther deliberation, and though he did not kill him on the spot, yet the wound proved mortal, and he died about fourteen days after.

This incident, however displeasing to the people, did yet, for a considerable time, awe them to their duty, and rendered them more submissive to the Captain's authority; but at last, when towards the middle of *October* the long-boat was nearly compleated, and they were preparing to put to sea, the additional provocation he gave them by covertly traversing their project of proceeding through the Streights of *Magellan,* and their fears that he might at length engage a party sufficient to overturn this favourite measure, made them resolve to make use of the death of *Cozens* as a reason for depriving him of his command, under pretence of carrying him a prisoner to *England,* to be tried for murder; and he was accordingly confined under a guard. But they never intended to carry him with them, as they too well knew what they had to apprehend on their return to *England,* if their Commander should be present to confront them.[1] And therefore, when they were just ready to put to sea, they set him at liberty, leaving him and the few who chose to take their fortunes with him, no other embarkation but the yawl, to which the barge was afterwards added, by the people on board her being prevailed on to return back.

When the ship was wreckt, there remained alive on board the *Wager* near an hundred and thirty persons; of these above thirty died during their stay upon the place, and near eighty went off in the long-boat, and the Cutter to the southward: So that there remained with the Captain, after their departure, no more than nineteen persons, which however was as many as the barge and the yawl, the only embarkations left them, could well carry off. It was the 13th of *October,* five months after the shipwreck, that the long-boat converted into a schooner, weighed, and stood to the southward, giving the Captain, who, with Lieutenant *Hamilton* of the land-forces and the surgeon, was then on the beach, three cheers at their departure. It was the 29th of *January* following before they arrived at *Rio Grande,* on the coast of *Brazil*: And having, by various accidents, left about twenty of their people on shore at the different places they touched at, and a greater number having perished by hunger during the course of their navigation, there were no more than thirty of them left, when they arrived in that Port. Indeed, the undertaking of itself was a most extraordinary one; for, not to mention the length of the run, the vessel was scarcely able to contain the number that first put to sea in her; and their stock of provisions (being only what they had saved out of the ship) was extremely slender, and the Cutter, the only boat they had with them, soon broke away from the stern, and was staved to pieces; so that when their provision and their water failed them, they had frequently no means of getting on shore to search for a fresh supply.

When the long boat and Cutter were gone, the Captain, and those who were left with him, proposed to pass to the northward in the barge and yawl: But the weather was so bad, and the difficulty of subsisting so great, that it was two months after the departure of the long-boat before he was able to put to sea. It seems, the place, where the *Wager* was cast away, was not a part of the Continent, as was first imagined, but an Island at some distance from the Main, which afforded no other sorts of provision but shelfish, and a few herbs; and as the greatest part of what they had gotten from the ship was carried off in the long-boat, the Captain and his people were often in great necessity, especially as they chose to preserve, what little sea-provisions remained, for their store when they should go to the northward. During their residence at this island, which was by the seamen denominated *Wager's Island,* they had now and then a straggling canoe or two of *Indians,* which came and bartered their fish and other provisions with our people. This was indeed some little succour, and at another season might perhaps have been greater; for as there were several *Indian* huts on the shore, it was supposed that in some years, during the height of summer, many of these savages might resort thither to fish: And from what has been related in the account of the *Anna Pink,* it should seem to be the general practice of those *Indians* to frequent this coast in the summer time for the benefit of fishing, and to retire in the winter into a better climate, more to the northward.

And on this mention of the *Anna Pink,* I cannot but observe, how much it is to be lamented, that the *Wager's* people had no knowledge of her being so near them on the coast; for as she was not above thirty leagues distant from them, and came into their neighbourhood about the same time the *Wager* was lost, and was a fine roomy ship, she could easily have taken them all on board, and have carried them to *Juan Fernandes.* Indeed, I suspect she was still nearer to them than what is here estimated; for several of the *Wager's* people, at different times, heard the report of a cannon, which I conceive could be no other than the evening gun fired from the *Anna Pink,*[1] especially as what was heard at *Wager's Island* was about the same time of the day. But to return to Captain *Cheap.*

Upon the 14th of *December,* the Captain and his people embarked in the barge and the yawl, in order to proceed to the northward, taking on board with them all the provisions they could amass from the wreck of the ship; but they had scarcely been an hour at sea, when the wind began to blow hard, and the sea ran so high, that they were obliged to throw the greatest part of their provisions over-board, to avoid immediate destruction. This was a terrible misfortune, in a part of the world where food is so difficult to be got: However, they still persisted in their design, putting on shore as often as they could to seek subsistance. But about a fortnight after, another dreadful accident befel them, for the yawl sunk at an anchor, and one of the men in her was drowned; and as the barge was incapable of carrying the whole company, they were now reduced to the hard necessity of leaving four marines behind them on that desolate shore. But they still kept on their course to the northwards, struggling with their disasters, and greatly delayed by the perverseness of the winds, and the frequent interruption which their search after food occasioned: Till at last, about the end of *January*, having made three unsuccessful attempts to double a head-land, which they supposed to be what the *Spaniards* called Cape *Tres Montes*, it was unanimously resolved to give over this expedition, the difficulties of which appeared insuperable, and to return again to *Wager Island*, where they got back about the middle of *February*, quite disheartned and dejected with their reiterated disappointments, and almost perishing with hunger and fatigue.

However, on their return they had the good luck to meet with several pieces of beef, which had been washed out of the ship, and were swimming in the sea. This was a most seasonable relief to them after the hardships they had endured: And to compleat their good fortune, there came, in a short time, two canoes of *Indians*, amongst which was a native of *Chiloe*, who spoke a little *Spanish*; and the surgeon, who was with Captain *Cheap*, understanding that language, he made a bargain with the *Indian*, that if he would carry the Captain and his people to *Chiloe* in the barge, he should have her, and all that belonged to her for his pains. Accordingly, on the 6th of *March*, the eleven persons to which the company was now reduced, embarked in the barge on this new expedition; but after having proceeded for a few days, the Captain and four of his principal officers being on shore, the six, who together with an *Indian* remained in the barge, put off with her to sea, and did not return.

By this means there were left on shore Captain *Cheap*, Mr. *Hamilton* Lieutenant of marines, the Honourable Mr. *Byron* and Mr. *Campbel*, Midshipmen, and Mr. *Elliot* the surgeon. One would have

147

thought that their distresses had long before this time been incapable of augmentation, but they found, on reflection, that their present situation was much more dismaying than any thing they had yet gone through, being left on a desolate coast without any provision, or the means of procuring any; for their arms, ammunition, and every conveniency they were masters of, except the tattered habits they had on, were all carried away in the barge.

But when they had sufficiently revolved in their own minds the various circumstances of this unexpected calamity, and were persuaded that they had no relief to hope for, they perceived a canoe at a distance, which proved to be that of the *Indian,* who had undertaken to carry them to *Chiloe,* he and his family being then on board it. He made no difficulty of coming to them; for it seems he had left Captain *Cheap* and his people a little before to go a fishing, and had in the mean time committed them to the care of the other *Indian,* whom the sailors had carried to sea in the barge. But when he came on shore, and found the barge gone and his companion missing, he was extremely concerned, and could with difficulty be persuaded that the other *Indian* was not murthered; but, being at last satisfied with the account that was given him, he still undertook to carry them to the *Spanish* settlements, and (as the *Indians* are well skilled in fishing and fowling) to procure them provisions by the way.

About the middle of *March,* Captain *Cheap* and the four who were left with him set out for *Chiloe,* the *Indian* having procured a number of canoes, and gotten many of his neighbours together for that purpose. Soon after they embarked, Mr. *Elliot* the surgeon died, so that there now remained only four of the whole company. At last, after a very complicated passage by land and water, Captain *Cheap,* Mr. *Byron,* and Mr. *Campbel,* arrived in the beginning of *June* at the Island of *Chiloe,* where they were received by the *Spaniards* with great humanity; but, on account of some quarrel among the *Indians,* Mr. *Hamilton* did not get thither till two months after. Thus, above a twelvemonth after the loss of the *Wager,* ended this fatiguing peregrination, which by a variety of misfortunes had diminished the company from twenty to no more than four, and those too brought so low, that, had their distresses continued but a few days longer, in all probability none of them would have survived. For the Captain himself was with difficulty recovered; and the rest were so reduced by the severity of the weather, their labour, and their want of all kinds of necessaries, that it was wonderful how they supported themselves so long. After some stay at *Chiloe*, the Captain and the three who were with him were sent to *Valparaiso*, and thence to St. *Jago*, the Capitol of *Chili*, where they continued above a year: But on the advice of a cartel being settled betwixt *Great-Britain* and *Spain*, Captain *Cheap*, Mr. *Byron*, and Mr. *Hamilton*, were permitted to return to *Europe* on board a *French* ship. The other Midshipman, Mr. *Campbel*, having changed his religion, whilst at St. *Jago*, chose to go back to *Buenos Ayres* with *Pizarro* and his officers, with whom he went afterwards to *Spain* on board the *Asia*; and there having failed in his endeavours to procure a commission from the Court of *Spain*, he returned to *England*, and attempted to get reinstated in the *British* Navy; and has since published a narration of his adventures, in which he complains of the injustice that had been done him, and strongly disavows his ever being in the *Spanish* service: But as the change of his religion, and his offering himself to the Court of *Spain*, (though not accepted) are matters which, he is conscious, are capable of being incontestably proved; on these two heads, he has been entirely silent.[1] And now, after this account of the accidents which befel the *Anna Pink*, and the catastrophe of the *Wager*, I shall again resume the thread of our own story.

CHAP. IV.

Conclusion of our proceedings at *Juan Fernandes*,
from the arrival of the *Anna Pink*, to our final
departure from thence.

ABOUT a week after the arrival of our Victualler, the *Tryal* Sloop,
that had been sent to the Island of *Masa-Fuero*, returned to an anchor
at *Juan Fernandes*, after having been round that Island, without meeting any part of our squadron. As, upon this occasion, the Island of
Masa-Fuero was more particularly examined, than I dare say it had
ever been before, or perhaps ever will be again; and as the knowledge
of it may, in certain circumstances, be of great consequence hereafter,
I think it incumbent on me to insert the accounts given of this place,
by the officers of the *Tryal* Sloop.

The *Spaniards* have generally mentioned two Islands, under the
name of *Juan Fernandes*, stiling them the greater and the less: The
greater being that Island where we anchored, and the less being the
Island we are now describing, which, because it is more distant from
the Continent, they have distinguished by the name of *Masa-Fuero*.
The *Tryal* Sloop found that it bore from the greater *Juan Fernandes*
W. by S, and was about twenty-two leagues distant. It is much larger
than has been generally reported; for former writers have represented
it as a barren rock, destitute of wood and water, and altogether inaccessible; whereas our people found it was covered with trees, and
that there were several fine falls of water pouring down its sides into
the sea: They found too, that there was a place where a ship might
come to an anchor on the North side of it, though indeed the anchorage
is inconvenient; for the bank extends but a little way, is steep to, and
has very deep water upon it, so that you must come to an anchor very
near the shore, and there lie exposed to all the winds but a southerly
one: And besides the inconvenience of the anchorage, there is also a
reef of rocks running off the eastern point of the Island, about two
miles in length; but there is little danger to be feared from them,
because they are always to be seen by the seas breaking over them.

This place has at present one advantage beyond the Island of *Juan Fernandes*; for it abounds with goats, who, not being accustomed to be disturbed, were no ways shy or apprehensive of danger, till they had been frequently fired at. These animals reside here in great tranquillity, the *Spaniards* having not thought the Island considerable enough to be frequented by their enemies, and therefore they have not been solicitous in destroying the provisions upon it; so that no dogs have been hitherto set on shore there. And besides the goats, our people found there vast numbers of seals and sea-lions: And upon the whole, they seemed to imagine, that though it was not the most eligible place for a ship to refresh at, yet in case of necessity it might afford some sort of shelter, and prove of considerable use, especially to a single ship, who might apprehend meeting with a superior force at *Fernandes*. The appearance of its N. E. side, and also of its West side, may be seen in the two annexed plates. This may suffice in relation to the Island of *Masa-Fuero*.

The latter part of the month of *August* was spent in unloading the provisions from the *Anna Pink*; and here we had the mortification to find that great quantities of our provisions, as bread, rice, groats, &c. were decayed, and unfit for use. This was owing to the water the *Pink* had made by her working and straining in bad weather; for hereby several of her casks had rotted, and her bags were soaked through. And now, as we had no farther occasion for her service, the Commodore, pursuant to his orders from the board of Admiralty, sent notice to Mr. *Gerard* her Master, that he discharged the *Anna Pink* from the service of attending the squadron; and gave him, at the same time, a certificate, specifying how long she had been employed. In consequence of this dismission, her Master was at liberty, either to return directly to *England*, or to make the best of his way to any Port, where he thought he could take in such a cargoe, as would answer the interest of his Owners. But the Master, being sensible of the bad condition of the ship and of her unfitness for any such voyage, wrote the next day an answer to the Commodore's message, acquainting Mr. *Anson*, that from the great quantity of water the *Pink* had made in her passage round Cape *Horn*, and since that, in the tempestuous weather he had met with on the coast of *Chili*, he had reason to apprehend that her bottom was very much decayed; and that besides, her upper works were rotten abaft; that she was extremely leaky;

that her fore-beam was broke; and that, in his opinion, it was impossible to proceed to sea with her before she had been thoroughly
refitted: He therefore requested the Commodore, that the Carpenters of the squadron might be directed to survey her, that their
judgment of her condition might be known. In compliance with this
desire, Mr. *Anson* immediately ordered the Carpenters to take a careful and strict survey of the *Anna Pink*, and to give him a faithful
report under their hands of the condition in which they found her,
directing them at the same time to proceed herein with such circumspection, that, if they should be hereafter called upon, they might be
able to make oath of the veracity of their proceedings. Pursuant to
these orders, the Carpenters immediately set about the examination,
and the next day made their report; which was, that the *Pink* had no
less than fourteen knees[1] and twelve beams broken and decayed; that
one breast-hook[2] was broken, and another rotten; that her water-
ways[3] were open and decayed; that two standards were broken, as
also several clamps, besides others which were rotten; that all her
iron-work was greatly decayed; that her spirkiting[4] and timbers were
very rotten; and that, having ripped off part of her sheathing, they
found her wales[5] and outside planks extremely defective, and her
bows and decks very leaky; and in consequence of these defects and
decays they certified, that in their opinion she could not depart from
the Island without great hazard, unless she was first of all thoroughly
refitted.

The thorough refitting of the *Anna Pink*, proposed by the Carpenters, was, in our present situation, impossible to be complied with,
as all the plank and iron in the squadron was insufficient for that
purpose. And now the Master finding his own sentiments confirmed
by the opinion of all the Carpenters, he offered a petition to the
Commodore in behalf of his Owners, desiring that, since it appeared
he was incapable of leaving the Island, Mr. *Anson* would please to
purchase the hull and furniture of the *Pink* for the use of the squadron.
Hereupon the Commodore ordered an inventory to be taken of every
particular belonging to the *Pink*, with its just value: And as by this
inventory it appeared, that there were many stores which would be
useful in refitting the other ships, and which were at present very
scarce in the squadron, by reason of the great quantities that had been
already expended, he agreed with Mr. *Gerard* to purchase the whole

together for 300 *l.* The *Pink* being thus broken up, Mr. *Gerard*, with
the hands belonging to the *Pink*, were sent on board the *Gloucester*;
as that ship had buried the greatest number of men in proportion to
her complement. But afterwards, one or two of them were received on
board the *Centurion* on their own petition, they being extremely
averse to sailing in the same ship with their old Master, on account of
some particular ill usage they conceived they had suffered from him.

This transaction brought us down to the beginning of *September*,
and our people by this time were so far recovered of the scurvy, that
there was little danger of burying any more at present; and therefore
I shall now sum up the total of our loss since our departure from
England, the better to convey some idea of our past sufferings, and of
our present strength. We had buried on board the *Centurion*, since
our leaving St. *Helens*, two hundred and ninety-two, and had now
remaining on board two hundred and fourteen. This will doubtless
appear a most extraordinary mortality: But yet on board the *Gloucester* it had been much greater; for out of a much smaller crew than ours
they had buried the same number, and had only eighty-two remaining
alive. It might be expected that on board the *Tryal*, the slaughter
would have been the most terrible, as her decks were almost constantly
knee-deep in water; but it happened otherwise, for she escaped more
favourably than the rest, since she only buried forty-two, and had now
thirty-nine remaining alive. The havock of this disease had fallen still
severer on the invalids and marines than on the sailors; for on board
the *Centurion*, out of fifty invalids and seventy-nine marines, there
remained only four invalids, including officers, and eleven marines;
and on board the *Gloucester* every invalid perished; and out of forty-
eight marines, only two escaped. From this account it appears, that the
three ships together departed from *England* with nine hundred and
sixty-one men on board, of whom six hundred and twenty-six were
dead before this time; so that the whole of our remaining crews,
which were now to be distributed amongst three ships, amounted to
no more than three hundred and thirty-five men and boys; a number,
greatly insufficient for the manning the *Centurion* alone, and barely
capable of navigating all the three, with the utmost exertion of their
strength and vigour. This prodigious reduction of our men was still
the more terrifying, as we were hitherto uncertain of the fate of
Pizarro's squadron, and had reason to suppose, that some part of it at

least had got round into these seas: Indeed, we were satisfied from our own experience, that they must have suffered greatly in their passage; but then every port in the *South-Seas* was open to them, and the whole power of *Chili* and *Peru* would doubtless be united in refreshing and refitting them, and recruiting the numbers they had lost. Besides, we had some obscure knowledge of a force to be fitted out from *Callao*; and, however contemptible the ships and sailors of this part of the world may have been generally esteemed, it was scarcely possible for any thing, bearing the name of a ship of force, to be feebler or less considerable than ourselves. And had there been nothing to be apprehended from the naval power of the *Spaniards* in this part of the world, yet our enfeebled condition would nevertheless give us the greatest uneasiness, as we were incapable of attempting any of their considerable places; for the risquing of twenty men, weak as we then were, was risquing the safety of the whole: So that we conceived we should be necessitated to content ourselves with what few prizes we could pick up at sea, before we were discovered; after which, we should in all probability be obliged to depart with precipitation, and esteem ourselves fortunate to regain our native country, leaving our enemies to triumph on the inconsiderable mischief they had received from a squadron, whose equipment had filled them with such dreadful apprehensions. This was a subject, on which we had reason to imagine the *Spanish* ostentation would remarkably exert itself; though the causes of our disappointment and their security were neither to be sought for in their valour nor our misconduct.

Such were the desponding reflections which at that time arose on the review and comparison of our remaining strength with our original numbers: Indeed our fears were far from being groundless, or disproportioned to our feeble and almost desperate situation. It is true, the final event proved more honourable than we had foreboded; but the intermediate calamities did likewise greatly surpass our most gloomy apprehensions, and could they have been predicted to us at this Island of *Juan Fernandes*, they would doubtless have appeared insurmountable. But to return from this digression.

In the beginning of *September*, as has been already mentioned, our men were tolerably well recovered; and now, the time of navigation in this climate drawing near, we exerted ourselves in getting our ships in readiness for the sea. We converted the fore-mast of the Victualler

into a main-mast for the *Tryal* Sloop; and still flattering ourselves
with the possibility of the arrival of some other ships of our squadron,
we intended to leave the main-mast of the Victualler, to make a
mizen-mast for the *Wager*. Thus all hands being employed in for-
warding our departure, we, on the 8th, about eleven in the morning,
espied a sail to the N. E, which continued to approach us, till her
courses[1] appeared even with the horizon. In this interval we all had
hopes she might prove one of our own squadron; but at length finding
she steered away to the eastward, without haling in for the Island, we
concluded she must be a *Spaniard*. And now great disputes were set
on foot about the possibility of her having discovered our tents on
shore, some of us strongly insisting, that she had doubtless been near
enough to have perceived something that had given her a jealousy
of an enemy, which had occasioned her standing to the eastward without haling in; but leaving these contents to be settled afterwards, it
was resolved to pursue her, and, the *Centurion* being in the greatest
forwardness, we immediately got all our hands on board, set up our
rigging, bent our sails, and by five in the afternoon got under sail.
We had at this time very little wind, so that all the boats were employed to tow us out of the bay; and even what wind there was lasted
only long enough to give us an offing of two or three leagues, when it
flatted to a calm. The night coming on we lost sight of the chace, and
were extremely impatient for the return of day-light, in hopes to find
that she had been becalmed as well as we; though I must confess, that
her greater distance from the land was a reasonable ground for suspecting the contrary, as we indeed found in the morning to our great
mortification; for though the weather continued perfectly clear, we
had no sight of the ship from the mast-head. But as we were now
satisfied that it was an enemy, and the first we had seen in these seas,
we resolved not to give over the search lightly; and, a small breeze
springing up from the W. N. W, we got up our top-gallant masts and
yards, set all the sails, and steered to the S. E, in hopes of retrieving
our chace, which we imagined to be bound to *Valparaiso*. We continued on this course all that day and the next, and then not getting
sight of our chace we gave over the pursuit, conceiving that by that
time she must, in all probability, have reached her Port. And now we
prepared to return to *Juan Fernandes*, and haled up to the S. W. with
that view, having but very little wind till the 12th, when, at three in

the morning, there sprung up a fresh gale from the W. S. W, and we tacked and stood to the N. W: And at day-break we were agreeably surprized with the sight of a sail on our weather-bow, between four and five leagues distant. On this we crouded all the sail we could, and stood after her, and soon perceived it not to be the same ship we originally gave chace to. She at first bore down upon us, showing *Spanish* colours, and making a signal as to her consort; but observing that we did not answer her signal, she instantly loofed close to the wind, and stood to the southward. Our people were now all in spirits, and put the ship about with great alacrity; and as the chace appeared to be a large ship, and had mistaken us for her consort, we conceived that she was a man of war, and probably one of *Pizarro*'s squadron: This induced the Commodore to order all the officers cabins to be knocked down and thrown over-board, with several casks of water and provisions which stood between the guns; so that we had soon a clear ship, ready for an engagement. About nine o'clock we had thick hazy weather and a shower of rain, during which we lost sight of the chace; and we were apprehensive, if the weather should continue, that by going upon the other tack, or by some other artifice, she might escape us; but it clearing up in less than an hour, we found that we had both weathered and fore-reached upon her considerably, and now we were near enough to discover that she was only a Merchantman, without so much as a single tire of guns. About half an hour after twelve, being then within a reasonable distance of her, we fired four shot amongst her rigging; on which, they lowered their top-sails, and bore down to us, but in very great confusion, their top-gallant sails and stay-sails all fluttering in the wind: This was owing to their having let run their sheets and halyards just as we fired at them; after which, not a man amongst them had courage enough to venture aloft (for there the shot had passed but just before) to take them in. As soon as the vessel came within hail of us, the Commodore ordered them to bring to under his lee-quarter, and then hoisted out the boat, and sent Mr. *Saumarez*, his first Lieutenant, to take possession of the prize, with directions to send all the prisoners on board the *Centurion*, but first the officers and passengers. When Mr. *Saumarez* came on board them, they received him at the side with the strongest tokens of the most abject submission; for they were all of them (especially the passengers, who were twenty-five in number) extremely terrified, and under the greatest apprehensions of meeting with very severe and cruel usage; but the Lieutenant endeavoured, with great courtesy, to dissipate their fright, assuring them, that their fears were altogether groundless, and that they would find a generous enemy in the Commodore, who was not less remarkable for his lenity and humanity, than for his resolution and courage. The prisoners, who were first sent on board the *Centurion*, informed us, that our prize was called *Nuestra Senora del Monte Carmelo*, and was commanded by Don *Manuel Zamorra*. Her cargoe consisted chiefly of sugar, and great quantities of blue cloth made in the province of *Quito*, somewhat resembling our *English* coarse broad-cloths, but inferiour to them. They had besides several bales of a coarser sort of cloth, of different colours, somewhat like *Colchester* bays, called by them *Pannia da Tierra*, with a few bales of cotton and tobacco; which, though strong, was not ill flavoured. These were the principal goods on board her; but we found besides, what was to us much more valuable than the rest of the cargoe: This was some trunks of wrought plate, and twenty-three serons[1] of dollars, each weighing upwards of 200 *l.* averdupois. The ship's burthen was about four hundred and fifty tuns; she had fifty-three sailors on board, both whites and blacks; she came from *Callao*, and had been twenty-seven days at sea, before she fell into our hands. She was bound to the port of *Valparaiso* in the kingdom of *Chili*, and proposed to have returned from thence loaded with corn and *Chili* wine, some gold, dried beef, and small cordage, which at *Callao* they convert into larger rope. Our prize had been built upwards of thirty years; yet as they lie in harbour all the winter months, and the climate is favourable, they esteemed it no very great age. Her rigging was very indifferent, as were likewise her sails, which were made of Cotton. She had only three four pounders, which were altogether unserviceable, their carriages being scarcely able to support them: And there were no small arms on board, except a few pistols belonging to the passengers. The prisoners informed us, that they left *Callao* in company with two other ships, whom they had parted with some days before, and that at first they conceived us to be one of their company; and by the description we gave them of the ship we had chased from *Juan Fernandes*, they assured us, she was of their number, but that the coming in sight of that Island was directly repugnant to the Merchant's instructions, who had expressly forbid it, as knowing that if any *English* squadron was in those seas, the Island of *Fernandes* was most probably the place of their rendezvous.

And now, after this short account of the ship and her cargoe, it is necessary that I should relate the important intelligence which we met with on board her, partly from the information of the prisoners, and partly from the letters and papers which fell into our hands. We here first learnd with certainty the force and destination of that squadron, which cruised off the *Maderas* at our arrival there, and afterwards chased the *Pearl* in our passage to port St. *Julian*. This we now knew was a squadron composed of five large *Spanish* ships, commanded by Admiral *Pizarro*, and purposely fitted out to traverse our designs, as hath been already more amply related in the 3d chapter of the 1st book. And we had, at the same time, the satisfaction to find, that *Pizarro*, after his utmost endeavours to gain his passage into these seas, had been forced back again into the river of *Plate*, with the loss of two of his largest ships: And besides this disappointment of *Pizarro*, which, considering our great debility, was no unacceptable intelligence, we farther learnt, that an embargo had been laid upon all shipping in these seas, by the Viceroy of *Peru*, in the month of *May* preceding, on a supposition that about that time we might arrive upon the coast. But on the account sent over-land by *Pizarro* of his own distresses, part of which they knew we must have encountered, as we were at sea during the same time, and on their having no news of us in eight months after we were known to set sail from St. *Catherine's*, they were fully persuaded that we were either shipwreck'd, or had perished at sea, or at least had been obliged to put back again; for it was conceived impossible for any ships to continue at sea during so long an interval: And therefore, on the application of the Merchants, and the firm persuasion of our having miscarried, the embargo had been lately taken off.

This last article made us flatter ourselves, that, as the enemy was still a stranger to our having got round Cape *Horn*, and the navigation of these seas was restored, we might meet with some considerable captures, and might thereby indemnify ourselves for the incapacity we were now under of attempting any of their considerable settlements on shore. And thus much we were certain of, from the information of our prisoners, that, whatever our success might be as to the prizes we might light on, we had nothing to fear, weak as we were, from the

Spanish force in this part of the world; though we discovered that we had been in most imminent peril from the enemy, when we least apprehended it, and when our other distresses were at the greatest height; for we learnt, from the letters on board, that *Pizarro*, in the express he dispatched to the Viceroy of *Peru*, after his return to the river of *Plate*, had intimated to him, that it was possible some part at least of the *English* squadron might get round; but that, as he was certain from his own experience, that if they did arrive in those seas it must be in a very weak and defenceless condition, he advised the Viceroy, in order to be secure at all events, to fit out what ships of force he had, and send them to the southward, where, in all probability, they would intercept us singly, and before we had an opportunity of touching any where for refreshment; in which case, he doubted not but we should prove an easy conquest. The Viceroy of *Peru* approved of this advice, and immediately fitted out four ships of force from *Callao*; one of fifty guns, two of forty guns, and one of twenty-four guns: Three of them were stationed off the Port of *Conception*, and one of them at the Island of *Fernandes*; and in these stations they continued cruising for us till the 6th of *June*, when not seeing any thing of us, and conceiving it to be impossible that we could have kept the seas so long, they quitted their cruise and returned to *Callao*, fully satisfied that we had either perished, or at least had been driven back. As the time of their quitting their station was but a few days before our arrival at the Island of *Fernandes*, it is evident, that had we made that Island on our first search for it, without haling in for the main to secure our easting, (a circumstance, which at that time we considered as very unfortunate to us, on account of the numbers which we lost by our longer continuance at sea) had we, I say, made the Island on the 28th of *May*, when we first expected to see it, and were in reality very near it, we had doubtless fallen in with some part of the *Spanish* squadron; and in the distressed condition we were then in, the meeting with a healthy well provided enemy, was an incident that could not but have been perplexing, and might perhaps have proved fatal, not only to us, but to the *Tryal*, the *Gloucester*, and the *Anna Pink*, who separately joined us, and who were each of them less capable than we were of making any considerable resistance. I shall only add, that these *Spanish* ships sent out to intercept us, had been greatly shattered by a storm during their cruise; and that, after their arrival at *Callao*, they had been laid up. And our prisoners assured us, that whenever intelligence was received at *Lima,* of our being in these seas, it would be at least two months before this armament could be again fitted out.

The whole of this intelligence was as favourable, as we in our reduced circumstances could wish for. And now we were fully satisfied as to the broken jars, ashes, and fish-bones, which we had observed at our first landing at *Juan Fernandes,* these things being doubtless the relics of the cruisers stationed off that Port. Having thus satisfied ourselves in the material articles, and having gotten on board the *Centurion* most of the prisoners, and all the silver, we, at eight in the same evening, made sail to the northward, in company with our prize, and at six the next morning discovered the Island of *Fernandes,* where, the next day, both we and our prize came to an anchor.

And here I cannot omit one remarkable incident which occurred, when the prize and her crew came into the bay, where the rest of the squadron lay. The *Spaniards* in the *Carmelo* had been sufficiently informed of the distresses we had gone through, and were greatly surprized that we had ever surmounted them: But when they saw the *Tryal* Sloop at anchor, they were still more astonished, that after all our fatigues we had the industry (besides refitting our other ships) to compleat such a vessel in so short a time, they taking it for granted that she had been built upon the spot. And it was with great difficulty they were prevailed on to believe, that she came from *England* with the rest of the squadron; they at first insisting, that it was impossible such a bawble as that could pass round Cape *Horn,* when the best ships of *Spain* were obliged to put back.

By the time we arrived at *Juan Fernandes,* the letters found on board our prize were more minutely examined: And, it appearing from them, and from the accounts of our prisoners, that several other Merchantmen were bound from *Callao* to *Valparaiso,* Mr. *Anson* dispatched the *Tryal* Sloop the very next morning, to cruise off the last-mentioned Port, reinforcing him with ten hands from on board his own ship. Mr. *Anson* likewise resolved, on the intelligence recited above, to separate the ships under his command, and employ them in distinct cruises, as he thought that by this means we should not only encrease our chance for prizes, but that we should likewise run a less risque of alarming the coast, and of being discovered. And now the spirits of our people being greatly raised, and their despondency dissipated by this earnest of success, they forgot all their past distresses, and resumed their wonted alacrity, and laboured indefatigably in compleating our water, receiving our lumber, and in preparing to take our farewel of the Island: But as these occupations took us up four or five days with all our industry, the Commodore, in that interval, directed that the guns belonging to the *Anna Pink*, being four six pounders, four four pounders, and two swivels, should be mounted on board the *Carmelo* our prize: And having sent on board the *Gloucester* six passengers, and twenty-three seamen to assist in navigating the ship, he directed Captain *Mitchel* to leave the Island as soon as possible, the service requiring the utmost dispatch, ordering him to proceed to the latitude of five degrees South, and there to cruise off the highland of *Paita*, at such a distance from shore, as should prevent his being discovered. On this station he was to continue till he should be joined by the Commodore, which would be whenever it should be known that the Viceroy had fitted out the ships at *Callao*, or on Mr. *Anson's* receiving any other intelligence, that should make it necessary to unite our strength. These orders being delivered to the Captain of the *Gloucester*, and all our business compleated, we, on the *Saturday* following, being the 19th of *September*, weighed our anchor, in company with our prize, and got out of the bay, taking our last leave of the Island of *Juan Fernandes*, and steering to the eastward, with an intention of joining the *Tryal* Sloop in her station off *Valparaiso*.

CHAP. V.

Our cruise from the time of our leaving *Juan Fernandes,* to the taking of the town of *Paita.*

ALTHOUGH the *Centurion,* with her prize the *Carmelo,* weighed from the bay of *Juan Fernandes* on the 19th of *September,* leaving the *Gloucester* at anchor behind her; yet, by the irregularity and fluctuation of the winds in the offing, it was the 22d of the same month in the evening, before we lost sight of the Island: After which, we continued our course to the eastward, in order to reach our station, and to join the *Tryal* off *Valparaiso.* The next night, the weather proved squally, and we split our maintop-sail, which we handed for the present, but got it repaired, and set it again the next morning. And now, on the 24th, a little before sun-set, we saw two sail to the eastward; on which, our prize stood directly from us, to avoid giving any suspicion of our being cruisers; whilst we, in the mean time, made ourselves ready for an engagement, and steered towards the two ships we had discovered with all our canvas. We soon perceived that one of these, which had the appearance of being a very stout ship, made directly for us, whilst the other kept at a very great distance. By seven o'clock we were within pistol-shot of the nearest, and had a broad-side ready to pour into her, the Gunners having their matches in their hands, and only waiting for orders to fire; but as we knew it was now impossible for her to escape us, Mr. *Anson,* before he permitted them to fire, ordered the Master to hail the ship in *Spanish;* on which the commanding officer on board her, who proved to be Mr. *Hughes,* Lieutenant of the *Tryal,* answered us in *English,* and informed us, that she was a prize taken by the *Tryal* a few days before, and that the other sail at a distance was the *Tryal* herself disabled in her masts. We were soon after joined by the *Tryal;* and Captain *Saunders* her Commander came on board the *Centurion.* He informed the Commodore, that he had taken this ship the 18th instant; that she was a prime sailor, and had cost him thirty-six hours chace, before he could come up with her; that for some time he gained so little upon her, that he began to despair of taking her; and the *Spaniards* though alarmed at first with seeing nothing but a cloud of sail in pursuit of them, the *Tryal's* hull being so low in the water that no part of it appeared, yet knowing the goodness of their ship, and finding how little the *Tryal* neared them, they at length laid aside their fears, and, recommending themselves to the blessed Virgin for protection, began to think themselves secure. And indeed their success was very near doing honour to their *Ave Marias*; for, altering their course in the night, and shutting up their windows to prevent any of their lights from being seen, they had some chance of escaping; but a small crevice in one of the shutters rendered all their invocations ineffectual; for through this crevice the people on board the *Tryal* perceived a light, which they chased, till they arrived within gun-shot; and then Captain *Saunders* alarmed them unexpectedly with a broadside, when they flattered themselves they were got out of his reach: However, for some time after they still kept the same sail abroad, and it was not observed that this first salute had made any impression on them; but, just as the *Tryal* was preparing to repeat her broadside, the *Spaniards* crept from their holes, lowered their sails, and submitted without any opposition. She was one of the largest Merchantmen employed in those seas, being about six hundred tuns burthen, and was called the *Arranzazu*. She was bound from *Callao* to *Valparaiso*, and had much the same cargoe with the *Carmelo* we had taken before, except that her silver amounted only to about 5000 *l.* sterling.

But to balance this success, we had the misfortune to find that the *Tryal* had sprung her main-mast, and that her maintop-mast had come by the board; and as we were all of us standing to the eastward the next morning, with a fresh gale at South, she had the additional ill-luck to spring her fore-mast: So that now she had not a mast left, on which she could carry sail. These unhappy incidents were still aggravated by the impossibility we were just then under of assisting her; for the wind blew so hard, and raised such a hollow sea, that we could not venture to hoist out our boat, and consequently could have no communication with her; so that we were obliged to lie to for the greatest part of forty-eight hours to attend her, as we could have no thought of leaving her to herself in her present unhappy situation: And as an accumulation to our misfortunes, we were all the while driving to the leeward of our station, at the very time when, by our intelligence, we had reason to expect several of the enemy's ships would appear upon the coast, who would now gain the port of *Valparaiso* without obstruction. And I am verily persuaded, that the embarrassment we received from the dismasting of the *Tryal*, and our absence from our intended station occasioned thereby, deprived us of some very considerable captures.

The weather proving somewhat more moderate on the 27th, we sent our boat for the Captain of the *Tryal*, who, when he came on board us, produced an instrument, signed by himself and all his officers, representing that the Sloop, besides being dismasted, was so very leaky in her hull, that even in moderate weather it was necessary to keep the pumps constantly at work, and that they were then scarcely sufficient to keep her free; so that in the late gale, though they had all been engaged at the pumps by turns, yet the water had encreased upon them; and, upon the whole, they apprehended her to be at present so very defective, that if they met with much bad weather, they must all inevitably perish; and therefore they petitioned the Commodore to take some measures for their future safety. But the refitting of the *Tryal*, and the repairing of her defects, was an undertaking that in the present conjuncture greatly exceeded his power; for we had no masts to spare her, we had no stores to compleat her rigging, nor had we any port where she might be hove down, and her bottom examined: Besides, had a port and proper requisites for this purpose been in our possession; yet it would have been extream imprudence, in so critical a conjuncture, to have loitered away so much time, as would have been necessary for these operations. The Commodore therefore had no choice left him, but that of taking out her people, and destroying her: But, at the same time, as he conceived it necessary for his Majesty's service to keep up the appearance of our force, he appointed the *Tryal's* prize (which had been often employed by the Viceroy of *Peru* as a man of war) to be a frigate in his Majesty's service, manning her with the *Tryal's* crew, and giving new commissions to the Captain and all the inferior officers accordingly. This new frigate, when in the *Spanish* service, had mounted thirty-two guns; but she was now to have only twenty, which were the twelve that were on board the *Tryal*, and eight that had belonged to the *Anna Pink*. When this affair was thus far regulated, Mr. *Anson* gave orders to Captain *Saunders* to put it in execution, directing him to take out of the Sloop the arms, stores, ammunition, and every thing that could be of any use to the other ships, and then to scuttle her and sink her. And after Captain *Saunders* had seen her destroyed, he was to proceed with his new frigate (to be called the *Tryal*'s Prize) and to cruise off the highland of *Valparaiso*, keeping it from him N. N. W, at the distance of twelve or fourteen leagues: For as all ships bound from *Valparaiso* to the northward steer that course, Mr. *Anson* proposed by this means to stop any intelligence, that might be dispatched to *Callao*, of two of their ships being missing, which might give them apprehensions of the *English* squadron being in their neighbourhood. The *Tryal*'s Prize was to continue on this station twenty-four days, and, if not joined by the Commodore at the expiration of that term, she was then to proceed down the coast to *Pisco* or *Nasca*, where she would be certain to meet with Mr. *Anson*. The Commodore likewise ordered Lieutenant *Saumarez*, who commanded the *Centurion*'s prize, to keep company with Captain *Saunders*, both to assist him in unloading the Sloop, and also that by spreading in their cruise, there might be less danger of any of the enemy's ships slipping by unobserved. These orders being dispatched, the *Centurion* parted from them at eleven in the evening, on the 27th of *September*, directing her course to the southward, with a view of cruising for some days to the windward of *Valparaiso*.

And now by this disposition of our ships we flattered ourselves, that we had taken all the advantages of the enemy that we possibly could with our small force, since our disposition was doubtless the most prudent that could be projected. For, as we might suppose the *Gloucester* by this time to be drawing near her station off the highland of *Paita*, we were enabled, by our separate stations, to intercept all vessels employed either betwixt *Peru* and *Chili* to the southward, or betwixt *Panama* and *Peru* to the northward: Since the principal trade from *Peru* to *Chili* being carried on to the port of *Valparaiso*, the *Centurion* cruising to the windward of *Valparaiso*, would, in all probability, meet with them, as it is the constant practice of those ships to fall in with the coast, to the windward of that port: And the *Gloucester* would, in like manner, be in the way of the trade bound from *Panama* or the northward, to any part of *Peru*; since the highland off which she was stationed is constantly made by all ships in that voyage. And whilst the *Centurion* and *Gloucester* were thus situated for interrupting the enemy's trade, the *Tryal*'s Prize and *Centurion*'s Prize were as conveniently stationed for preventing all intelligence, by intercepting all ships bound from *Valparaiso* to the northward; for it was on board these vessels that it was to be feared some account of us might possibly be sent to *Peru*.

But the most prudent dispositions carry with them only a probability of success, and can never ensure its certainty: Since those chances, which it was reasonable to overlook in deliberations, are sometimes of most powerful influence in execution. Thus in the present case, the distress of the *Tryal*, and the quitting our station to assist her (events which no degree of prudence could either foresee or obviate) gave an opportunity to all the ships, bound to *Valparaiso*, to reach that port without molestation, during this unlucky interval. So that though, after leaving Captain *Saunders*, we were very expeditious in regaining our station, where we got the 29th at noon, yet in plying on and off till the 6th of *October*, we had not the good fortune to discover a sail of any sort: And then having lost all hopes of making any advantage by a longer stay, we made sail to the leeward of the port, in order to join our prizes; but when we arrived on the station appointed for them, we did not meet with them, though we continued there four or five days. We supposed that some chace had occasioned their leaving the station, and therefore we proceeded down the coast to the highland of *Nasca*, where Captain *Saunders* was directed to join us. Here we arrived on the 21st, and were in great expectation of meeting with some of the enemy's ships on the coast, as both the accounts of former voyages, and the information of our prisoners assured us, that all ships bound to *Callao* constantly make this land, to prevent the danger of running to the leeward of the port. But notwithstanding the advantages of this station, we saw no sail till the 2d of *November*, when two ships appeared in sight together; we immediately gave them chace, but soon perceived that they were the *Tryal's* and *Centurion's* prizes: As they had the wind of us, we brought to and waited their coming up; when Captain *Saunders* came on board us, and acquainted the Commodore, that he had cleared the *Tryal* pursuant to his orders, and having scuttled her, he remained by her till she sunk, but that it was the 4th of *October* before this was effected; for there ran so large and hollow a sea, that the Sloop, having neither masts nor sails to steady her, rolled and pitched so violently, that it was impossible for a boat to lay a long-side of her, for the greatest part of the time: And during this attendance on the Sloop, they were all driven so far to the

North-west, that they were afterwards obliged to stretch a long way to the westward to regain the ground they had lost; which was the reason that we had not met with them on their station as we expected. We found they had not been more fortunate in their cruise than we were, for they had seen no vessel since they separated from us. The little success we all had, and our certainty, that had any ships been stirring in these seas for some time past we must have met with them, made us believe, that the enemy at *Valparaiso*, on the missing of the two ships we had taken, had suspected us to be in the neighbourhood, and had consequently laid an embargo on all the trade in the southern parts. We likewise apprehended, that they might by this time be fitting out the men of war at *Callao*; for we knew that it was no uncommon thing for an express from *Valparaiso* to reach *Lima* in twenty-nine or thirty days, and it was now more than fifty since we had taken our first prize. These apprehensions of an embargo along the coast, and of the equipment of the *Spanish* squadron at *Callao*, determined the Commodore to hasten down to the leeward of *Callao*, and to join Captain *Mitchel* (who was stationed off *Paita*) as soon as possible, that our strength being united, we might be prepared to give the ships from *Callao* a warm reception, if they dared to put to sea. With this view we bore away the same afternoon, taking particular care to keep at such a distance from the shore, that there might be no danger of our being discovered from thence; for we knew that all the country ships were commanded, under the severest penalty, not to sail by the port of *Callao* without stopping; and as this order was constantly complied with, we should undoubtedly be known for enemies, if we were seen to act contrary to it. In this new navigation, not being certain whether we might not meet the *Spanish* squadron in our route, the Commodore took on board the *Centurion* part of his crew, with which he had formerly manned the *Carmelo*. And now standing to the northward, we, before night came on, had a view of the small Island called St. *Gallan*, which bore from us N. N. E. $\frac{1}{2}$ E, about seven leagues distant. This Island lies in the latitude of about fourteen degrees South, and about five miles to the northward of a highland, called *Morro veijo*, or the old man's head. I mention this Island, and the highland near it, more particularly, because between them is the most eligible station on that coast for cruising upon the enemy; as all ships bound to *Callao*, whether from the northward or the southward, run well in with the land in this part. By the 5th of *November*, at three in the afternoon, we were advanced within view of the high land of *Barranca*, lying in the latitude of 10°:36' South, bearing from us N. E. by E, distant eight or nine leagues; and an hour and an half afterwards we had the satisfaction we had so long wished for, of seeing a sail. She first appeared to leeward, and we all immediately gave her chace; but the *Centurion* so much outsailed the two prizes, that we soon ran them out of sight, and gained considerably on the chace: However, night coming on before we came up with her, we, about seven o'clock, lost sight of her, and were in some perplexity what course to steer; but at last Mr. *Anson* resolved, as we were then before the wind, to keep all his sails set, and not to change his course: For though we had no doubt but the chace would alter her course in the night; yet, as it was uncertain what tack she would go upon, it was thought more prudent to keep on our course, as we must by this means unavoidably near her, than to change it on conjecture; when, if we should mistake, we must infallibly lose her. Thus then we continued the chace about an hour and an half in the dark, some one or other on board us constantly imagining they discerned her sails right a-head of us; but at last Mr. *Brett*, then our second Lieutenant, did really discover her about four points on the larboard-bow, steering off to the seaward: We immediately clapped the helm a weather, and stood for her; and in less than an hour came up with her, and having fired fourteen shot at her, she struck. Our third Lieutenant, Mr. *Dennis*, was sent in the boat with sixteen men, to take possession of the prize, and to return the prisoners to our ship. This ship was named the *Santa Teresa de Jesus*, built at *Guaiaquil*, of about three hundred tuns burthen, and was commanded by *Bartolome Urrunaga*, a *Biscayer*: She was bound from *Guaiaquil* to *Callao*; her loading consisted of timber, cocao, coco-nuts, tobacco, hides, *Pito* thread (which is very strong, and is made of a species of grass) *Quito* cloth, wax, &c. The species on board her was inconsiderable, being principally small silver money, and not amounting to more than 170 *l.* sterling. It is true, her cargoe was of great value, could we have disposed of it; but, the *Spaniards* having strict orders never to ransom their ships, all the goods that we took in these seas, except what little we had occasion for ourselves, were of no advantage to us. Indeed, though we could make no profit thereby ourselves, it was some satisfaction to us to consider, that it was so much really lost to the enemy, and that the despoiling them was no contemptible branch of that service, in which we were now employed by our country.

Besides our prize's crew, which amounted to forty-five hands, there were on board her ten passengers, consisting of four men and three women, who were natives of the country, born of *Spanish* parents, and three black female slaves that attended them. The women were a mother and her two daughters, the eldest about twenty-one, and the youngest about fourteen. It is not to be wondered at, that women of these years should be excessively alarmed at the falling into the hands of an enemy, whom, from the former outrages of the Buccaneers, and by the artful insinuations of their Priests, they had been taught to consider as the most terrible and brutal of all mankind. These apprehensions too were in the present instance exaggerated by the singular beauty of the youngest of the women, and the riotous disposition which they might well expect to find in a set of sailors, that had not seen a woman for near a twelvemonth. Full of these terrors, the women all hid themselves when our officer went on board, and when they were found out, it was with great difficulty that he could persuade them to approach the light: However, he soon satisfied them, by the humanity of his conduct and his assurances of their future security and honourable treatment, that they had nothing to fear. And the Commodore being informed of the matter sent directions that they should be continued on board their own ship, with the use of the same apartments, and with all the other conveniencies they had enjoyed before, giving strict orders that they should receive no kind of inquietude or molestation whatever: And that they might be the more certain of having these orders complied with, or of complaining if they were not, the Commodore permitted the Pilot, who in *Spanish* ships is generally the second person on board, to stay with them, as their guardian and protector. He was particularly chosen for this purpose by Mr *Anson*, as he seemed to be extremely interested in all that concerned the women, and had at first declared that he was married to the youngest of them; though it afterwards appeared, both from the information of the rest of the prisoners, and other circumstances, that he had asserted this with a view, the better to secure them from the insults they expected on their first falling into our hands. By this compassionate and indulgent behaviour of the Commodore, the consternation of our female prisoners entirely subsided, and they continued easy and chearful during the whole time they were with us, as I shall have occasion to mention more particularly hereafter.

I have before observed, that at the beginning of this chace the *Centurion* ran her two consorts out of sight, for which reason we lay by all the night, after we had taken the prize, for Captain *Saunders* and Lieutenant *Saumarez* to join us, firing guns, and making false fires every half hour, to prevent their passing us unobserved; but they were so far a-stern, that they neither heard nor saw any of our signals, and were not able to come up with us till broad day-light. When they had joined us we proceeded together to the northward, being now four sail in company. We here found the sea, for many miles round us, of a beautiful red colour: This, upon examination, we imputed to an immense quantity of spawn spread upon its surface; and taking up some of the water in a wine-glass, it soon changed from a dirty aspect to a clear chrystal, with only some red globules of a slimy nature floating on the top. And now having a supply of timber on board our new prize, the Commodore ordered our boats to be repaired, and a swivel gunstock to be fixed in the bow both of the barge and pinnace, in order to encrease their force, in case we should be obliged to have recourse to them for boarding ships, or for any attempts on shore.

As we stood from hence to the northward, nothing remarkable occurred for two or three days, though we spread our ships in such a manner, that it was not probable any vessel of the enemy could escape us. In our run along this coast we generally observed, that there was a current which set us to the northward, at the rate of ten or twelve miles each day. And now being in about eight degrees of South latitude, we began to be attended with vast numbers of flying fish and bonitos, which were the first we saw after our departure from the coast of *Brazil*. But it is remarkable, that on the East side of South *America* they extended to a much higher latitude than they do on the West side; for we did not lose them on the coast of *Brazil*, till we approached the southern tropic. The reason for this diversity is doubtless the different degrees of heat obtaining in the same latitude on different sides of that Continent. And on this occasion, I must beg leave to make a short digression on the heat and cold of different climates, and on the varieties which occur in the same place in different parts of the year, and in different places lying in the same degree of latitude.

The Ancients, as appears in many places, conceived that of the five zones, into which they divided the surface of the globe, two only were habitable, supposing that all between the tropics was too hot, and all within the polar circle too cold to be supported by mankind. The falshood of this reasoning has been long evinced; but the particular comparisons of the heat and cold of these various climates, has as yet been very imperfectly considered. However, enough is known safely to determine this position, that all places between the tropics are far from being the hottest on the globe, as many of those within the polar circles are far from enduring that extreme degree of cold, to which their situation should seem to subject them: That is to say, in other words, that the temperature of a place depends much more upon other circumstances, than upon its distance from the pole, or its proximity to the equinoctial.

This proposition relates to the general temperature of places, taking the whole year round; and in this sense it cannot be denied, but that the city of *London*, for instance, enjoys much warmer seasons than the bottom of *Hudson*'s bay, which is nearly in the same latitude with it; for there the severity of the winter is so great, that it will scarcely permit the hardiest of our garden plants to live. And if the comparison be made between the coast of *Brazil* and the western shore of South *America*, as, for example, betwixt *Bahia* and *Lima*, the difference will be still more remarkable; for though the coast of *Brazil* is extremely sultry, yet the coast of the *South-Seas* in the same latitude is perhaps as temperate and tolerable as any part of the globe; since in ranging along it, we did not once meet with so warm weather, as is frequent in a summer's day in *England*: And this was the more remarkable, as there never fell any rains to refresh and cool the air.

The causes of this temperature in the *South-Seas* are not difficult to be assigned, and shall be hereafter mentioned. I am now only solicitous to establish the truth of this assertion, that the latitude of a place alone is no rule whereby to judge of the degree of heat and cold which obtains there. Perhaps this position might be more briefly confirmed, by observing, that on the tops of the *Andes*, though under the equinoctial, the snow never melts the whole year round; a criterion of cold, stronger than what is known to take place in many parts far removed within the polar circle.

I have hitherto considered the temperature of the air all the year through, and the gross estimations of heat and cold which every one

171

makes from his own sensation. If this matter be examined by means of Thermometers, which in respect to the absolute degree of heat and cold are doubtless the most unerring evidences; if this be done, the result will be indeed most wonderful: For it will appear that the heat in very high latitudes, as at *Petersburgh* for instance, is at particular times much greater than any that has been hitherto observed between the tropics; and that even at *London* in the year 1746, there was the part of one day considerably hotter than what was at any time felt by a ship of Mr. *Anson's* squadron, in running from hence to Cape *Horn* and back again, and passing twice under the sun; for in the summer of that year, the thermometer in *London* (being one of those graduated according to the method of *Farenheit*) stood once at 78°; and the greatest height at which a thermometer of the same kind stood in the foregoing ship, I find to be 76°: This was at St. *Catherine's*, in the latter end of *December*, when the sun was within about three degrees of the vertex. And as to *Petersburgh*, I find, by the acts of the academy established there, that in the year 1734, on the 20th and 25th of *July*, the thermometer rose to 98° in the shade, that is, it was twenty-two divisions higher than it was found to be at St. *Catherine's*; which is a degree of heat that, were it not authorized by the regularity and circumspection with which the observations seem to have been made, would appear altogether incredible.

If it should be asked, how it comes to pass then, that the heat in many places between the tropics is esteemed so violent and insufferable, when it appears by these instances, that it is sometimes rivalled or exceeded in very high latitudes not far from the polar circle? I should answer, that the estimation of heat in any particular place, ought not to be founded upon that degree of heat which may now and then obtain there, but is rather to be deduced from the medium observed in a whole season, or perhaps in a whole year: And in this light it will easily appear, how much more intense the same degree of heat may prove, by being long continued without remarkable variation. For instance, in comparing together St. *Catherine's* and *Petersburgh*, we will suppose the summer heat at St. *Catherine's* to be 76°, and the winter heat to be twenty divisions short of it: I do not make use of this last conjecture upon sufficient observation; but I am apt to suspect, that the allowance is full large. Upon this supposition then, the medium heat all the year round will be 66°, and this perhaps by night as well as day, with no great variation: Now those who have attended to thermometers will readily own, that a continuation of this degree of heat for a length of time would by the generality of mankind be stiled violent and suffocating. But now at *Petersburgh*, though a few times in the year the heat, by the thermometer, may be considerably greater than at St. *Catherine's*, yet, as at other times the cold is immensely sharper, the medium for a year, or even for one season only, would be far short of 66°. For I find, that the variation of the thermometer at *Petersburgh* is at least five times greater, from its highest to its lowest point, than what I have supposed to take place at St. *Catherine's*.

But besides this estimation of the heat of a place, by taking the medium for a considerable time together, there is another circumstance which will still augment the apparent heat of the warmer climates, and diminish that of the colder, though I do not remember to have seen it remarked in any author. To explain myself more distinctly upon this head, I must observe, that the measure of absolute heat, marked by the thermometer, is not the certain criterion of the sensation of heat, with which human bodies are affected: For as the presence and perpetual succession of fresh air is necessary to our respiration, so there is a species of tainted or stagnated air, which is often produced by the continuance of great heats, which never fails to excite in us an idea of sultriness and suffocating warmth, much beyond what the mere heat of the air alone, supposing it pure and agitated, would occasion. Hence it follows, that the mere inspection of the thermometer will never determine the heat which the human body feels from this cause; and hence it follows too, that the heat in most places between the tropics must be much more troublesome and uneasy, than the same degree of absolute heat in a high latitude: For the equability and duration of the tropical heat contribute to impregnate the air with a multitude of steams and vapours from the soil and water, and these being, many of them, of an impure and noxious kind, and being not easily removed, by reason of the regularity of the winds in those parts, which only shift the exhalations from place to place, without dispersing them, the atmosphere is by this means rendered less proper for respiration, and mankind are consequently affected with what they stile a most intense and stifling heat: Whereas in the higher latitudes these vapours are probably raised in smaller quantities, and the irregularity and violence of the winds frequently disperse them;

so that, the air being in general pure and less stagnant, the same degree of absolute heat is not attended with that uneasy and suffocating sensation. This may suffice in general with respect to the present speculation; but I cannot help wishing, as it is a subject in which mankind, especially travellers of all sorts, are very much interested, that it were more thoroughly and accurately examined, and that all ships bound to the warmer climates would furnish themselves with thermometers of a known fabric, and would observe them daily, and register their observations; for considering the turn to philosophical subjects, which has obtained in *Europe* for the last fourscore years, it is incredible how very rarely any thing of this kind hath been attended to. For my own part, I do not recollect that I have ever seen any observations of the heat and cold, either in the *East* or *West-Indies*, which were made by mariners or officers of vessels, except those made by Mr. *Anson's* order, on board the *Centurion*, and by Captain *Leg* on board the *Severn*, which was another ship of our squadron.

This digression I have been in some measure drawn into, by the consideration of the fine weather we met with on the coast of *Peru*, even under the equinoctial itself, but the particularities of this weather I have not yet described: I shall now therefore add, that in this climate every circumstance concurred, that could render the open air and the day-light desirable. For in other countries the scorching heat of the sun in summer renders the greater part of the day unapt either for labour or amusement; and the frequent rains are not less troublesome in the more temperate parts of the year. But in this happy climate the sun rarely appears: Not that the heavens have at any time a dark and gloomy look; but there is constantly a chearful grey sky, just sufficient to screen the sun, and to mitigate the violence of its perpendicular rays, without obscuring the air, or tinging the day-light with an unpleasant or melancholy hue. By this means all parts of the day are proper for labour or exercise abroad, nor is there wanting that refreshment and pleasing refrigeration of the air, which is sometimes produced in other climates by rains; for here the same effect is brought about, by the fresh breezes from the cooler regions to the southward. It is reasonable to suppose, that this fortunate complexion of the heavens is principally owing to the neighbourhood of those vast hills, called the *Andes*, which running nearly parallel to the shore, and at a small distance from it, and extending themselves immensely higher than any other mountains upon the globe, form upon their sides and declivities a prodigious tract of country, where, according to the different approaches to the summit, all kinds of climates may at all seasons of the year be found. These mountains, by intercepting great part of the eastern winds which generally blow over the Continent of South *America*, and by cooling that part of the air which forces its way over their tops, and by keeping besides a prodigious extent of the atmosphere perpetually cool, by its contiguity to the snows with which they are covered; these hills, I say, by thus extending the influence of their frozen crests to the neighbouring coasts and seas of *Peru*, are doubtless the cause of the temperature and equability which constantly prevail there. For when we were advanced beyond the equinoctial, where these mountains left us, and had nothing to screen us to the eastward, but the high lands on the Isthmus of *Panama*, which are but mole-hills to the *Andes*, we then soon found that in a short run we had totally changed our climate, passing in two or three days from the temperate air of *Peru*, to the sultry burning atmosphere of the *West-Indies*. But it is time to return to our narration.

On the 10th of *November* we were three leagues South of the southermost Island of *Lobos*, lying in the latitude of 6° : 27′ South; There are two Islands of this name; this called *Lobos de la Mar*; and another, which lies to the northward of it, very much resembling it in shape and appearance, and often mistaken for it, called *Lobos de tierra*. We were now drawing near to the station appointed to the *Gloucester*, for which reason, fearing to miss her, we made an easy sail all night. The next morning, at day-break, we saw a ship in shore, and to windward, plying up the coast: She had passed by us with the favour of the night, and we soon perceiving her not to be the *Gloucester*, got our tacks on board, and gave her chace; but it proving very little wind, so that neither of us could make much way, the Commodore ordered the barge, his pinnace, and the *Tryal's* pinnace to be manned and armed, and to pursue the chace and board her. Lieutenant *Brett*, who commanded the barge, came up with her first, about nine o'clock, and running along side of her, he fired a volley of small shot between the masts, just over the heads of the people on board, and then instantly entered with the greatest part of his men; but the enemy made no resistance, being sufficiently frightened by the dazzling of the cutlasses, and the volley they had just received. Lieutenant *Brett* ordered the sails to be trimmed, and bore down to the Commodore, taking up in his way the two pinnaces. When he was arrived within about four miles of us he put off in the barge, bringing with him a number of the prisoners, who had given him some material intelligence, which he was desirous the Commodore should be acquainted with as soon as possible. On his arrival we learnt, that the prize was called *Nuestra Senora del Carmin*, of about two hundred and seventy tuns burthen; she was commanded by *Marcos Morena*, a native of *Venice*, and had on board forty-three mariners: She was deep laden with steel, iron, wax, pepper, cedar, plank, snuff, rosarios, *European* bale goods, powder blue, cinnamon, *Romish* indulgences, and other species of merchandize: And though this cargoe, in our present circumstances, was but of little value to us, yet with respect to the *Spaniards*, it was the most considerable capture that fell into our hands in this part of the world; for it amounted to upwards of 400,000 dollars prime cost at *Panama*. This ship was bound to *Callao*, and had stopped at *Paita* in her passage, to take in a recruit of water and provisions, and had not left that place above twenty-four hours, before she fell into our hands.

I have mentioned that Mr. *Brett* had received some important intelligence from the prisoners, which he endeavoured to acquaint the Commodore with immediately. The first person he received it from (though upon further examination it was confirmed by the other prisoners) was one *John Williams* an *Irishman*, whom he found on board the *Spanish* vessel. *Williams* was a Papist, who worked his passage from *Cadiz*, and had travelled over all the kingdom of *Mexico* as a Pedlar: He pretended, that by this business he had got 4 or 5000 dollars; but that he was embarrassed by the Priests, who knew he had money, and was at last stript of all he had. He was indeed at present all in rags, being but just got out of *Paita* goal, where he had been confined for some misdemeanor; he expressed great joy upon seeing his countrymen, and immediately informed them, that, a few days before, a vessel came into *Paita*, where the Master of her informed the Governor, that he had been chased in the offing by a very large ship, which from her size, and the colour of her sails, he was persuaded must be one of the *English* squadron: This we then conjectured to have been the *Gloucester*, as we afterwards found it was. The Governor, upon examining the Master, was fully satisfied of his relation, and immediately sent away an express to *Lima* to acquaint the Vice-

roy therewith: And the Royal Officer residing at *Paita*, being apprehensive of a visit from the *English*, was busily employed in removing
the King's treasure and his own to *Piura*, a town within land, about
fourteen leagues distant. We further learnt from our prisoners, that
there was a very considerable sum of money belonging to some Merchants at *Lima*, that was now lodged at the Custom-house at *Paita*;
and that this was intended to be shipped on board a vessel, which was
then in the port of *Paita*, and was preparing to sail with the utmost
expedition, being bound for the bay of *Sonsonnate*, on the coast of
Mexico, in order to purchase a part of the cargoe of the *Manila* ship.
This vessel at *Paita* was esteemed a prime sailor, and had just received a new coat of tallow on her bottom; and, in the opinion of the
prisoners, she might be able to sail the succeeding morning. The
character they gave us of this vessel, on which the money was to be
shipped, left us little reason to believe that our ship, which had been
in the water near two years, could have any chance of coming up with
her, if we once suffered her to escape out of the Port. And therefore,
as we were now discovered, and the coast would be soon alarmed, and
as our cruising in these parts any longer would answer no purpose,
the Commodore resolved to surprize the place, having first minutely
informed himself of its strength and condition, and being fully satisfied, that there was little danger of losing many of our men in the
attempt. This surprize of *Paita*, besides the treasure it promised us,
and its being the only enterprize it was in our power to undertake, had
these other advantages attending it, that we should in all probability
supply ourselves with great quantities of live provision, of which we
were at this time in want: And we should likewise have an opportunity of setting our prisoners on shore, who were now very numerous, and made a greater consumption of our food than our stock that
remained was capable of furnishing long. In all these lights the attempt
was a most eligible one, and what our necessities, our situation, and
every prudential consideration, prompted us to. How it succeeded,
and how far it answered our expectations, shall be the subject of the
following chapter.

CHAP. VI.

The taking of *Paita*, and our proceedings till we left the coast of *Peru*.

THE town of *Paita* is situated in the latitude of 5° : 12 South, in a most barren soil, composed only of sand and slate: The extent of it (as may be seen in the annexed plan of it) is but small, containing in all less than two hundred families. The houses are only ground-floors; the walls built of split cane and mud, and the roofs thatched with leaves: These edifices, though extremely slight, are abundantly sufficient for a climate, where rain is considered as a prodigy, and is not seen in many years: So that it is said, that a small quantity of rain falling in this country in the year 1728, it ruined a great number of buildings, which mouldered away, and as it were melted before it. The inhabitants of *Paita* are principally *Indians* and black slaves, or at least a mixed breed, the whites being very few. The port of *Paita*, though in reality little more than a bay, is esteemed the best on that part of the coast; and is indeed a very secure and commodious anchorage. It is greatly frequented by all vessels coming from the North; since it is here only that the ships from *Acapulco, Sonsonnate, Realeijo* and *Panama*, can touch and refresh in their passage to *Callao*: And the length of these voyages (the wind for the greatest part of the year being full against them) renders it impossible to perform them without calling upon the coast for a recruit of fresh water. It is true, *Paita* is situated on so parched a spot, that it does not itself furnish a drop of fresh water, or any kind of greens or provisions, except fish and a few goats: But there is an *Indian* town called *Colan*, about two or three leagues distant to the northward, from whence water, maize, greens, fowls, &c. are brought to *Paita* on balsas or floats, for the conveniency of the ships that touch here; and cattle are sometimes brought from *Piura*, a town which lies about fourteen leagues up in the country. The water brought from *Colan* is whitish, and of a disagreeable appearance, but is said to be very wholsome: For it is pretended by the inhabitants, that it runs through large woods of sarsaparilla, and that it is sensibly impregnated therewith. This port of *Paita*, besides fur-

178

nishing the northern trade bound to *Callao*, with water and necessaries, is the usual place where passengers from *Acapulco* or *Panama*, bound to *Lima*, disembark; for, as it is two hundred leagues from hence to *Callao*, the port of *Lima*, and as the wind is generally contrary, the passage by sea is very tedious and fatiguing, but by land there is a tolerable good road parallel to the coast, with many stations and villages for the accommodation of travellers.

It appears by the plan, that the town of *Paita* is itself an open place; so that its sole protection and defence is the fort marked (B) in the plan. It was of consequence to us to be well informed of the fabrick and strength of this fort; and by the examination of our prisoners we found, that there were eight pieces of cannon mounted in it, but that it had neither ditch nor outwork, being only surrounded by a plain brick wall; and that the garrison consisted of only one weak company, but the town itself might possibly arm three hundred men more.

Mr. *Anson* having informed himself of the strength of the place, resolved (as hath been said in the preceding chapter) to attempt it that very night. We were then about twelve leagues distant from the shore, far enough to prevent our being discovered; yet not so far, but that by making all the sail we could, we might arrive in the bay with our ships in the night. However, the Commodore prudently considered, that this would be an improper method of proceeding, as our ships, being such large bodies, might be easily discovered at a distance even in the night, and might thereby alarm the inhabitants, and give them an opportunity of removing their valuable effects. He therefore, as the strength of the place did not require our whole force, resolved to attempt it with our boats only, ordering the eighteen oared barge, and our own and the *Tryal's* pinnaces on that service; and having picked out fifty-eight men to man them, well provided with arms and ammunition, he gave the command of the expedition to Lieutenant *Brett*, and gave him his necessary orders. And the better to prevent the disappointment and confusion which might arise from the darkness of the night, and the ignorance of the streets and passages of the place, two of the *Spanish* Pilots were ordered to attend the Lieutenant, and to conduct him to the most convenient landing-place, and were afterwards to be his guides on shore; and that we might have the greater security for their faithful behaviour on this occasion, the Commodore took care to assure all our prisoners, that,

179

if the Pilots acted properly, they should all of them be released, and set on shore at this place; but in case of any misconduct or treachery, he threatened them that the Pilots should be instantly shot, and that he would carry all the rest of the *Spaniards*, who were on board him, prisoners to *England*. So that the prisoners themselves were interested in our success, and therefore we had no reason to suspect our Conductors either of negligence or perfidy.

And on this occasion I cannot but remark a singular circumstance of one of the Pilots employed by us in this business. It seems (as we afterwards learnt) he had been taken by Captain *Clipperton* above twenty years before, and had been forced to lead *Clipperton* and his people to the surprize of *Truxillo*, a town within land to the southward of *Paita*, where however he contrived to alarm his countrymen, and to save them, though the place was taken. Now that the only two attempts on shore, which were made at so long an interval from each other, should be guided by the same person, and he too a prisoner both times, and forced upon the employ contrary to his inclination, is an incident so very extraordinary, that I could not help taking notice of it. But to return to the matter in hand.

During our preparations, the ships themselves stood towards the Port with all the sail they could make, being secure that we were yet at too great a distance to be seen. But about ten o'clock at night, the ships being then within five leagues of the place, Lieutenant *Brett*, with the boats under his command, put off, and arrived at the mouth of the bay without being discovered; but no sooner had he entered it, than some of the people, on board a vessel riding at anchor there, perceived him, who instantly put off in their boat, rowing towards the fort, shouting and crying, *the English, the English dogs*, &c. by which the whole town was suddenly alarmed, and our people soon observed several lights hurrying backwards and forwards in the fort, and other marks of the inhabitants being in great motion. Lieutenant *Brett*, on this, encouraged his men to pull briskly up to the shore, that they might give the enemy as little time as possible to prepare for their defence. However, before our boats could reach the shore, the people in the fort had got ready some of their cannon, and pointed them towards the landing-place; and though in the darkness of the night it might be well supposed that chance had a greater share than skill in their direction, yet the first shot passed extremely near one of the

A Sea-Lion and Lioness

The burning of the Town of Payr

coast of Santa Fee in the South Sea

A View of the Watering Place at Tenian

boats, whistling just over the heads of the crew. This made our people redouble their efforts; so that they had reached the shore, and were in part disembarked by the time the second gun fired. As soon as our men landed, they were conducted by one of the *Spanish* Pilots to the entrance of a narrow street, not above fifty yards distant from the beach, where they were covered from the fire of the fort; and being formed in the best manner the shortness of the time would allow, they immediately marched for the parade, which was a large square at the end of this street, the fort being one side of the square, and the Governor's house another, as may be seen more distinctly in the plan, where likewise the road they took from their landing to the fort is marked out by a prickt line. In this march (though performed with tolerable regularity) the shouts and clamours of threescore sailors, who had been confined so long on shipboard, and were now for the first time on shore in an enemy's country, joyous as they always are, when they land, and animated besides in the present case with the hopes of an immense pillage; the huzza's, I say, of this spirited detachment, joined with the noise of their drums, and favoured by the night, had augmented their numbers, in the opinion of the enemy, to at least three hundred; by which persuasion the inhabitants were so greatly intimidated, that they were much more solicitous about the means of their flight than of their resistance: So that though upon entering the parade, our people received a volley from the Merchants who owned the treasure then in the town, and who, with a few others, had ranged themselves in a gallery that ran round the Governor's house, yet that post was immediately abandoned upon the first fire made by our people, who were thereby left in quiet possession of the parade.

On this success Lieutenant *Brett* divided his men into two parties, ordering one of them to surround the Governor's house, and if possible to secure the Governor, whilst he himself with the other marched to the fort, with an intent to force it. But, contrary to his expectation, he entered it without opposition; for the enemy, on his approach, abandoned it, and made their escape over the walls. By this means the whole place was mastered in less than a quarter of an hour's time from the first landing, with no other loss than that of one man killed on the spot, and two wounded; one of which was the *Spanish* Pilot of the *Terefa*, who received a slight bruise by a ball which grazed on his wrist: Indeed another of the company, the Honourable Mr. *Kepple*, son to the Earl of *Albemarle*, had a very narrow escape; for having on a jocky cap, one side of the peak was shaved off close to his temple by a ball, which however did him no other injury.[1]

And now Lieutenant *Brett*, after this success, placed a guard at the fort, and another at the Governor's house, and appointed centinels at all the avenues of the town, both to prevent any surprize from the enemy, and to secure the effects in the place from being embezzled. And this being done, his next care was to seize on the Custom-house where the treasure lay, and to examine if any of the inhabitants remained in the town, that he might know what farther precautions it was necessary to take; but he soon found that the numbers left behind were no ways formidable: For the greatest part of them (being in bed when the place was surprized) had run away with so much precipitation, that they had not given themselves time to put on their cloaths. And in this precipitate rout the Governor was not the last to secure himself, for he fled betimes half naked, leaving his wife, a young Lady of about seventeen years of age, to whom he had been married but three or four days, behind him, though she too was afterwards carried off in her shift by a couple of centinels, just as the detachment, ordered to invest the house, arrived before it. This escape of the Governor was an unpleasing circumstance, as Mr. *Anson* had particularly recommended it to Lieutenant *Brett* to secure his person, if possible, in hopes that by that means we might be able to treat for the ransom of the place: But it seems his alertness rendered it impossible to seize him. The few inhabitants who remained were confined in one of the churches under a guard, except some stout Negroes which were found in the place; these, instead of being shut up, were employed the remaining part of the night to assist in carrying the treasure from the Custom-house and other places to the fort: However, there was care taken that they should be always attended by a file of musqueteers.

The transporting the treasure from the Custom-house to the fort, was the principal occupation of Mr. *Brett*'s people, after he had got possession of the place. But the sailors, while they were thus employed, could not be prevented from entring the houses which lay near them, in search of private pillage. And the first things which occurred to them, being the cloaths which the *Spaniards* in their flight had left behind them, and which, according to the custom of the country, were most of them either embroidered or laced, our people eagerly seized these glittering habits, and put them on over their own dirty trowsers and jackets, not forgetting, at the same time, the tye or bag-wig and laced hat, which were generally found with the cloaths; and when this practice was once begun, there was no preventing the whole detachment from imitating it: And those, who came latest into the fashion, not finding mens cloaths sufficient to equip themselves, they were obliged to take up with womens gowns and petticoats, which (provided there was finery enough) they made no scruple of putting on, and blending with their own greasy dress. So that when a party of them thus ridiculously metamorphised first appeared before Mr. *Brett*, he was extreamly surprized at their appearance, and could not immediately be satisfied they were his own people.[1]

These were the transactions of our detachment on shore at *Paita* the first night. And now to return to what was done on board the *Centurion* in that interval. I must observe, that after the boats were gone off, we lay by till one o'clock in the morning, and then supposing our detachment to be near landing, we made an easy sail for the bay. About seven in the morning we began to open the bay, and soon after we had a view of the town; and though we had no reason to doubt of the success of the enterprize, yet it was with great joy that we first discovered an infallible signal of the certainty of our hopes; this was by means of our perspectives, for through them we saw an *English* flag hoisted on the flag-staff of the fort, which to us was an incontestable proof that our people had got possession of the town. We plied into the bay with as much expedition as the wind, which then blew off shore, would permit us: And at eleven, the *Tryal's* boat came on board us, loaden with dollars and church-plate; and the officer who commanded her informed us of the preceding night's transactions, such as we have already related them. About two in the afternoon we came to an anchor in ten fathom and a half, at a mile and a half distance from the town, and were consequently near enough to have a more immediate intercourse with those on shore. And now we found that Mr. *Brett* had hitherto gone on in collecting and removing the treasure without interruption; but that the enemy had rendezvoused from all parts of the country on a hill, at the back of the town, where they made no inconsiderable appearance: For amongst the rest of their force, there were two hundred horse seemingly very well armed,

183

and mounted, and, as we conceived, properly trained and regimented, being furnished with trumpets, drums and standards. These troops paraded about the hill with great ostentation, sounding their military musick, and practising every art to intimidate us, (as our numbers on shore were by this time not unknown to them) in hopes that we might be induced by our fears to abandon the place before the pillage was compleated. But we were not so ignorant as to believe, that this body of horse, which seemed to be what the enemy principally depended on, would dare to venture in streets and amongst houses, even had their numbers been three times as great; and therefore, notwithstanding their menaces, we went on, as long as the day-light lasted, calmly, in sending off the treasure, and in employing the boats to carry on board the refreshments, such as hogs, fowls, &c. which we found here in great abundance. But at night, to prevent any surprize, the Commodore sent on shore a reinforcement, who posted themselves in all the streets, leading to the parade; and for their greater security, they traversed the streets with barricadoes six feet high: And the enemy continuing quiet all night, we, at day-break, returned again to our labour of loading the boats, and sending them off.

By this time we were convinced of what consequence it would have been to us, had fortune seconded the prudent views of the Commodore, by permitting us to have secured the Governor. For we found in the place many store-houses full of valuable effects, which were useles to us at present, and such as we could not find room for on board. But had the Governor been in our power, he would, in all probability, have treated for a ransom, which would have been extremely advantageous both to him and us: Whereas, he being now at liberty, and having collected all the force of the country for many leagues round, and having even got a body of militia from *Piura*, which was fourteen leagues distant, he was so elated with his numbers, and so fond of his new military command, that he seemed not to trouble himself about the fate of his Government. So that though Mr. *Anson* sent several messages to him by the inhabitants, who were in our power, desiring him to enter into a treaty for the ransom of the town and goods, giving him, at the same time, an intimation that he should be far from insisting on a rigorous equivalent, but perhaps might be satisfied with some live cattle, and a few necessaries for the use of the squadron, and assuring him too, that if he would not condescend at least to treat, he would set fire to the town, and all the warehouses: Yet the Governor was so imprudent and arrogant, that he despised all these reiterated applications, and did not deign even to return the least answer to them.

On the second day of our being in possession of the place, several Negro slaves deserted from the enemy on the hill, and coming into the town, voluntarily entered into our service: One of these was well known to a Gentleman on board, who remembered him formerly at *Panama*. And the *Spaniards* without the town being in extreme want of water, many of their slaves crept into the place by stealth, and carried away several jars of water to their masters on the hill; and though some of them were seized by our men in the attempt, yet the thirst amongst the enemy was so pressing, that they continued this practice till we left the place. And now, on this second day we were assured, both by the deserters and by these prisoners we took, that the *Spaniards* on the hill, who were by this time encreased to a formidable number, had resolved to storm the town and fort the succeeding night; and that one *Gordon*, a *Scotch* Papist, and Captain of a ship in those seas, was to have the command of this enterprize. But we notwithstanding, continued sending off our boats, and prosecuted our work without the least hurry or precipitation till the evening; and then a reinforcement was again sent on shore by the Commodore, and Lieutenant *Brett* doubled his guards at each of the barricadoes; and our posts being connected by the means of centinels placed within call of each other, and the whole being visited by frequent rounds, attended with a drum, these marks of our vigilance which the enemy could not be ignorant of, as they could doubtless hear the drum, if not the calls of the centinels; these marks, I say, of our vigilance, and of our readiness to receive them, cooled their resolution, and made them forget the vaunts of the preceding day; so that we passed this second night with as little molestation as we had done the first.

We had finished sending the treasure on board the *Centurion* the evening before; so that the third morning, being the 15th of *November*, the boats were employed in carrying off the most valuable part of the effects that remained in the town. And the Commodore intending to sail this day, he, about ten o'clock, pursuant to his promise, sent all his prisoners, amounting to eighty-eight, on shore, giving orders to Lieutenant *Brett* to secure them in one of the churches under a strict guard, till he was ready to embark his men. Mr. *Brett* was at the same time ordered to set the whole town on fire, except the two churches (which by good fortune stood at some distance from the other houses) and then he was to abandon the place, and to come on board. These orders were punctually complied with; for Mr. *Brett* immediately set his men to work, to distribute pitch, tar, and other combustibles (of which great quantities were found here) into houses situated in different streets of the town, so that, the place being fired in many quarters at the same time, the destruction might be more violent and sudden, and the enemy, after our departure, might not be able to extinguish it. These preparations being made, he, in the next place, ordered the cannon, which he found in the fort, to be nailed up; and then setting fire to those houses which were most to windward, he collected his men, and marched towards the beach, where the boats waited to carry them off. And the part of the beach where he intended to embark being an open place without the town, near where the churches are marked in the foregoing plan, the *Spaniards* on the hill perceiving he was retreating, resolved to try if they could not precipitate his departure, and thereby lay some foundation for their future boasting. And for this purpose a small squadron of their horse, consisting of about sixty, picked out, as I suppose, for this service, marched down the hill with much seeming resolution; so that, had we not been prepossessed with a juster opinion of their prowess, we might have suspected, that now we were on the open beach with no advantage of situation, they would certainly have charged us: But we presumed (and we were not mistaken) that this was mere ostentation. For, notwithstanding the pomp and parade they advanced with, Mr. *Brett* had no sooner ordered his men to halt and face about, but the enemy stopped their career, and never dared to advance a step further.

When our people were arrived at their boats, and were ready to go on board, they were for some time delayed, by missing one of their number; but being unable, by their mutual enquiries amongst each other, to inform themselves where he was left, or by what accident he was detained, they, after a considerable delay, resolved to get into their boats, and to put off without him. And the last man was actually embarked, and the boats just putting off, when they heard him calling to them to take him in. The town was by this time so thoroughly on fire, and the smoke covered the beach so effectually, that they could scarcely see him, though they heard his voice. The Lieutenant instantly ordered one of the boats to his relief, who found him up to the chin in water, for he had waded as far as he durst, being extremely frightned with the apprehensions of falling into the hands of an enemy, enraged, as they doubtless were, with the pillage and destruction of their town. On enquiring into the cause of his staying behind, it was found that he had taken that morning too large a dose of brandy, which had thrown him into so sound a sleep, that he did not awake till the fire came near enough to scorch him. He was strangely amazed on first opening his eyes, to see the place all in a blaze on one side, and several *Spaniards* and *Indians* not far from him on the other. The greatness and suddenness of his fright instantly reduced him to a state of sobriety, and gave him sufficient presence of mind to push thro' the thickest of the smoke, as the likeliest means to escape the enemy; and making the best of his way to the beach, he ran as far into the water as he durst, (for he could not swim) before he ventured to look back.

And here I cannot but observe, to the honour of our people, that though there were great quantities of wine and spirituous liquors found in the place, yet this man was the only one who was known to have so far neglected his duty, as to get drunk. Indeed, their whole behaviour, while they were on shore, was much more regular than could well have been expected from sailors, who had been so long confined to a ship: And though part of this prudent demeanor must doubtless be imputed to the diligence of their Officers, and to the excellent discipline to which they had been long inured on board the Commodore, yet it was doubtless no small reputation to the men, that they should in general refrain from indulging themselves in those intoxicating liquors, which they found ready to their hands in almost every warehouse.

And having mentioned this single instance of drunkenness, I cannot pass by another oversight, which was likewise the only one of its kind, and which was attended with very particular circumstances. There was an *Englishman*, who had formerly wrought as a ship-carpenter in the yard at *Portsmouth*, but leaving his country, had afterwards entered into the *Spanish* service, and was employed by them at the port of *Guaiaquil*; and it being well known to his friends in *England* that he was then in that part of the world, they put letters on board the *Centurion*, directed to him. This man being then by accident amongst

187

the *Spaniards*, who were retired to the hill at *Paita*, he was desirous (as it should seem) of acquiring some reputation amongst his new Masters. With this view he came down unarmed to a centinel of ours, who was placed at some distance from the fort towards the enemy, and pretended to be desirous of surrendring himself, and of entering into our service. Our centinel had a cock'd pistol, but being deceived by the other's fair speeches, he was so imprudent as to let him approach much nearer than he ought; so that the Shipwright, watching his opportunity, rushed on the centinel, and seizing his pistol, wrenched it out of his hand, and instantly ran away with it up the hill. By this time, two of our people, who seeing the fellow advance had suspected his intention, were making towards him, and were thereby prepared to pursue him; but he got to the top of the hill before they could reach him, and then turning about fired the pistol; at which instant his pursuers fired at him, and though he was at a great distance, and the crest of the hill hid him as soon as they had fired, so that they took it for granted they had missed him, yet we afterwards learnt that he was shot through the body, and had fallen down dead the very next step he took after he was out of sight. The centinel too, who had been thus grossly imposed upon, did not escape unpunished; for he was ordered to be severely whipt for being thus shamefully surprized upon his post, and for having given an example of carelessness, which, if followed in other instances, might prove fatal to us all. But to return:

By the time our people had taken their comrade out of the water, and were making the best of their way for the squadron, the flames had taken possession of every part of the town, and had got such hold, both by means of combustibles that had been distributed for that purpose, and by the slightness of the materials of which the houses were composed, and their aptitude to take fire, that it was sufficiently apparent, no efforts of the enemy (though they flocked down in great numbers) could possibly put a stop to it, or prevent the entire destruction of the place, and all the merchandize contained therein. A whole town on fire at once, especially a place that burnt with such facility and violence, being a very singular spectacle, Mr. *Brett* had the curiosity to delineate its appearance, together with that of the ships in the harbour, which may be seen in the annexed plate.[1]

Our detachment under Lieutenant *Brett* having safely joined the squadron, the Commodore prepared to leave the place the same evening. He found, when he first came into the bay, six vessels of the enemy at anchor; one of which was the ship, which, according to our intelligence, was to have sailed with the treasure to the coast of *Mexico*, and which, as we were persuaded she was a good sailor, we resolved to take with us: The others were two Snows, a Bark, and two Row-gallies of thirty-six oars a-piece: These last, as we were afterwards informed, with many others of the same kind built at different ports, were intended to prevent our landing in the neighbourhood of *Callao*: For the *Spaniards*, on the first intelligence of our squadron and its force, expected that we would attempt the city of *Lima*. The Commodore, having no occasion for these other vessels, had ordered the masts of all five of them to be cut away on his first arrival; and now, at his leaving the place, they were towed out of the harbour, and scuttled and sunk; and the command of the remaining ship, called the *Solidad*, being given to Mr. *Hughes* the Lieutenant of the *Tryal*, who had with him a crew of ten men to navigate her, the squadron, towards midnight, weighed anchor, and sailed out of the bay, being now augmented to six sail, that is, the *Centurion* and the *Tryal* Prize, together with the *Carmelo*, the *Teresa*, the *Carmin*, and our last acquired vessel the *Solidad*.

And now, before I entirely quit the account of our transactions at this place, it may not perhaps be improper to give a succinct relation of the booty we made here, and of the loss the *Spaniards* sustained. I have before observed, that there were great quantities of valuable effects in the town; but as the greatest part of them were what we could neither dispose of nor carry away, the total amount of this merchandize can only be rudely guessed at. But the *Spaniards*, in the representations they made to the Court of *Madrid*, (as we were afterwards assured) estimated their whole loss at a million and a half of dollars: And when it is considered, that no small part of the goods we burnt there were of the richest and most expensive species, as broadcloaths, silks, cambrics, velvets, &c. I cannot but think their valuation sufficiently moderate. As to our parts, our acquisition, though inconsiderable in comparison of what we destroyed, was yet in itself far from despicable; for the wrought plate dollars and other coin which fell into our hands amounted to upwards of 30,000 *l.* sterling, besides several rings, bracelets, and jewels, whose intrinsick value we could not then determine; and over and above all this, the plunder, which

189

became the property of the immediate captors, was very great; so that upon the whole it was by much the most important booty we made upon that coast.

There remains, before I take leave of this place, another particularity to be mentioned, which, on account of the great honour which our national character in those parts has thence received, and the reputation which our Commodore in particular has thereby acquired, merits a distinct and circumstantial discussion. It has been already related, that all the prisoners taken by us in our preceding prizes were put on shore, and discharged at this place; amongst which, there were some persons of considerable distinction, particularly a youth of about seventeen years of age, son of the Vice-President of the Council of *Chili*. As the barbarity of the Buccaneers, and the artful use the Ecclesiasticks had made of it, had filled the natives of those countries with the most terrible ideas of the *English* cruelty, we always found our prisoners, at their first coming on board us, to be extremely dejected, and under great horror and anxiety. In particular this youth, whom I last mentioned, having never been from home before, lamented his captivity in the most moving manner, regretting, in very plaintive terms, his parents, his brothers, his sisters, and his native country; of all which he was fully persuaded he had taken his last farewel, believing that he was now devoted, for the remaining part of his life, to an abject and cruel servitude; nor was he singular in his fears, for his companions on board, and indeed all the *Spaniards* that came into our power, had the same desponding opinion of their situation. Mr. *Anson* constantly exerted his utmost endeavours to efface these inhuman impressions they had received of us; always taking care, that as many of the principal people among them as there was room for should dine at his table by turns; and giving the strictest orders too, that they should at all times, and in every circumstance, be treated with the utmost decency and humanity. But notwithstanding this precaution, it was generally observed, that for the first day or two they did not quit their fears, but suspected the gentleness of their usage to be only preparatory to some unthought of calamity. However, being confirmed by time, they grew perfectly easy in their situation and remarkably chearful, so that it was often disputable, whether or no they considered their being detained by us as a misfortune. For the youth I have above-mentioned, who was near two months on board us, had at last so far conquered his melancholy surmises, and had taken such an affection to Mr. *Anson*, and seemed so much pleased with the manner of life, totally different from all he had ever seen before, that it is doubtful to me whether, if his own opinion had been taken, he would not have preferred a voyage to *England* in the *Centurion*, to the being set on shore at *Paita*, where he was at liberty to return to his country and his friends.

This conduct of the Commodore to his prisoners, which was continued without interruption or deviation, gave them all the highest idea of his humanity and benevolence, and induced them likewise (as mankind are fond of forming general opinions) to entertain very favourable thoughts of the whole *English* Nation. But whatever they might be disposed to think of Mr. *Anson* before the taking of the *Teresa*, their veneration for him was prodigiously increased by his conduct towards those women, whom (as I have already mentioned) he took in that vessel: For the leaving them in the possession of their apartments, the strict orders given to prevent all his people on board from approaching them, and the permitting the Pilot to stay with them as their guardian, were measures that seemed so different from what might be expected from an enemy and an heretick, that the *Spaniards* on board, though they had themselves experienced his beneficence, were surprized at this new instance of it, and the more so, as all this was done without his ever having seen the women, though the two daughters were both esteemed handsome, and the youngest was celebrated for her uncommon beauty. The women themselves too were so sensible of the obligations they owed him, for the care and attention with which he had protected them, that they absolutely refused to go on shore at *Paita*, till they had been permitted to wait on him on board the *Centurion*, to return him thanks in person. Indeed, all the prisoners left us with the strongest assurances of their grateful remembrance of his uncommon treatment. A Jesuit in particular, whom the Commodore had taken, and who was an Ecclesiastick of some distinction, could not help expressing himself with great thankfulness for the civilities he and his countrymen had found on board, declaring, that he should consider it as his duty to do Mr. *Anson* justice at all times; adding, that his usage of the men prisoners was such as could never be forgot, and such as he could never fail to acknowledge and recite upon all occasions: But that his behaviour to the women was so extraordinary, and so extremely honourable, that he doubted all the regard due to his own ecclesiastical character, would be scarcely sufficient to render it credible. And indeed we were afterwards informed, that both he and the rest of our prisoners had not been silent on this head, but had, both at *Lima* and at other places, given the greatest encomiums to our Commodore; the Jesuit in particular, as we were told, having, on his account, interpreted in a lax and hypothetical sense that article of his Church, which asserts the impossibility of hereticks being saved.

And let it not be imagined, that the impressions which the *Spaniards* hence received to our advantage, is a matter of small import; for, not to mention several of our countrymen who have already felt the good effects of these prepossessions, the *Spaniards* are a Nation, whose good opinion of us is doubtless of more consequence than that of all the world besides: Not only as the commerce we have formerly carried on with them, and perhaps may again hereafter, is so extremely valuable; but also as the transacting it does so immediately depend on the honour and good faith of those who are entrusted with its management. But however, had no national conveniencies attended it, the Commodore's equity and good temper would not less have deterred him from all tyranny and cruelty to those, whom the fortune of war had put into his hands. I shall only add, that by his constant attachment to these humane and prudent maxims, he has acquired a distinguished reputation amongst the *Creolian Spaniards*, which is not confined merely to the coast of the *South-Seas*, but is extended through all the *Spanish* settlements in *America*; so that his name is frequently to be met with in the mouths of most of the *Spanish* inhabitants of that prodigious Empire.[1]

CHAP. VII.

From our departure from *Paita*, to our arrival at *Quibo*.

WHEN we got under sail from the road of *Paita*, (which, as I have already observed, was about midnight, on the 16th of *November*) we stood to the westward, and in the morning the Commodore gave orders, that the whole squadron should spread themselves, in order to look out for the *Gloucester*. For we now drew near to the station where Captain *Mitchel* had been directed to cruise, and hourly expected to get sight of him; but the whole day passed without seeing him.

And now a jealousy, which had taken its rise at *Paita*, between those who had been ordered on shore for the attack, and those who had continued on board, grew to such a height, that the Commodore, being made acquainted with it, thought it necessary to interpose his authority to appease it. The ground of this animosity was the plunder gotten at *Paita*, which those who had acted on shore had appropriated to themselves, and considered it as a reward for the risks they had run, and the resolution they had shown in that service. But those, who had remained on board, considered this as a very partial and unjust procedure, urging, that had it been left to their choice, they should have preferred the acting on shore to the continuing on board; that their duty, while their comrades were on shore, was extremely fatiguing; for besides the labour of the day, they were constantly under arms all night to secure the prisoners, whose numbers exceeded their own, and of whom it was then necessary to be extremely watchful, to prevent any attempts they might have formed in that critical conjuncture: That upon the whole it could not be denied, but that the presence of a sufficient force on board was as necessary to the success of the enterprize, as the action of the others on shore, and therefore those who had continued on board insisted, that they could not be deprived of their share of the plunder, without manifest injustice. These were the contests amongst our men, which were carried on with great heat on both sides: And though the plunder in question was a very trifle, in comparison of the treasure taken in the place, (in

193

which there was no doubt but those on board had an equal right) yet as the obstinacy of sailors is not always regulated by the importance of the matter in dispute, the Commodore thought it necessary to put a stop to this ferment betimes. And accordingly, the morning after our leaving of *Paita*, he ordered all hands upon the quarter-deck; where, addressing himself to those who had been detached on shore, he commended their behaviour, and thanked them for their services on that occasion: But then representing to them the reasons urged, by those who had continued on board, for an equal distribution of the plunder, he told them, that he thought these reasons very conclusive, and that the expectations of their comrades were justly founded; and therefore he ordered, that not only the men, but all the officers likewise, who had been employed in taking the place, should produce the whole of their plunder immediately upon the quarter-deck; and that it should be impartially divided amongst the whole crew, in proportion to each man's rank and commission: And to prevent those who had been in possession of the plunder from murmuring at this diminution of their share, the Commodore added, that as an encouragement to others who might be hereafter employed on like services, he would give his entire share to be distributed amongst those who had been detached for the attack of the place. Thus this troublesome affair, which if permitted to have gone on, might perhaps have been attended with mischievous consequences, was by the Commodore's prudence soon appeased, to the general satisfaction of the ship's company: Not but there were some few, whose selfish dispositions were uninfluenced by the justice of this procedure, and who were incapable of discerning the force of equity, however glaring, when it tended to deprive them of any part of what they had once got into their hands.[1]

This important business employed the best part of the day, after we came from *Paita*. And now, at night, having no sight of the *Gloucester*, the Commodore ordered the squadron to bring to, that we might not pass her in the dark. The next morning we again looked out for her, and at ten we saw a sail, to which we gave chace; and at two in the afternoon we came near enough to her to discover her to be the *Gloucester*, with a small vessel in tow. About an hour after, we were joined by them; and then we learnt that Captain *Mitchel*, in the whole time of his cruise, had only taken two prizes; one of them being a small Snow, whose cargoe consisted chiefly of wine, brandy, and olives in jars, with about 7000 *l*. in specie; and the other a large boat or launch, which the *Gloucester's* barge came up with near the shore. The prisoners on board this vessel alleged, that they were very poor, and that their loading consisted only of cotton; though the circumstances in which the barge surprized them, seemed to insinuate that they were more opulent than they pretended to be; for the *Gloucester's* people found them at dinner upon pidgeon-pye, served up in silver dishes. However, the Officer who commanded the barge having opened several of the jars on board, to satisfy his curiosity, and finding nothing in them but cotton, he was inclined to believe the account the prisoners gave him: But the cargoe being taken into the *Gloucester*, and there examined more strictly, they were agreeably surprised to find, that the whole was a very extraordinary piece of false package; and that there was concealed amongst the cotton, in every jar, a considerable quantity of double doubloons and dollars, to the amount in the whole of near 12,000 *l*. This treasure was going to *Paita*, and belonged to the same Merchants who were the proprietors of the greatest part of the money we had taken there; so that had this boat escaped the *Gloucester*, it is probable her cargoe would have fallen into our hands. Besides these two prizes which we have mentioned, the *Gloucester's* people told us, that they had been in sight of two or three other ships of the enemy which had escaped them; and one of them we had reason to believe, from some of our intelligence, was of an immense value.[1]

Being now joined by the *Gloucester* and her prize, it was resolved that we should stand to the northward, and make the best of our way either to Cape St. *Lucas* on *California*, or to Cape *Corientes* on the coast of *Mexico*. Indeed the Commodore, when at *Juan Fernandes*, had determined with himself to touch in the neighbourhood of *Panama*, and to endeavour to get some correspondence over land with the fleet under the command of Admiral *Vernon*. For when we departed from *England*, we left a large force at *Portsmouth*, which was intended to be sent to the *West-Indies*, there to be employed in an expedition against some of the *Spanish* settlements. And Mr. *Anson* taking it for granted, that this enterprize had succeeded, and that *Porto Bello* perhaps might be then garrisoned by *British* troops, he hoped, that on his arrival at the *Isthmus*, he should easily procure an intercourse with our countrymen on the other side, either by the *Indians*, who were greatly disposed in our favour, or even by the *Spaniards* themselves, some of whom, for proper rewards, might be induced to carry on this intelligence, which, after it was once begun, might be continued with very little difficulty; so that Mr. *Anson* flattered himself, that he might by this means have received a reinforcement of men from the other side, and that by settling a prudent plan of operations with our Commanders in the *West-Indies*, he might have taken even *Panama* itself; which would have given to the *British* Nation the possession of that *Isthmus*, whereby we should have been in effect masters of all the treasures of *Peru*; and should have had in our hands an equivalent for any demands, however extraordinary, which we might have been induced to have made on either of the branches of the House of *Bourbon*.

Such were the projects which the Commodore resolved in his thoughts at the Island of *Juan Fernandes*, notwithstanding the feeble conditions to which he was then reduced. And indeed, had the success of our force in the *West-Indies* been answerable to the general expectation, it cannot be denied but these views would have been the most prudent that could have been thought of. But in examining the papers which were found on board the *Carmelo*, the first prize we took, we learnt (though I then omitted to mention it) that our attempt against *Carthagena* had failed, and that there was no probability that our fleet, in that part of the world, would engage in any new enter-prize, that would at all facilitate this plan. And therefore Mr. *Anson* gave over all hopes of being reinforced a-cross the *Isthmus*, and consequently had no inducement at present to proceed to *Panama*, as he was incapable of attacking the place; and there was great reason to believe, that by this time there was a general embargo on all the coast.

The only feasible measure then which was left us, was to get as soon as possible to the southern parts of *California*, or to the adjacent coast of *Mexico*, there to cruise for the *Manila* Galeon, which we knew was now at sea, bound to the port of *Acapulco*. And we doubted not to get on that station, time enough to intercept her; for this ship does not actually arrive at *Acapulco* till towards the middle of *January*, and we were now but in the middle of *November*, and did not conceive that our passage thither would cost us above a month or five weeks; so that we imagined, we had near twice as much time as was necessary for our purpose. Indeed there was a business which we foresaw would occasion some delay, but we flattered ourselves that it would be dispatched in four or five days, and therefore could not interrupt our project. This was the recruiting of our water; for the number of prisoners we had entertained on board, since our leaving the Island of *Fernandes*, had so far exhausted our stock, that it was impossible to think of venturing upon this passage to the coast of *Mexico*, till we had procured a fresh supply; especially as at *Paita*, where we had some hopes of getting a quantity, we did not find enough for our consumption during the time we stayed there. It was for some time a matter of deliberation, where we should take in this necessary article; but by consulting the accounts of former Navigators, and examining our prisoners, we at last resolved for the Island of *Quibo*, situated at the mouth of the bay of *Panama*: Nor was it but on good grounds that the Commodore conceived this to be the properest place for watering the squadron. Indeed, there was a small Island called *Cocos*, which was less out of our way than *Quibo*, where some of the Buccaneers have pretended they found water; but none of our prisoners knew any thing of it, and it was thought too hazardous to risque the safety of the squadron, and expose ourselves to the hazard of not meeting with water when we came there, on the mere authority of these legendary writers, of whose misrepresentations and falsities we had almost daily experience. Besides, by going to *Quibo* we were not without hopes that some of the enemies ships bound to or from *Panama* might fall into our hands, particularly such of them as were put to sea, before they had any intelligence of our squadron.

Having determined therefore to go to *Quibo*, we directed our course to the northward, being eight sail in company, and consequently having the appearance of a very formidable fleet; and on the 19th, at day-break, we discovered Cape *Blanco*, bearing S. S. E. $\frac{1}{2}$ E, seven miles distant. This Cape lies in the latitude of 4°:15′ South, and is always made by ships bound either to windward or to leeward; so that off this Cape is a most excellent station to cruise upon the enemy. By this time we found that our last prize, the *Solidad* was far from answering the character given her of a good sailor; and she and the *Santa Teresa* delaying us considerably, the Commodore ordered them both to be cleared of every thing that might prove useful to the rest of the ships, and then to be burnt; and having given proper instructions, and a rendezvous to the *Gloucester* and the other prizes, we proceeded in our course for *Quibo*; and, on the 22d in the morning, saw the Island of *Plata*, bearing East, distant four leagues. Here one of our prizes was ordered to stand close in with it, both to discover if there were any ships between that Island and the Continent, and likewise to look out for a stream of fresh water, which was reported to be there, and which would have saved us the trouble of going to *Quibo*; but she returned without having seen any ship, or finding any water. At three in the afternoon point *Manta* bore S. E. by E. seven miles distant; and there being a town of the same name in the neighbourhood, Captain *Mitchel* took this opportunity of sending away several of his prisoners from the *Gloucester* in the *Spanish* launch. The boats were now daily employed in distributing provisions on board the *Tryal* and other prizes, to compleat their stock for six months: And that the *Centurion* might be the better prepared to give the *Manila* ship (one of which we were told was of an immense size) a warm reception, the Carpenters were ordered to fix eight stocks in the main and fore-tops, which were properly fitted for the mountings of swivel guns.

On the 25th we had a sight of the Island of *Gallo*, bearing E. S. E. $\frac{1}{2}$ E, four leagues distant; and from hence we crossed the bay of *Panama* with a N. W. course, hoping that this would have carried us in a direct line to the Island of *Quibo*. But we afterwards found that we ought to have stood more to the westward; for the winds in a short time began to incline to that quarter, and made it difficult for us to gain the Island. And now, after passing the equinoctial, (which we did on the 22d) and leaving the neighbourhood of the *Cordilleras*, and standing more and more towards the *Isthmus*, where the communication of the atmosphere to the eastward and the westward was no longer interrupted, we found in very few days an extraordinary alteration in the climate. For instead of that uniform temperature, where neither the excess of heat or cold was to be complained of, we had now for several days together close and sultry weather, resembling what we had before met with on the coast of *Brazil*, and in other parts between the tropics on the eastern side of *America*. We had besides frequent calms and heavy rains; which we at first ascribed to the neighbourhood of the line, where this kind of weather is generally found to prevail at all seasons of the year; but observing that it attended us to the latitude of seven degrees North, we were at length induced to believe, that the stormy season, or, as the *Spaniards* call it, the Vandevals, was not yet over; though many writers, particularly Captain *Shelvocke*, positively assert, that this season begins in *June*, and is ended in *November*; and our prisoners all affirmed the same thing. But perhaps its end may not be always constant, and it might last this year longer than usual.

On the 27th, Captain *Mitchel* having finished the clearing of his largest prize, she was scuttled, and set on fire; but we still consisted of five ships, and were fortunate enough to find them all good sailors; so that we never occasioned any delay to each other. Being now in a rainy climate, which we had been long disused to, we found it necessary to caulk the decks and sides of the *Centurion*, to prevent the rain-water from running into her.

On the 3d of *December* we had a view of the Island of *Quibo*; the East end of which then bore from us N.N.W, four leagues distant, and the Island of *Quicara* W.N.W, at about the same distance. Here we struck ground with sixty-five fathom of line, and found the bottom to consist of grey sand, with black specks. There is hereafter inserted (being contained in the same plate with the view of the hill of *Petaplan*) a view of these two Islands, where (*a*) represents the S. E. end of *Quibo*, bearing N. by W. four leagues distant: And (*b*) the Island of *Quicara*, which bears from the point (*a*) W.S.W. ½ S, and is distant from it four leagues, the point (*a*) being itself in the latitude of 7°: 20′ North. When we had thus got sight of the land, we found the wind to hang westerly; and therefore, night coming on, we thought it advise-able to stand off till morning, as there are said to be some shoals in the entrance of the channel. At six the next morning point *Mariato* bore N.E. ½ N, three or four leagues distant. In weathering this point all the squadron, except the *Centurion*, were very near it; and the *Gloucester* being the leewardmost ship, was forced to tack and stand to the southward, so that we lost sight of her. At nine, the Island *Sebaco* bore N. W. by N, four leagues distant; but the wind still proving unfavourable, we were obliged to ply on and off for the succeeding twenty-four hours, and were frequently taken aback. However, at eleven the next morning the wind happily settled in the S. S. W, and we bore away for the S. S. E. end of the Island, and about three in the afternoon entered the *Canal Bueno*, passing round a shoal which stretches off about two miles from the South point of the Island. This

Canal Bueno, or *Good Channel,* is at least six miles in breadth; and as we had the wind large,[1] we kept in a good depth of water, generally from twenty-eight to thirty-three fathom, and came not within a mile and a half distance of the breakers; though, in all probability, if it had been necessary, we might have ventured much nearer, without incurring the least danger. At seven in the evening we came to an anchor in thirty-three fathom muddy ground; the South point of the Island bearing S. E. by S, a remarkable high part of the Island W. by N, and the Island *Sebaco* E. by N. Being thus arrived at this Island of *Quibo,* the account of the place, and of our transactions there, shall be referred to the ensuing chapter.

CHAP. VIII.

Our proceedings at *Quibo*, with an account of the place.

THE next morning, after our coming to an anchor, an officer was dispatched on shore to discover the watering place, who having found it, returned before noon; and then we sent the long boat for a load of water, and at the same time we weighed and stood farther in with our ships. At two we came again to an anchor in twenty-two fathom, with a bottom of rough gravel intermixed with broken shells, the watering place now bearing from us N. W. ½ N, only three quarters of a mile distant. A plan of the road where we lay and of the East-end Island is annexed, where the soundings are laid down, such as we found them, the latitude of the S. E. point of the Island being, as hath been already mentioned, 7°:20′ North.

This Island of *Quibo* is extremely convenient for wooding and watering; for the trees grow close to the high-water mark, and a large rapid stream of fresh water runs over the sandy beach into the sea: So that we were little more than two days in laying in all the wood and water we wanted. The whole Island is of a very moderate height, excepting one part. It consists of a continued wood spread over the whole surface of the country, which preserves its verdure all the year round. Amongst the other wood, we found there abundance of cassia, and a few lime-trees. It appeared singular to us, that considering the climate and the shelter, we should see no other birds there than parrots, parroquets, and mackaws; indeed of these last there were prodigious flights. Next to these birds, the animals we found there in most plenty were monkeys and guanos, and these we frequently killed for food; for tho' there were many herds of deer upon the place, yet the difficulty of penetrating the woods prevented our coming near them, so that though we saw them often, we killed only two during our stay. Our prisoners assured us, that this Island abounded with tygers; and we did once discover the print of a tyger's paw upon the beach, but the tygers themselves we never saw. The *Spaniards* too informed us, that there was often found in the woods a most mischievous serpent, called the flying snake, which they said darted itself from the boughs of trees on either man or beast that came within its reach; and whose sting, they believed, to be inevitable death. Besides these mischievous land-animals, the sea hereabouts is infested with great numbers of alligators of an extraordinary size; and we often observed a large kind of flat-fish, jumping a considerable height out of the water, which we supposed to be the fish that is said frequently to destroy the pearl-divers, by clasping them in its fins as they rise from the bottom; and we were told that the divers, for their security, are now always armed with a sharp knife, which, when they are entangled, they stick into the belly of the fish, and thereby disengage themselves from its embraces.

Whilst the ship continued here at anchor, the Commodore, attended by some of his officers, went in a boat to examine a bay which lay to the northward; and they afterwards ranged all along the eastern side of the Island. And in the places where they put on shore in the course of this expedition, they generally found the soil to be extremely rich, and met with great plenty of excellent water. In particular, near the N. E. point of the Island, they discovered a natural cascade, which surpassed, as they conceived, every thing of this kind, which human art or industry hath hitherto produced. It was a river of transparent water, about forty yards wide, which ran down a declivity of near a hundred and fifty yards in length. The channel it ran in was very irregular; for it was entirely formed of rock, both its sides and bottom being made up of large detached blocks; and by these the course of the water was frequently interrupted: For in some places it ran sloping with a rapid but uniform motion, while in other parts it tumbled over the ledges of rocks with a perpendicular descent. All the neighbourhood of this stream was fine wood; and even the huge masses of rock which overhung the water, and which, by their various projections, formed the inequalities of the channel, were covered with lofty forest trees. Whilst the Commodore, and those who were with him, were attentively viewing this place, and were remarking the different blendings of the water, the rocks and the wood, there came in sight (as it were with an intent still to heighten and animate the prospect) a prodigious flight of mackaws, which hovering over this spot, and often wheeling and playing on the wing about it, afforded a most brilliant appearance, by the glittering of the sun on their variegated plumage; so that some of the spectators cannot refrain from a kind of transport, when they recount the complicated beauties which occurred in this extraordinary water-fall.

In this expedition, which the boat made along the eastern side of the Island, though they met with no inhabitants, yet they saw many huts upon the shore, and great heaps of shells of fine mother of pearl scattered up and down in different places: These were the remains left by the pearl-fishers from *Panama,* who often frequent this place in the summer season; for the pearl oysters, which are to be met with every where in the bay of *Panama,* are so plenty at *Quibo,* that by advancing a very little way into the sea, you might stoop down and reach them from the bottom. They are usually very large, and out of curiosity we opened some of them with a view of tasting them, but we found them extremely tough and unpalatable. And having mentioned these oysters and the pearl-fishery, I must beg leave to recite a few particulars relating thereto.

The oysters most productive of pearls are those found in considerable depths; for though what are taken up by wading near shore are of the same species, yet the pearls found in them are very rare and very small. It is said too, that the pearl partakes in some degree of the quality of the bottom on which the oyster is found; so that if the bottom be muddy, the pearl is dark and ill-coloured.

The taking up oysters from great depths for the sake of the pearls they contain, is a work performed by Negro slaves, of which the inhabitants of *Panama* and the neighbouring coast formerly kept great numbers, which were carefully trained to this business. And these are said not to be esteemed compleat divers, till they have by degrees been able to protract their stay under water so long, that the blood gushes out from their nose, mouth and ears. And it is the tradition of the country, that when this accident has once befallen them, they dive for the future with much greater facility than before; and they have no apprehension either that any inconvenience can attend it, the bleeding generally stopping of itself, or that there is any probability of their being ever subject to it a second time. But to return from this digression.

Though the pearl oyster, as hath been said, was incapable of being eaten, yet the sea at this place furnished us with another dainty, in the greatest plenty and perfection: This was the turtle, of which we took here what quantity we pleased. There are generally reckoned four species of turtle; that is, the trunk turtle, the loggerhead, the hawk-bill, and the green turtle. The two first are rank and unwholesome; the hawkbill (which furnishes the tortois-shell) is but indifferent food, though better than the other two; but the green turtle is generally esteemed, by the greatest part of those who are acquainted with its taste, to be the most delicious of all eatables; and that it is a most wholsome food, we are amply convinced by our own experience: For we fed on this last species, or the green turtle, for near four months, and consequently had it been in any degree noxious, its ill effects could not possibly have escaped us. At this Island we took what quantity we pleased with great facility; for as they are an amphibious animal, and get on shore to lay their eggs, which they generally deposit in a large hole in the sand, just above the high-water mark, covering them up, and leaving them to be hatched by the heat of the sun, we usually dispersed several of our men along the beach, whose business it was to turn them on their backs when they came on land; and the turtle being thereby prevented from getting away, we carried them off at our leisure: By this means we not only secured a sufficient stock for the time we stayed on the Island, but we took a number of them with us to sea, which proved of great service both in lengthning out our store of provision, and in heartning the whole crew with an almost constant supply of fresh and palatable food; for the turtle being large, they generally weighing about 200 *lb.* weight each, those we took with us lasted us near a month, and by that time we met with a fresh recruit on the coast of *Mexico*, where we often saw them in the heat of the day floating in great numbers on the surface of the water fast asleep; when we discovered them, we usually sent out our boat with a man in the bow, who was a dextrous diver, and when the boat came within a few yards of the turtle, the diver plunged into the water, and took care to rise close upon it; and seizing the shell near the tail, and pressing down the hinder parts, the turtle, when awakened, began to strike with its claws, which motion supported both it and the diver, till the boat came up and took them in. By this management we never wanted turtle for the succeeding four months in which we continued at sea; and though, when at *Quibo*, we had already been three months on board, without otherwise putting our foot on shore, than in the few days we stayed at this Island of *Quibo*, (except those employed in the attack of *Paita*) yet in the whole seven months, from our leaving *Juan*

Fernandes to our anchoring in the harbour of *Chequetan*, we buried no more in the whole squadron than two men; a most incontestable proof, that the turtle, on which we fed for the last four months of this term, was at least innocent, if not something more.

Considering the scarcity of provisions on some part of the coast of these seas, it appears wonderful, that a species of food so very palatable and salubrious as turtle, and so much abounding in those parts, should be proscribed by the *Spaniards* as unwholesome, and little less than poisonous. Perhaps the strange appearance of this animal may have been the foundation of this ridiculous and superstitious aversion, which is strongly rooted in all the inhabitants of that coast, and of which we had many instances in the course of this navigation. I have already observed, that we put our *Spanish* prisoners on shore at *Paita*, and that the *Gloucester* sent theirs to *Manta*; but as we had taken in our prizes some *Indian* and Negro slaves, we did not set these on shore with their masters, but continued them on board, as our crews were thin, to assist in navigating our ships. These poor people being possessed with the prejudices of the country they came from, were astonished at our feeding on turtle, and seemed fully persuaded that it would soon destroy us; but finding that none of us died, nor even suffered in our health by a continuation of this diet, they at last got so far the better of their aversion, as to be persuaded to taste it, to which the absence of all other kinds of fresh provisions might not a little contribute. However, it was with great reluctance, and very sparingly, that they first began to eat of it: But the relish improving upon them by degrees, they at last grew extremely fond of it, and preferred it to every other kind of food, and often felicitated each other on the happy experience they had acquired, and the delicious and plentiful repasts it would be always in their power to procure, when they should again return back to their country. Those who are acquainted with the manner of life of these unhappy wretches, need not be told, that next to large draughts of spirituous liquors, plenty of tolerable food is the greatest joy they know, and consequently the discovering a method which would always supply them with what quantity they pleased, of a food more luxurious to the palate than any their haughty Lords and Masters could indulge in, was doubtless a circumstance, which they considered as the most fortunate that could befal them.

After this digression, which the prodigious quantity of turtle on this

Island of *Quibo*, and the store of it we thence took to sea, in some measure led me into, I shall now return to our own proceedings.

In three days time we had compleated our business at this place, and were extremely impatient to put to sea, that we might arrive time enough on the coast of *Mexico* to intercept the *Manila* galeon. But the wind being contrary detained us a night, and the next day, when we got into the offing (which we did through the same channel by which we entered) we were obliged to keep hovering about the Island, in hopes of getting sight of the *Gloucester*, who, as I have in the last chapter mentioned, was separated from us on our first arrival. It was the 9th of *December*, in the morning, when we put to sea, and continuing to the southward of the Island, looking out for the *Gloucester*, we, on the 10th, at five in the afternoon, discerned a small sail to the north-ward of us, to which we gave chace, and coming up with her took her. She proved to be a bark from *Panama*, bound to *Cheripe*, an inconsider-able village on the Continent, and was called the *Jesu Nazareno*. She had nothing on board but some oakum, about a tun of rock salt, and between 30 and 40 *l.* in specie, most of it consisting of small silver money, intended for purchasing a cargoe of provisions at *Cheripe*.

And on occasion of this prize I cannot but observe, for the use of future cruisers, that had we been in want of provisions, we had by this capture an obvious method of supplying ourselves. For at *Cheripe*, whither she was bound, there is a constant store of provisions pre-pared for the vessels who go thither every week from *Panama*, the market of *Panama* being chiefly supplied from thence: So that by putting a few of our hands on board our prize, we might easily have seized a large store without any hazard, since *Cheripe* is a place of no strength. And as provisions are the staple commodity of that place and of its neighbourhood, the knowledge of this circumstance may be of great use to such cruisers, as find their provisions grow scant, and yet are desirous of continuing on that coast as long as possible. But to return:

On the 12th of *December* we were at last relieved from the perplexity we had suffered, by the separation of the *Gloucester*; for on that day she joined us, and informed us, that in tacking to the southward, on our first arrival, she had sprung her fore-top-mast, which had disabled her from working to windward, and prevented her from joining us sooner. And now we scuttled and sunk the *Jesu Nazareno*, the prize we took last; and having the greatest impatience to get into a proper station for the galeon, we stood all together to the westward, leaving the Island of *Quibo* (notwithstanding all the impediments we met with) in about nine days after our first coming in sight of it.

CHAP. IX.

From *Quibo* to the coast of *Mexico*.

ON the 12th of *December* we stood from *Quibo* to the westward, and the same day the Commodore delivered fresh instructions to the Captains of the men of war, and the commanders of our prizes, appointing them the rendezvouses they were to make, and the courses they were to steer in case of a separation. And first, they were directed to use all possible dispatch in getting to the northward of the harbour of *Acapulco*, where they were to endeavour to fall in with the land, between the latitudes of 18 and 19 degrees; from thence, they were to beat up the coast at eight or ten leagues distance from the shore, till they came a-breast of Cape *Corientes*, in the latitude of 20° : 20′. When they arrived there, they were to continue cruising on that station till the 14th of *February*; and then they were to proceed to the middle Island of the *Tres Marias*, in the latitude of 21° : 25′, bearing from Cape *Corientes* N. W. by N, twenty-five leagues distant. And if at this Island they did not meet the Commodore, they were there to recruit their wood and water, and then to make the best of their way to the Island of *Macao*, on the coast of *China*. These orders being distributed to all the ships, we had little doubt of arriving soon upon our intended station, as we expected, upon the encreasing our offing from *Quibo*, to fall in with the regular trade-wind. But, to our extream vexation, we were baffled for near a month, either with tempestuous weather from the western quarter, or with dead calms and heavy rains, attended with a sultry air; so that it was the 25th of *December* before we got a sight of the Island of *Cocos*, which by our reckoning was only a hundred leagues from the Continent; and we had the mortification to make so little way, that we did not lose sight of it again in five days. This Island we found to be in the latitude of 5° : 20′ North. It has a high hummock towards the western part, which descends gradually, and at last terminates in a low point to the eastward. From the Island of *Cocos* we stood W. by N, and were till the 9th of *January* in running an hundred leagues more. We had at first flattered ourselves, that the uncertain weather and western gales we met with were owing to the neighbourhood of the Continent, from which, as we got more distant, we expected every day to be relieved, by falling in with the eastern trade-wind: But as our hopes were so long baffled, and our patience quite exhausted, we began at length to despair of succeeding in the great purpose we had in view, that of intercepting the *Manila* galeon; and this produced a general dejection amongst us, as we had at first considered this project as almost infallible, and had indulged ourselves in the most boundless hopes of the advantages we should thence receive. However, our despondency was at last somewhat alleviated, by a favourable change of the wind; for, on the 9th of *January*, a gale for the first time sprung up from the N. E, and on this we took the *Carmelo* in tow, as the *Gloucester* did the *Carmin*, making all the sail we could to improve the advantage, for we still suspected that it was only a temporary gale, which would not last long; but the next day we had the satisfaction to find, that the wind did not only continue in the same quarter, but blew with so much briskness and steadiness, that we now no longer doubted of its being the true trade-wind. And as we advanced a-pace towards our station, our hopes began to revive, and our former despair by degrees gave place to more sanguine prejudices: For though the customary season of the arrival of the galeon at *Acapulco* was already elapsed, yet we were by this time unreasonable enough to flatter ourselves, that some accidental delay might, for our advantage, lengthen out her passage beyond its usual limits.

When we got into the trade-wind, we found no alteration in it till the 17th of *January*, when we were advanced to the latitude of 12° : 50', but on that day it shifted to the westward of the North: This change we imputed to our having haled up too soon, though we then esteemed our selves full seventy leagues from the coast, which plainly shows, that the trade-wind doth not take place, but at a considerable distance from the Continent. After this, the wind was not so favourable to us as it had been: However, we still continued to advance, and, on the 26th of *January*, being then to the northward of *Acapulco*, we tacked and stood to the eastward, with a view of making the land.

In the preceding fortnight we caught some turtle on the surface of the water, and several dolphins, bonitos, and albicores. One day, as one of the sail-makers mates was fishing from the end of the gibboom, he lost his hold and dropped into the sea; and the ship, which was then going at the rate of six or seven knots, went directly over him: But as we had the *Carmelo* in tow, we instantly called out to the people on board her, who threw him over several ends of ropes, one of which he fortunately caught hold of, and twisting it round his arm, they haled him into the ship, without his having received any other injury than a wrench in his arm, of which he soon recovered.

When, on the 26th of *January*, we stood to the eastward, we expected, by our reckonings, to have fallen in with the land on the 28th; but though the weather was perfectly clear, we had no sight of it at sun-set, and therefore we continued on our course, not doubting but we should see it by the next morning. About ten at night we discovered a light on the larboard-bow, bearing from us N. N. E. The *Tryal*'s prize too, who was about a mile a head of us, made a signal at the same time for seeing a sail; and as we had none of us any doubt but what we saw was a ship's light, we were all extremely animated with a firm persuasion, that it was the *Manila* galeon, which had been so long the object of our wishes: And what added to our alacrity, was our expectation of meeting with two of them instead of one, for we took it for granted, that the light in view was carried in the top of one ship for a direction to her consort. We immediately cast off the *Carmelo*, and pressed forward with all our canvass, making a signal for the *Gloucester* to do the same. Thus we chased the light, keeping all our hands at their respective quarters, under an expectation of engaging in the next half hour, as we sometimes conceived the chace to be about a mile distant, and at other times to be within reach of our guns; and some on board us positively averred, that besides the light, they could plainly discern her sails. The Commodore himself was so fully persuaded that we should be soon along side of her, that he sent for his first Lieutenant, who commanded between decks, and directed him to see all the great guns loaded with two round-shot for the first broadside, and after that with one round-shot and one grape, strictly charging him, at the same time, not to suffer a gun to be fired, till he, the Commodore, should give orders, which he informed the Lieutenant would not be till we arrived within pistol-shot of the enemy. In this constant and eager attention we continued all night, always presuming that another quarter of an hour would bring us up with this *Manila* ship, whose wealth, with that of her supposed consort, we now estimated by round millions. But when the morning broke, and day-light came on, we were most strangely and vexatiously disappointed, by finding that the light which had occasioned all this bustle and expectancy, was only a fire on the shore. Indeed the circumstances of this deception are so extraordinary as to be scarcely credible; for, by our run during the night and the distance of the land in the morning, there was no doubt to be made but this fire, when we first discovered it, was above twenty-five leagues from us: And yet I believe there was no person on board, who doubted of its being a ship's light, or of its being near at hand. It was indeed upon a very high mountain, and continued burning for several days afterwards; it was not a vulcano, but rather, as I suppose, stubble or heath set on fire for some purpose of agriculture.

At sun-rising, after this mortifying delusion, we found ourselves about nine leagues off the land, which extended from the N. W. to E. ½ N. On this land we observed two remarkable hummocks, such as are usually called paps, which bore North from us: These a *Spanish* Pilot and two *Indians*, who were the only persons amongst us that pretended to have traded in this part of the world, affirmed to be over the harbour of *Acapulco*. Indeed, we very much doubted their knowledge of the coast; for we found these paps to be in the latitude of 17° : 56′, whereas those over *Acapulco* are said to be in 17 degrees only; and we afterwards found our suspicions of their skill to be well grounded: However, they were very confident, and assured us, that the height of the mountains was itself an infallible mark of the harbour; the coast, as they pretended (though falsly) being generally low to the eastward and westward of it.

And now being in the track of the *Manila* galeon, it was a great doubt with us (as it was near the end of *January*) whether she was or was not arrived: But examining our prisoners about it, they assured us, that she was sometimes known to come in after the middle of *February*; and they endeavoured to persuade us, that the fire we had seen on shore was a proof that she was as yet at sea, it being customary, as they said, to make use of these fires as signals for her direction, when she continued longer out than ordinary. On this information, strengthened by our propensity to believe them in a matter which so pleasingly flattered our wishes, we resolved to cruise for her for some days; and we accordingly spread our ships at the distance of twelve leagues from the coast, in such a manner, that it was impossible she should pass us unobserved: However, not seeing her soon, we were at intervals inclined to suspect that she had gained her port already; and as we now began to want a harbour to refresh our people, the uncertainty of our present situation gave us great uneasiness, and we were very solicitous to get some positive intelligence, which might either set us at liberty to consult our necessities, if the galeon was arrived, or might animate us to continue on our present cruise with chearfulness, if she was not. With this view the Commodore, after examining our prisoners very particularly, resolved to send a boat, under colour of the night, into the harbour of *Acapulco*, to see if the *Manila* ship was there or not, one of the *Indians* being very positive that this might be done without the boat itself being discovered. To execute this project, the barge was dispatched the 6th of *February*, with a sufficient crew and two officers, who took with them a *Spanish* Pilot, and the *Indian* who had insisted on the practicability of this measure, and had undertaken to conduct it. Our barge did not return to us again till the eleventh, when the officers acquainted Mr. *Anson*, that, agreeable to our suspicion, there was nothing like a harbour in the place where the *Spanish* Pilots had at first asserted *Acapulco* to lie; that when they had satisfied themselves in this particular, they steered to the eastward, in hopes of discovering it, and had coasted along shore thirty-two leagues; that in this whole range they met chiefly with sandy beaches of a great length, over which the sea broke with so much violence, that it was impossible for a boat to land; that at the end of their run they could just discover two paps at a very great distance to the eastward, which from their appearance and their latitude, they concluded to be those in the neighbourhood of *Acapulco*; but that not having a sufficient quantity of fresh water and provision for their passage thither and back again, they were obliged to return to the Commodore, to acquaint him with their disappointment. On this intelligence we all made sail to the eastward, in order to get into the neighbourhood of that port, the Commodore resolving to send the barge a second time upon the same enterprize, when we were arrived within a moderate distance. And the next day, which was the 12th of *February*, we being by that time considerably advanced, the barge was again dispatched, and particular instructions given to the officers to preserve themselves from being seen from the shore. On the 13th we espied a high land to the eastward, which we first imagined to be that over the harbour of *Acapulco*; but we afterwards found that it was the high land of *Seguateneio*, where there is a small harbour, of which we shall have occasion to make more ample mention hereafter. And now, having waited six days without any news of our barge, we began to be uneasy for her safety; but, on the 7th day, that is, on the 19th of *February*, she returned. The officers informed the Commodore, that they had discovered the harbour of *Acapulco*, which they esteemed to bear from us E. S. E. at least fifty leagues distant: That on the 17th, about two in the morning, they were got within the Island that lies at the mouth of the harbour, and yet neither the *Spanish* Pilot, nor the *Indian* who were with them, could give them any information where they then were; but that while they were lying upon their oars in suspence what to do, being ignorant that they were then at the very place they sought for, they discerned a small light upon the surface of the water, on which they instantly plied their paddles, and moving as silently as possible towards it, they found it to be in a fishing canoe, which they surprized, with three Negroes that belonged to it. It seems the Negroes at first attempted to jump overboard; and being so near the land they would easily have swam on shore; but they were prevented by presenting a piece at them, on which they readily submitted, and were taken into the barge. The officers further added, that they had immediately turned the canoe adrift against the face of a rock, where it would inevitably be dashed to pieces by the fury of the sea: This they did to deceive those who perhaps might be sent from the town to search after the canoe; for upon seeing several pieces of a wreck, they would immediately conclude that the people on board her had been drowned, and would have no suspicion of their having fallen into our hands. When the crew of the barge had taken this precaution, they exerted their utmost strength in pulling out to sea, and by dawn of day had gained such an offing, as rendered it impossible for them to be seen from the coast.

And now having gotten the three Negroes in our possession, who were not ignorant of the transactions at *Acapulco*, we were soon satisfied about the most material points which had long kept us in suspence: And on examination we found, that we were indeed disappointed in our expectation of intercepting the galeon before her arrival at *Acapulco*; but we learnt other circumstances which still revived our hopes, and which, we then conceived, would more than balance the opportunity we had already lost: For tho' our Negroe prisoners informed us that the galeon arrived at *Acapulco* on our 9th of *January*, which was about twenty days before we fell in with this coast, yet they at the same time told us, that the galeon had delivered her cargoe, and was taking in water and provisions for her return, and that the Viceroy of *Mexico* had by proclamation, fixed her departure from *Acapulco* to the 14th of *March*, *N. S.*[1] This last news was most joyfully received by us, as we had no doubt but she must certainly fall into our hands, and as it was much more eligible to seize her on her return, than it would have been to have taken her before her arrival, as the species for which she had sold her cargoe and which she would now have on board, would be prodigiously more to be esteemed by us than the cargoe itself; great part of which would have perished on our hands, and no part of it could have been disposed of by us at so advantageous a mart as *Acapulco*.

Thus we were a second time engaged in an eager expectation of meeting with this *Manila* ship, which, by the fame of its wealth, we had been taught to consider as the most desirable prize that was to be met with in any part of the globe. As all our future projects will be in some sort regulated with a view to the possession of this celebrated galeon, and as the commerce which is carried on by means of these vessels between the city of *Manila* and the port of *Acapulco* is perhaps the most valuable, in proportion to its quantity, of any in the known world, I shall endeavour, in the ensuing chapter, to give as distinct an account as I can of all the particulars relating thereto, both as it is a matter in which I conceive the public to be in some degree interested, and as I flatter myself, that from the materials which have fallen into my hands, I am enabled to describe it with more distinctness than has hitherto been done, at least in our language.

CHAP. X.

An account of the commerce carried on between the city of *Manila* on the Island of *Luconia*, and the port of *Acapulco* on the Coast of *Mexico*.

ABOUT the end of the 15th Century and the beginning of the 16th, the discovery of new countries and of new branches of commerce was the reigning passion of several of the *European* Princes. But those who engaged most deeply and fortunately in these pursuits were the Kings of *Spain* and *Portugal*; the first of these having discovered the immense and opulent Continent of *America* and its adjacent Islands, whilst the other, by doubling the Cape of *Good Hope*, had opened to his fleets a passage to the southern coast of *Asia*, usually called the *East-Indies*, and by his settlements in that part of the globe, became possessed of many of the manufactures and natural productions with which it abounded, and which, for some ages, had been the wonder and delight of the more polished and luxurious part of mankind.

In the mean time, these two Nations of *Spain* and *Portugal*, who were thus prosecuting the same views, though in different quarters of the world, grew extremely jealous of each other, and became apprehensive of mutual encroachments. And therefore to quiet their jealousies, and to enable them with more tranquillity to pursue the propagation of the Catholick Faith in these distant countries, (they having both of them given distinguished marks of their zeal for their mother church, by their butchery of innocent Pagans) Pope *Alexander* VI. granted to the *Spanish* Crown the property and dominion of all places, either already discovered, or that should be discovered an hundred leagues to the westward of the Islands of *Azores*, leaving all the unknown countries to the eastward of this limit, to the industry and future disquisition of the *Portuguese*: And this boundary being afterwards removed two hundred and fifty leagues more to the westward, by the agreement of both Nations, it was imagined that by this regulation all the seeds of future contests were suppressed. For the *Spaniards* presumed, that the *Portuguese* would be hereby prevented from meddling with their colonies in *America*: And the *Portuguese* supposed that their *East-Indian* settlements, and particularly the spice Islands, which they had then newly discovered, were secured from any future attempts of the *Spanish* Nation.

But it seems the infallibility of the Holy Father had, on this occasion, deserted him, and for want of being more conversant in geography, he had not foreseen that the *Spaniards*, by pushing their discoveries to the West, and the *Portuguese* to the East, might at last meet with each other, and be again embroiled; as it actually happened within a few years afterwards. For *Frederick Magellan*, who was an officer in the King of *Portugal's* service, having received some disgust from that Court, either by the defalcation of his pay, or by having his parts, as he conceived, too cheaply considered, he entered into the service of the King of *Spain*; and being as it appears a man of ability, he was very desirous of signalizing his talents by some enterprize, which might prove extremely vexatious to his former Masters, and might teach them to estimate his worth by the greatness of the mis-chief he brought upon them, this being the most obvious and natural turn of all fugitives, and more especially of those, who, being really men of capacity, have quitted their country by reason of the small account that has been made of them. *Magellan*, in pursuance of these vindictive views, knowing that the *Portuguese* Court considered their possession of the spice islands as their most important acquisition in the *East-Indies*, resolved with himself to instigate the Court of *Spain* to an enterprize, which, by still pushing their discoveries, would give them a right to interfere both in the property and commerce of those renowned *Portuguese* settlements; and the King of *Spain* approving of this project, *Magellan*, in the year 1519, set sail from the port of *Sevil*, in order to carry this enterprize into execution. He had with him a considerable force, consisting of five ships and two hundred and thirty-four men, with which he stood for the coast of South *America*, and ranging along shore, he at last, towards the end of *October* 1520, had the good fortune to discover those Streights, which have since been denominated from him, and which opened him a passage into the *Pacific* Ocean. And this first part of his scheme being thus happily accomplished, he, after some stay on the coast of *Peru*, set sail again to the westward, with a view of falling in with the spice islands. In this extensive run he first discovered the *Ladrones* or *Marian* Islands; and continuing on his course, he at length reached the *Philippine*

Islands, which are the most eastern part of *Asia*, where, venturing on shore in an hostile manner, and skirmishing with the *Indians*, he was slain.

By the death of *Magellan*, the original project of securing some of the spice islands was defeated; for those who were left in command contented themselves with ranging through them, and purchasing some spices from the natives; after which they returned home round the Cape of *Good Hope*, being the first ships which had ever surrounded this terraqueous globe; and thereby demonstrated, by a palpable experiment obvious to the grossest and most vulgar capacity, the reality of its long disputed spherical figure.

But though *Spain* did not hereby acquire the property of any of the spice islands, yet the discovery made in this expedition of the *Philippine* Islands, was thought too considerable to be neglected; for these were not far distant from those places which produced spices, and were very well situated for the *Chinese* trade, and for the commerce of other parts of *India*; and therefore a communication was soon established, and carefully supported between these Islands and the *Spanish* colonies on the coast of *Peru*: So that the city of *Manila*, (which was built on the Island of *Luconia*, the chief of the *Philippines*) soon became the mart for all *Indian* commodities, which were bought up by the inhabitants, and were annually sent to the *South-Seas* to be there vended on their account; and the returns of this commerce to *Manila* being principally made in silver, the place by degrees grew extremely opulent and considerable, and its trade so far encreased, as to engage the attention of the Court of *Spain*, and to be frequently controlled and regulated by royal edicts.

In the infancy of this trade, it was carried on from the port of *Callao* to the city of *Manila*, in which voyage the trade-wind continually favoured them; so that notwithstanding these places were distant between three and four thousand leagues, yet the voyage was often made in little more than two months: But then the return from *Manila* was extremely troublesome and tedious, and is said to have sometimes taken them up above a twelve month, which, if they pretended to ply up within the limits of the trade-wind, is not at all to be wondered at; and it is asserted, that in their first voyages they were so imprudent and unskilful as to attempt this course. However, that route was soon laid aside by the advice, as it is said, of a Jesuit, who

217

persuaded them to steer to the northward till they got clear of the trade-winds, and then by the favour of the westerly winds, which generally prevail in high latitudes, to stretch away for the coast of *California*. This has been the practice for at least a hundred and sixty years past: For Sir *Thomas Cavendish,* in the year 1586 engaged off the South end of *California* a vessel bound from *Manila* to the *American* coast. And it was in compliance with this new plan of navigation, and to shorten the run both backwards and forwards, that the staple of this commerce to and from *Manila* was removed from *Callao* on the coast of *Peru,* to the port of *Acapulco* on the coast of *Mexico,* where it continues fixed at this time.

Such was the commencement, and such were the early regulations of this commerce; but its present condition being a much more interesting subject, I must beg leave to dwell longer on this head, and to be indulged in a more particular narration, beginning with a description of the Island of *Luconia,* and of the port and bay of *Manila.*

The Island of *Luconia,* though situated in the latitude of 15° North, is esteemed to be in general extremely healthy, and the water, that is found upon it, is said to be the best in the world: It produces all the fruits of the warm climates, and abounds in a most excellent breed of horses, supposed to be carried thither first from *Spain*: It is very well situated for the *Indian* and *Chinese* trade; and the bay and port of *Manila,* which lies on its western side, is perhaps the most remarkable on the whole globe, the bay being a large circular bason, near ten leagues in diameter, and great part of it entirely land-locked. On the east side of this bay stands the city of *Manila,* which is very large and populous; and which, at the beginning of this war, was only an open place, its principal defence consisting in a small fort, which was in great measure surrounded on every side by houses; but they have lately made considerable additions to its fortifications, though I have not yet learnt in what manner. The port, peculiar to the city, is called *Cabite,* and lies near two leagues to the southward; and in this port all the ships employed in the *Acapulco* trade are usually stationed. As I have never seen but one engraved plan of this bay, and that in a very scarce book, I have hereafter added, towards the beginning of the third book, a plan which fell into my hands, and which differs considerably from that already published: But I cannot pretend to decide which of the two is most to be relied on.

The city of *Manila* itself is in a very healthy situation, is well watered, and is in the neighbourhood of a very fruitful and plentiful country; but as the principal business of this place is its trade to *Acapulco*, it lies under some disadvantage, from the difficulty there is in getting to sea to the eastward: For the passage is among islands and through channels where the *Spaniards*, by reason of their unskilfulness in marine affairs, waste much time, and are often in great danger. These difficulties will be better apprehended by the reader by the annexed draughts of the Island of *Luconia*, and of its neighbouring isles, which was taken from the enemy, and had been newly drawn and corrected but a short time before.

The trade carried on from this place to *China* and different parts of *India*, is principally for such commodities as are intended to supply the Kingdoms of *Mexico* and *Peru*. These are spices, all sorts of *Chinese* silks and manufactures; particularly silk stockings, of which I have heard that no less than fifty thousand pair were the usual number shipped on board the annual ship; vast quantities of *Indian* stuffs, as callicoes and chints, which are much worn in *America*, together with other minuter articles, as goldsmiths work, &c. which is principally done at the city of *Manila* itself by the *Chinese*; for it is said there are at least twenty thousand *Chinese* who constantly reside there, either as servants, manufacturers, or brokers. All these different commodities are collected at *Manila*, thence to be transported annually in one or more ships, to the port of *Acapulco*, in the Kingdom of *Mexico*.

But this trade to *Acapulco* is not laid open to all the inhabitants of *Manila*, but is confined by very particular regulations, somewhat analogous to those by which the trade of the register ships from *Cadiz* to the *West-Indies* is restrained. The ships employed herein are found by the King of *Spain*, who pays the officers and crew; and the tunnage is divided into a certain number of bales, all of the same size: These are distributed amongst the Convents at *Manila*, but principally to the Jesuits, as a donation for the support of their missions for the propagation of the Catholick Faith; and these Convents have thereby a right to embark such a quantity of goods on board the *Manila* ship, as the tunnage of their bales amounts to; or if they chuse not to be concerned in trade themselves, they have the power of selling this privilege to others; and as the Merchants to whom they grant their shares are often unprovided of a stock, it is usual for the Convents to lend them considerable sums of money on bottomry.

The trade is by the royal edicts limited to a certain value, which the annual cargoe ought not to exceed. Some *Spanish* manuscripts, I have seen, mention this limitation to be 600,000 dollars; but the annual cargoe does certainly surpass this sum; and though it may be difficult to fix its exact value, yet from many comparisons I conclude, that the return cannot be greatly short of three millions of dollars.

It is sufficiently obvious, that the greatest part of the treasure, returned from *Acapulco* to *Manila*, does not remain in that place, but is again dispersed into different parts of *India*. And as all *European* Nations have generally esteemed it good policy to keep their *American* settlements in an immediate dependence on their mother country, without permitting them to carry on directly any gainful traffick with other powers, these considerations have occasioned many remonstrances to be presented to the Court of *Spain* against the *Indian* trade, hereby allowed to the Kingdom of *Peru* and *Mexico*; it having been urged, that the silk manufactures of *Valencia* and other parts of *Spain* are hereby greatly prejudiced, and the linnens carried from *Cadiz* are much injured in their sale: Since the *Chinese* silks coming almost directly to *Acapulco*, can be afforded much cheaper there than any *European* manufactures of equal goodness; and the cottons from the *Coromondel* coast, make the *European* linnens almost useless. So that the *Manila* trade renders both *Mexico* and *Peru* less dependent upon *Spain* for a supply of their necessities than they ought to be; and exhausts those countries of a considerable quantity of silver, the greatest part of which, were this trade prohibited, would center in *Spain*, either in payment for *Spanish* commodities, or in gains to the *Spanish* Merchant; whereas now the only advantage which arises from it is, the enriching the Jesuits and a few particular persons besides, at the other extremity of the world. These arguments did so far influence Don *Joseph Patinho*, who was then prime Minister, but an enemy to the Jesuits, that about the year 1725, he had resolved to abolish this trade, and to have permitted no *Indian* commodities to be introduced into any of the *Spanish* ports in the *West-Indies*, but what were carried there in the register ships from *Europe*. But the powerful intrigues of the Jesuits prevented this regulation from taking place.

This trade from *Manila* to *Acapulco* and back again, is usually carried on in one or at most two annual ships, which set sail from *Manila* about *July*, and arrive at *Acapulco* in the *December, January,* or *February* following, and having there disposed of their effects, return for *Manila* sometime in *March*, where they generally arrive in *June*; so that the whole voyage takes up very near an entire year: For this reason, though there is often no more than one ship employed at a time, yet there is always one ready for the sea when the other arrives; and therefore the commerce at *Manila* are provided with three or four stout ships, that in case of any accident, the trade may not be suspended. The largest of these ships, whose name I have not learnt, is described as little less than one of our first rate men of war, and indeed she must be of an enormous size; for it is known, that when she was employed with other ships from the same port, to cruise for our *China* trade, she had no less than twelve hundred men on board.[1] Their other ships, though far inferior in bulk to this, are yet stout large vessels, of the burthen of twelve hundred tun and upwards, and usually carry from three hundred and fifty to six hundred hands, passengers included, with fifty odd guns. As these are all King's ships commissioned and paid by him, there is usually one of the Captains, who is stiled the General, and who carries the royal standard of *Spain* at the main-top gallant mast-head, as we shall more particularly observe hereafter.

And now having described the port of *Manila* and the shipping they employ, it is necessary to give a more circumstantial detail of their navigation. The ship having received her cargoe on board, and being fitted for the sea, generally weighs from the mole of *Cabite* about the middle of *July*, taking the advantage of the westerly monsoon, which then sets in, to carry them to sea. It appears by the chart already inserted, that the getting through the *Boccadero* to the eastward must be a troublesome navigation, and in fact, it is sometimes the end of *August* before they get clear of the land. When they have got through this passage, and are clear of the Islands, they stand to the northward of the east, in order to get into the latitude of 30 odd degrees, where they expect to meet with westerly winds, before which they run away for the coast of *California*. To give a better idea of the track which they hold in this navigation, I have inserted, towards the latter end of the third book, the copy of a manuscript chart, which was taken on board one of these ships, containing all that Ocean between the

221

Philippine Islands and the coast of *Mexico,* in which I have laid down the particular route of this vessel, both in her passage from *Manila* to *Acapulco,* and from *Acapulco* back again. In this chart (as it was drawn for the use of the *Spanish* General) there are contained all the discoveries which the *Manila* ships have at any time made in traversing this vast Ocean; whence it appears what minute and inconsiderable fragments of land are dispersed in that prodigious sea; and it is most remarkable, that by the concurrent testimony of all the *Spanish* Navigators, there is not one port, nor even a tolerable road as yet found out betwixt the *Philippine* Islands and the coast of *California* and *Mexico*; so that from the time the *Manila* ship first loses sight of land, she never lets go her anchor till she arrives on the coast of *California,* and very often not till she gets to its southermost extremity: And therefore as this voyage is rarely of less than six months continuance, and the ship is deep laden with merchandize and crowded with people, it may appear wonderful how they can be supplied with a stock of fresh water for so long a time; and indeed their method of procuring it is extremely singular, and deserves a very particular recital.

It is well known to those who are acquainted with the *Spanish* customs in the *South-Seas,* that their water is preserved on shipboard not in casks but in earthern jars, which in some sort resemble the large oil jars we often see in *Europe.* When the *Manila* ship first puts to sea, they take on board a much greater quantity of water than can be stowed between decks, and the jars which contain it are hung all about the shrouds and stays, so as to exhibit at a distance a very odd appearance. And though it is one convenience of their jars that they are much more manageable than casks, and are liable to no leekage, unless they are broken, yet it is sufficiently obvious, that a sixth, or even a three months store of water could never be stowed in a ship so loaded, by any management whatever; and therefore without some other supply, this navigation could not be performed: A supply indeed they have, but the reliance upon it seems at first sight so extremely precarious, that it is wonderful such numbers should risque the perishing by the most dreadful of all deaths, on the expectation of so casual a circumstance. In short, their only method of recruiting their water is by the rains, which they meet with between the latitudes of 30 and 40° North, and which they are always prepared to catch: For this purpose they take to sea with them a great number of mats, which they place slopingly against the gunwale, whenever the rain descends; these mats extend from one end of the ship to the other, and their lower edges rest on a large split bamboe, so that all the water which falls on the mats drains into the bamboe, and by this, as a trough, is conveyed into a jar; and this method of supplying their water, however accidental and extraordinary it may at first sight appear, hath never been known to fail them, so that it is common for them, when their voyage is a little longer than usual, to fill all their water jars several times over.

However, though their distresses for fresh water are much short of what might be expected in so tedious a navigation, yet there are other inconveniencies generally attendant upon a long continuance at sea, from which they are not exempted. The principal of these is the scurvy, which sometimes rages with extreme violence, and destroys great numbers of the people; but at other times their passage to *Acapulco* (of which alone I would be here understood to speak) is performed with little loss.

The length of time employed in this passage, so much beyond what usually occurs in any other known navigation, is perhaps in part to be imputed to the indolence and unskilfulness of the *Spanish* sailors, and to an unnecessary degree of caution and concern for so rich a vessel: For it is said, that they never set their main sail in the night, and often lie by unnecessarily. And indeed the instructions given to their Captains (which I have seen) seem to have been drawn up by such as were more apprehensive of too strong a gale, though favourable, than of the inconveniencies and mortality attending a lingring and tedious voyage; for the Captain is particularly ordered to make his passage in the latitude of 30 degrees if possible, and to be extremely careful to stand no farther to the northward than is absolutely necessary for the getting a westerly wind. This, according to our conceptions, appears to be a very absurd restriction; since it can scarcely be doubted, but that in the higher latitudes the westerly winds are much steadier and brisker than in the latitude of 30 degrees: So that the whole conduct of this navigation seems liable to very great censure. For if instead of steering E. N. E. into the latitude of 30 odd degrees, they at first stood N. E. or even still more northerly, into the latitude of 40 or 45 degrees, in part of which course the trade-winds would greatly assist them, I doubt not but by this management they might considerably contract their voyage, and perhaps perform it in half the time, which is now allotted for it; for in the journals I have seen of these voyages it appears, that they are often a month or six weeks after their laying the land, before they get into the latitude of 30 degrees; whereas, with a more northerly course, it might easily be done in a fourth part of the time; and when they were once well advanced to the northward, the westerly winds would soon blow them over to the coast of *California,* and they would be thereby freed from the other embarassments, to which they are now subjected, only at the expence of a rough sea and a stiff gale. And this is not merely matter of speculation; for I am credibly informed, that about the year 1721, a *French* ship, by pursuing this course, ran from the coast of *China* to the valley of *Vanderas* on the coast of *Mexico,* in less than fifty days: But it was said that this ship, notwithstanding the shortness of her passage, suffered prodigiously by the scurvy, so that she had only four or five of her crew left when she arrived in *America.*

However, I shall descant no longer on the probability of performing this voyage in a much shorter time, but shall content myself with reciting the actual occurrences of the present navigation. The *Manila* ship having stood so far to the northward as to meet with a westerly wind, stretches away nearly in the same latitude for the coast of *California*: And when she has run into the longitude of 96 degrees from Cape *Espiritu Santo,* she generally meets with a plant floating on the sea, which, being called *Porra* by the *Spaniards,* is, I presume, a species of sea-leek. On the sight of this plant they esteem themselves sufficiently near the *Californian* shore, and immediately stand to the southward; and they rely so much on this circumstance, that on the first discovery of the plant the whole ship's company chaunt a solemn *Te Deum,* esteeming the difficulties and hazards of their passage to be now at an end; and they constantly correct their longitude thereby, without ever coming within sight of land. After falling in with these Signs, as they denominate them, they steer to the southward, without endeavouring to fall in with the coast, till they have run into a lower latitude; for as there are many islands, and some shoals adjacent to *California,* the extreme caution of the *Spanish* Navigators makes them very apprehensive of being engaged with the land; however, when they draw near its southern extremity, they venture to hale in, both for the sake of making Cape St. *Lucas* to ascertain their reckoning, and also to receive intelligence from the *Indian* inhabitants, whether or no there are any enemies on the coast; and this last circumstance, which is a particular article in the Captain's instructions, makes it necessary to mention the late proceedings of the Jesuits amongst the *Californian Indians.*

Since the first discovery of *California*, there have been various wandring Missionaries who have visited it at different times, though to little purpose; but of late years the Jesuits, encouraged and supported by a large donation from the Marquis *de Valero*, a most munificent bigot, have fixed themselves upon the place, and have established a very considerable mission. Their principal settlement lies just within Cape St. *Lucas*, where they have collected a great number of savages, and have endeavoured to inure them to agriculture and other mechanic arts: And their efforts have not been altogether ineffectual; for they have planted vines at their settlements with very good success, so that they already make a considerable quantity of wine, resembling in flavour the inferior sorts of *Madera*, which begins to be esteemed in the neighbouring kingdom of *Mexico.*

The Jesuits then being thus firmly rooted on *California*, they have already extended their jurisdiction quite across the country from sea to sea, and are endeavouring to spread their influence farther to the northward; with which view they have made several expeditions up the gulf between *California* and *Mexico*, in order to discover the nature of the adjacent countries, all which they hope hereafter to bring under their power. And being thus occupied in advancing the interests of their society, it is no wonder if some share of attention is engaged about the security of the *Manila* ship, in which their Convents at *Manila* are so deeply concerned. For this purpose there are refreshments, as fruits, wine, water, &c. constantly kept in readiness for her; and there is besides care taken at Cape St. *Lucas*, to look out for any ship of the enemy, which might be cruising there to intercept her; this being a station where she is constantly expected, and where she has been often waited for and fought with, though generally with little success. In consequence then of the measures mutually settled between the Jesuits of *Manila* and their brethren at *California*, the Captain of the galeon is ordered to fall in with the land to the northward of Cape St. *Lucas*, where the inhabitants are directed, on sight of the vessel, to make the proper signals with fires; and on discovering these fires, the Captain is to send his launch on shore with twenty men, well armed, who are to carry with them the letters from the Convents at *Manila* to the *Californian* Missionaries, and are to bring back the refreshments which will be prepared for them, and likewise intelligence whether or no there are any enemies on the coast. And if the Captain finds, from the account which is sent him, that he has nothing to fear, he is directed to proceed for Cape St. *Lucas,* and thence to Cape *Corientes,* after which he is to coast it along for the port of *Acapulco.*

The most usual time of the arrival of the galeon at *Acapulco* is towards the middle of *January*: But this navigation is so uncertain, that she sometimes gets in a month sooner, and at other times has been detained at sea above a month longer. The port of *Acapulco* is by much the securest and finest in all the northern parts of the *Pacific* Ocean, being, as it were, a bason surrounded by very high mountains: But the town is a most wretched place, and extremely unhealthy, for the air about it is so pent up by the hills, that it has scarcely any circulation. The place is besides destitute of fresh water, except what is brought from a considerable distance, and is in all respects so inconvenient, that except at the time of the mart, whilst the *Manila* galeon is in the port, it is almost deserted. To compensate in some measure for the shortness of this description, I have added in the third book, in the same plate with the bay of *Manila* abovementioned, a plan of this place and of its port and citadel, in which are likewise drawn the new works which were added on their first intelligence of the equipment of our squadron. As this plan was taken from the *Spaniards,* I cannot answer for its accuracy; but having seen two or three other *Spanish* draughts of the place, I conceive, by comparing them together, that this I have here inserted is not very distant from the truth.

When the galeon arrives in this port, she is generally moored on its western side to the two trees marked in the plan, and her cargoe is delivered with all possible expedition. And now the town of *Acapulco,* from almost a solitude, is immediately thronged with Merchants from all parts of the kingdom of *Mexico.* The cargoe being landed and disposed of, the silver and the goods intended for *Manila* are taken on board, together with provisions and water, and the ship prepares to put to sea with the utmost expedition. There is indeed no time to be lost; for it is an express order to the Captain to be out of the port of *Acapulco* on his return, before the first day of *April, N. S.*

And having mentioned the goods intended for *Manila*, I must observe, that the principal return is always made in silver, and consequently the rest of the cargoe is but of little account, the other articles, besides the silver, being some cochineal and a few sweetmeats, the produce of the *American* settlements, together with *European* millinery ware for the women at *Manila*, and some *Spanish* wines, such as tent and sherry, which are intended for the use of their Priests in the administration of the Sacrament.

And this difference in the cargoe of the ship to and from *Manila*, occasions a very remarkable variety in the manner of equipping the ship for these two different voyages. For the galeon, when she sets sail from *Manila*, being deep laden with a variety of bulky goods, she has not the conveniency of mounting her lower tire of guns, but carries them in her hold, till she draws near Cape St. *Lucas*, and is apprehensive of an enemy. Her hands too are as few as is consistent with the safety of the ship, that she may be less pestered with the stowage of provisions. But on her return from *Acapulco*, as her cargoe lies in less room, her lower tire is (or ought to be) always mounted before she leaves the port, and her crew is augmented with a supply of sailors, and with one or two companies of foot, which are intended to reinforce the garrison at *Manila*. And there being besides many Merchants who take their passage to *Manila* on board the galeon, her whole number of hands on her return is usually little short of six hundred, all which are easily provided for, by reason of the small stowage necessary for the silver.

The galeon being thus fitted for her return, the Captain, on leaving the port of *Acapulco*, steers for the latitude of 13° or 14°, and runs on that parallel, till he gets sight of the Island of *Guam*, one of the *Ladrones*. In this run the Captain is particularly directed to be careful of the shoals of St. *Bartholomew*, and of the Island of *Gasparico*. He is also told in his instructions, that to prevent his passing the *Ladrones* in the dark, there are orders given that, through all the month of *June*, fires shall be lighted every night on the highest part of *Guam* and *Rota*, and kept in till the morning.

At *Guam* there is a small *Spanish* garrison, (as will be more particularly mentioned hereafter) purposely intended to secure that place for the refreshment of the galeon, and to yield her all the assistance in their power. However, the danger of the road at *Guam* is so great, that though the galeon is ordered to call there, yet she rarely stays above a day or two, but getting her water and refreshments on board as soon as possible, she steers away directly for Cape *Espiritu Santo*, on the Island of *Samal.* Here the Captain is again ordered to look out for signals; and he is told, that centinels will be posted not only on that Cape, but likewise in *Catanduanas, Butusan, Birriborongo,* and on the Island of *Batan.* These centinels are instructed to make a fire when they discover the ship, which the Captain is carefully to observe: For if, after this first fire is extinguished, he perceives that four or more are lighted up again, he is then to conclude that there are enemies on the coast; and on this he is immediately to endeavour to speak with the centinel on shore, and to procure from him more particular intelligence of their force, and of the station they cruise in; pursuant to which, he is to regulate his conduct, and to endeavour to gain some secure port amongst those Islands, without coming in sight of the enemy; and in case he should be discovered when in port, and should be apprehensive of an attack, he is then to land his treasure, and to take some of his artillery on shore for its defence, not neglecting to send frequent and particular accounts to the city of *Manila* of all that passes. But if, after the first fire on shore, the Captain observes that two others only are made by the centinels, he is then to conclude, that there is nothing to fear: And he is to pursue his course without interruption, and to make the best of his way to the port of *Cabite,* which is the port to the city of *Manila,* and the constant station for all the ships employed in this commerce to *Acapulco.*

CHAP. XI.

Our cruise off the port of *Acapulco* for the *Manila* ship.

I HAVE already mentioned, in the ninth chapter, that the return of our barge from the port of *Acapulco*, where she had surprized three Negro fishermen, gave us inexpressible satisfaction, as we learnt from our prisoners, that the galeon was then preparing to put to sea, and that her departure was fixed, by an edict of the Viceroy of *Mexico*, to the 14th of *March*, *N. S.* that is, to the 3d of *March*, according to our reckoning.

What related to this *Manila* ship being the matter to which we were most attentive, it was necessarily the first article of our examination; but having satisfied ourselves upon this head, we then indulged our curiosity in enquiring after other news; when the prisoners informed us, that they had received intelligence at *Acapulco*, of our having plundered and burnt the town of *Paita*; and that, on this occasion, the Governor of *Acapulco* had augmented the fortifications of the place, and had taken several precautions to prevent us from forcing our way into the harbour; that in particular, he had placed a guard on the Island which lies at the harbour's mouth, and that this guard had been withdrawn but two nights before the arrival of our barge: So that had the barge succeeded in her first attempt, or had she arrived at the port the second time two days sooner, she could scarcely have avoided being seized on, or if she had escaped, it must have been with the loss of the greatest part of her crew, as she would have been under the fire of the guard, before she had known her danger.

The withdrawing of this guard was a circumstance that greatly encouraged us, as it seemed to demonstrate, not only that the enemy had not as yet discovered us, but likewise that they had now no farther apprehensions of our visiting their coast. Indeed the prisoners assured us, that they had no knowledge of our being in those seas, and that they had therefore flattered themselves, that, in the long interval since our taking of *Paita*, we had steered another course. But we did not consider the opinion of these Negro prisoners as so authentick a proof of our being hitherto concealed, as the withdrawing of the guard from the harbour's mouth; for this being the action of the Governor, was of all arguments the most convincing, as he might be supposed to have intelligence, with which the rest of the inhabitants were unacquainted.

Satisfied therefore that we were undiscovered, and that the time was fixed for the departure of the galeon from *Acapulco*, we made all necessary preparations, and waited with the utmost impatience for the important day. As this was the 3d of *March*, and it was the 19th of *February* when the barge returned and brought us our intelligence, the Commodore resolved to continue the greatest part of the intermediate time on his present station, to the westward of *Acapulco*, conceiving that in this situation there would be less danger of his being seen from the shore, which was the only circumstance that could deprive us of the immense treasure, on which we had at present so eagerly fixed our thoughts. During this interval, we were employed in scrubbing and cleansing our ships bottoms, in bringing them into their most advantageous trim, and in regulating the orders, signals and stations to be observed, when we should arrive off *Acapulco*, and the time of the departure of the galeon should draw nigh.

And now, on the first of *March*, we made the high lands, usually called the paps over *Acapulco*, and got with all possible expedition into the situation prescribed by the Commodore's orders. The distribution of our squadron on this occasion, both for the intercepting the galeon, and for the avoiding a discovery from the shore, was so very judicious, that it well merits to be distinctly described. The order of it was thus:

The *Centurion* brought the paps over the harbour to bear N.N.E, at fifteen leagues distance, which was a sufficient offing to prevent our being seen by the enemy. To the westward of the *Centurion* there was stationed the *Carmelo*, and to the eastward were the *Tryal* Prize, the *Gloucester*, and the *Carmin*: These were all ranged in a circular line, each ship was three leagues distant from the next: so that the *Carmelo* and the *Carmin*, which were the two extremes, were twelve leagues distant from each other: And, as the galeon could, without doubt, be discerned at six leagues distance from either extremity, the whole sweep of our squadron, within which nothing could pass undiscovered, was at least twenty-four leagues in extent; and yet we were so connected by our signals, as to be easily and speedily informed of what was seen in any part of the line: And to render this disposition still more compleat, and to prevent even the possibility of the galeon's escaping us in the night, the two Cutters belonging to the *Centurion* and the *Gloucester* were both manned and sent in shore, and were ordered to lie all day at the distance of four or five leagues from the entrance of the port, where, by reason of their smallness, they could not possibly be discovered; but in the night they were directed to stand nearer to the harbour's mouth, and as the light of the morning came on, they were to return back again to their day-posts. When the Cutters should first discover the *Manila* ship, one of them was ordered to return to the squadron, and to make a signal, whether the galeon stood to the eastward or to the westward; whilst the other was to follow the galeon at a distance, and if it grew dark, was to direct the squadron in their chace, by shewing false fires. The particular situation of each ship and of the Cutters, and the bearings from each other, which they were to observe in order to keep their stations, will be better understood by the delineation exhibited in the annexed plate; a draught of which was delivered to each of the Commanders at the same time with their orders.

Besides the care we had taken to prevent the galeon from passing by us unobserved, we had not been inattentive to the means of engaging her to advantage, when we came up with her: For considering the thinness of our hands, and the vaunting accounts given by the *Spaniards* of her size, her guns, and her strength,[1] this was a consideration not to be neglected. As we supposed that none of our ships but the *Centurion* and the *Gloucester* were capable of lying along side of her, we took on board the *Centurion* all the hands belonging to the *Carmelo* and the *Carmin*, except what were just sufficient to navigate those ships; and Captain *Saunders* was ordered to send from the *Tryal* Prize ten *Englishmen*, and as many Negroes, to reinforce the crew of the *Gloucester*: And for the encouragement of our Negroes, of which we had a considerable number on board, we promised them, that on their good behaviour they should all have their freedom; and as they had been almost every day trained to the management of the great guns for the two preceding months, they were very well qualified to be of service to us; and from their hopes of liberty, and in return for the usage they had met with amongst us, they seemed disposed to exert themselves to the utmost of their power.

And now being thus prepared for the reception of the galeon, we expected, with the utmost impatience, the so often mentioned 3d of *March*, the day fixed for her departure. And on that day we were all of us most eagerly engaged in looking out towards *Acapulco*; and we were so strangely prepossessed with the certainty of our intelligence, and with an assurance of her coming out of port, that some or other on board us were constantly imagining that they discovered one of our Cutters returning with a signal. But to our extreme vexation, both this day and the succeeding night passed over, without any news of the galeon: However, we did not yet despair, but were all heartily disposed to flatter ourselves, that some unforeseen accident had intervened, which might have put off her departure for a few days; and suggestions of this kind occurred in plenty, as we knew that the time fixed by the Viceroy for her sailing, was often prolonged on the petition of the Merchants of *Mexico*. Thus we kept up our hopes, and did not abate of our vigilance; and as the 7th of *March* was *Sunday* the beginning of Passion week, which is observed by the Papists with great strictness, and a total cessation from all kinds of labour, so that no ship is permitted to stir out of port during the whole week, this quieted our apprehensions for some days, and disposed us not to expect the galeon till the week following. On the *Friday* in this week our Cutters returned to us, and the officers on board them were very confident that the galeon was still in port, for that she could not possibly have come out but they must have seen her. On the *Monday* morning succeeding passion week, that is, on the 15th of *March*, the Cutters were again dispatched to their old station, and our hopes were once more indulged in as sanguine prepossessions as before; but in a week's time our eagerness was greatly abated, and a general dejection and despondency took place in its room. It is true, there were some few amongst us who still kept up their spirits, and were very ingenious in finding out reasons to satisfy themselves, that the disappointment we had hitherto met with had only been occasioned by a casual delay of the galeon, which a few days would remove, and not by a total suspension of her departure for the whole season: But these speculations were not relished by the generality of our people; for they were persuaded that the enemy had, by some accident, discovered our being upon the coast, and had therefore laid an embargo on the galeon till the next year. And indeed this persuasion was but too well founded; for we afterwards learnt, that our barge, when sent on the discovery of the port of *Acapulco*, had been seen from the shore; and that this circumstance (no embarkations but canoes ever frequenting that coast) was to them a sufficient proof of the neighbourhood of our squadron; on which, they stopped the galeon till the succeeding year.

The Commodore himself, though he declared not his opinion, was yet in his own thoughts very apprehensive that we were discovered, and the departure of the galeon was put off and he had, in consequence of this opinion, formed a plan for possessing himself of *Acapulco*; for he had no doubt but the treasure as yet remained in the town, even though the orders for the dispatching of the galeon were countermanded. Indeed the place was too well defended to be carried by an open attempt; for besides the garrison and the crew of the galeon, there were in it at least a thousand men well armed, who had marched thither as guards to the treasure, when it was brought down from the city of *Mexico*: For the roads thereabout are so much infested either by independent *Indians* or fugitives, that the *Spaniards* never trust the silver without an armed force to protect it. And besides, had the strength of the place been less considerable, and such as might have appeared not superior to the efforts of our squadron, yet a declared attack would have prevented us from receiving any advantages from its success; since upon the first discovery of our squadron, all the treasure would have been ordered into the country, and in a few hours would have been out of our reach; so that our conquest would have been only a desolate town, where we should have found nothing that could have been of the least consequence to us.

For these reasons, the surprisal of the place was the only method that could at all answer our purpose; and therefore the manner in which Mr. *Anson* proposed to conduct this enterprize was, by setting sail with the squadron in the evening, time enough to arrive at the port in the night; and as there is no danger on that coast, he would have stood boldly for the harbour's mouth, where he expected to arrive, and might perhaps have entered it, before the *Spaniards* were acquainted with his designs: As soon as he had run into the harbour, he intended to have pusht two hundred of his men on shore in his boats, who were immediately to attempt the fort markt (C) in the plan mentioned in the preceding chapter, and inserted towards the beginning of the third book; whilst he, the Commodore, with his ships, was employed in firing upon the town, and the other batteries. And these different operations, which would have been executed with great regularity, could hardly have failed of succeeding against an enemy, who would have been prevented by the suddenness of the attack, and by the want of day-light, from concerting any measures for their defence; so that it was extremely probable that we should have carried the fort by storm; and then the other batteries, being open behind, must have been soon abandoned; after which, the town, and its Inhabitants, and all the treasure, must necessarily have fallen into our hands; for the place is so cooped up with mountains, that it is scarcely possible to escape out of it, but by the great road, markt (H.H.) in the plan, which passes under the fort. This was the project which the Commodore had settled in general in his thoughts; but when he began to inquire into such circumstances as were necessary to be considered in order to regulate the particulars of its execution, he found there was a difficulty, which, being insuperable, occasioned the enterprize to be laid aside: For on examining the prisoners about the winds which prevail near the shore, he learnt (and it was afterwards confirmed by the officers of our cutters) that nearer in shore there was always a dead calm for the greatest part of the night, and that towards morning, when a gale sprung up, it constantly blew off the land; so that the setting sail from our present station in the evening, and arriving at *Acapulco* before day-light, was impossible.

This scheme, as hath been said, was formed by the Commodore, upon a supposition that the galeon was detained till the next year: But as this was a matter of opinion only, and not founded on intelligence, and there was a possibility that she might still put to sea in a short time, the Commodore thought it prudent to continue his cruise upon this station, as long as the necessary attention to his stores of wood and water, and to the convenient season for his future passage to *China*, would give him leave; and therefore, as the Cutters had been ordered to remain before *Acapulco* till the 23d of *March*, the squadron did not change its position till that day; when the Cutters not appearing, we were in some pain for them, apprehending they might have suffered either from the enemy or the weather; but we were relieved from our concern the next morning, when we discovered them, though at a great distance and to the leeward of the squadron: We bore down to them and took them up, and were informed by them, that, conformable to their orders, they had left their station the day before, without having seen any thing of the galeon; and we found, that the reason of their being so far to the leeward of us was a strong current, which had driven the whole squadron to windward.

And here it is necessary to mention, that, by information which was afterwards received, it appeared that this prolongation of our cruise was a very prudent measure, and afforded us no contemptible chance of seizing the treasure, on which we had so long fixed our thoughts. For it seems, after the embargo was laid on the galeon, as is before mentioned, the persons principally interested in the cargoe sent several expresses to *Mexico*, to beg that she might still be permitted to depart: For as they knew, by the accounts sent from *Paita*, that we had not more than three hundred men in all, they insisted that there was nothing to be feared from us; for that the galeon (carrying above twice as many hands as our whole squadron) would be greatly an overmatch for us. And though the Viceroy was inflexible, yet, on the account of their representation, she was kept ready for the sea for near three weeks after the first order came to detain her.

When we had taken up the Cutters, all the ships being joined, the Commodore made a signal to speak with their Commanders; and upon enquiry into the stock of fresh water remaining on board the squadron, it was found to be so very slender, that we were under a necessity of quitting our station to procure a fresh supply: And consulting what place was the properest for this purpose, it was agreed, that the harbour of *Seguataneo* or *Chequetan* being the nearest to us, was, on that account, the most eligible; and it was therefore immediately resolved to make the best of our way thither: And that, even while we were recruiting our water, we might not totally abandon our views upon the galeon, which perhaps, upon certain intelligence of our being employed at *Chequetan*, might venture to slip out to sea, our Cutter, under the command of Mr. *Hughes*, the Lieutenant of the *Tryal* Prize, was ordered to cruise off the port of *Acapulco* for twenty-four days; that if the galeon should set sail in that interval, we might be speedily informed of it. In pursuance of these resolutions we endeavoured to ply to the westward, to gain our intended port, but were often interrupted in our progress by calm and adverse currents: In these intervals we employed ourselves in taking out the most valuable part of the cargoes of the *Carmelo* and *Carmin* prizes, which two ships we intended to destroy as soon as we had tolerably cleared them. By the first of *April* we were so far advanced towards *Seguataneo*, that we thought it expedient to send out two boats, that they might range along the coast, and discover the watering place; they were gone some days, and our water being now very short, it was a particular felicity to us that we met with daily supplies of turtle, for had we been entirely confined to salt provisions, we must have suffered extremely in so warm a climate. Indeed our present circumstances were sufficiently alarming, and gave the most considerate amongst us as much concern as any of the numerous perils we had hitherto encountered; for our boats, as we conceived by their not returning, had not as yet discovered a place proper to water at, and by the leakage of our cask and other accidents, we had not ten days water on board the whole squadron: So that from the known difficulty of procuring water on this coast, and the little reliance we had on the Buccaneer writers (the only guides we had to trust to) we were apprehensive of being soon exposed to a calamity, the most terrible of any in the long disheartning catalogue of the distresses of a seafaring life.

But these gloomy suggestions were soon happily ended; for our boats returned on the 5th of *April*, having discovered a place proper for our purpose, about seven miles to the westward of the rocks of *Seguataneo*, which, by the description they gave of it, appeared to be the port, called by *Dampier* the harbour of *Chequetan*.[1] The success of our boats was highly agreeable to us, and they were ordered out again the next day, to sound the harbour and its entrance, which they had represented as very narrow. At their return they reported the place to be free from any danger; so that on the 7th we stood in, and that evening came to an anchor in eleven fathom. The *Gloucester* came to an anchor at the same time with us; but the *Carmelo* and the *Carmin* having fallen to leeward, the *Tryal* Prize was ordered to join them, and to bring them in, which in two or three days she effected.

Thus, after a four months continuance at sea from the leaving of *Quibo*, and having but six days water on board, we arrived in the harbour of *Chequetan*, the description of which, and of the adjacent coast, shall be the business of the ensuing chapter.

CHAP. XII.

Description of the harbour of *Chequetan*, and of the adjacent coast and country.

THE harbour of *Chequetan*, which we here propose to describe, lies in the latitude of 17° : 36′ North, and is about thirty leagues to the westward of *Acapulco*. It is easy to be discovered by any ship that will keep well in with the land, especially by such as range down coast from *Acapulco*, and will attend to the following particulars.

There is a beach of sand, which extends eighteen leagues from the harbour of *Acapulco* to the westward, against which the sea breaks with such violence, that it is impossible to land in any part of it : But yet the ground is so clean, that ships, in the fair season, may anchor in great safety, at the distance of a mile or two from the shore. The land adjacent to this beach is generally low, full of villages, and planted with a great number of trees; and on the tops of some small eminencies there are several look-out towers; so that the face of the country affords a very agreeable prospect: For the cultivated part, which is the part here described, extends some leagues back from the shore, and there appears to be bounded by the chain of mountains, which stretch to a considerable distance on either side of *Acapulco*. It is a most remarkable particularity, that in this whole extent, being, as hath been mentioned, eighteen leagues, and containing, in appearance, the most populous and best planted district of the whole coast, there should be neither canoes, boats, nor any other embarkations either for fishing, coasting, or for pleasure.

The beach here described is the surest guide for finding the harbour of *Chequetan*; for five miles to the westward of the extremity of this beach there appears a hummock, which at first makes like an island, and is in shape not very unlike the hill of *Petaplan* hereafter mentioned, though much smaller. Three miles to the westward of this hummock is a white rock lying near the shore, which cannot easily be passed by unobserved: It is about two cables length from the land, and lies in a large bay about nine leagues over. The westward point of this bay is the hill of *Petaplan*, which is represented in the same plate with the

237

view of the Island of *Quicara* and *Quibo,* and is here inserted. This hill too, like the forementioned hummock, may be at first mistaken for an island, though it be, in reality, a peninsula, which is joined to the Continent by a low and narrow Isthmus, covered over with shrubs and small trees. The bay of *Seguataneo* extends from this hill a great way to the westward; and it appears, by a plan of the bay of *Petaplan,* which is part of that of *Seguataneo,* and is here annexed, that at a small distance from the hill, and opposite to the entrance of the bay, there is an assemblage of rocks, which are white from the excrements of boobies and tropical birds. Four of these rocks are high and large, and, together with several smaller ones, are by the help of a little imagination, pretended to resemble the form of a cross, and are called the *White Friars.* These rocks, as appears by the plan, bear W. by N. from *Petaplan;* and about seven miles to the westward of them lies the harbour of *Chequetan,* which is still more minutely distinguished by a large and single rock, that rises out of the water a mile and an half distant from its entrance, and bears $S\frac{1}{2}$ W. from the middle of it. The appearance of the entrance of this harbour is very accurately represented in the annexed plate, where (e) is the East point of the harbour, and (d) the West, the forementioned rock being marked (f). In the same view (a) is a large sandy bay, but where there is no landing; (b) are four remarkable white rocks; and from the island (c) there runs a large bay to the westward.

These are the infallible marks by which the harbour of *Chequetan* may be known to those who keep well in with the land; and I must add, that the coast is no ways to be dreaded from the middle of *October* to the beginning of *May,* nor is there then any danger from the winds: Though in the remaining part of the year there are frequent and violent tornadoes, heavy rains, and hard gales in all directions of the compass. But as to those who keep at any considerable distance from the coast, there is no other method to be taken by them for finding this harbour, than that of making it by its latitude: For there are so many ranges of mountains rising one upon the back of another within land, that no drawings of the appearance of the coast can be at all depended on, when off at sea; for every little change of distance or variation of position brings new mountains in view, and produces an infinity of different prospects, which would render all attempts of delineating the aspect of the coast impossible.

This may suffice as to the methods of discovering the harbour of *Chequetan*. A plan of the harbour itself is represented in the annexed plate; where it appears, that its entrance is but about half a mile broad; the two points which form it, and which are faced with rocks that are almost perpendicular, bear from each other S. E. and N. W. The harbour is invironed on all sides, except to the westward, with high mountains overspread with trees. The passage into it is very safe on either side of the rock that lies off the mouth of it, though we, both in coming in and going out, left it to the eastward. The ground without the harbour is gravel mixed with stones, but within it is a soft mud: And it must be remembered, that in coming to an anchor a good allowance should be made for a large swell which frequently causes a great send of the sea; as likewise, for the ebbing and flowing of the tide, which we observed to be about five feet, and that it set nearly E. and W.

The watering place is situated in that part of the harbour, which is taken notice of in the plan for fresh water. This, during the whole time of our stay, had the appearance of a large standing lake, without any visible outlet into the sea, from which it is separated by a part of the strand. The origin of this lake is a spring; that bubbles out of the ground near half a mile within the country. We found the water a little brackish, but more considerably so towards the sea-side; for the nearer we advanced towards the spring-head the softer and fresher it proved. This laid us under a necessity of filling all our casks from the furthest part of the lake, and occasioned us some trouble; and would have proved still more difficult, had it not been for our particular management, which for the conveniency of it deserves to be recommended to all who shall hereafter water at this place. Our method consisted in making use of canoes which drew but little water; for, loading them with a number of small cask, they easily got up the lake to the spring-head, and the small cask being there filled were in the same manner transported back again to the beach, where some of our hands always attended to start them into other casks of a larger size.

Though this lake, during our continuance there, appeared to have no outlet into the sea, yet there is reason to suppose that in the wet season it overflows the strand, and communicates with the ocean; for *Dampier*, who was formerly here, speaks of it as a large river. Indeed there must be a very great body of water amassed before the lake can rise high enough to overflow the strand; for the neighbouring country is so low, that great part of it must be covered with water, before it can run out over the beach.

As the country in the neighbourhood, particularly the tract which we have already described, appeared to be well peopled, and cultivated, we hoped thence to have procured fresh provision and other refreshments which we stood in need of. With this view, the morning after we came to an anchor, the Commodore ordered a party of forty men, well armed, to march into the country, and to endeavour to discover some town or village, where they were to attempt to set on foot a correspondence with the inhabitants; for we doubted not, if we could have any intercourse with them, but that by presents of some of the coarse merchandise, with which our prizes abounded (which, though of little consequence to us, would to them be extremely valuable) we should allure them to furnish us with whatever fruits or fresh provisions were in their power. Our people were directed on this occasion to proceed with the greatest circumspection, and to make as little ostentation of hostility as possible; for we were sensible, that we could meet with no wealth here worth our notice, and that what necessaries we really wanted, we should in all probability be better supplied with by an open amicable traffic, than by violence and force of arms. But this endeavour of opening an intercourse with the inhabitants proved ineffectual; for towards evening, the party which had been ordered to march into the country, returned greatly fatigued with their unusual exercise, and some of them so far spent as to have fainted by the way, and to be obliged to be brought back upon the shoulders of their companions. They had marched in all, as they conceived, about ten miles, in a beaten road, where they often saw the fresh dung of horses or mules. When they had got about five miles from the harbour, the road divided between the mountains into two branches, one running to the East, and the other to the West: After some deliberation about the course they should take, they agreed to pursue the eastern road, which, when they had followed for some time, led them at once into a large plain or Savannah; on one side of which they discovered a centinel on horseback with a pistol in his hand: It was supposed that when they first saw him he was asleep, but his horse startled at the glittering of their arms, and turning round suddenly rode off with his master, who was very near being unhorsed in the surprize, but he recovered his seat, and escaped with the loss only of his hat and his pistol which he dropped on the ground. Our people ran after him, in hopes of discovering some village or habitation which he would retreat to, but as he had the advantage of being on horseback, he soon lost sight of them. However, they were unwilling to come back without making some discovery, and therefore still followed the track they were in; but the heat of the day encreasing, and finding no water to quench their thirst, they were first obliged to halt, and then resolved to return; for as they saw no signs of plantations or cultivated land, they had no reason to believe that there was any village or settlement near them: But to leave no means untried of procuring some inter-course with the people, the officers stuck up several poles in the road, to which were affixed declarations, written in *Spanish*, encouraging the inhabitants to come down to the harbour, and to traffic with us, giving the strongest assurances of a kind reception, and faithful pay-ment for any provisions they should bring us. This was doubtless a very prudent measure, but yet it produced no effect; for we never saw any of them during the whole time of our continuance at this port of *Chequetan*. But had our men upon the division of the path, taken the western road instead of the eastern, it would soon have led them to a village or town, which in some *Spanish* manuscripts is mentioned as being in the neighbourhood of this port, and which we afterwards learnt was not above two miles from that turning.

And on this occasion I cannot help mentioning another adventure, which happened to some of our people in the bay of *Petaplan*, as it may help to give the reader a just idea of the temper of the inhabitants of this part of the world. Sometime after our arrival at *Chequetan*, Lieutenant *Brett* was sent by the Commodore, with two of our boats under his command, to examine the coast to the eastward, particularly to make observations on the bay and watering place of *Petaplan*, a plan of which has been already inserted in this chapter. As Mr. *Brett* with one of the boats was preparing to go on shore towards the hill of *Petaplan*, he, accidentally looking across the bay, perceived, on the opposite strand, three small squadrons of horse parading upon the beach, and seeming to advance towards the place where he proposed to land. On sight of this he immediately put off the boat, though he had but sixteen men with him, and stood over the bay towards them: And he soon came near enough to perceive that they were mounted on very sightly horses, and were armed with carbines and lances. On seeing him make towards them, they formed upon the beach, and seemed resolved to dispute his landing, firing several distant shot at him as he drew near; till at last the boat being arrived within a reasonable distance of the most advanced squadron, Mr. *Brett* ordered his people to fire, upon which this resolute cavalry instantly ran in great confusion into the wood, through a small opening which appears in the plan. In this precipitate flight one of their horses fell down and threw his rider; but, whether he was wounded or not, we could not learn, for both man and horse soon got up again, and followed the rest into the wood. In the mean time the other two squadrons, who were drawn up at a great distance behind, out of the reach of our shot, were calm spectators of the rout of their comrades; for they had halted on our first approach, and never advanced afterwards. It was doubtless fortunate for our people that the enemy acted with so little prudence, and exerted so little spirit; for had they concealed themselves till our men had landed, it is scarcely possible but the whole boat's crew must have fallen into their hands; since the *Spaniards* were not much short of two hundred, and the whole number with Mr. *Brett*, as hath been already mentioned, only amounted to sixteen.[1] However, the discovery of so considerable a force, collected in this bay of *Petaplan*, obliged us constantly to keep a boat or two before it: For we were apprehensive that the Cutter, which we had left to cruise off *Acapulco*, might, on her return, be surprized by the enemy, if she did not receive timely information of her danger. But now to proceed with the account of the harbour of *Chequetan*.

After our unsuccessful attempt to engage the people of the country, to furnish us with the necessaries we wanted, we desisted from any more endeavours of the same nature, and were obliged to be contented with what we could procure for ourselves in the neighbourhood of the port. We caught fish here in tolerable quantities, especially when the smoothness of the water permitted us to hale the Seyne. Amongst the rest, we got here cavallies, breams, mullets, soles, fiddle-fish, sea eggs, and lobsters: And we here, and in no other place, met with that extraordinary fish called the *Torpedo*, or numbing fish, which is in shape very like the fiddle-fish, and is not to be known from it but by a brown circular spot of about the bigness of a crown piece near the center of its back; perhaps its figure will be better understood, when I say it is a flat fish, much resembling the thornback. This fish, the *Torpedo*, is indeed of a most singular nature, productive of the strangest effects on the human body: For whoever handles it, or happens even to set his foot upon it, is presently seized with a numbness all over him; but which is more distinguishable, in that limb which was in immediate contact with it. The same effect too will be in some degree produced by touching the fish with any thing held in the hand; for I myself had a considerable degree of numbness conveyed to my right arm, through a walking cane which I rested on the body of the fish for some time; and I make no doubt but I should have been much more sensibly affected, had not the fish been near expiring when I made the experiment: For it is observable that this influence acts with most vigour when the fish is first taken out of the water, and entirely ceases when it is dead, so that it may be then handled or even eaten without any inconvenience. I shall only add that the numbness of my arm on this occasion did not go off on a sudden, as the accounts of some Naturalists gave me reason to expect, but diminished gradually, so that I had some sensation of it remaining till the next day.

To the account given of the fish we met with here, I must add, that though turtle now grew scarce, and we met with none in this harbour of *Chequetan*, yet our boats, which, as I have mentioned, were stationed off *Petaplan*, often supplied us therewith; and though this was a food that we had now been so long as it were confined to, (for it was the only fresh provisions which we had tasted for next six months) yet we were far from being cloyed with it, or from finding that the relish we had of it at all diminished.

The animals we met with on shore were principally guanos, with which the country abounds, and which are by some reckoned delicious food. We saw no beasts of prey here, except we should esteem that amphibious animal, the alligator, as such, several of which our people discovered, but none of them very large. However, we were satisfied that there were great numbers of tygers in the woods, though none of them came in sight; for we every morning found the beach near the watering place imprinted very thick with their footsteps: But we never apprehended any mischief from them; for they are by no means so fierce as the *Asiatic* or *African* tyger, and are rarely, if ever known, to attack mankind. Birds were here in sufficient plenty; for we had abundance of pheasants of different kinds, some of them of an uncommon size, but they were very dry and tasteless food. And besides these we had a variety of smaller birds, particularly parrots, which we often killed for food.

The fruits and vegetable refreshments at this place were neither plentiful, nor of the best kinds: There were, it is true, a few bushes scattered about the woods, which supplied us with limes, but we scarcely could procure enough for our present use; and these, with a small plumb of an agreeable acid, called in *Jamaica* the *Hog-Plumb*, together with another fruit called a *Papah*, were the only fruits to be found in the woods. Nor is there any other useful vegetable here worth mentioning, except brook-lime: This indeed grew in great quantities near the fresh-water banks; and, as it was esteemed an antiscorbutic, we fed upon it frequently, though its extreme bitterness made it very unpalatable.

These are the articles most worthy of notice in this harbour of *Chequetan*. I shall only mention a particular of the coast lying to the westward of it, that to the eastward having been already described. As Mr. *Anson* was always attentive to whatever might be of consequence to those who might frequent these seas hereafter; and, as we had observed, that there was no double land to the westward of *Chequetan*, which stretched out to a considerable distance, with a kind of opening, which appeared not unlike the inlet to some harbour, the Commodore, soon after we came to an anchor, sent a boat to discover it more accurately, and it was found, on a nearer examination, that the two hills, which formed the double land, were joined together by a valley, and that there was no harbour nor shelter between them.

By all that hath been said it will appear, that the conveniencies of this port of *Chequetan*, particularly in the articles of refreshment, are not altogether such as might be desired: But yet, upon the whole, it is a place of considerable consequence, and the knowledge of it may be of great import to future cruisers. For it is the only secure harbour in a vast extent of coast, except *Acapulco*, which is in the hands of the enemy. It lies at a proper distance from *Acapulco* for the convenience of such ships as may have any designs on the *Manila* galeon; and it is a place, where wood and water may be taken in with great security, in despight of the efforts of the inhabitants of the adjacent district: For there is but one narrow path which leads through the woods into the country, and this is easily to be secured by a very small party, against all the strength the *Spaniards* in that neighbourhood can muster. After this account of *Chequetan*, and the coast contiguous to it, we shall return to the recital of our own proceedings.

CHAP. XIII.

Our proceedings at *Chequetan* and on the adjacent coast, till our setting sail for *Asia*.

THE next morning, after our coming to an anchor in the harbour of *Chequetan*, we sent about ninety of our men well armed on shore, forty of whom were ordered to march into the country, as hath been mentioned, and the remaining fifty were employed to cover the watering place, and to prevent any interruption from the natives.

Here we compleated the unloading of the *Carmelo* and *Carmin*, which we had begun at sea; at least, we took out of them the indico, cacao, and cochineal, with some iron for ballast, which were all the goods we intended to preserve, though they did not amount to a tenth of their cargoes. Here too it was agreed, after a mature consultation, to destroy the *Tryal*'s Prize, as well as the *Carmelo* and *Carmin*, whose fate had been before resolved on. Indeed the ship was in good repair and fit for the sea; but as the whole numbers on board our squadron did not amount to the complement of a fourth rate man of war, we found it was impossible to divide them into three ships, without rendering them incapable of navigating in safety in the tempestuous weather we had reason to expect on the coast of *China*, where we supposed we should arrive about the time of the change of the monsoons. These considerations determined the Commodore to destroy the *Tryal* Prize, and to reinforce the *Gloucester* with the greatest part of her crew.[1] And in consequence of this resolve, all the stores on board the *Tryal* Prize were removed into the other ships, and the Prize herself, with the *Carmelo* and *Carmin*, were prepared for scuttling with all the expedition we were masters of; but the greatest difficulties we were under in laying in a store of water (which have been already touched on) together with the necessary repairs of our rigging and other unavoidable occupations, took us up so much time, and found us such unexpected employment, that it was near the end of *April* before we were in a condition to leave the place.

During our stay here, there happened an incident, which, as it proved the means of convincing our friends in *England* of our safety, which for some time they had despaired of, and were then in doubt about, I shall beg leave particularly to recite. I have observed, in the preceding chapter, that from this harbour of *Chequetan* there was but one path-way which led through the woods into the country. This we found much beaten, and were thence convinced, that it was well known to the inhabitants. As it passed by the spring-head, and was the only avenue by which the *Spaniards* could approach us, we, at some distance beyond the spring-head, felled several large trees, and laid them one upon the other across the path; and at this barricadoe we constantly kept a guard: And we besides ordered our men employed in watering to have their arms ready, and, in case of any alarm, to march instantly to this post. And though our principal intention was to prevent our being disturbed by any sudden attack of the enemy's horse, yet it answered another purpose, which was not in itself less important; this was to hinder our own people from straggling singly into the country, where we had reason to believe they would be surprized by the *Spaniards*, who would doubtless be extremely solicitous to pick up some of them, in hopes of getting intelligence of our future designs. To avoid this inconvenience, the strictest orders were given to the centinels, to let no person whatever pass beyond their post: But notwithstanding this precaution, we missed one *Lewis Leger*, who was the Commodore's Cook; and as he was a *Frenchman*, and suspected to be a Papist, it was by some imagined that he had deserted, with a view of betraying all that he knew to the enemy; but this appeared, by the event, to be an ill-grounded surmise; for it was afterwards known, that he had been taken by some *Indians*, who carried him prisoner to *Acapulco*, from whence he was transferred to *Mexico*, and then to *Vera Cruz*, where he was shipped on board a vessel bound to *Old Spain*: And the vessel being obliged by some accident to put into *Lisbon*, *Leger* escaped on shore, and was by the *British* Consul sent from thence to *England*; where he brought the first authentick account of the safety of the Commodore, and of what he had done in the *South-Seas*.[1] The relation he gave of his own seizure was, that he rambled into the woods at some distance from the barricadoe, where he had first attempted to pass, but had been stopped and threatned to be punished; that his principal view was to get a quantity of limes for his Master's store; and that in this occupation he was surprized unawares by four *Indians*, who stripped him naked, and carried him in that condition to *Acapulco*, exposed to the scorching heat of the sun, which at that time of the year shone with its greatest violence: And afterwards at *Mexico* his treatment in prison was sufficiently severe, and the whole course of his captivity was a continued instance of the hatred, which the *Spaniards* bear to all those who endeavour to disturb them in the peaceable possession of the coasts of the *South-Seas*. Indeed *Leger's* fortune was, upon the whole, extremely singular; for after the hazards he had run in the Commodore's squadron, and the severities he had suffered in his long confinement amongst the enemy, a more fatal disaster attended him on his return to *England*: For though, when he arrived in *London*, some of Mr. *Anson's* friends interested themselves in relieving him from the poverty to which his captivity had reduced him; yet he did not long enjoy the benefit of their humanity, for he was killed in an insignificant night brawl, the cause of which could scarcely be discovered.

And here I must observe, that though the enemy never appeared in sight during our stay in this harbour, yet we perceived that there were large parties of them incamped in the woods about us; for we could see their smokes, and could thence determine that they were posted in a circular line surrounding us at a distance; and just before our coming away they seemed, by the increase of their fires, to have received a considerable reinforcement. But to return:

Towards the latter end of *April*, the unloading of our three prizes, our wooding and watering, and, in short, all our proposed employments at the harbour of *Chequetan*, were compleated: So that, on the 27th of *April*, the *Tryal's* Prize, the *Carmelo* and the *Carmin*, all which we here intended to destroy, were towed on shore and scuttled, and a quantity of combustible materials were distributed in their upper works; and the next morning the *Centurion* and the *Gloucester* weighed anchor, but as there was but little wind, and that not in their favour, they were obliged to warp out of the harbour. When they had reached the offing, one of the boats was dispatched back again to set fire to our prizes, which was accordingly executed. And a canoe was left fixed to a grapnel in the middle of the harbour, with a bottle in it well corked, inclosing a letter to Mr. *Hughes,* who commanded the Cutter, which was ordered to cruise before the port of *Acapulco*, when we came off that station. And on this occasion I must mention more particularly than I have yet done, the views of the Commodore in leaving the Cutter before that port.

When we were necessitated to make for *Chequetan* to take in our water, Mr. *Anson* considered that our being in that harbour would soon be known at *Acapulco*; and therefore he hoped, that on the intelligence of our being employed in port, the galeon might put to sea, especially as *Chequetan* is so very remote from the course generally steered by the galeon: He therefore ordered the Cutter to cruise twenty-four days off the port of *Acapulco*, and her Commander was directed, on perceiving the galeon under sail, to make the best of his way to the Commodore at *Chequetan*. As the *Centurion* was doubtless a much better sailor than the galeon, Mr. *Anson*, in this case, resolved to have got to sea as soon as possible, and to have pursued the galeon across the *Pacific* Ocean: And supposing he should not have met with her in his passage (which considering that he would have kept nearly the same parallel, was not very improbable) yet he was certain of arriving off Cape *Espiritu Santo*, on the Island of *Samal*, before her; and that being the first land she makes on her return to the *Philippines*, we could not have failed to have fallen in with her, by cruising a few days in that station. But the Viceroy of *Mexico* ruined this project, by keeping the galeon in the port of *Acapulco* all that year.

The letter left in the canoe for Mr. *Hughes*, the Commander of the Cutter, (the time of whose return was now considerably elapsed) directed him to go back immediately to his former station before *Acapulco*, where he would find Mr. *Anson*, who resolved to cruise for him there for a certain number of days; after which it was added, that the Commodore would return to the southward to join the rest of the squadron. This last article was inserted to deceive the *Spaniards*, if they got possession of the canoe, (as we afterwards learnt they did) but could not impose on Mr. *Hughes*, who well knew that the Commodore had no squadron to join, nor any intention of steering back to *Peru*.

Being now in the offing of *Chequetan*, bound cross the vast *Pacific* Ocean in our way to *China*, we were impatient to run off the coast as soon as possible; for as the stormy season was approaching apace, and as we had no further views in the *American* seas, we had hoped that nothing would have prevented us from standing to the westward, the moment we got out of the harbour of *Chequetan*: And it was no small mortification to us, that our necessary employment there had detained us so much longer than we expected; and now we were farther detained by the absence of the Cutter, and the standing towards *Acapulco* in search of her. Indeed, as the time of her cruise had been expired for near a fortnight, we suspected that she had been discovered from the shore; and that the Governor of *Acapulco* had thereupon sent out a force to seize her, which, as she carried but six hands, was no very difficult enterprize. However, this being only conjecture, the Commodore, as soon as he was got clear of the harbour of *Chequetan,* stood along the coast to the eastward in search of her: And to prevent her from passing by us in the dark, we brought to every night; and the *Gloucester,* whose station was a league within us towards the shore, carried a light, which the Cutter could not but perceive, if she kept along shore, as we supposed she would do; and as a farther security, the *Centurion* and the *Gloucester* alternately showed two false fires every half hour. Indeed, had she escaped us, she would have found orders in the canoe to have returned immediately before *Acapulco,* where Mr. *Anson* proposed to cruise for her some days.

By *Sunday,* the 2d of *May,* we were advanced within three leagues of *Acapulco,* and having seen nothing of our boat, we gave her over for lost, which, besides the compassionate concern for our ship-mates, and for what it was apprehended they might have suffered, was in itself a misfortune, which, in our present scarcity of hands, we were all greatly interested in: For the crew of the Cutter, consisting of six men and the Lieutenant, were the very flower of our people, purposely pickt out for this service, and known to be every one of them of tried and approved resolution, and as skilful seamen as ever trod a deck. However, as it was the general belief among us that they were taken and carried into *Acapulco,* the Commodore's prudence suggested a project which we hoped would recover them. This was founded on our having many *Spanish* and *Indian* prisoners in our possession, and a number of sick Negroes, who could be of no service to us in the navigating of the ship. The Commodore therefore wrote a letter the same day to the Governor of *Acapulco,* telling him, that he would release them all, provided the Governor returned the Cutter's crew; and the letter was dispatched the same afternoon by a *Spanish* officer, of whose honour we had a good opinion, and who was furnished with a launch belonging to one of our prizes, and a crew of six other prisoners who all gave their parole for their return. The officer too, besides the Commodore's letter, carried with him a joint petition signed by all the rest of the prisoners, beseeching his Excellence to acquiesce in the terms proposed for their liberty. From a consideration of the number of our prisoners, and the quality of some of them, we did not doubt but the Governor would readily comply with Mr *Anson's* proposal, and therefore we kept plying on and off the whole night, intending to keep well in with the land, that we might receive an answer at the limited time, which was the next day, being *Monday*: But both on the *Monday* and *Tuesday* we were driven so far off shore, that we could not hope to receive any answer; and on the *Wednesday* morning we found ourselves fourteen leagues from the harbour of *Acapulco*; but as the wind was now favourable, we pressed forwards with all our sail, and did not doubt of getting in with the land in a few hours. Whilst we were thus standing in, the man at the mast-head called out that he saw a boat under sail at a considerable distance to the South eastward: This we took for granted was the answer of the Governor to the Commodore's message, and we instantly edged towards it; but when we drew nearer, we found to our unspeakable joy that it was our own Cutter. While she was still at a distance we imagined that she had been discharged out of the port of *Acapulco* by the Governor; but when she drew nearer, the wan and meager countenances of the crew, the length of their beards, and the feeble and hollow tone of their voices, convinced us that they had suffered much greater hardships than could be expected from even the severities of a *Spanish* prison. They were obliged to be helped into the ship, and were immediately put to bed, and with rest, and nourishing diet, which they were plentifully supplied with from the Commodore's table, they recovered their health and vigour apace: And now we learnt that they had kept the sea the whole time of their absence, which was above six weeks, that when they had finished their cruise before *Acapulco*, and had just begun to ply to the westward in order to join the squadron, a strong adverse current had forced them down the coast to the eastward in spight of all their efforts; that at length their water being all expended, they were obliged to search the coast farther on to the eastward, in quest of some convenient landing-place, where they might get a fresh supply; that in this distress they ran upwards of eighty leagues to leeward, and found every where so large a surf, that there was not the least possibility of their landing; that they passed some days in this dreadful situation, without water, and having no other means left them to allay their thirst than sucking the blood of the turtle, which they caught; and at last, giving up all hopes of relief, the heat of the climate too augmenting their necessities, and rendring their sufferings insupportable, they abandoned themselves to despair, fully persuaded that they should perish by the most terrible of all deaths; but that they were soon after happily relieved by a most unexpected incident, for there fell so heavy a rain, that by spreading their sails horizontally, and by putting bullets in the centers of them to draw them to a point, they caught as much water, as filled all their cask; that immediately upon this fortunate supply they stood to the westward in quest of the Commodore; and being now luckily favoured by a strong current, they joined us in less than fifty hours, from the time they stood to the westward, after having been absent from us full forty-three days. Those who have an idea of the inconsiderable size of a Cutter belonging to a sixty gun ship, (being only an open boat about twenty-two feet in length) and who will attend to the various accidents to which she was exposed during a six weeks continuance alone, in the open ocean, on so impracticable and dangerous a coast, will readily own, that her return to us at last, after all the difficulties which she actually experienced, and the hazards to which she was each hour exposed, may be considered as little short of miraculous.

I cannot finish the article of this Cutter, without remarking how little reliance Navigators ought to have on the accounts of the Buccaneer writers: For though in this run of hers, eighty leagues to the eastward of *Acapulco*, she found no place where it was possible for a boat to land, yet those writers have not been ashamed to feign harbours and convenient watering places within these limits, thereby exposing such as should confide in their relations, to the risque of being destroyed by thirst.

I must farther add on this occasion, that when we stood near the port of *Acapulco*, in order to send our message to the Governor, and to receive his answer, Mr. *Brett* took that opportunity of delineating a view of the entrance of the port, and of the neighbouring coast, which, added to the plan of the place formerly mentioned, may be of considerable use hereafter, and is therefore annexed. In this plate (*a*) is the west point of the harbour called the *Griffo*, being in the latitude of

16° : 45'; (*b c*) is the Island bearing from the observer N. by E, three leagues distant; (*d*) is the east point of the harbour; (*e*) port *Marquis*; (*f*) *Sierra di Brea*; (*h*) a white rock in the harbour, and (*g*) watch towers.

And now having received our Cutter, the sole object of our coming a second time before *Acapulco*, the Commodore resolved not to lose a moment's time longer, but to run off the coast with the utmost expedition, both as the stormy season on the coast of *Mexico* was now approaching apace, and as we were apprehensive of having the westerly monsoon to struggle with when we came upon the coast of *China*; and therefore he no longer stood towards *Acapulco*, as he now wanted no answer from the Governor; but yet he resolved not to deprive his prisoners of the liberty, which he had promised them; so that they were all immediately embarked in two launches which belonged to our prizes, those from the *Centurion* in one launch, and those from the *Gloucester* in the other. The launches were well equipped with masts, sails and oars; and least the wind might prove unfavourable, they had a stock of water and provisions put on board them sufficient for fourteen days. There were discharged thirty-nine persons from on board the *Centurion*, and eighteen from the *Gloucester*, the greatest part of them *Spaniards*, the rest *Indians* and sick Negroes: But as our crews were very weak, we kept the Mulattoes and some of the stoutest of the Negroes, with a few *Indians* to assist us;[1] but we dismissed every *Spanish* prisoner whatever. We have since learnt, that these two launches arrived safe at *Acapulco*, where the prisoners could not enough extol the humanity with which they had been treated; and that the Governor, before their arrival, had returned a very obliging answer to the Commodore's letter, and had attended it with a present of two boats laden with the choicest refreshments and provisions which were to be got at *Acapulco*; but that these boats not having found our ships, were at length obliged to put back again, after having thrown all their provisions over-board in a storm which threatened their destruction.

The sending away our prisoners was our last transaction on the *American* coast; for no sooner had we parted with them, than we and the *Gloucester* made sail to the S. W, proposing to get a good offing from the land, where we hoped, in a few days, to meet with the regular trade-wind, which the accounts of former Navigators had represented as much brisker and steadier in this ocean, than in any other part of the globe: For it has been esteemed no uncommon passage, to run from hence to the eastermost parts of *Asia*, in two months; and we flattered ourselves that, we were as capable of making an expeditious passage, as any ships that had ever run this course before us: So that we hoped soon to gain the coast of *China*, for which we were now bound. And conformable to the general idea of this navigation given by former Voyagers, we considered it as free from all kinds of embarrassment of bad weather, fatigue, or sickness; and consequently we undertook it with alacrity, especially as it was no contemptible step towards our arrival at our native country, for which many of us by this time began to have great longings. Thus, on the 6th of *May*, we, for the last time, lost sight of the mountains of *Mexico*, persuaded, that in a few weeks we should arrive at the river of *Canton* in *China*, where we expected to meet with many *English* ships, and numbers of our countrymen; and hoped to enjoy the advantages of an amicable well frequented port, inhabited by a polished people, and abounding with the conveniencies and indulgencies of a civilized life; blessings, which now for near twenty months had never been once in our power. But there yet remains (before we take our leave of *America*) the consideration of a matter well worthy of attention, the discussion of which shall be referred to the ensuing chapter.

CHAP. XIV.

A brief account of what might have been expected from our squadron, had it arrived in the *South-Seas* in good time.

AFTER the recital of the transactions of the Commodore, and the ships under his command, on the coasts of *Peru* and *Mexico*, as contained in the preceding part of this book, it will be no useless digression to examine what the whole squadron might have been capable of achieving, had it arrived in those seas in so good a plight, as it would probably have done, had the passage round Cape *Horn* been attempted in a more seasonable time of the year. This disquisition may be serviceable to those who shall hereafter form projects of the like nature for that part of the world, or may be entrusted with their execution. And therefore I propose, in this chapter, to consider as succinctly as I can, the numerous advantages which the Public might have received from the operations of the squadron, had it set sail from *England* a few months sooner.

And first, I must suppose, that in the summer time we might have got round Cape *Horn* with an inconsiderable loss, and without any damage to our ships or rigging. For the Duke and Duchess of *Bristol*, who between them had above three hundred men, buried no more than two, from the coast of *Brazil* to *Juan Fernandes*,[1] and out of a hundred and eighty-three hands which were on board the Duke, there were only twenty-one sick of the scurvy, when they arrived at that Island: Whence as men of war are much better provided with all conveniencies than privateers, we might doubtless have appeared before *Baldivia* in full strength, and in a condition of entering immediately on action; and therefore, as that place was in a very defenceless state, its cannon incapable of service, and its garrison in great measure unarmed, it was impossible that it could have opposed our force, or that its half starved inhabitants, most of whom are convicts banished thither from other parts, could have had any other thoughts than that of submitting; and *Baldivia*, which is a most excellent port, being once taken, we should immediately have been terrible to the whole kingdom of *Chili*, and should doubtless have awed the most distant parts of the *Spanish* Empire. Indeed, it is far from improbable that, by a prudent use of our advantages, we might have given a violent shock to the authority of *Spain* on that whole Continent; and might have rendered some, at least, of her provinces independent. This would doubtless have turned the whole attention of the *Spanish* Ministry to that part of the world, where the danger would have been so pressing: And thence *Great-Britain*, and her Allies, might have been rid of the numerous embarrassments, which the wealth of the *Spanish Indies*, operating in conjunction with the *Gallick* intrigues, have constantly thrown in her way.

And that I may not be thought to over-rate the force of this squadron, by ascribing to it a power of overturning the *Spanish* Government in *America*, it is necessary to premise a few observations on the condition of the provinces bordering on the *South-Seas*, and on the disposition of the inhabitants, both *Spaniards* and *Indians*, at that time; by which it will appear, that there was great dissension amongst the Governors, and disaffection among the *Creolians*; that they were in want of arms and stores, and had fallen into a total neglect of all military regulations in their garrisons; and that as to the *Indians* on their frontier, they were universally discontented, and seemed to be watching with impatience for the favourable moment, when they might take a severe revenge for the barbarities they had groaned under for more than two ages; so that every circumstance concurred to facilitate the enterprizes of our squadron. Of all these particulars we were amply informed by the letters we took on board our prizes, none of these vessels, as I remember, having had the precaution to throw her papers over-board.

The ill blood amongst the Governors was greatly augmented by their apprehensions of our squadron; for every one being willing to have it believed, that the bad condition of his Government was not the effect of negligence, there were continual demands and remonstrances amongst them, in order to throw the blame upon each other. Thus, for instance, the President of St. *Jago* in *Chili*, the President of *Panama*, and many other Governors, and military officers, were perpetually soliciting the Viceroy of *Peru* to furnish them with the necessary supplies of money for putting their provinces and places in a proper state of defence to oppose our designs: But the customary answer of the

Viceroy to these representations was the emptiness of the royal chest at *Lima*, and the difficulties he was under to support the expences of his own Government; and in one of his letters, (which we intercepted,) he mentioned his apprehensions that he might even be necessitated to stop the pay of the troops and of the garrison of *Callao*, the key of the whole kingdom of *Peru*. Indeed he did at times remit to these Governors some part of their demands; but as what he sent them was greatly short of their wants, it rather tended to the raising jealousies and heartburnings amongst them, than contributed to the purposes for which it was intended.

And besides these mutual janglings amongst the Governors, the whole body of the people were extremely dissatisfied; for they were fully persuaded that the affairs of *Spain* for many years before had been managed by the influence of a particular foreign interest, which was altogether detached from the advantages of the *Spanish* Nation: So that the inhabitants of these distant provinces believed themselves to be sacrificed to an ambition, which never considered their convenience or interests, or paid any regard to the reputation of their name, or the honour of their country. That this was the temper of the *Creolian Spaniards* at that time, might be evinced from a hundred instances; but I shall content myself with one, which is indeed conclusive: This is the testimony of the *French* Mathematicians sent into *America*, to measure the magnitude of an equatorial degree of latitude. For in the relation of the murther of a surgeon belonging to their company in one of the cities of *Peru*, and of the popular tumult occasioned thereby, written by one of those astronomers, the author confesses, that the inhabitants, during the uproar, all joined in imprecations on their bad Governors, and bestowed the most abusive language upon the *French*, detesting them, in all probability, more particularly as belonging to a nation, to whose influence in the *Spanish* Counsels the *Spaniards* imputed all their misfortunes.

And whilst the *Creolian Spaniards* were thus dissatisfied, it appears by the letters we intercepted, that the *Indians*, on almost every frontier, were ripe for a revolt, and would have taken up arms on the slightest encouragement; in particular, the *Indians* in the southern parts of *Peru*; as likewise the *Arraucos*, and the rest of the *Chilian Indians*, the most powerful and terrible to the *Spanish* name of any on that Continent. For it seems, that in the disputes between the *Spaniards*

257

and the *Indians*, which happened some time before our arrival, the *Spaniards* had insulted the *Indians* with an account of the force, which they expected from *Old Spain* under the command of Admiral *Pizarro*, and had vaunted that he was coming thither to compleat the great work, which had been left unfinished by his ancestors. These threats alarmed the *Indians*, and made them believe that their extirpation was resolved on: For the *Pizarro's* being the first conquerors of that coast, the *Peruvian Indians* held the name, and all that bore it, in execration; not having forgot the destruction of their Monarchy, the massacre of their beloved *Inca*, *Atapalipa*, the extinction of their religion, and the slaughter of their ancestors; all perpetrated by the family of the *Pizarro's*. The *Chilian Indians* too abhorred a Chief descended from those, who, by their Lieutenants, had first attempted to inslave them, and had necessitated their Tribes, for more than a Century, to be continually wasting their blood in defence of their independency.

And let it not be supposed, that among those barbarous nations the traditions of such distant transactions could not be continued till the present times; for all who have been acquainted with that part of the world agree, that the *Indians*, in their publick feasts, and annual solemnities, constantly revive the memory of these tragick incidents; and those who have been present at these spectacles, have observed, that all the recitals and representations of this kind were received with an enthusiastick rage, and with such vehement emotions, as plainly evinced how strongly the memory of their former wrongs was implanted in them, and how acceptable the means of revenge would at all times prove. To this account I must add too, that the *Spanish* Governors themselves were so fully informed of the disposition of the *Indians*, and were so apprehensive of a general defection among them, that they employed all their industry to reconcile the most dangerous tribes, and to prevent them from immediately taking up arms: Among the rest, the President of *Chili* in particular made large concessions to the *Arraucos*, and the other *Chilian Indians*, by which, and by distributing considerable presents to their leading men, he at last got them to consent to a prolongation of the truce between the two nations. But these negotiations were not concluded at the time when we might have been in the *South-Seas*; and had they been compleated, yet the hatred of these *Indians* to the *Spaniards* was so great, that it would have been impossible for their Chiefs to have prevented their joining us.

Thus then it appears, that on our arrival in the *South-Sea* we might have found the whole coast unprovided with troops, and destitute even of arms: For we well knew from very particular intelligence, that there were not three hundred fire-arms, of which too the greatest part were matchlocks, in all the province of *Chili*. At the same time, the *Indians* would have been ready to revolt, the *Spaniards* disposed to mutiny, and the Governors enraged with each other, and each prepared to rejoice at the disgrace of his antagonist; whilst we, on the other hand, might have consisted of near two thousand men, the greatest part in health and vigour, all well-armed, and united under a Chief, whose enterprising genius (as we have seen) could not be depressed by a continued series of the most sinister events, and whose equable and prudent turn of temper would have remained unvaried, in the midst of the greatest degree of good success; and who besides possessed, in a distinguished manner, the two qualities, the most necessary in these uncommon undertakings; I mean, that of maintaining his authority, and preserving, at the same time, the affections of his people. Our other officers too, of every rank, appear, by the experience the Public hath since had of them, to have been equal to any enterprize they might have been charged with by their Commander: And our men (at all times brave if well conducted) in such a cause where treasure was the object, and under such leaders, would doubtless have been prepared to rival the most celebrated atchievements hitherto performed by *British* Mariners.

It cannot then be contested, but that *Baldivia* must have surrendered on the appearance of our squadron: After which, it may be presumed, that the *Arraucos*, the *Pulches* and *Penguinches*, inhabiting the banks of the river *Imperial*, about twenty-five leagues to the northward of this place, would have immediately taken up arms, being disposed as hath been already related, and encouraged by the arrival of so considerable a force in their neighbourhood. As these *Indians* can bring into the field near thirty thousand men, the greatest part of them horse, their first step would doubtless have been the invading the province of *Chili*, which they would have found totally unprovided of ammunition and weapons; and as its inhabitants are a luxurious and effeminate race, they would have been incapable, on such an emergency, of giving any opposition to this rugged enemy: So that it is no strained conjecture to imagine, that the *Indians* would have been soon masters of the whole country. And the other *Indians* on the frontiers of *Peru* being equally disposed with the *Arraucos* to shake off the *Spanish* yoke, it is highly probable, that they likewise would have embraced the occasion, and that a general insurrection would have taken place through all the *Spanish* territories in *South America*; in which case, the only resource left to the *Creolians* (dissatisfied as they were with the *Spanish* Government) would have been to have made the best terms they could with their *Indian* neighbours, and to have withdrawn themselves from the obedience of a Master, who had shown so little regard to their security. This last supposition may perhaps appear chimerical to those, who measure the possibility of all events by the scanty standard of their own experience; but the temper of the times, and the strong dislike of the natives to the measures then pursued by the *Spanish* Court, sufficiently evince at least its possibility. But not to insist on the presumption of a general revolt, it is sufficient for our purpose to conclude, that the *Arraucos* would scarcely have failed of taking arms on our appearance: For this alone would so far have embarrassed the enemy, that they would no longer have thought of opposing us; but would have turned all their care to the *Indian* affairs; as they still remember, with the utmost horror, the sacking of their cities, the rifling of their convents, the captivity of their wives and daughters, and the desolation of their country by these resolute savages, in the last war between the two nations. For it must be remembered, that this tribe of *Indians* have been frequently successful against the *Spaniards*, and possess at this time a large tract of country, which was formerly full of *Spanish* towns and villages, whose inhabitants were all either destroyed, or carried into captivity by the *Arraucos* and the neighbouring *Indians*, who, in a war against the *Spaniards*, never fail to join their forces.

But even, independent of an *Indian* revolt, there were but two places on all the coast of the *South-Sea*, which could be supposed capable of resisting our squadron; these were the cities of *Panama* and *Callao*: As to the first of these, its fortifications were so decayed, and it was so much in want of powder, that the Governor himself, in an intercepted letter, acknowledged it was incapable of being defended; so that I take it for granted, it would have given us but little trouble, especially if we had opened a communication across the Isthmus with our fleet on the other side: And for the city and port of *Callao*, its condition was not much better than that of *Panama*; for its walls are built upon the plain ground, without either outwork or ditch before them, and consist only of very slender feeble masonry, without any earth behind them; so that a battery of five or six pieces of cannon, raised any where within four or five hundred paces of the place, would have had a full view of the whole rampart, and would have opened it in a short time; and the breach hereby formed, as the walls are so extremely thin, could not have been difficult of ascent; for the ruins would have been but little higher than the surface of the ground; and it would have yielded this particular advantage to the assailants, that the bullets, which grazed upon it, would have driven before them such shivers of brick and stone, as would have prevented the garrison from forming behind it, supposing that the troops employed in the defence of the place, should have so far surpassed the usual limits of *Creolian* bravery, as to resolve to stand a general assault: Indeed, such a resolution cannot be imputed to them; for the garrison and people were in general dissatisfied with the Viceroy's behaviour, and were never expected to act a vigorous part. The Viceroy himself greatly apprehended that the Commodore would make him a visit at *Lima*, the capitol of the kingdom of *Peru*; to prevent which, if possible, he had ordered twelve gallies to be built at *Guaiaquil* and other places, which were intended to oppose the landing of our boats, and to hinder us from pushing our men on shore. But this was an impracticable project, and proceeded on the supposition that our ships, when we should land our men, would keep at such a distance, that these gallies, by drawing little water, would have been out of the reach of their guns; whereas the Commodore, before he had made such an attempt, would doubtless have been possessed of several prize ships, which he would not have hesitated to have run on shore for the protection of his boats; and besides there were many places on that coast, and one in particular in the neighbourhood of *Callao*, where there was good anchoring, though a great depth of water, within a cable's length of the shore; so that the cannon of the men of war would have swept all the coast to above a mile's distance from the water's edge, and would have effectually prevented any force from assembling, to oppose the landing and forming of our men: And the place had this additional advantage, that it was but two leagues distant from the city of *Lima*; so that we might have been at that city within four hours after we should have been first discovered from the shore. The place I have here in view is about two leagues South of *Callao*, and just to the northward of the head-land called, in *Frezier's* draught of that coast, *Morro Solar*. Here there is seventy or eighty fathom of water, within two cables length of the shore; and the *Spaniards* themselves were so apprehensive of our attempting to land there, that they had projected to build a fort close to the water; but there being no money in the royal chests, they could not go on with that work, and therefore they contented themselves with keeping a guard of an hundred horse there, that they might be sure to receive early notice of our appearance on that coast. Indeed some of them (as we were told) conceiving our management at sea to be as pusillanimous as their own, pretended that the Commodore would never dare to bring in his ships there, for fear that in so great a depth of water their anchors could not hold them.

And here let it not be imagined, that I am proceeding upon groundless and extravagant presumptions, when I conclude, that fifteen hundred or a thousand of our people, well conducted, should have been an over-match for any numbers the *Spaniards* could muster in *South America*. For not to mention the experience we had of them at *Paita* and *Petaplan*, it must be remembered, that our Commodore was extremely solicitous to have all his men trained to the dexterous use of their fire-arms; whereas the *Spaniards*, in this part of the world, were in great want of arms, and were very awkward in the management of the few they had: And though, on their repeated representations, the Court of *Spain* had ordered several thousand firelocks to be put on board *Pizarro's* squadron, yet those, it is evident, could not have been in *America* time enough to have been employed against us; so that by our arms, and our readiness in the use of them (not to insist on the timidity and softness of our enemy) we should in some degree have had the same advantages, which the *Spaniards* themselves had, in the first discovery of this country, against its naked and unarmed inhabitants.

And now let it be considered what were the events which we had to fear, or what were the circumstances which could have prevented us from giving law to all the coast of *South America*, and thereby cutting off from *Spain* the resources which she drew from those immense provinces. By sea there was no force capable of opposing us; for how soon soever we had sailed, *Pizarro's* squadron could not have sailed sooner than it did, and therefore could not have avoided the fate it met with: As we should have been masters of the port of *Chili*, we could there have supplied ourselves with the provisions we wanted in the greatest plenty; and from *Baldivia* to the equinoctial we ran no risque of losing our men by sickness, (that being of all climates the most temperate and healthy) nor of having our ships disabled by bad weather; and had we wanted hands to assist in the navigating our squadron, whilst a considerable part of our men were employed on shore, we could not have failed to getting whatever numbers we pleased in the ports we should have taken, and the prizes which would have fallen into our hands; and I must observe that the *Indians*, who are the principal sailors in that part of the world, are extremely docile, and dexterous, and though they are not fit to struggle with the inclemencies of a cold climate, yet in temperate seas they are most useful and laborious seamen.

Thus then it appears, what important revolutions might have been brought about by our squadron, had it departed from *England* as early as it ought to have done: And from hence it is easy to conclude, what immense advantages might have thence accrued to the public. For, as on our success it would have been impossible for the kingdom of *Spain* to have received any treasure from the provinces bordering on the *South-Seas*, or even to have had any communication with them, it is certain that the whole attention of that Monarchy must have been immediately employed in regaining the possession of these inestimable territories, either by force or compact. By the first of these methods it was scarcely possible they could succeed; for it must have been at least a twelvemonth from our arrival, before any ships from *Spain* could get into the *South-Seas*, and those perhaps separated, disabled, and sickly; and by that time they would have had no port in their possession, either to rendezvous at or to refit; whilst we might have been supplied across the Isthmus with whatever necessaries, stores, or even men we wanted, and might thereby have maintained our squadron in as good a plight, as when it first set sail from St. *Helens*. In short, it required but little prudence in the conduct of this business to have rendered all the efforts of *Spain*, seconded by the power of *France*, ineffectual, and to have maintained our conquests in defiance of them both: So that they must either have resolved to have left *Great-Britain* masters of the wealth of *South America*, (the principal support of all their destructive projects) or they must have submitted to her terms, and have been contented to receive these provinces back again, as an equivalent for those restrictions to their future ambition, which her prudence should have dictated to them.[1] Having thus discussed the prodigious weight which the operations of our Squadron might have added to the national influence of this kingdom, I shall here end this second book, referring to the next, the passage of the shattered remains of our force across the *Pacific* Ocean, and all their future transactions till the Commodore's arrival in *England*.

END OF BOOK II

BOOK III.

CHAP. I.

The run from the coast of *Mexico* to the *Ladrones* or *Marian* Islands.

WHEN, on the 6th of *May* 1742, we left the coast of *America*, we stood to the S. W. with a view of meeting with the N. E. trade-wind, which the accounts of former writers made us expect at seventy or eighty leagues distance from the land: We had besides another reason for standing to the southward, which was the getting into the latitude of 13 or 14° North; that being the parallel where the *Pacific* Ocean is most usually crossed, and consequently where the navigation is esteemed the safest: This last purpose we had soon answered, being in a day or two sufficiently advanced to the South. At the same time we were also farther from the shore, than we had presumed was necessary for the falling in with the trade-wind: But in this particular we were most grievously disappointed; for the wind still continued to the westward, or at best variable. As the getting into the N. E. trade was to us a matter of the last consequence, we stood more to the southward, and made many experiments to meet with it; but all our efforts were for a long time unsuccessful: So that it was seven weeks, from our leaving the coast, before we got into the true trade-wind. This was an interval, in which we believed we should well nigh have reached the eastermost parts of *Asia*: But we were so baffled with the contrary and variable winds, which for all that time perplexed us, that we were not as yet advanced above a fourth part of the way. The delay alone would have been a sufficient mortification; but there were other circumstances attending it, which rendered this situation not less terrible, and our apprehensions perhaps still greater than in any of our past distresses. For our two ships were by this time extremely crazy; and many days had not passed, before we discovered a spring in the foremast of the *Centurion,* which rounded about twenty-six inches of its circumference, and which was judged to be at least four inches deep:

And no sooner had our Carpenters secured this with fishing it, but the *Gloucester* made a signal of distress; and we learnt that she had a dangerous spring in her main-mast, twelve feet below the trussel-trees;[1] so that she could not carry any sail upon it. Our Carpenters, on a strict examination of this mast, found it so very rotten and decayed, that they judged it necessary to cut it down as low as it appeared to have been injured; and by this it was reduced to nothing but a stump, which served only as a step to the top-mast. These accidents augmented our delay, and occasioned us great anxiety about our future security: For on our leaving the coast of *Mexico*, the scurvy had begun to make its appearance again amongst our people; though from our departure from *Juan Fernandes* we had till then enjoyed a most uninterrupted state of health. We too well knew the effects of this disease, from our former fatal experience, to suppose that any thing but a speedy passage could secure the great part of our crew from perishing by it: And as, after being seven weeks at sea, there did not appear any reason that could persuade us, we were nearer the trade-wind, than when we first set out, there was no ground for us to suppose, but our passage would prove at least three times as long as we at first expected; and consequently we had the melancholy prospect, either of dying by the scurvy, or perishing with the ship for want of hands to navigate her. Indeed, some amongst us were at first willing to believe, that in this warm climate, so different from what we felt in passing round Cape *Horn*, the violence of this disease, and its fatality, might be in some degree mitigated; as it had not been unusual to suppose that its particular virulence in that passage was in a great measure owing to the severity of the weather: But the havock of the distemper, in our present circumstances, soon convinced us of the falsity of this speculation; as it likewise exploded some other opinions, which usually pass current about the cause and nature of this disease.

For it has been generally presumed, that plenty of fresh provisions, and of water are effectual preventives of this malady; but it happened that in the present instance we had a considerable stock of fresh provisions on board, as hogs and fowls,[2] which were taken at *Paita*; and we besides almost every day caught great abundance of bonito's, dolphins, and albicores; and the unsettled season, which deprived us of the benefit of the trade-wind, proved extremely rainy; so that we were enabled to fill up our water cask, almost as fast as they were empty; and each man had five pints of water allowed him every day, during the passage. But notwithstanding this plenty of water, and that the fresh provisions were distributed amongst the sick, and the whole crew often fed upon fish,[1] yet neither were the sick hereby relieved, nor the progress and advancement of the disease retarded: Nor was it in these instances only that we found ourselves disappointed; for though it has been usually esteemed a necessary piece of management to keep all ships, where the crews are large, as clean and airy between decks as possible; and it hath been believed by many, that this particular, if well attended to, would prevent the appearance of the scurvy, or at least, mitigate its effects; yet we observed, during the latter part of our run, that though we kept all our ports open, and took uncommon pains in cleansing and sweetning the ships, yet neither the progress, nor the virulence of the disease were thereby sensibly abated.

However, I would not be understood to assert, that fresh provisions, plenty of water, and a constant fresh supply of sweet air between decks, are matters of no moment: I am, on the contrary, well satisfied, that they are all of them articles of great importance, and are doubtless extremely conducive to the health and vigour of a crew, and may in many cases prevent the fatal malady we are now speaking of from taking place. All I have aimed at, in what I have advanced, is only to shew that in some instances, both the cure, and prevention of this disease, is impossible to be effected by any management, or by the application of any remedies which can be made use of at sea. Indeed, I am myself fully persuaded, that when it has once got to a certain head, there are no other means in nature for relieving the diseased, but carrying them on shore, or at least bringing them into the neighbourhood of land. Perhaps a distinct and adequate knowledge of the source of this disease may never be discovered; but in general, there is no difficulty in conceiving, that as a continued supply of fresh air is necessary to all animal life, and as this air is so particular a fluid, that without losing its elasticity, or any of its obvious properties, it may be rendered unfit for this purpose, by the mixing with it some very subtle and otherwise imperceptible effluvia; it may be conceived, I say, that the steams arising from the ocean may have a tendency to render the air they are spread through less properly adapted to the support of the life of terrestrial animals, unless these steams are corrected by effluvia of another kind, and which perhaps the land alone can supply.

To what hath been already said in relation to this disease, I shall add, that our surgeon (who during our passage round Cape *Horn*, had ascribed the mortality we suffered to the severity of the climate) exerted himself in the present run to the utmost, and at last declared, that all his measures were totally ineffectual, and did not in the least avail his patients.[1] On which it was resolved by the Commodore to try the effects of two medicines, which, just before his departure from *England*, were the subject of much discourse, I mean the pill and drop of Mr. *Ward*. For however violent the effects of these medicines are said to have sometimes proved, yet in the present instance, where destruction seemed inevitable without some remedy, the experiment at least was thought adviseable: And therefore, one or both of them, at different times, were given to persons in every stage of the distemper. Out of the numbers that took them, one, soon after swallowing the pill, was seized with a violent bleeding at the nose: He was before given over by the surgeon, and lay almost at the point of death; but he immediately found himself much better, and continued to recover, though slowly, till we arrived on shore, which was near a fortnight after. A few others too were relieved for some days, but the disease returned again with as much violence as ever; though neither did these, nor the rest, who received no benefit, appear to be reduced to a worse condition than they would have been if they had taken nothing. The most remarkable property of these medicines, and what was obvious in almost every one that took them, was, that they operated in proportion to the vigour of the patient; so that those who were within two or three days of dying were scarcely affected; and as the patient was differently advanced in the disease, the operation was either a gentle perspiration, an easy vomit, or a moderate purge: But if they were taken by one in full strength, they then produced all the beforementioned effects with considerable violence, which sometimes continued for six or eight hours together with little intermission. But to return to the prosecution of our voyage.

I have already observed, that, a few days after our running off the coast of *Mexico*, the *Gloucester* had her main-mast cut down to a stump, and we were obliged to fish our fore-mast; and that these misfortunes were greatly aggravated, by our meeting with contrary and variable winds for near seven weeks. I shall now add, that when we reached the trade-wind, and it settled between the North and the East, yet it seldom blew with so much strength, but the *Centurion* might have carried all her small sails abroad with the greatest safety; so that now had we been a single ship, we might have run down our longitude apace, and have reached the *Ladrones* soon enough to have recovered great numbers of our men, who afterwards perished. But the *Gloucester*, by the loss of her mainmast, sailed so very heavily, that we had seldom any more than our top-sails set, and yet were frequently obliged to lie too for her: And, I conceive, that in the whole we lost little less than a month by our attendance upon her, in consequence of the various mischances she encountered. In all this run it was remarkable, that we were rarely many days together, without seeing great numbers of birds; which is a proof that there are many islands, or at least rocks, scattered all along, at no very considerable distance from our track. Some indeed there are marked in the *Spanish* chart, hereafter inserted; but the frequency of the birds seem to evince, that there are many more than have been hitherto discovered: For the greatest part of the birds, we observed, were such as are known to roost on shore; and the manner of their appearance sufficiently made out, that they came from some distant haunt every morning, and returned thither again in the evening; for we never saw them early or late; and the hour of their arrival and departure gradually varied, which we supposed was occasioned by our running nearer their haunts, or getting farther from them.

The trade-wind continued to favour us without any fluctuation, from the end of *June* till towards the end of *July*. But on the 26th of *July*, being then, as we esteemed, about three hundred leagues distant from the *Ladrones*, we met with a westerly wind, which did not come about again to the eastward in four days time. This was a most dispiriting incident, as it at once damped all our hopes of speedy relief, especially too as it was attended with a vexatious accident to the *Gloucester*: For in one part of these four days the wind flatted to a calm, and the ships rolled very deep; by which means the *Gloucester*'s forecap[1] split, and her top-mast came by the board, and broke her fore-yard directly in the slings. As she was hereby rendered incapable of making any sail for some time, we were obliged, as soon as a gale sprung up, to take her in tow; and near twenty of the healthiest and ablest of our seamen were taken from the business of our own ship, and were employed for eight or ten days together on board the *Gloucester* in repairing her damages: But these things, mortifying as we thought them, were but the beginning of our disasters; for scarce had our people finished their business in the *Gloucester*, before we met with a most violent storm in the western board, which obliged us to lie to. In the beginning of this storm our ship sprung a leak, and let in so much water, that all our people, officers included, were employed continually in working the pumps: And the next day we had the vexation to see the *Gloucester*, with her top-mast once more by the board; and whilst we were viewing her with great concern for this new distress, we saw her main-top mast, which had hitherto served her as a jury[1] main-mast, share the same fate. This compleated our misfortunes, and rendered them without resource; for we knew the *Gloucester*'s crew were so few and feeble, that without our assistance they could not be relieved: And our sick were now so far encreased, and those that remained in health so continually fatigued with the additional duty of our pumps, that it was impossible for us to lend them any aid. Indeed we were not as yet fully apprized of the deplorable situation of the *Gloucester*'s crew; for when the storm abated, (which during its continuance prevented all communication with them) the *Gloucester* bore up under our stern; and Captain *Mitchel* informed the Commodore, that besides the loss of his masts, which was all that had appeared to us, the ship had then no less than seven feet of water in her hold, although his officers and men had been kept constantly at the pump for the last twenty-four hours.

This last circumstance was indeed a most terrible accumulation to the other extraordinary distresses of the *Gloucester*, and required, if possible, the most speedy and vigorous assistance; which Captain *Mitchel* begged the Commodore to send him: But the debility of our people, and our own immediate preservation, rendered it impossible for the Commodore to comply with his request. All that could be done was to send our boat on board for a more particular condition of the ship; and it was soon suspected that the taking her people on board us, and then destroying her, was the only measure that could be prosecuted in the present emergency, both for the security of their lives and of our own.

Our boat soon returned with a representation of the state of the *Gloucester*, and of her several defects, signed by Captain *Mitchel* and all his officers; by which it appeared, that she had sprung a leak by the stern post being loose, and working with every roll of the ship, and by two beams a midships being broken in the orlope;[1] no part of which the Carpenters reported was possible to be repaired at sea: That both officers and men had worked twenty-four hours at the pump without intermission, and were at length so fatigued, that they could continue their labour no longer; but had been forced to desist, with seven feet of water in the hold, which covered their cask, so that they could neither come at fresh water, nor provision: That they had no mast standing, except the fore-mast, the mizen-mast, and the mizen top-mast, nor had they any spare masts to get up in the room of those they had lost: That the ship was besides extremely decayed, in every part, for her knees and clamps were all worked quite loose and her upper works in general were so loose, that the quarter-deck was ready to drop down: And that her crew was greatly reduced, for there remained alive on board her no more than seventy-seven men, eighteen boys, and two prisoners, officers included; and that of this whole number, only sixteen men, and eleven boys were capable of keeping the deck, and several of these very infirm.

The Commodore, on the perusal of this melancholy representation, presently ordered them a supply of water and provisions, of which they seemed to be in immediate want, and at the same time sent his own Carpenter on board them, to examine into the truth of every particular; and it being found, on the strictest enquiry, that the preceding account was in no instance exaggerated, it plainly appeared, that there was no possibility of preserving the *Gloucester* any longer, as her leaks were irreparable, and the united hands on board both ships, capable of working, would not be able to free her, even if our own ship should not employ any part of them. What then could be resolved on, when it was the utmost we ourselves could do to manage our own pumps? Indeed there was no room for deliberation; the only step to be taken was, the saving the lives of the few that remained on board the *Gloucester*, and getting out of her as much as was possible before she was destroyed. And therefore the Commodore immediately sent an order to Captain *Mitchel*, as the weather was now calm and favourable, to send his people on board the *Centurion*, as expeditiously as he could; and to take out such stores as he could get at, whilst the ship could be kept above water. And as our leak required less attention, whilst the present easy weather continued, we sent our boats with as many men as we could spare, to Captain *Mitchel's* assistance.

The removing the *Gloucester's* people on board us, and the getting out such stores as could most easily be come at, gave us full employment for two days. Mr. *Anson* was extremely desirous to have gotten two of her cables and an anchor, but the ship rolled so much, and the men were so excessively fatigued, that they were incapable of effecting it; nay, it was even with the greatest difficulty that the prize money, which the *Gloucester* had taken in the *South-Seas*, was secured, and sent on board the *Centurion*: However, the prize goods on board her, which amounted to several thousand pounds in value, and were principally the *Centurion's* property, were entirely lost; nor could any more provision be got out than five cask of flower, three of which were spoiled by the salt-water. The sick men amounting to near seventy, were removed into the boats with as much care as the circumstances of that time would permit; but three or four of them expired as they were hoisting them into the *Centurion*.

It was the 15th of *August*, in the evening, before the *Gloucester* was cleared of every thing that was proposed to be removed; and though the hold was now almost full of water, yet, as the Carpenters were of opinion that she might still swim for some time, if the calm should continue, and the water become smooth, she was set on fire; for we knew not how near we might now be to the Island of *Guam*, which was in the possession of our enemies, and the wreck of such a ship would have been to them no contemptible acquisition. When she was set on fire, Captain *Mitchel* and his officers left her, and came on board the *Centurion*: And we immediately stood from the wreck, not without some apprehensions (as we had now only a light breeze) that if she blew up soon, the concussion of the air might damage our rigging; but she fortunately burnt, though very fiercely, the whole night, her guns firing successively, as the flames reached them. And it was six in the morning, when we were about four leagues distant, before she blew up; the report she made upon this occasion was but a small one, but there was an exceeding black pillar of smoke, which shot up into the air to a very considerable height.[1]

Thus perished his Majesty's ship the *Gloucester*. And now it might have been expected, that being freed from the embarrassments which her frequent disasters had involved us in, we might proceed on our way much brisker than we had hitherto done, especially as we had received some small addition to our strength, by the taking on board the *Gloucester*'s crew; but our anxieties were not yet to be relieved; for, notwithstanding all that we had hitherto suffered, there remained much greater distresses, which we were still to struggle with. For the late storm, which had proved so fatal to the *Gloucester*, had driven us to the northward of our intended course; and the current setting the same way, after the weather abated, had forced us still a degree or two farther, so that we were now in $17° \frac{1}{4}$ of North latitude, instead of being in $13° \frac{1}{2}$, which was the parallel we proposed to keep, in order to reach the Island of *Guam*: And as it had been a perfect calm for some days since the cessation of the storm, and we were ignorant how near we were to the meridian of the *Ladrones*, and supposed ourselves not to be far from it, we apprehended that we might be driven to the leeward of them by the current, without discovering them: In this case, the only land we could make would be some of the eastern parts of *Asia*, where, if we could arrive, we should find the western monsoon in its full force, so that it would be impossible for the stoutest best manned ship to get in. And this coast being removed between four and five hundred leagues farther, we, in our languishing circumstances, could expect no other than to be destroyed by the scurvy, long before the most favourable gale could carry us to such a distance: For our deaths were now extremely alarming, no day passing in which we did not bury eight or ten, and sometimes twelve of our men; and those, who had hitherto continued healthy, began to fall down apace. Indeed we made the best use we could of the present calm, by employing our Carpenters in searching after the leak, which was now considerable notwithstanding the little wind we had: The Carpenters at length discovered it to be in the Gunner's fore store-room, where the water rushed in under the breast-hook, on each side of the stem; but though they found where it was, they agreed that it was impossible to stop it, till we should get into port, and till they could come at it on the outside: However, they did the best they could within board, and were fortunate enough to reduce it, which was a considerable relief to us.

We had hitherto considered the calm which succeeded the storm, and which continued for some days, as a very great misfortune; since the currents were driving us to the northward of our parallel, and we thereby risqued the missing of the *Ladrones*, which we now conceived ourselves to be very near. But when a gale sprung up, our condition was still worse; for it blew from the S. W, and consequently was directly opposed to the course we wanted to steer: And though it soon veered to the N. E, yet this served only to tantalize us, for it returned back again in a very short time to its old quarter. However, on the 22d of *August* we had the satisfaction to find that the current was shifted; and had set us to the southward: And the 23d, at day-break, we were cheered with the discovery of two Islands in the western board: This gave us all great joy, and raised our drooping spirits; for before this an universal dejection had seized us, and we almost despaired of every seeing land again: The nearest of these Islands we afterwards found to be *Anatacan*; we judged it to be full fifteen leagues from us, and it seemed to be high land, though of an indifferent length: The other was the Island of *Serigan*; and had rather the appearance of a high rock, than a place we could hope to anchor at. The view of these Islands is inserted at the top of the annexed plan. We were extremely impatient to get in with the nearest Island, where we expected to meet with anchoring ground, and an opportunity of refreshing our sick: But the wind proved so variable all day, and there was so little of it, that we advanced towards it but slowly; however, by the next morning we were got so far to the westward, that we were in view of a third Island which was that of *Paxaros*, though marked in the chart only as a rock. This was small and very low land, and we had passed within less than a mile of it, in the night, without seeing it: And now at noon, being within four miles of the Island of *Anatacan*, the boat was sent away to examine the anchoring ground and the produce of the place; and we were not a little solicitous for her return, as we then conceived our fate to depend upon the report we should receive: For the other two Islands were obviously enough incapable of furnishing us with any assistance, and we knew not then that there were any others which we could reach. In the evening the boat came back, and the crew informed us that there was no place for a ship to anchor, the bottom being every where foul ground, and all except one small spot, not less than fifty fathom in depth; that on that spot there was thirty fathom, though not above half a mile from the shore; and that the bank was steep to, and could not be depended on:

They farther told us, that they had landed on the Island, but with some difficulty on account of the greatness of the swell; that they found the ground was every where covered with a kind of wild cane, or rush; but that they met with no water, and did not believe the place to be inhabited; though the soil was good, and abounded with groves of coco-nut-trees.

This account of the impossibility of anchoring at this Island occasioned a general melancholy on board; for we considered it as little less than the prelude to our destruction; and our despondency was encreased by a disappointment we met with the succeeding night; for, as we were plying under top-sails, with an intention of getting nearer to the Island, and of sending our boat on shore to load with coco-nuts for the refreshment of our sick, the wind proved squally, and blew so strong off shore, that we were driven so far to the southward, that we dared not to send off our boat. And now the only possible circumstance, that could secure the few which remained alive from perishing, was the accidental falling in with some other of the *Ladrone* Islands, better prepared for our accommodation; and as our knowledge of these Islands was extremely imperfect, we were to trust entirely to chance for our guidance; only as they are all of them usually laid down near the same meridian, and we had conceived those we had already seen to be part of them, we concluded to stand to the southward, as the most probable means of falling in with the next. Thus, with the most gloomy persuasion of our approaching destruction, we stood from the Island of *Anatacan*, having all of us the strongest apprehensions (and those not ill founded) either of dying of the scurvy, or of perishing with the ship, which, for want of hands to work her pumps, might in a short time be expected to founder.[1]

CHAP. II.

Our arrival at *Tinian*, and an account of the Island, and of our proceedings there, till the *Centurion* drove out to sea.

IT was the 26th of *August* 1742, in the morning, when we lost sight of *Anatacan*. The next morning we discovered three other Islands to the eastward, which were from ten to fourteen leagues from us. These were, as we afterwards learnt, the Islands of *Saypan*, *Tinian*, and *Aguigan*. We immediately steered towards *Tinian*, which was the middlemost of the three, but had so much of calms and light airs, that tho' we were helped forwards by the currents, yet next day, at day-break, we were at least five leagues distant from it. However, we kept on our course, and about ten in the morning we perceived a proa under sail to the southward, between *Tinian* and *Aguigan*. As we imagined from hence that these Islands were inhabited, and knew that the *Spaniards* had always a force at *Guam*, we took the necessary precautions for our own security, and for preventing the enemy from taking advantage of our present wretched circumstances, of which they would be sufficiently informed by the manner of our working the ship; we therefore mustered all our hands, who were capable of standing to their arms, and loaded our upper and quarter-deck guns with grape-shot; and that we might the more readily procure some intelligence of the state of these Islands, we showed *Spanish* colours, and hoisted a red flag at the fore top-mast-head, to give our ship the appearance of the *Manila* galeon, hoping thereby to decoy some of the inhabitants on board us. Thus preparing ourselves, and standing towards the land, we were near enough, at three in the afternoon, to send the Cutter in shore, to find out a proper birth for the ship; and we soon perceived that a proa came off the shore to meet the Cutter, fully persuaded, as we afterwards found, that we were the *Manila* ship. As we saw the Cutter returning back with the proa in tow, we immediately sent the Pinnace to receive the proa and the prisoners, and to bring them on board, that the Cutter might proceed on her errand. The Pinnace came back with a *Spaniard* and four *Indians*, which were the people taken in the proa. The *Spaniard* was immediately examined as to the produce and circumstances of this Island of *Tinian*, and his account of it surpassed even our most sanguine hopes; for he informed us that it was uninhabited, which, in our present defenceless condition, was an advantage not to be despised, especially as it wanted but few of the conveniencies that could be expected in the most cultivated country; for he assured us, that there was great plenty of very good water, and that there were an incredible number of cattle, hogs, and poultry running wild on the Island, all of them excellent in their kind; that the woods produced sweet and sour oranges, limes, lemons and coco-nuts in great plenty, besides a fruit peculiar to these Islands (called by *Dampier, Bread-fruit*); that from the quantity and goodness of the provisions produced here, the *Spaniards* at *Guam* made use of it as a store for supplying the garrison; that he himself was a Serjeant of that garrison, and was sent here with twenty-two *Indians* to jerk beef, which he was to load for *Guam* on board a small bark of about fifteen tun, which lay at anchor near the shore.

This account was received by us with inexpressible joy: Part of it we were ourselves able to verify on the spot, as we were by this time near enough to discover several numerous herds of cattle feeding in different places of the Island; and we did not any ways doubt the rest of his relation, as the appearance of the shore prejudiced us greatly in its favour, and made us hope, that not only our necessities might be there fully relieved, and our diseased recovered, but that, amidst those pleasing scenes which were then in view, we might procure ourselves some amusement and relaxation, after the numerous fatigues we had undergone: For the prospect of the country did by no means resemble that of an uninhabited and uncultivated place, but had much more the air of a magnificent plantation, where large lawns and stately woods had been laid out together with great skill, and where the whole had been so artfully combined, and so judiciously adapted to the slopes of the hills, and the inequalities of the ground, as to produce a most striking effect, and to do honour to the invention of the contriver. Thus, (an event not unlike what we had already seen) we were forced upon the most desirable and salutary measures by accidents, which at first sight we considered as the greatest of misfortunes; for had we not been driven by the contrary winds and currents to the northward of our course, (a circumstance, which at that time gave us the most terrible apprehensions) we should, in all probability, never have arrived at this delightful Island, and consequently we should have missed of that place, where alone all our wants could be most amply relieved, our sick recovered, and our enfeebled crew once more re-freshed, and enabled to put again to sea.

The *Spanish* Serjeant, from whom we received the account of the Island, having informed us that there were some *Indians* on shore under his command, employed in jerking beef, and that there was a bark at anchor to take it on board, we were desirous, if possible, to prevent the *Indians* from escaping, who doubtless would have given the Governor of *Guam* intelligence of our arrival; and we therefore immediately dispatched the Pinnace to secure the bark, which the Serjeant told us was the only imbarkation on the place; and then, about eight in the evening, we let go our anchor in twenty-two fathom; and though it was almost calm, and whatever vigour and spirit was to be found on board was doubtless exerted to the utmost on this pleasing occasion, when, after having kept the sea for some months, we were going to take possession of this little paradise, yet we were full five hours in furling our sails: It is true, we were somewhat weakened by the crews of the Cutter and Pinnace which were sent on shore; but it is not less true, that, including those absent with the boats and some Negroe and *Indian* prisoners, all the hands we could muster capable of standing at a gun amounted to no more than seventy-one, most of which number too were incapable of duty; but on the greatest emergencies this was all the force we could collect, in the present enfeebled condition, from the united crews of the *Centurion*, the *Gloucester*, and the *Tryal*, which, when we departed from *England*, consisted all together of near a thousand hands.

When we had furled our sails, the remaining part of the night was allowed to our people for their repose, to recover them from the fatigue they had undergone; and in the morning a party was sent on shore well armed, of which I myself was one, to make ourselves masters of the landing place, as we were not certain what opposition might be made by the *Indians* on the Island: We landed without diffi-culty, for the *Indians* having perceived, by our seizure of the bark the night before, that we were enemies, they immediately fled into the woody parts of the Island. We found on shore many huts which they had inhabited, and which saved us both the time and trouble of erecting tents; one of these huts which the *Indians* made use of for a store-house was very large, being twenty yards long, and fifteen broad; this we immediately cleared of some bales of jerked beef, which we found in it, and converted it into an hospital for our sick, who as soon as the place was ready to receive them were brought on shore, being in all a hundred and twenty-eight: Numbers of these were so very helpless, that we were obliged to carry them from the boats to the hospital upon our shoulders, in which humane employment (as before at *Juan Fernandes*) the Commodore himself, and every one of his officers, were engaged without distinction; and, notwithstanding the great debility and the dying aspects of the greatest part of our sick, it is almost incredible how soon they began to feel the salutary influence of the land; for, though we buried twenty-one men on this and the preceding day, yet we did not loose above ten men more during our whole two months stay here; and in general, our diseased received so much benefit from the fruits of the Island, particularly the fruits of the acid kind, that, in a week's time, there were but few who were not so far recovered, as to be able to move about without help.[1]

And now being in some sort established at this place, we were enabled more particularly to examine its qualities and productions; and that the reader may the better judge of our manner of life here, and future Navigators be better apprized of the conveniencies we met with, I shall, before I proceed any farther in the history of our own adventures, throw together the most interesting particulars that came to our knowledge, in relation to the situation, soil, produce, and conveniencies of this Island of *Tinian*.

This Island lies in the latitude of $15° : 8'$ North, and longitude from *Acapulco* $114° : 50'$ West. Its length is about twelve miles, and its breadth about half as much; it extending from the S. S. W. to N. N. E. The soil is every where dry and healthy, and somewhat sandy, which being less disposed than other soils to a rank and over luxuriant vegetation, occasions the meadows and the bottoms of the woods to be much neater and smoother than is customary in hot climates. The land rises by easy slopes, from the very beach where we watered to the middle of the Island; tho' the general course of its ascent is often interrupted and traversed by gentle descents and

vallies; and the inequalities, that are formed by the different combinations of these gradual swellings of the ground, are most beauti-
fully diversified with large lawns, which are covered with a very fine
trefoil, intermixed with a variety of flowers, and are skirted by woods
of tall and well-spread trees, most of them celebrated either for their
aspect or their fruit. The turf of the lawns is quite clean and even, and
the bottoms of the woods in many places clear of all bushes and under-
woods; and the woods themselves usually terminate on the lawns with
a regular outline, not broken, nor confused with straggling trees, but
appearing as uniform, as if laid out by art. Hence arose a great variety
of the most elegant and entertaining prospects, formed by the mixture
of these woods and lawns, and their various intersections with each
other, as they spread themselves differently through the vallies, and
over the slopes and declivities with which the place abounds. The
fortunate animals too, which for the greatest part of the year are the
sole lords of this happy soil, partake in some measure of the romantic
cast of the Island, and are no small addition to its wonderful scenery:
For the cattle, of which it is not uncommon to see herds of some
thousands feeding together in a large meadow, are certainly the most
remarkable in the world; for they are all of them milk-white, except
their ears, which are generally black. And though there are no inhabitants here, yet the clamour and frequent parading of domestic poultry,
which range the woods in great numbers, perpetually excite the ideas
of the neighbourhood of farms and villages, and greatly contribute to
the chearfulness and beauty of the place. The cattle on the Island we
computed were at least ten thousand; and we had no difficulty in
getting near them, as they were not shy of us. Our first method of
killing them was shooting them; but at last, when, by accidents to be
hereafter recited, we were obliged to husband our ammunition, our
men ran them down with ease. Their flesh was extremely well tasted,
and was believed by us to be much more easily digested, than any we
had ever met with. The fowls too were exceeding good, and were
likewise run down with little trouble; for they could scarce fly further
than an hundred yards at a flight, and even that fatigued them so much,
that they could not readily rise again; so that, aided by the openness
of the woods, we could at all times furnish ourselves with whatever
number we wanted. Besides the cattle and the poultry, we found here
abundance of wild hogs: These were most excellent food; but as they

were a very fierce animal, we were obliged either to shoot them, or to hunt them with large dogs, which we found upon the place at our landing, and which belonged to the detachment which was then upon the Island amassing provisions for the garrison of *Guam*. As these dogs had been purposely trained to the killing of the wild hogs, they followed us very readily, and hunted for us; but though they were a large bold breed, the hogs fought with so much fury, that they frequently destroyed them, so that we by degrees lost the greatest part of them.

But this place was not only extremely grateful to us from the plenty and excellency of its fresh provisions, but was as much perhaps to be admired for its fruits and vegetable productions, which were most fortunately adapted to the cure of the sea scurvy, which had so terribly reduced us. For in the woods there were inconceivable quantities of coco-nuts, with the cabbages growing on the same tree: There were besides guavoes, limes, sweet and sower oranges, and a kind of fruit, peculiar to these Islands, called by the *Indians Rima*, but by us the *Bread Fruit*,[1] for it was constantly eaten by us during our stay upon the Island instead of bread, and so universally preferred to it, that no ship's bread was expended during that whole interval. It grew upon a tree which is somewhat lofty, and which, towards the top, divides into large and spreading branches. The leaves of this tree are of a remarkable deep green, are notched about the edges, and are generally from a foot to eighteen inches in length. The fruit itself grows indifferently on all parts of the branches; it is in shape rather eliptical than round, is covered with a rough rind, and is usually seven or eight inches long; each of them grows singly and not in clusters. This fruit is fittest to be used, when it is full grown, but is still green; in which state, its taste has some distant resemblance to that of an artichoke bottom, and its texture is now very different, for it is soft and spungy. As it ripens it grows softer and of a yellow colour, and then contracts a luscious taste, and an agreeable smell, not unlike a ripe peach; but then it is esteemed unwholesome, and is said to produce fluxes. In the annexed view of the watering place, there is drawn one of the trees bearing this fruit, it being that marked with the letter (*c*). Besides the fruits already enumerated, there were many other vegetables extremely conducive to the cure of the malady we had long laboured under, such as water-melons, dandelion, creeping purslain, mint, scurvy-grass, and sorrel;

all which, together with the fresh meats of the place, we devoured with great eagerness, prompted thereto by the strong inclination, which nature never fails of exciting in scorbutic disorders for these powerful specifics.

It will easily be conceived from what hath been already said, that our cheer upon this Island was in some degree luxurious, but I have not yet recited all the varieties of provision which we here indulged in. Indeed we thought it prudent totally to abstain from fish, the few we caught at our first arrival having surfeited those who eat of them; but considering how much we had been inured to that species of food, we did not regard this circumstance as a disadvantage, especially as the defect was so amply supplied by the beef, pork and fowls already mentioned, and by great plenty of wild fowl; for I must observe, that near the center of the Island there were two considerable pieces of fresh water, which abounded with duck, teal and curlew: Not to mention the whistling plover, which we found there in prodigious plenty.

And now perhaps it may be wondered at, that an Island, so exquisitely furnished with the conveniencies of life, and so well adapted, not only to the subsistence, but likewise to the enjoyment of mankind, should be entirely destitute of inhabitants, especially as it is in the neighbourhood of other Islands, which in some measure depend upon this for their support. To obviate this difficulty, I must observe, that it is not fifty years since the Island was depopulated. The *Indians* we had in our custody assured us, that formerly the three Islands of *Tinian, Rota* and *Guam*, were all full of inhabitants; and that *Tinian* alone contained thirty thousand souls: But a sickness raging amongst these Islands, which destroyed multitudes of the people, the *Spaniards* to recruit their numbers at *Guam*, which were greatly diminished by this mortality, ordered all the inhabitants of *Tinian* thither; where, languishing for their former habitations, and their customary method of life, the greatest part of them in a few years died of grief. Indeed, independent of that attachment which all mankind have ever shown to the places of their birth and bringing up, it should seem, from what has been already said, that there were few countries more worthy to be regretted than this of *Tinian*.

These poor *Indians* might reasonably have expected, at the great distance from *Spain*, where they were placed, to have escaped the violence and cruelty of that haughty Nation, so fatal to a large proportion of the whole human race: But it seems their remote situation could not protect them from sharing in the common destruction of the western world, all the advantage they received from their distance being only to perish an age or two later. It may perhaps be doubted, if the number of the inhabitants of *Tinian*, who were banished to *Guam*, and who died there pining for their native home, was so great, as what we have related above; but, not to mention the concurrent assertion of our prisoners, and the commodiousness of the Island, and its great fertility, there are still remains to be met with on the place, which evince it to have been once extremely populous: For there are, in all parts of the Island, a great number of ruins of a very particular kind; they usually consist of two rows of square pyramidal pillars, each pillar being about six feet from the next, and the distance between the rows being about twelve feet; the pillars themselves are about five feet square at the base, and about thirteen feet high; and on the top of each of them there is a semi-globe, with the flat part upwards; the whole of the pillars and semi-globe is solid, being composed of sand and stone cemented together, and plaistered over. This odd fabrick will be better understood, by inspecting the view of the watering place inserted above,[1] where an assemblage of these pillars is drawn, and is denoted by the letter (*a*). If the account our prisoners gave us of these structures was true, the Island must indeed have been extremely populous; for they assured us, that they were the foundations of particular buildings set apart for those *Indians* only, who had engaged in some religious vow; and monastic institutions are often to be met with in many Pagan nations. However, if these ruins were originally the basis of the common dwelling-houses of the natives, their numbers must have been considerable; for in many parts of the Island they are extremely thick planted, and sufficiently evince the great plenty of former inhabitants. But to return to the present state of the Island.

Having mentioned the conveniencies of this place, the excellency and quantity of its fruits and provisions, the neatness of its lawns, the stateliness, freshness and fragrance of its woods, the happy inequality of its surface, and the variety and elegance of the views it afforded, I must now observe that all these advantages were greatly enhanced by the healthiness of its climate, by the almost constant breezes which prevail there, and by the frequent showers which fall, and which, though of a very short and almost momentary duration, are extremely grateful and refreshing, and are perhaps one cause of the salubrity of the air, and of the extraordinary influence it was observed to have upon us, in increasing and invigorating our appetites and digestion. This was so remarkable, that those amongst our officers, who were at all other times spare and temperate eaters, who, besides a slight breakfast, made but one moderate repast a day, were here, in appearance, transformed into gluttons; for instead of one reasonable flesh-meal, they were now scarcely satisfied with three, and each of them so prodigious in quantity, as would at another time have produced a fever or a surfeit: And yet our digestion so well corresponded with the keeness of our appetites, that we were neither disordered nor even loaded by this repletion; for after having, according to the custom of the Island, made a large beef breakfast, it was not long before we began to consider the approach of dinner as a very desirable, though somewhat tardy incident.

And now having been thus large in my encomiums on this Island, in which however, I conceive, I have not done it justice, it is necessary I should speak of those circumstances in which it is defective, whether in point of beauty or utility.

And first, with respect to its water. I must own, that before I had seen this spot, I did not conceive that the absence of running water, of which it is entirely destitute, could have been so well replaced by any other means, as it is in this Island; for though there are no streams, yet the water of the wells and springs, which are to be met with every where near the surface, is extremely good; and in the midst of the Island there are two or three considerable pieces of excellent water, whose edges are as neat and even, as if they had been basons purposely made for the decoration of the place. It must however be confessed, that with regard to the beauty of the prospects, the want of rills and streams is a very great defect, not to be compensated either by large pieces of standing water, or by the neighbourhood of the sea, though that, by reason of the smallness of the Island, generally makes a part of every extensive view.

As to the residence upon the Island, the principal inconvenience attending it is the vast numbers of muscatos, and various other species of flies, together with an insect called a tick, which, though principally attached to the cattle, would yet frequently fasten upon our limbs and bodies, and if not perceived and removed in time, would bury its head under the skin, and raise a painful inflammation. We found here too centipedes and scorpions, which we supposed were venemous, but none of us ever received any injury from them.

But the most important and formidable exception to this place remains still to be told. This is the inconvenience of the road, and the little security there is at some seasons for a ship at anchor. The only proper anchoring place for ships of burthen is at the S. W. end of the Island. As a direction for readily finding it, there is annexed a very accurate view of the S. W. side of the Island, where (*a*) is the peak of *Saypan*, seen over the northern part of *Tinian*, and bearing N. N. E. ½ E. And (*b*) is the anchoring place, distant eight miles from the observer. And as an additional assistance, there is also added a near view of the anchoring place itself, which represents it so exactly, that none hereafter can possibly mistake it. In this place the *Centurion* anchored in twenty and twenty-two fathom water, opposite to a sandy bay, and about a mile and an half distant from the shore. The bottom of this road is full of sharp-pointed coral rocks, which, during four months of the year, that is, from the middle of *June* to the middle of *October*, renders it a very unsafe place to lie at. This is the season of the western monsoons, when near the full and change of the moon, but more particularly at the change, the wind is usually variable all round the compass, and seldom fails to blow with such fury, that the stoutest cables are not to be confided in; what adds to the danger at these times, is the excessive rapidity of the tide of flood which sets to the S. E, between this Island and that of *Aguiguan*, a small Island near the southern extremity of *Tinian*, which is represented in the general chart, hereafter inserted, only by a dot. This tide runs at first with a vast head and overfall of water, and occasions such a hollow and overgrown sea, as is scarcely to be conceived; so that (as will be hereafter more particularly mentioned) we were under the dreadful apprehension of being pooped[1] by it, though we were in a sixty-gun ship. In the remaining eight months of the year, that is, from the middle of *October* to the middle of *June*, there is a constant season of settled weather, when, if the cables are but well armed, there is scarcely any danger of their being so much as rubbed: So that during all that interval, it is as secure a road as could be wished for. I shall only add, that the anchoring bank is very shelving, and stretches along the

S. W. end of the Island, and that it is entirely free from shoals, except a reef of rocks which is visible, and lies about half a mile from the shore, and affords a narrow passage into a small sandy bay, which is the only place where boats can possibly land. After this account of the Island, and its produce, it is necessary to return to our own history.

Our first undertaking, after our arrival, was the removal of our sick on shore, as hath been mentioned. Whilst we were thus employed, four of the *Indians* on shore, being part of the *Spanish* Serjeant's detachment, came and surrendered themselves to us, so that with those we took in the proa, we had now eight of them in our custody. One of the four who submitted undertook to show us the most convenient place for killing cattle, and two of our men were ordered to attend him on that service; but one of them unwarily trusting the *Indian* with his firelock and pistol, the *Indian* escaped with them into the woods: His countrymen, who remained behind, were apprehensive of suffering for this perfidy of their comrade, and therefore begged leave to send one of their own party into the country, who they engaged should both bring back the arms, and persuade the whole detachment from *Guam* to submit to us. The Commodore granted their request; and one of them was dispatched on this errand, who returned next day, and brought back the firelock and pistol, but assured us, he had met with them in a path way in the wood, and protested that he had not been able to meet with any one of his countrymen. This report had so little the air of truth, that we suspected there was some treachery carrying on, and therefore to prevent any future communication amongst them, we immediately ordered all the *Indians* who were in our power on board the ship, and did not permit them to return any more on shore.[1]

When our sick were well settled on the Island, we employed all the hands that could be spared from attending them, in arming the cables with a good rounding, several fathom from the anchor, to secure them from being rubbed by the coral rocks, which here abounded: And this being compleated, our next attention was our leak, and in order to raise it out of water, we, on the first of *September*, began to get the guns aft to bring the ship by the stern; and now the Carpenters, being able to come at it on the outside, ripped of the old sheathing that was left, and caulked all the seams on both sides the cut-water,[2] and leaded them over, and then new sheathed the bows to the surface of the water: By this means we conceived the defect was sufficiently secured; but upon our beginning to bring the guns into their places, we had the mortification to perceive, that the water rushed into the ship in the old place, with as much violence as ever: Hereupon we were necessitated to begin again; and that our second attempt might be more effectual, we cleared the fore store-room, and sent a hundred and thirty barrels of powder on board the small *Spanish* bark we had seized here, by which means we raised the ship about three feet out of the water forwards, and the Carpenters ripped of the sheathing lower down, and new caulked all the seams, and afterwards laid on new sheathing; and then, supposing the leak to be effectually stopped, we began to move the guns forwards; but the upper deck guns were scarcely in their places, when, to our amazement, it burst out again; and now, as we durst not cut away the lining within board, least a but-end or a plank might start, and we might go down immediately, we had no other resource left than chincing[1] and caulking within board; and indeed by this means the leak was stopped for some time; but when our guns were all in their places, and our stores were taken on board, the water again forced its way through a hole in the stem, where one of the bolts was driven in; and on this we desisted from all farther efforts, being now well assured, that the defect was in the stem itself, and that it was not to be remedied till we should have an opportunity of heaving down.[2]

Towards the middle of *September*, several of our sick were tolerably recovered by their residence on shore; and, on the 12th of *September*, all those who were so far relieved, since their arrival, as to be capable of doing duty, were sent on board the ship: And then the Commodore, who was himself ill of the scurvy, had a tent erected for him on shore, where he went with the view of staying a few days for the recovery of his health, being convinced by the general experience of his people, that no other method but living on the land was to be trusted to for the removal of this dreadful malady. The place, where his tent was pitched on this occasion, was near the well, whence we got all our water, and was indeed a most elegant spot. A view of it hath been already inserted[3] under the title of the watering place, where (*b*) is the Commodore's tent, and (*d*) the well where we watered.

As the crew on board were now reinforced by the recovered hands returned from the Island, we began to send our cask on shore to be fitted up, which till now could not be done, for the Coopers were not well enough to work. We likewise weighed our anchors, that we might examine our cables, which we suspected had by this time received considerable damage. And as the new moon was now approaching, when we apprehended violent gales, the Commodore, for our greater security, ordered that part of the cables next to the anchors to be armed with the chains of the fire-grapnels; and they were besides cackled twenty fathom from the anchors, and seven fathom from the service, with a good rounding of a 4½ inch hawser; and to all these precautions we added that of lowering the main and fore-yard close down, that in case of blowing weather the wind might have less power upon the ship, to make her ride a strain.

Thus effectually prepared, as we conceived, we expected the new moon, which was the 18th of *September*, and riding safe that and the three succeeding days, (though the weather proved very squally and uncertain) we flattered ourselves (for I was then on board) that the prudence of our measures had secured us from all accidents; but, on the 22d, the wind blew from the eastward with such fury, that we soon despaired of riding out the storm; and therefore we should have been extremely glad that the Commodore and the rest of our people on shore, which were the greatest part of our hands, had been on board with us, since our only hopes of safety seemed to depend on our putting immediately to sea; but all communication with the shore was now effectually cut off, for there was no possibility that a boat could live, so that we were necessitated to ride it out, till our cables parted. Indeed it was not long before this happened, for the small bower parted at five in the afternoon, and the ship swung off to the best bower; and as the night came on, the violence of the wind still encreased; but notwithstanding its inexpressible fury, the tide ran with so much rapidity, as to prevail over it; for the tide having set to the northward in the beginning of the storm, turned suddenly to the southward about six in the evening, and forced the ship before it in despight of the storm, which blew upon the beam: And now the sea broke most surprizingly all round us, and a large tumbling swell threatened to poop us; the long boat, which was at this time moored a-stern, was on a sudden canted so high, that it broke the transom of the Commodore's gallery, whose cabin was on the quarter-deck, and would doubtless have risen as high as the tafferel, had it not been for this stroke which stove the boat all to pieces; but the poor boat-keeper, though extremely bruised, was saved almost by miracle. About eight, the tide slackened, but the wind did not abate; so that at eleven, the best bower cable, by which alone we rode, parted. Our sheet anchor,[1] which was the only one we had left, was instantly cut from the bow; but before it could reach the bottom, we were driven from twenty-two into thirty-five fathom; and after we had veered away one whole cable, and two thirds of another, we could not find ground with sixty fathom of line: This was a plain indication, that the anchor lay near the edge of the bank, and could not hold us long. In this pressing danger, Mr. *Saumarez*, our first Lieutenant, who now commanded on board, ordered several guns to be fired, and lights to be shown, as a signal to the Commodore of our distress; and in a short time after, it being then about one o'clock, and the night excessively dark, a strong gust, attended with rain and lightning, drove us off the bank, and forced us out to sea, leaving behind us, on the Island, Mr. *Anson*, with many more of our officers, and great part of our crew, amounting in the whole to an hundred and thirteen persons. Thus were we all, both at sea and on shore, reduced to the utmost despair by this catastrophe, those on shore conceiving they had no means left them ever to leave the Island, and we on board utterly unprepared to struggle with the fury of the seas and winds, we were now exposed to, and expecting each moment to be our last.[2]

CHAP. III.

Transactions at *Tinian* after the departure of the *Centurion*

THE storm, which drove the *Centurion* to sea, blew with too much turbulence to permit either the Commodore or any of the people on shore from hearing the guns, which she fired as signals of distress; and the frequent glare of the lightning had prevented the explosions from being observed: So that, when at day-break it was perceived from the shore that the ship was missing, there was the utmost consternation amongst them: For much the greatest part of them immediately concluded that she was lost, and intreated the Commodore that the boat might be sent round the Island to look for the wreck; and those who believed her safe, had scarcely any expectation that she would ever be able to make the Island again: For the wind continued to blow strong at East, and they knew how poorly she was manned and provided for struggling with so tempestuous a gale. And if the *Centurion* was lost, or should be incapable of returning, there appeared in either case no possibility of their ever getting off the Island: For they were at least six hundred leagues from *Macao*, which was their nearest port; and they were masters of no other vessel than the small *Spanish* bark, of about fifteen tun, which they seized at their first arrival, and which would not even hold a fourth part of their number: And the chance of their being taken off the Island by the casual arrival of any other ship was altogether desperate; as perhaps no *European* ship had ever anchored here before, and it were madness to expect that like incidents should send another here in an hundred ages to come: So that their desponding thoughts could only suggest to them the melancholy prospect of spending the remainder of their days on this Island, and bidding adieu for ever to their country, their friends, their families, and all their domestic endearments.

Nor was this the worst they had to fear: For they had reason to expect, that the Governor of *Guam*, when he should be informed of their situation, might send a force sufficient to overpower them, and to remove them to that Island; and then, the most favourable treatment they could hope for would be to be detained prisoners for life; since, from the known policy and cruelty of the *Spaniards* in their distant settlements, it was rather to be expected, that the Governor, if he once had them in his power, would make their want of commissions (all of them being on board the *Centurion*) a pretext for treating them as pirates, and for depriving them of their lives with infamy.

In the midst of these gloomy reflections, Mr. *Anson* had doubtless his share of disquietude; but he always kept up his usual composure and steadiness: And having soon projected a scheme for extricating himself and his men from their present anxious situation, he first communicated it to some of the most intelligent persons about him; and having satisfied himself that it was practicable, he then endeavoured to animate his people to a speedy and vigorous prosecution of it. With this view he represented to them, how little foundation there was for their apprehension of the *Centurion*'s being lost: That he should have hoped, they had been all of them better acquainted with sea-affairs, than to give way to the impression of so chimerical a fright; and that he doubted not, but if they would seriously consider what such a ship was capable of enduring, they would confess that there was not the least probability of her having perished: That he was not without hopes that she might return in a few days; but if she did not, the worst that could be supposed was, that she was driven so far to the leeward of the Island that she could not regain it, and that she would consequently be obliged to bear away for *Macao* on the coast of *China*: That as it was necessary to be prepared against all events, he had, in this case, considered of a method of carrying them off the Island, and joining their old ship the *Centurion* again at *Macao*: That this method was to hale the *Spanish* bark on shore, to saw her asunder, and to lengthen her twelve feet, which would enlarge her to near forty tun burthen, and would enable her to carry them all to *China*: That he had consulted the Carpenters, and they had agreed that this proposal was very feazible, and that nothing was wanting to execute it, but the united resolution and industry of the whole body: He added, that for his own part he would share the fatigue and labour with them, and would expect no more from any man than what he, the Commodore himself, was ready to submit to; and concluded with representing to them the importance of saving time; and that, in order to be the better prepared for all events, it was necessary to set to work immediately, and to take it for granted, that the *Centurion* would not be able to put back (which was indeed the Commodore's secret opinion); since if she did return, they should only throw away a few days application; but if she did not, their situation, and the season of the year, required their utmost dispatch.

These remonstrances, though not without effect, did not immediately operate so powerfully as Mr. *Anson* could have wished: He indeed raised their spirits, by showing them the possibility of their getting away, of which they had before despaired; but then, from their confidence of this resource, they grew less apprehensive of their situation, gave a greater scope to their hopes, and flattered themselves that the *Centurion* would return and prevent the execution of the Commodore's scheme, which they could easily foresee would be a work of considerable labour: By this means, it was some days before they were all of them heartily engaged in the project; but at last, being in general convinced of the impossibility of the ship's return, they set themselves zealously to the different tasks allotted them, and were as industrious and as eager as their Commander could desire, punctually assembling at day-break at the rendezvous, whence they were distributed to their different employments, which they followed with unusual vigour till night came on.

And here I must interrupt the course of this transaction for a moment, to relate an incident which for some time gave Mr. *Anson* more concern than all the preceding disasters. A few days after the ship was driven off, some of the people on shore cried out, *a sail*. This spread a general joy, every one supposing that it was the ship returning; but presently, a second sail was descried, which quite destroyed their first conjecture, and made it difficult to guess what they were. The Commodore eagerly turned his glass towards them, and saw they were two boats; on which it immediately occurred to him, that the *Centurion* was gone to the bottom, and that these were her two boats coming back with the remains of her people; and this sudden and unexpected suggestion wrought on him so powerfully, that, to conceal his emotion, he was obliged (without speaking to any one) instantly to retire to his tent, where he past some bitter moments, in the firm belief that the ship was lost, and that now all his views of farther distressing the enemy, and of still signalizing his expedition by some important exploit, were at an end.

But he was soon relieved from these disturbing thoughts, by discovering that the two boats in the offing were *Indian* proas; and perceiving that they stood towards the shore, he directed every appearance that could give them any suspicion to be removed, and concealed his people, in the adjacent thickets, prepared to secure the *Indians* when they should land: But, after the proas had stood in within a quarter of a mile of the land, they suddenly stopt short, and remaining there motionless for near two hours, they then made sail again, and stood to the southward. But to return to the projected enlargement of the bark.

If we examine how they were prepared for going through with this undertaking, on which their safety depended, we shall find, that, independent of other matters which were of as much importance, the lengthning of the bark alone was attended with great difficulty. Indeed, in a proper place, where all the necessary materials and tools were to be had, the embarrasment would have been much less; but some of these tools were to be made, and many of the materials were wanting; and it required no small degree of invention to supply all these deficiencies. And when the hull of the bark should be compleated, this was but one article; and there were many others of equal weight, which were to be well considered: These were the rigging it, the victualling it, and lastly, the navigating it, for the space of six or seven hundred leagues, thro' unknown seas, where no one of the company had ever passed before. In some of these particulars such obstacles occurred, that, without the intervention of very extraordinary and unexpected accidents, the possibility of the whole enterprize would have fallen to the ground, and their utmost industry and efforts must have been fruitless. Of all these circumstances I shall make a short recital.

It fortunately happened that the Carpenters, both of the *Gloucester* and of the *Tryal*, with their chests of tools, were on shore when the ship drove out to sea; the Smith too was on shore, and had with him his forge and some tools, but unhappily his bellows had not been brought from on board; so that he was incapable of working, and without his assistance they could not hope to proceed with their design: Their first attention therefore was to make him a pair of bellows, but in this they were for some time puzzled, by their want of leather; however, as they had hides in sufficient plenty, and they had found a hogshead of lime, which the *Indians* or *Spaniards* had prepared for their own use, they tanned some hides with this lime; and though we may suppose the workmanship to be but indifferent, yet the leather they thus made served tolerably well, and the bellows (to which a gun-barrel served for a pipe) had no other inconvenience, than that of being somewhat strong scented from the imperfection of the Tanner's work.

Whilst the Smith was preparing the necessary iron-work, others were employed in cutting down trees, and sawing them into planks; and this being the most laborious task, the Commodore wrought at it himself for the encouragement of his people.[1] As there were neither blocks nor cordage sufficient for tackles to hale the bark on shore, it was proposed to get her up on rollers; and for these, the body of the coco-nut tree was extremely useful; for its smoothness and circular turn prevented much labour, and fitted it for the purpose with very little workmanship: A number of these trees were therefore felled, and the ends of them properly opened for the reception of hand-spikes; and in the mean time a dry dock was dug for the bark, and ways laid from thence quite into the sea, to facilitate the bringing her up. And besides those who were thus occupied in preparing measures for the future enlargement of the bark, a party was constantly ordered for the killing and preparing of provisions for the rest: And tho' in these various employments, some of which demanded considerable dexterity, it might have been expected there would have been great confusion and delay; yet good order being once established, and all hands engaged, their preparations advanced apace. Indeed, the common men, I presume, were not the less tractable for their want of spirituous liquors: For, there being neither wine nor brandy on shore, the juice of the coco-nut was their constant drink, and this, though extremely pleasant, was not at all intoxicating, but kept them very cool and orderly.

And now the officers began to consider of all the articles necessary for the fitting out the bark; when it was found, that the tents on shore, and the spare cordage accidentally left there by the *Centurion*, together with the sails and rigging already belonging to the bark, would serve to rig her indifferently well, when she was lengthened: And as they had tallow in plenty, they proposed to pay her bottom with a mixture of tallow and lime, which it was known was well adapted to that purpose: So that with respect to her equipment, she would not have been very defective. There was, however, one exception, which would have proved extremely inconvenient, and that was her size: For as they could not make her quite forty tun burthen, she would have been incapable of containing half the crew below the deck, and she would have been so top-heavy, that if they were all at the same time ordered upon deck, there would be no small hazard of her oversetting; but this was a difficulty not to be removed, as they could not augment her beyond the size already proposed. After the manner of rigging and fitting up the bark was considered and regulated, the next essential point to be thought on was, how to procure a sufficient stock of provisions for their voyage; and here they were greatly at a loss what course to take; for they had neither grain nor bread of any kind on shore, their bread fruit, which would not keep at sea, having all along supplied its place: And though they had live cattle enough, yet they had no salt to cure beef for a sea-store, nor would meat take salt in that climate. Indeed, they had preserved a small quantity of jerked beef, which they found upon the place at their landing; but this was greatly disproportioned to the run of near six hundred leagues, which they were to engage in, and to the number of hands they should have on board. It was at last, however, resolved to take on board as many coco-nuts as they possibly could; to make the most of their jerked beef, by a very sparing distribution of it; and to endeavour to supply their want of bread by rice; to furnish themselves with which, it was proposed, when the bark was fitted up, to make an expedition to the Island of *Rota*, where they were told, that the *Spaniards* had large plantations of rice under the care of the *Indian* inhabitants: But as this last measure was to be executed by force, it became necessary to examine what ammunition had been left on shore, and to preserve it carefully; and on this enquiry, they had the mortification to find, that the utmost that could be collected, by the strictest search, did not amount to more than ninety charges of powder for their fire locks, which was considerably short of one a-piece for each of the company, and was indeed a very slender stock of ammunition, for such as were to eat no grain or bread for a month, but what they were to procure by force of arms.

But the most alarming circumstance, and what, without the providential interposition of very improbable events, had rendered all their schemes abortive, remains yet to be related. The general idea of the fabric and equipment of the vessel was settled in a few days; and when this was done, it was not difficult to make some estimation of the time necessary to compleat her. After this, it was natural to expect that the officers would consider on the course they were to steer, and the land they were to make. These reflections led them to the disheartning discovery, that there was neither compass nor quadrant on the Island. Indeed the Commodore had brought a pocket-compass on shore for his own use; but Lieutenant *Brett* had borrowed it to determine the position of the neighbouring Islands, and he had been driven to sea in the *Centurion*, without returning it: And as to a quadrant, that could not be expected to be found on shore, for as it was of no use at land, there could be no reason for bringing it from on board the ship. It was eight days, from the departure of the *Centurion*, before they were in any degree relieved from this terrible perplexity: At last, in rumaging a chest belonging to the *Spanish* bark, they found a small compass, which, though little better than the toys usually made for the amusement of school-boys, was to them an invaluable treasure. And a few days after, by a similar piece of good fortune, they found a quadrant on the sea-shore, which had been thrown overboard amongst other lumber belonging to the dead: The quadrant was eagerly seized, but on examination, it unluckily wanted vanes, and therefore in its present state was altogether useless; however, fortune still continuing in a favourable mood, it was not long before a person out of curiosity pulling out the drawer of an old table, which had been driven on shore, found therein some vanes, which fitted the quadrant very well; and it being thus compleated, it was examined by the known latitude of the place, and was found to answer to a sufficient degree of exactness.

And now, all these obstacles being in some degree removed, (which were always as much as possible concealed from the vulgar, that they might not grow remiss with the apprehension of labouring to no purpose)[1] the work proceeded very successfully and vigorously: The necessary iron-work was in great forwardness; and the timbers and planks (which, though not the most exquisite performances of the Sawyer's art, were yet sufficient for the purpose) were all prepared; so that, on the 6th of *October*, being the 14th day from the departure of the ship, they haled the bark on shore, and, on the two succeeding days she was sawn asunder, (though with great care not to cut her planks) and her two parts were separated the proper distance from each other, and, the materials being all ready before hand, they, the next day, being the 9th of *October*, went on with great dispatch in their proposed enlargement of her; and by this time they had all their future operations so fairly in view, and were so much masters of them, that they were able to determine when the whole would be finished, and had accordingly, fixed the 5th of *November* for the day of their putting to sea. But their projects and labours were now drawing to a speedier and happier conclusion; for on the 11th of *October*, in the afternoon, one of the *Gloucester's* men, being upon a hill in the middle of the Island, perceived the *Centurion* at a distance, and running down with his utmost speed towards the landing place, he, in the way, saw some of his comrades, to whom he hallowed out with great extasy, *The ship, the ship*. This being heard by Mr. *Gordon*, a Lieutenant of marines, who was convinced by the fellow's transport that his report was true, Mr. *Gordon* ran towards the place where the Commodore and his people were at work, and being fresh and in breath, easily outstripped the *Gloucester's* man, and got before him to the Commodore, who, on hearing this happy and unexpected news, threw down his axe with which he was then at work, and by his joy broke through, for the first time, the equable and unvaried character which he had hitherto preserved; the others, who were with him, instantly ran down to the seaside in a kind of frenzy, eager to feast themselves with a sight they had so ardently wished for, and of which they had now for a considerable time despaired. By five in the evening, the *Centurion* was visible in the offing to them all; and, a boat being sent off with eighteen men to reinforce her, and with fresh meat and fruits for the refreshment of her crew, she, the next afternoon, happily came to an anchor in the road, where the Commodore immediately came on board her, and was received by us with the sincerest and heartiest acclamations: For, from the following short recital of the fears, the dangers and fatigues we in the ship underwent, during our nineteen days absence from *Tinian*, it may be easily conceived, that a harbour, refreshments, repose, and the joining of our Commander and Shipmates, were not less pleasing to us, than our return was to them.

CHAP. IV.

Proceedings on board the *Centurion*, when driven
out to sea.

THE *Centurion* being now once more safely arrived at *Tinian*, to the mutual respite of the labours of our divided crew, it is high time that the reader, after the relation already given of the projects and employment of those left on shore, should be apprized of the fatigues and distresses, to which we, who were driven off to sea, were exposed during the long interval of nineteen days that we were absent from the Island.

It has been already mentioned, that it was the 22d of *September*, about one o'clock, in an extreme dark night, when by the united violence of a prodigious storm, and an exceeding rapid tide, we were driven from our anchors, and forced to sea. Our condition then was truly deplorable; we were in a leaky ship, with three cables in our hawses, to one of which hung our only remaining anchor; we had not a gun on board lashed, nor a port barred in; our shrowds were loose, and our top-masts unrigged, and we had struck our fore and main-yards close down, before the storm came on, so that there were no sails we could set, except our mizen. In this dreadful extremity we could muster no more strength on board, to navigate the ship, than an hundred and eight hands, several Negroes and *Indians* included: This was scarcely the fourth part of our complement; and of these the greater number were either boys, or such as, being lately recovered from the scurvy, had not yet arrived at half their former vigour. No sooner were we at sea, but by the violence of the storm, and the working of the ship, we made a great quantity of water through our hawse-holes, ports and scuppers, which, added to the constant effect of our leak, rendered our pumps alone a sufficient employment for us all: But though this leakage, by being a short time neglected, would inevitably end in our destruction; yet we had other dangers then impending, which occasioned this to be regarded as a secondary consideration only. For we all imagined, that we were driving directly on the neighbouring Island of *Aguiguan*, which was about two leagues distant; and as we had lowered our main and fore-yards close down, we had no sails

298

we could set but the mizen, which was altogether insufficient to carry us clear of this instant peril: We therefore immediately applied ourselves to work, endeavouring, by the utmost of our efforts, to heave up the main and fore-yards, in hopes that, if we could but be enabled to make use of our lower canvas, we might possibly weather the Island, and thereby save ourselves from this impending shipwreck. But after full three hours ineffectual labour, the jeers broke, and the men being quite jaded, we were obliged, by mere debility, to desist, and quietly to expect our fate, which we then conceived to be unavoidable: For we imagined ourselves, by this time, to be driven just upon the shore, and the night was so extremely dark, that we expected to discover the Island no otherwise than by striking upon it; so that the belief of our destruction, and the uncertainty of the point of time when it would take place, occasioned us to pass several hours, under the most serious apprehensions, that each succeeding moment would send us to the bottom. Nor did these continued terrors, of instantly striking and sinking, end but with the day-break; when we with great transport perceived, that the Island, we had thus dreaded, was at a considerable distance, and that a strong northern current had been the cause of our preservation.

The turbulent weather, which forced us from *Tinian*, did not begin to abate, till three days after; and then we swayed up the fore-yard, and began to heave up the main-yard, but the jeers[1] broke and killed one of our men, and prevented us at that time from proceeding. The next day, being the 26th of *September*, was a day of most severe fatigue to us all; for it must be remembred, that in these exigencies no rank or office exempted any person from the manual application and bodily labour of a common sailor. The business of this day was no less than an attempt to heave up the sheet-anchor, which we had hitherto dragged at our bows with two cables an end. This was a work of great importance to our future preservation: For, not to mention the impediment to our navigation, and the hazard it would be to our ship, if we attempted to make sail with the anchor in its present situation, we had this most interesting consideration to animate us, that it was the only anchor we had left; and, without securing it, we should be under the utmost difficulties and hazards, when ever we made the land again; and therefore, being all of us fully apprized of the consequence of this enterprize, we laboured at it with the severest application for full twelve hours, when we had indeed made a considerable progress, having brought the anchor in sight; but, it then growing dark, and we being excessively fatigued, we were obliged to desist, and to leave our work unfinished, till the next morning, when, by the benefit of a night's rest, we compleated it, and hung the anchor at our bow.

It was the 27th of *September* in the morning, that is, five days after our departure, when we thus secured our anchor; and the same day, we got up our main-yard: And having now conquered in some degree the distress and disorder which we were necessarily involved in at our first driving out to sea, and being enabled to make use of our canvass, we set our courses, and for the first time stood to the eastward, in hopes of regaining the Island of *Tinian*, and joining our Commodore in a few days: For we were then, by our accounts, only forty-seven leagues to the South West of *Tinian*; so that on the first day of *October*, having then run the distance necessary for making the Island according to our reckoning, we were in full expectation of seeing it; but we were unhappily disappointed, and were thereby convinced, that a current had driven us to the westward. And as we could not judge how much we might hereby have deviated, and consequently how long we might still expect to be at sea, we had great apprehensions that our stock of water might prove deficient; for we were doubtful about the quantity we had on board, and found many of our casks so decayed, as to be half leaked out. However, we were delivered from our uncertainty the next day by having a sight of the Island of *Guam*, by which we discovered that the currents had driven us forty-four leagues to the westward of our accounts. This sight of land having satisfied us of our situation, we kept plying to the eastward, though with excessive labour, for, the wind continuing fixed in the eastern board, we were obliged to tack often, and our crew was so weak, that, without the assistance of every man on board, it was not in our power to put the ship about: This severe employment lasted till the 11th of *October*, being the nineteenth day from our departure; when arriving in the offing of *Tinian*, we were reinforced from the shore, as hath been already mentioned; and on the evening of the same day, we, to our inexpressible joy, came to an anchor in the road, thereby procuring to our shipmates on shore, as well as to ourselves, a cessation from the fatigues and apprehensions, which this disastrous incident had given rise to.

CHAP. V.

Employment at *Tinian*, till the final departure of the
Centurion from thence; with a description
of the *Ladrones*.

WHEN the Commodore came on board the *Centurion*, on her return to
Tinian, as already mentioned, he resolved to stay no longer at the
Island than was absolutely necessary to compleat our stock of water,
a work which we immediately set ourselves about. But the loss of our
long-boat, which was staved against our poop, when we were driven
out to sea, put us to great inconveniencies in getting our water on
board; for we were obliged to raft off all our cask, and the tide ran so
strong, that, besides the frequent delays and difficulties it occasioned,
we more than once lost the whole raft. Nor was this our only misfortune; for, on the 14th of *October*, being but the third day after our
arrival, a sudden gust of wind brought home our anchor, forced us off
the bank, and drove the ship out to sea a second time. The Commodore, it is true, and the principal officers were now on board; but we
had near seventy men on shore, who had been employed in filling our
water, and procuring provisions: These had with them our two
Cutters; but as they were too many for the Cutters to bring off at once,
we sent the eighteen oared barge to assist them; and at the same time
made a signal for all that could to embark. The two Cutters soon
came off to us full of men; but forty of the company, who were employed in killing cattle in the wood, and in bringing them down to the
landing-place, were left behind; and though the eighteen oared barge
was left for their conveyance, yet, as the ship soon drove to a considerable distance, it was not in their power to join us. However, as
the weather was favourable, and our crew was now stronger than
when we were first driven out, we, in about five days time, returned
again to an anchor at *Tinian*, and relieved those we had left behind us
from their second fears of being deserted by their ship.

On our arrival, we found that the *Spanish* bark, the old object of
their hopes, had undergone a new metamorphosis: For those we had
left on shore began to despair of our return, and conceiving that the

lengthening the bark, as formerly proposed, was both a toilsome and unnecessary measure, considering the small number they consisted of, they had resolved to join her again, and to restore her to her first state; and in this scheme they had made some progress; for they had brought the two parts together, and would have soon compleated her, had not our coming back put a period to their labours and disquietudes.

These people we had left behind informed us, that, just before we were seen in the offing, two proas had stood in very near the shore, and had continued there for some time; but, on the appearance of our ship, they crowded away, and were presently out of sight. And, on this occasion, I must mention an incident, which, though it happened during the first absence of the ship, was then omitted, to avoid interrupting the course of the narration.

It hath been already observed, that a part of the detachment, sent to this Island under the command of the *Spanish* Serjeant, lay concealed in the woods; and we were the less solicitous to find them out, as our prisoners all assured us, that it was impossible for them to get off, and consequently that it was impossible for them to send any intelligence about us to *Guam*. But when the *Centurion* drove out to sea, and left the Commodore on shore, he one day, attended by some of his officers, endeavoured to make the tour of the Island: In this expedition, being on a rising ground, they perceived in the valley beneath them the appearance of a small thicket, which, by observing more nicely, they found had a progressive motion: This at first surprized them; but they soon discovered, that it was no more than several large coco bushes, which were dragged along the ground, by persons concealed beneath them. They immediately concluded that these were some of the Serjeant's party (which was indeed true); and therefore the Commodore and his people made after them, in hopes of finding out their retreat. The *Indians* soon perceived they were discovered, and hurried away with precipitation; but Mr. *Anson* was so near them, that he did not lose sight of them till they arrived at their cell, which he and his officers entering found to be abandoned, there being a passage from it down a precipice contrived for the conveniency of flight. They found here an old firelock, or two, but no other arms. However, there was a great quantity of provisions, particularly salted sparibs of pork, which were excellent; and from what our people saw here, they concluded, that the extraordinary appetite, which they had found at this Island, was not confined to themselves alone; for, it being about noon, the *Indians* had laid out a very plentiful repast considering their numbers, and had their bread-fruit and coco-nuts prepared ready for eating, and in a manner which plainly evinced, that, with them too, a good meal was neither an uncommon nor an unheeded article. The Commodore having in vain endeavoured to discover the path by which the *Indians* had escaped, he and his officers contented themselves with sitting down to the dinner, which was thus luckily fitted to their present appetites; after which, they returned back to their old habitation, displeased at missing the *Indians*, as they hoped to have engaged them in our service, if they could have had any conference with them. But notwithstanding what our prisoners had asserted, we were afterwards assured, that these *Indians* were carried off to *Guam* long before we left the place. But to return to our history.

On our coming to an anchor again, after our second driving off to sea, we laboured indefatigably in getting in our water; and having, by the 20th of *October*, compleated it to fifty tun, which we supposed would be sufficient for our passage to *Macao*, we, on the next day, sent one of each mess on shore, to gather as large a quantity of oranges, lemons, coco-nuts, and other fruits of the Island, as they possibly could, for the use of themselves and their mess-mates, when at sea. And, these purveyors returning on board us on the evening of the same day, we then set fire to the bark and proa, hoisted in our boats, and got under sail, steering away for the South end of the Island of *Formosa*, and taking our leaves, for the third and last time, of the Island of *Tinian*: An Island, which, whether we consider the excellence of its productions, the beauty of its appearance, the elegance of its woods and lawns, the healthiness of its air, or the adventures it gave rise to, may in all these views be truly stiled romantic.

And now, postponing for a short time our run to *Formosa*, and thence to *Canton*, I shall interrupt the narration with a description of that range of Islands, usually called the *Ladrones*, or *Marian* Islands, of which this of *Tinian* is one.

These Islands were discovered by *Magellan* in the year 1521; and by the account given of the two he first fell in with, it should seem that they were the Islands of *Saypan* and *Tinian*; for they are described in his expedition as very beautiful Islands, and as lying between 15 and 16 degrees of North latitude. These characteristics are particularly applicable to the two above mentioned places; for the pleasing appearance of *Tinian* hath occasioned the *Spaniards* to give it the additional name of *Buenavista*; and *Saypan*, which is in the latitude of 15°: 22' North, affords no contemptible prospect when seen from the sea, as may be sufficiently evinced from the annexed view of its North West side, taken at three leagues distance.

There are usually reckoned twelve of these Islands; but it will appear, from the chart of the North part of the *Pacific* Ocean hereafter inserted, that if the small islets and rocks are counted in, then their whole number will amount to above twenty. They were formerly most of them well inhabited; and, even not sixty years ago, the three principal Islands, *Guam, Rota,* and *Tinian* together, are said to have contained above fifty thousand people: But since that time *Tinian* hath been entirely depopulated; and only two or three hundred *Indians* have been left at *Rota*, to cultivate rice for the Island of *Guam*; so that now no more than *Guam* can properly be said to be inhabited. This Island of *Guam* is the only settlement of the *Spaniards*; here they keep a governor and garrison, and here the *Manila* ship generally touches for refreshment, in her passage from *Acapulco* to the *Philippines*. It is esteemed to be about thirty leagues in circumference, and contains, by the *Spanish* accounts, near four thousand inhabitants, of which a thousand are said to live in the city of *San Ignatio de Agand*, where the Governor generally resides, and where the houses are represented as considerable, being built with stone and timber, and covered with tiles, a very uncommon fabric for these warm climates and savage countries: Besides this city, there are upon the Island thirteen or fourteen villages. As this is a post of some consequence, on account of the refreshment it yields to the *Manila* ship, there are two castles on the sea-shore; one is the castle of St. *Angelo*, which lies near the road, where the *Manila* ship usually anchors, and is but an insignificant fortress, mounting only five guns eight pounders; the other is the castle of St. *Lewis*, which is N. E. from St. *Angelo*, and four leagues distant, and is intended to protect a road where a small vessel anchors, which arrives here every other year from *Manila*. This fort mounts the same number of guns as the former: And besides these forts, there is a battery of five pieces of cannon on an eminence near the sea-shore. The *Spanish* troops employed on this Island, consist of three companies of foot, from forty to fifty men each; and this is the principal strength the

Governor has to depend on; for he cannot rely on any assistance from the *Indian* inhabitants, being generally upon ill terms with them, and so apprehensive of them, that he has debarred them the use of firearms or lances.

The rest of these Islands, though not inhabited, do yet abound with many kinds of refreshment and provision; but there is no good harbour or road to be met with amongst them all: Of that of *Tinian* we have treated largely already; nor is the road of *Guam* much better; for it is not unusual for the *Manila* ship, though she proposes to stay there but twenty-four hours, to be forced to sea, and to leave her boat behind her. This is an inconvenience so sensibly felt by the commerce at *Manila*, that it is always recommended to the Governor of *Guam*, to use his best endeavours for the discovery of some safe port in this part of the world. How industrious he may be to comply with his instructions, I know not; but this is certain, that, notwithstanding the many Islands already found out between the coast of *Mexico* and the *Philippines*, there is not yet known any one safe port in that whole tract; though in other parts of the world it is not uncommon for very small Islands to furnish most excellent harbours.

From what has been said it appears, that the *Spaniards*, on the *Island* of *Guam*, are extremely few, compared to the *Indian* inhabitants; and formerly the disproportion was still greater, as may be easily conceived from what hath been said, in another chapter, of the numbers heretofore on *Tinian* alone. These *Indians* are a bold well-limbed people; and it should seem from some of their practices, that they are no ways defective in understanding; for their flying proas in particular, which have been for ages the only vessels used by them, are so singular and extraordinary an invention, that it would do honour to any nation, however dexterous and acute. For if we consider the aptitude of this proa to the particular navigation of these Islands, which lying all of them nearly under the same meridian, and within the limits of the trade-wind, require the vessels made use of in passing from one to the other, to be particularly fitted for sailing with the wind upon the beam; or, if we examine the uncommon simplicity and ingenuity of its fabric and contrivance, or the extraordinary velocity with which it moves, we shall, in each of these articles, find it worthy of our admiration, and meriting a place amongst the mechanical productions of the most civilized nations, where arts and sciences have most eminently flourished. As former Navigators, though they have mentioned these vessels, have yet treated of them imperfectly, and, as I conceive, that, besides their curiosity, they may furnish both the shipwright and seaman with no contemptible observations, I shall here insert a very exact description of the built, rigging, and working of these vessels, which I am well enabled to do, for one of them, as I have mentioned, fell into our hands at our first arrival at *Tinian*, and Mr. *Brett* took it to pieces, on purpose to delineate its fabric and dimensions with greater accuracy: So that the following account may be relied on.

The name of flying proa given to these vessels, is owing to the swiftness with which they sail. Of this the *Spaniards* assert such stories, as appear altogether incredible to those who have never seen these vessels move; nor are the *Spaniards* the only people who relate these extraordinary tales of their celerity. For those who shall have the curiosity to enquire at the dock at *Portsmouth*, about a trial made there some years since, with a very imperfect one built at that place, will meet with accounts not less wonderful than any the *Spaniards* have given. However, from some rude estimations made by our people, of the velocity with which they crossed the horizon at a distance, while we lay at *Tinian*, I cannot help believing, that with a brisk trade-wind they will run near twenty miles an hour: Which though, greatly short of what the *Spaniards* report of them, is yet a prodigious degree of swiftness. But let us give a distinct idea of its figure.

The construction of this proa is a direct contradiction to the practice of all the rest of mankind. For as the rest of the world make the head of their vessels different from the stern, but the two sides alike; the proa, on the contrary, has her head and stern exactly alike, but her two sides very different; the side, intended to be always the lee-side, being flat; and the windward-side made rounding, in the manner of other vessels: And, to prevent her oversetting, which from her small breadth, and the straight run of her leeward-side, would, without this precaution, infallibly happen, there is a frame laid out from her to windward, to the end of which is fastened a log, fashioned into the shape of a small boat, and made hollow: The weight of the frame is intended to ballance the proa, and the small boat is by its buoyance (as it is always in the water) to prevent her oversetting to windward; and this frame is usually called an outrigger. The body of the proa (at least of that we took) is made of two pieces joined end-ways, and sowed together with bark, for there is no iron used about her: She is about two inches thick at the bottom, which at the gunwale is reduced to less than one: The dimensions of each part will be better known from the uprights and views contained in the annexed plate,[1] which were drawn from an exact mensuration; these I shall endeavour to explain as minutely and distinctly as I can.

Fig. 1. Represents the proa with her sail set, as she appears when viewed from the leeward.

Fig. 2. Is a view of her from the head, with the outrigger to the windward.

Fig. 3. Is the plan of the whole; where (A B) is the lee-side of the proa; (C D) the windward-side; (E F G H) the outrigger or frame laid out to windward; (K L) the boat at the end of it; (M N P Q) two braces from the head and stern to steady the frame; (R S) a thin plank placed to windward, to prevent the proa from shipping of water, and for a seat to the *Indian* who bales, and sometimes goods are carried upon it; (I) is the part of the middle outrigger, on which the mast itself is supported (*Fig.* 2,) by the shore (C D), and by the shrowd (E F), and by two stays, one of which may be seen, in *Fig.* 1, marked (C D), the other is hid by the sail: The sail (E F G), in *Fig.* 1, is made of matting, and the mast, yard, boom. and outriggers, are all made of bamboo: The heel of the yard is always lodged in one of the sockets (T) or (V), *Fig.* 3, according to the tack the proa goes on; and when she alters her tack, they bear away a little to bring her stern up to the wind, then by easing the halyard, and raising the yard, and carrying the heel of it along the lee-side of the proa, they fix it in the opposite socket; whilst the boom at the same time, by letting fly the sheet (M), and haling the sheet (N), *Fig.* 1, shifts into a contrary situation to what it had before, and that which was the stern of the proa, now becomes the head, and she is trimmed on the other tack. When it is necessary to reef or furl the sail, this is done by rolling it round the boom. The proa generally carries six or seven *Indians*; two of which are placed in the head and stern, who steer the vessel alternately with a paddle according to the tack she goes on, he in the stern being the steersman; the other *Indians* are employed either in baling out the water which she accidentally ships, or in setting and trimming the sail. From the description of these vessels it is sufficiently obvious, how dexterously they are fitted for ranging this collection of Islands called the *Ladrones*: For as these Islands lie nearly N. and S. of each other, and are all within the limits of the trade-wind, the proas, by sailing most excellently on a wind, and with either end foremost, can run from one of these Islands to the other and back again, only by shifting the sail, without ever putting about; and, by the flatness of their lee-side, and their small breadth, they are capable of lying much nearer the wind than any other vessel hitherto known, and thereby have an advantage, which no vessels that go large can ever pretend to: The advantage I mean is that of running with a velocity nearly as great, and perhaps sometimes greater than that with which the wind blows. This, however paradoxical it may appear, is evident enough in similar instances on shore: For it is well known, that the sails of a windmill often move faster than the wind; and one great superiority of common windmills over all others, that ever were, or ever will be contrived to move with an horizontal motion, is analogous to the case we have mentioned of a vessel upon a wind and before the wind: For the sails of an horizontal windmill, the faster they move, the more they detract from the impulse of the wind upon them; whereas the common windmills, by moving perpendicular to the torrent of air, are nearly as forcibly acted on by the wind, when they are in motion, as when they are at rest.

Thus much may suffice as to the description and nature of these singular embarkations. I must add, that vessels bearing some obscure resemblance to these, are to be met with in various parts of the *East-Indies*, but none of them, that I can learn, to be compared with those of the *Ladrones*, either in their construction or celerity;[1] which should induce one to believe, that this was originally the invention of some genius of these Islands, and was afterwards imperfectly copied by the neighbouring nations: For though the *Ladrones* have no immediate intercourse with any other people, yet there lie to the S. and S. W. of them a great number of Islands, which are supposed to extend to the coast of *New Guinea*. These Islands are so near the *Ladrones*, that canoes from them have sometimes, by distress, been driven to *Guam*; and the *Spaniards* did once dispatch a bark for their discovery, which left two Jesuits amongst them, who were afterwards murthered: And the inhabitants of the *Ladrones*, with their proas, may, by like accident, have been driven amongst these Islands. Indeed I should conceive, that the same range of Islands extends to the S. E. as well as the S. W, and that to a prodigious distance: For *Schouten*, who traversed the South part of the *Pacific* Ocean in the year 1615, met with a large double canoe full of people, at above a thousand leagues distance from the *Ladrones* towards the S. E. If this double canoe was any distant imitation of the flying proa, which is no very improbable conjecture, this can only be accounted for, by supposing that there is a range of Islands, near enough to each other to be capable of an accidental communication, which is extended from the *Ladrones* thither. And indeed all those who have crossed from *America* to the *East-Indies* in a southern latitude, have never failed to meeting with several very small Islands scattered over that immense ocean.

And as there may be hence some reason to suppose, that the *Ladrones* are only a part of an extensive chain of Islands, spreading themselves to the southward, towards the unknown boundaries of the *Pacific* Ocean; so it appears from the *Spanish* chart hereafter inserted, that the same chain is extended from the northward of the *Ladrones* to *Japan*: So that in this light the *Ladrones* will be only one small portion of a range of Islands reaching from *Japan*, perhaps to the unknown southern Continent.[1] After this short account of these places, I shall now return to the prosecution of our voyage.

CHAP. VI.

From *Tinian* to *Macao.*

I HAVE already mentioned, that, on the 21st of *October*, in the evening, we took our leave of the Island of *Tinian*, steering the proper course for *Macao* in *China*. The eastern monsoon was now, we reckoned, fairly settled; and we had a constant gale blowing right upon our stern: So that we generally run from forty to fifty leagues a day. But we had a large hollow sea pursuing us, which occasioned the ship to labour much; whence we received great damage in our rigging, which was grown very rotten, and our leak was augmented: But happily for us, our people were now in full health; so that there were no complaints of fatigue, but all went through their attendance on the pumps, and every other duty of the ship, with ease and chearfulness.

Having now no other but our sheet-anchor left, except our prize anchors, which were stowed in the hold and were too light to be depended on, we were under great concern how we should manage on the coast of *China*, where we were all entire strangers, and where we should doubtless be frequently under the necessity of coming to an anchor. Our sheet-anchor being obviously much too heavy for a coasting anchor, it was at length resolved, to fix two of our largest prize anchors into one stock, and to place between their shanks two guns, four pounders, which was accordingly executed, and it was to serve as a best bower: And a third prize-anchor being in like manner joined with our stream-anchor, with guns between them, we thereby made a small bower; so that, besides our sheet-anchor, we had again two others at our bows, one of which weighed 3900, and the other 2900 pounds.

The 3d of *November*, about three in the afternoon, we saw an Island, which at first we imagined to be the Island of *Botel Tobago Xima*: But on our nearer approach we found it to be much smaller than that is usually represented; and about an hour after we saw another Island, five or six miles farther to the westward. As no chart, nor any journal we had seen, took notice of any other Island to the eastward of *Formosa*, than *Botel Tobago Xima*, and as we had no observation of our

310

latitude at noon, we were in some perplexity, being apprehensive that an extraordinary current had driven us into the neighbourhood of the *Bashee Islands*; and therefore, when night came on, we brought to, and continued in this posture till the next morning, which proving dark and cloudy, for some time prolonged our uncertainty; but it cleared up about nine o'clock, when we again discerned the two Islands above-mentioned; we then prest forwards to the westward, and by eleven got a sight of the southern part of the Island of *Formosa*. This satisfied us that the second Island we saw was *Botel Tobago Xima*, and the first a small island or rock, lying five or six miles due East from it, which, not being mentioned by any of our books or charts, was the occasion of our fears.

When we got sight of the Island of *Formosa*, we steered W. by S, in order to double its extremity, and kept a good look-out for the rocks of *Vele Rete*, which we did not see till two in the afternoon. They then bore from us W. N. W, three miles distant, the South end of *Formosa* at the same time bearing N. by W $\frac{1}{2}$ W, about five leagues distant. To give these rocks a good birth, we immediately haled up S. by W, and so left them between us and the land. Indeed we had reason to be careful of them; for though they appeared as high out of the water as a ship's hull, yet they are environed with breakers on all sides, and there is a shoal stretching from them at least a mile and an half to the southward, whence they may be truly called dangerous. The course from *Botel Tobago Xima* to these rocks, is S. W. by W, and the distance about twelve or thirteen leagues: And the South end of *Formosa*, off which they lie, is in the latitude of 21° : 50' North, and in 23° : 50' West longitude from *Tinian*, according to our most approved reckonings, though by some of our accounts above a degree more.

While we were passing by these rocks of *Vele Rete*, there was an outcry of fire on the fore-castle; this occasioned a general alarm, and the whole crew instantly flocked together in the utmost confusion, so that the officers found it difficult for some time to appease the uproar: But having at last reduced the people to order, it was perceived that the fire proceeded from the furnace; and pulling down the brick-work, it was extinguished with great facility, for it had taken its rise from the bricks, which, being overheated, had begun to communicate the fire to the adjacent wood-work. In the evening we were surprized with a view of what we at first sight conceived to have been breakers, but, on a stricter examination, we found them to be only a great number of fires on the Island of *Formosa*. These, we imagined, were intended by the inhabitants of that Island as signals for us to touch there, but that suited not our views, we being impatient to reach the port of *Macao* as soon as possible. From *Formosa* we steered W. N. W, and sometimes still more northerly, proposing to fall in with the coast of *China*, to the eastward of *Pedro Blanco*; for the rock so called is usually esteemed an excellent direction for ships bound to *Macao*. We continued this course till the following night, and then frequently brought to, to try if we were in soundings: But it was the 5th of *November*, at nine in the morning, before we struck ground, and then we had forty-two fathom, and a bottom of grey sand mixed with shells. When we had got about twenty miles farther W. N. W, we had thirty-five fathom and the same bottom, from whence our soundings gradually decreased from thirty-five to twenty-five fathom; but soon after, to our great surprize, they jumped back again to thirty fathom: This was an alteration we could not very well account for, since all the charts laid down regular soundings every where to the northward of *Pedro Blanco*; and for this reason we kept a very careful look-out, and altered our course to N. N. W, and having run thirty-five miles in this direction, our soundings again gradually diminished to twenty-two fathom, and we at last, about midnight, got sight of the main land of *China*, bearing N. by W. four leagues distant: We then brought the ship to, with her head to the sea, proposing to wait for the morning; and before sunrise we were surprized to find ourselves in the midst of an incredible number of fishing boats, which seemed to cover the surface of the sea as far as the eye could reach. I may well stile their number incredible, since I cannot believe, upon the lowest estimate, that there were so few as six thousand, most of them manned with five hands, and none of those we saw with less than three. Nor was this swarm of fishing vessels peculiar to this spot; for, as we ran on to the westward, we found them as abundant on every part of the coast. We at first doubted not but we should procure a Pilot from them to carry us to *Macao*; but though many of them came close to the ship, and we endeavoured to tempt them by showing them a number of dollars, a most alluring bait for *Chinese* of all ranks and professions, yet we could not entice them on board us, nor procure any directions from them; though, I presume, the only difficulty was their not comprehending what we wanted them to do, for we could have no communication with them but by signs: Indeed we often pronounced the word *Macao*; but this we had reason to suppose they understood in a different sense; for in return they sometimes held up fish to us, and we afterwards learnt, that the *Chinese* name for fish is of a somewhat similar sound. But what surprised us most was the inattention and want of curiosity, which we observed in this herd of fishermen: A ship like ours had doubtless never been in those seas before; perhaps, there might not be one, amongst all the *Chinese* employed in this fishery, who had ever seen any *European* vessel; so that we might reasonably have expected to have been considered by them as a very uncommon and extraordinary object; but though many of their vessels came close to the ship, yet they did not appear to be at all interested about us, nor did they deviate in the least from their course to regard us; which insensibility, especially in maritime persons, about a matter in their own profession, is scarcely to be credited, did not the general behaviour of the *Chinese*, in other instances, furnish us with continual proofs of a similar turn of mind: It may perhaps be doubted, whether this cast of temper be the effect of nature or education; but, in either case, it is an incontestable symptom of a mean and contemptible disposition, and is alone a sufficient confutation of the extravagant panegyrics, which many hypothetical writers have bestowed on the ingenuity and capacity of this Nation.[1] But to return:

Not being able to procure any information from the *Chinese* fishermen about our proper course to *Macao*, it was necessary for us to rely entirely on our own judgment; and concluding from our latitude, which was 23°: 42' North, and from our soundings, which were only seventeen or eighteen fathoms, that we were yet to the eastward of *Pedro Blanco*, we stood to the westward: And for the assistance of future Navigators, who may hereafter doubt about the parts of the coast they are upon, I must observe, that besides the latitude of *Pedro Blanco*, which is 22°: 18', and the depth of water, which to the westward of that rock is almost every where twenty fathoms, there is another circumstance which will give great assistance in judging of the position of the ship: This is the kind of ground; for, till we came within thirty miles of *Pedro Blanco*, we had constantly a sandy bottom; but there the bottom changed to soft and muddy, and continued so quite to the Island of *Macao*; only while we were in sight of *Pedro Blanco* and very near it, we had for a short space a bottom of greenish mud, intermixed with sand.

It was on the 5th of *November*, at midnight, when we first made the coast of *China*; and the next day, about two o'clock, as we were standing to the westward within two leagues of the coast, and still surrounded by fishing vessels in as great numbers as at first, we perceived that a boat a-head of us waved a red flag, and blew a horn: This we considered as a signal made to us, either to warn us of some shoal, or to inform us that they would supply us with a Pilot, and in this belief we immediately sent our Cutter to the boat, to know their intentions; but we were soon made sensible of our mistake, and found that this boat was the Commodore of the whole fishery, and that the signal she had made, was to order them all to leave off fishing, and to return in shore, which we saw them instantly obey. On this disappointment we kept on our course, and soon after passed by two very small rocks, which lay four or five miles distant from the shore; but night came on before we got sight of *Pedro Blanco*, and we therefore brought to till the morning, when we had the satisfaction to discover it. It is a rock of a small circumference, but of a moderate height, and, both in shape and colour, resembles a sugar loaf, and is about seven or eight miles from the shore. We passed within a mile and an half of it, and left it between us and the land, still keeping on to the westward; and the next day, being the 7th, we were a-breast of a chain of Islands, which stretched from East to West. These, as we afterwards found, were called the Islands of *Lema*; they are rocky and barren, and are in all, small and great, fifteen or sixteen; and there are, besides, a great number of other Islands between them and the main land of *China*. There is annexed a view of these Islands, and likewise a view of the grand *Ladrone* hereafter mentioned, as it appears when (R), the westermost of the Islands of *Lema*, bears W. N. W, at the distance of a mile and half. These Islands we left on the starboard-side, passing within four miles of them, where we had twenty-four fathom water. We were still surrounded by fishing boats; and we once more sent the Cutter on board one of them, to endeavour to procure a Pilot, but could not prevail; however, one of the *Chinese* directed us by signs to sail round the westermost of the islands or rocks of *Lema*, and then to hale up. We followed this direction, and in the evening came to an anchor in eighteen fathom; at which time, the rock (R) in the foregoing draught bore S. S. E. five miles distant, and the grand *Ladrone* W. by S, about two leagues distant. The rock (R) is a most excellent direction for ships coming from the eastward: Its latitude is 21° : 52′ North, and it bears from *Pedro Blanco* S. 64° W, distant twenty-one leagues. You are to leave it on the starboard-side, and you may come within half a mile of it in eighteen fathom water: And then you must steer N. by W. ½ W. for the channel, between the Islands of *Cabouce* and *Bamboo*, which are to the northward of the grand *Ladrone*.

After having continued at anchor all night, we, on the 9th, at four in the morning, sent our Cutter to sound the channel, where we proposed to pass; but before the return of the Cutter, a *Chinese* Pilot put on board us, and told us, in broken *Portuguese*, he would carry us to *Macao* for thirty dollars: These were immediately paid him, and we then weighed and made sail; and soon after, several other Pilots came on board us, who, to recommend themselves, produced certificates from the Captains of several ships they had pilotted in, but we continued the ship under the management of the *Chinese* who came first on board. By this time we learnt, that we were not far distant from *Macao*, and that there were in the river of *Canton*, at the mouth of which *Macao* lies, eleven *European* ships, of which four were *English*. Our Pilot carried us between the Islands of *Bamboo* and *Cabouce*, but the winds hanging in the northern board, and the tides often setting strongly against us, we were obliged to come frequently to an anchor, so that we did not get through between the two Islands till the 12th of *November*, at two in the morning. In passing through, our depth of water was from twelve to fourteen fathom; and as we still steered on N. by W. ½ W, between a number of other Islands, our soundings underwent little or no variation till towards the evening, when they encreased to seventeen fathom; in which depth (the wind dying away) we anchored not far from the Island of *Lantoon*, which is the largest of all this range of Islands. At seven in the morning we weighed again, and steering W. S. W. and S. W. by W, we at ten o'clock happily anchored in *Macao* road, in five fathom water, the city of *Macao* bearing W. by N, three leagues distant; the peak of *Lantoon* E. by N, and the grand *Ladrone* S. by E, each of them about five leagues distant. Thus, after a fatiguing cruise of about two years continuance, we once more arrived in an amicable port, in a civilized country; where the conveniencies of life were in great plenty; where the naval stores,

315

which we now extremely wanted, could be in some degree procured; where we expected the inexpressible satisfaction of receiving letters from our relations and friends; and where our country men, who were lately arrived from *England,* would be capable of answering the numerous enquiries we were prepared to make, both about public and private occurrences, and to relate to us many particulars, which, whether of importance or not, would be listned to by us with the utmost attention, after the long suspension of our correspondence with our country, to which the nature of our undertaking had hitherto subjected us.

CHAP. VII.

Proceedings at *Macao*.

THE city of *Macao*, in the road of which we came to an anchor on the 12th of *November*, is a *Portuguese* settlement, situated in an Island at the mouth of the river of *Canton*. It was formerly a very rich and populous city, and capable of defending itself against the power of the adjacent *Chinese* Governors: But at present it is much fallen from its ancient splendor; for though it is inhabited by *Portuguese*, and hath a Governor nominated by the King of *Portugal*, yet it subsists merely by the sufferance of the *Chinese*, who can starve the place, and dispossess the *Portuguese* whenever they please: This obliges the Governor of *Macao* to behave with great circumspection, and carefully to avoid every circumstance that may give offence to the *Chinese*. The river of *Canton*, at the mouth of which this city lies, is the only *Chinese* port, frequented by *European* ships; and this river is indeed a more commodious harbour, on many accounts, than *Macao*: But the peculiar customs of the *Chinese*, only adapted to the entertainment of trading ships, and the apprehensions of the Commodore, least he should embroil the *East-India* Company with the Regency of *Canton*, if he should insist on being treated upon a different footing than the Merchantmen, made him resolve to go first to *Macao*, before he ventured into the port of *Canton*. Indeed, had not this reason prevailed with him, he himself had nothing to fear: For it is certain that he might have entered the port of *Canton*, and might have continued there as long as he pleased, and afterwards have left it again, although the whole power of the *Chinese* Empire had been brought together to oppose him.

The Commodore, not to depart from his usual prudence, no sooner came to an anchor in *Macao* road, than he dispatched an officer with his compliments to the *Portuguese* Governor of *Macao*, requesting his Excellency, by the same officer, to advise him in what manner it would be proper to act, to avoid offending the *Chinese*, which, as there were then four of our ships in their power at *Canton*, was a matter worthy of attention. The difficulty, which the Commodore principally apprehended, related to the duty usually paid by all ships in the river of *Canton*, according to their tunnage. For as men of war are exempted in every foreign harbour from all manner of port charges, the Commodore thought it would be derogatory to the honour of his country, to submit to this duty in *China*: And therefore he desired the advice of the Governor of *Macao*, who, being an *European*, could not be ignorant of the privileges claimed by a *British* man of war, and consequently might be expected to give us the best lights for avoiding this perplexity. Our boat returned in the evening with two officers sent by the Governor, who informed the Commodore, that it was the Governor's opinion, that if the *Centurion* ventured into the river of *Canton*, the duty would certainly be demanded; and therefore, if the Commodore approved of it, he would send him a Pilot, who should conduct us into another safe harbour called the *Typa*, which was every way commodious for careening the ship (an operation we were resolved to begin upon as soon as possible) and where the abovementioned duty would, in all probability, be never asked for.

This proposal the Commodore agreed to, and in the morning we weighed anchor, and, under the direction of the *Portuguese* Pilot, steered for the intended harbour. As we entered two Islands, which form the eastern passage to it, we found our soundings decreased to three fathom and a half: But the Pilot assuring us that this was the least depth we should meet with, we continued our course, till at length the ship struck fast in the mud, with only eighteen foot water abaft; and, the tide of ebb making, the water fewed to sixteen feet, but the ship remained perfectly up right; we then sounded all round us, and finding the water deepned to the northward, we carried out our small bower with two hawsers on end, and at the return of the tide of flood hove the ship a float; and a small breeze springing up at the same instant, we set the fore-top-sail, and slipping the hawser run into the harbour, where we moored in about five fathom water. This harbour of the *Typa* is formed by a number of Islands, and is about six miles distant from *Macao*. Here we saluted the castle of *Macao* with eleven guns, which were returned by an equal number.

The next day the Commodore paid a visit in person to the Governor, and was saluted at his landing by eleven guns; which were returned by the *Centurion*. Mr. *Anson*'s business in this visit, was to solicit the Governor to grant us a supply of provisions, and to furnish us with such stores as were necessary to refit the ship. The Governor seemed really inclined to do us all the service he could; and assured the Commodore, in a friendly manner, that he would privately give us all the assistance in his power; but he, at the same time, frankly owned, that he dared not openly furnish us with any thing we demanded, unless we first procured an order for it from the Viceroy of *Canton*; for that he neither received provisions for his garrison nor any other necessaries, but by permission from the *Chinese* Government; and as they took care only to furnish him from day to day, he was indeed no other than their vassal, whom they could at all times compel to submit to their own terms, only by laying an embargo on his provisions.

On this declaration of the Governor, Mr. *Anson* resolved himself to go to *Canton*, to procure a licence from the Viceroy; and he accordingly hired a *Chinese* boat for himself and his attendants; but just as he was ready to embark, the *Hoppo*[1] or *Chinese* Custom-house officer at *Macao* refused to grant a permit to the boat, and ordered the watermen not to proceed at their peril. The Commodore at first endeavoured to prevail with the *Hoppo* to withdraw his injunction, and to grant a permit; and the Governor of *Macao* employed his interest with the *Hoppo* to the same purpose. Mr. *Anson*, finding the officer inflexible, told him, the next day, that if he longer refused to grant the permit, he would man and arm his own boats, to carry him thither; asking the *Hoppo*, at the same time, who he imagined would dare to oppose him. This threat immediately brought about what his intreaties had laboured for in vain: The permit was granted, and Mr. *Anson* went to *Canton*. On his arrival there, he consulted with the Supercargoes and Officers of the *English* ships, how to procure an order from the Viceroy for the necessaries he wanted: But in this he had reason to suppose, that the advice they gave him, though doubtless well intended, was yet not the most prudent: For as it is the custom with these Gentlemen, never to apply to the supreme Magistrate himself, whatever difficulties they labour under, but to transact all matters relating to the Government, by the mediation of the principal *Chinese* Merchants, Mr. *Anson* was advised to follow the same method upon this occasion, the *English* promising (in which they were doubtless sincere) to exert all their interest to engage the Merchants in his favour. And when the *Chinese* Merchants were applied to, they readily undertook the management of it, and promised to answer for its success; but after near a month's delay, and reiterated excuses, during which interval they pretended to be often upon the point of compleating the business, they at last (being pressed, and measures being taken for delivering a letter to the Viceroy) threw off the mask, and declared they neither had applied to the Viceroy, nor could they; for he was too great a man, they said, for them to approach on any occasion.[1] And not contented with having themselves thus grossly deceived the Commodore, they now used all their persuasion with the *English* at *Canton*, to prevent them from intermeddling with any thing that regarded him, representing to them, that it would in all probability embroil them with the Government, and occasion them a great deal of unnecessary trouble; which groundless insinuations had indeed but too much weight with those they were applied to.

It may be difficult to assign a reason for this perfidious conduct of the *Chinese* Merchants: Interest indeed is known to exert a boundless influence over the inhabitants of that Empire; but how their interest could be affected in the present case is not easy to discover; unless they apprehended that the presence of a ship of force might damp their *Manila* trade, and therefore acted in this manner with a view of forcing the Commodore to *Batavia*: But it might be as natural in this light to suppose, that they would have been eager to have got him dispatched. I therefore rather impute their behaviour to the unparalleled pusillanimity of the Nation, and to the awe they are under of the Government: For as such a ship as the *Centurion*, fitted for war only, had never been seen in those parts before, she was the horror of these dastards,[2] and the Merchants were in some degree terrified even with the idea of her, and could not think of applying to the Viceroy (who is doubtless fond of all opportunities of fleecing them) without representing to themselves the pretences which a hungry and tyrannical Magistrate might possibly find, for censuring their intermeddling in so unusual a transaction, in which he might pretend the interest of the State was immediately concerned. However, be this as it may, the Commodore was satisfied that nothing was to be done by the interposition of the Merchants, as it was on his pressing them to deliver a letter to the Viceroy, that they had declared they durst not intermeddle, and had confessed, that notwithstanding all their pretences of serving him, they had not yet taken one step towards it. Mr. *Anson* therefore told them, that he would proceed to *Batavia*, and refit his ship there; but informed them, at the same time, that this was impossible to be done, unless he was supplied with a stock of provisions sufficient for his passage. The Merchants, on this, undertook to procure him provisions, but assured him, that it was what they durst not engage in openly, but proposed to manage it in a clandestine manner, by putting a quantity of bread, flower and other provision on board the *English* ships, which were now ready to sail; and these were to stop at the mouth of the *Typa*, where the *Centurion*'s boats were to receive it. This article, which the Merchants represented as a matter of great favour, being settled, the Commodore, on the 16th of *December*, returned from *Canton* to the ship, seemingly resolved to proceed to *Batavia* to refit, as soon as he should get his supplies of provision on board.

But Mr. *Anson* (who never intended going to *Batavia*) found, on his return to the *Centurion*, that her main-mast was sprung in two places, and that the leak was considerably encreased; so that, upon the whole, he was fully satisfied, that though he should lay in a sufficient stock of provisions, yet it would be impossible for him to put to sea without refitting: For, if he left the port with his ship in her present condition, she would be in the utmost danger of foundring; and therefore, notwithstanding the difficulties he had met with, he resolved at all events to have her hove down, before he left *Macao*. He was fully convinced, by what he had observed at *Canton*, that his great caution not to injure the *East-India* Company's affairs, and the regard he had shown to the advice of their officers, had occasioned all his embarrasments. For he now saw clearly, that if he had at first carried his ship into the river of *Canton*, and had immediately applied himself to the *Mandarines*, who are the chief officers of State, instead of employing the Merchants to apply for him, he would, in all probability, have had all his requests granted, and would have been soon dispatched. He had already lost a month, by the wrong measures he had been put upon, but he resolved to lose as little more time as possible; and therefore, the 17th of *December*, being the next day after his return from *Canton*, he wrote a letter to the Viceroy of that place, acquainting him, that he was Commander in chief of a squadron of his *Britannick* Majesty's ships of war, which had been cruising for two years past in the *South-Seas* against the *Spaniards*, who were at war with the King his

Master; that, in his way back to *England*, he had put into the port of *Macao*, having a considerable leak in his ship, and being in great want of provisions, so that it was impossible for him to proceed on his voyage, till his ship was repaired, and he was supplied with the necessaries he wanted; that he had been at *Canton*, in hopes of being admitted to a personal audience of his Excellency; but being a stranger to the customs of the country, he had not been able to inform himself what steps were necessary to be taken to procure such an audience, and therefore was obliged to apply to him in this manner, to desire his Excellency to give orders, for his being permitted to employ Carpenters and proper workmen to refit his ship, and to furnish himself with provisions and stores, thereby to enable him to pursue his voyage to *Great-Britain* with this monsoon, hoping, at the same time, that these orders would be issued with as little delay as possible, least it might occasion his loss of the season, and he might be prevented from departing till the next winter.

This letter was translated into the *Chinese* language, and the Commodore delivered it himself to the *Hoppo* or chief officer of the Emperor's customs at *Macao*, desiring him to forward it to the Viceroy of *Canton*, with as much expedition as he could. The officer at first seemed unwilling to take charge of it, and raised many difficulties about it, so that Mr. *Anson* suspected him of being in league with the Merchants of *Canton*, who had always shown a great apprehension of the Commodore's having any immediate intercourse with the Viceroy or *Mandarines*; and therefore the Commodore, with some resentment, took back his letter from the *Hoppo*, and told him, he would immediately send an officer with it to *Canton* in his own boat, and would give him positive orders not to return without an answer from the Viceroy. The *Hoppo* perceiving the Commodore to be in earnest, and fearing to be called to an account for his refusal, begged to be entrusted with the letter, and promised to deliver it, and to procure an answer as soon as possible. And now it was soon seen how justly Mr. *Anson* had at last judged of the proper manner of dealing with the *Chinese*; for this letter was written but the 17th of *December*, as hath been already observed; and, on the 19th in the morning, a *Mandarine* of the first rank, who was Governor of the city of *Janson*, together with two *Mandarines* of an inferior class, and a great retinue of officers and servants, having with them eighteen half gallies, decorated with a great number of streamers, and furnished with music, and full of men, came to grapnel a-head of the *Centurion*; whence the *Mandarine* sent a message to the Commodore, telling him, that he (the *Mandarine*) was ordered, by the Viceroy of *Canton*, to examine the condition of the ship, and desiring the ship's boat might be sent to fetch him on board. The *Centurion*'s boat was immediately dispatched, and preparations were made for receiving him; for a hundred of the most sightly of the crew were uniformly drest in the regimentals of the marines,[1] and were drawn up under arms on the main-deck, against his arrival. When he entered the ship he was saluted by the drums, and what other military music there was on board; and passing by the new-formed guard, he was met by the Commodore on the quarter-deck, who conducted him to the great cabbin. Here the *Mandarine* explained his commission, declaring, that his business was to examine all the particulars mentioned in the Commodore's letter to the Viceroy, and to confront them with the representation that had been given of them; that he was particularly instructed to inspect the leak, and had for that purpose brought with him two *Chinese* Carpenters; and that for the greater regularity and dispatch of his business, he had every head of enquiry separately wrote down on a sheet of paper, with a void space opposite to it, where he was to insert such information and remarks thereon, as he could procure by his own observation.

This *Mandarine* appeared to be a person of very considerable parts, and endowed with more frankness and honesty, than is to be found in the generality of the *Chinese*. After the proper enquiries had been made, particularly about the leak, which the *Chinese* Carpenters reported to be as dangerous as it had been represented, and consequently that it was impossible for the *Centurion* to proceed to sea without being refitted, the *Mandarine* expressed himself satisfied with the account given in the Commodore's letter. And this Magistrate, as he was more intelligent than any other person of his nation that came to our knowledge, so likewise was he more curiou_ ..._d inquisitive, viewing each part of the ship with particular attention, and appearing greatly surprized at the largeness of the lower deck guns, and at the weight and size of the shot. The Commodore, observing his astonishment, thought this a proper opportunity to convince the *Chinese* of the prudence of granting him a speedy and ample supply of all he wanted: With this view he told the *Mandarine*, and those who were with him, that, besides the demands he made for a general supply, he had a particular complaint against the proceedings of the Custom-house of *Macao*; that at his first arrival the *Chinese* boats had brought on board plenty of greens, and variety of fresh provisions for daily use, for which they had always been paid to their full satisfaction, but that the Custom house officers at *Macao* had soon forbid them, by which means he was deprived of those refreshments which were of the utmost consequence to the health of his men, after their long and sickly voyage; that as they, the *Mandarines*, had informed themselves of his wants, and were eye-witnesses of the force and strength of his ship, they might be satisfied it was not for want of power to supply himself, that he desired the permission of the Government to purchase what provisions he stood in need of; that they must be convinced that the *Centurion* alone was capable of destroying the whole navigation of the port of *Canton*, or of any other port in *China*, without running the least risque from all the force the *Chinese* could collect; that it was true, this was not the manner of proceeding between nations in friendship with each other, but it was likewise true, that it was not customary for any nation to permit the ships of their friends to starve and sink in their ports, when those friends had money to supply their wants, and only desired liberty to lay it out; that they must confess, he and his people had hitherto behaved with great modesty and reserve, but that, as his wants were each day encreasing, hunger would at last prove too strong for any restraint, and necessity was acknowledged in all countries to be superior to every other law; and therefore it could not be expected that his crew would long continue to starve in the midst of that plenty to which their eyes were every day witnesses: To this the Commodore added, (though perhaps with a less serious air) that if by the delay of supplying him with provision his men should be reduced to the necessity of turning cannibals, and preying upon their own species, it was easy to be foreseen that, independent of their friendship to their comrades, they would, in point of luxury, prefer the plump well fed *Chinese* to their own immaciated shipmates. The first *Mandarine* acquiesced in the justness of this reasoning, and told the Commodore, that he should that night proceed for *Canton*; that on his arrival, a Council of *Mandarines* would be summoned, of which he himself was a Member, and that by being employed in the present Commission, he was of course the Commodore's Advocate; that, as he was fully convinced of the urgency of Mr. *Anson's* necessity, he did not doubt but, on his representation, the Council would be of the same opinion; and that all that was demanded would be amply and speedily granted: And with regard to the Commodore's complaint of the Custom-house of *Macao*, he undertook to rectify that immediately by his own authority; for desiring a list to be given him of the quantity of provision necessary for the expence of the ship for a day, he wrote a permit under it, and delivered it to one of his attendants, directing him to see that quantity sent on board early every morning; and this order, from that time forwards, was punctually complied with.

When this weighty affair was thus in some degree regulated, the Commodore invited him and his two attendant *Mandarines* to dinner, telling them at the same time, that if his provision, either in kind or quantity, was not what they might expect, they must thank themselves for having confined him to so hard an allowance. One of his dishes was beef, which the *Chinese* all dislike, though Mr. *Anson* was not apprized of it; this seems to be derived from the *Indian* superstition, which for some ages past has made a great progress in *China*. However, his guests did not entirely fast; for the three *Mandarines* compleatly finished the white part of four large fowls. But they were extremely embarrassed with their knives and forks, and were quite incapable of making use of them: So that, after some fruitless attempts to help themselves, which were sufficiently awkward, one of the attendants was obliged to cut their meat in small pieces for them. But whatever difficulty they might have in complying with the *European* manner of eating, they seemed not to be novices in drinking. The Commodore excused himself in this part of the entertainment, under the pretence of illness; but there being another Gentleman present, of a florid and jovial complexion, the chief *Mandarine* clapped him on the shoulder, and told him by the interpreter, that certainly he could not plead sickness, and therefore insisted on his bearing him company; and that Gentleman perceiving, that after they had dispatched four or five bottles of *Frontiniac*, the *Mandarine* still continued unruffled, he ordered a bottle of citron-water to be brought up, which the *Chinese* seemed much to relish, and this being near finished, they arose from table, in appearance cool and uninfluenced by what they had drank, and the Commodore having, according to custom, made the *Mandarine* a present, they all departed in the same vessels that brought them.

After their departure, the Commodore with great impatience expected the resolution of the Council, and the necessary licences for his refitment. For it must be observed, as hath already appeared from the preceding narration, that he could neither purchase stores nor necessaries with his money, nor did any kind of workmen dare to engage themselves to work for him, without the permission of the Government first obtained. And in the execution of these particular injunctions, the Magistrates never fail of exercising great severity, they, notwithstanding the fustian elogiums bestowed upon them by the Catholic Missionaries and their *European* copiers,[1] being composed of the same fragile materials with the rest of mankind, and often making use of the authority of the law, not to suppress crimes, but to enrich themselves by the pillage of those who commit them; for capital punishments are rare in *China*, the effeminate genius of the nation, and their strong attachment to lucre, disposing them rather to make use of fines; and hence arises no inconsiderable profit to those who compose their tribunals: Consequently prohibitions of all kinds, particularly such, as the alluring prospect of great profit may often tempt the subject to infringe, cannot but be favourite institutions in such a Government. But to return:

Some time before this, Captain *Saunders* took his passage to *England* on board a *Swedish* ship, and was charged with dispatches from the Commodore; and soon after, in the month of *December*, Captain *Mitchel*, Colonel *Cracherode*, and Mr. *Tassel*, one of the Agent-Victuallers, with his nephew, Mr. *Charles Herriot*, embarked on board some of our Company's ships; and I, having obtained the Commodore's leave to return home, embarked with them.[2] I must observe too, (having omitted it before) that whilst we lay here at *Macao*, we were informed by some of the officers of our *Indiamen*, that the *Severn* and *Pearl*, the two ships of our squadron, which had separated from us off Cape *Noir*, were safely arrived at *Rio Janeiro* on the coast of *Brazil*. I have formerly taken notice, that at the time of their separation, we apprehended them to be lost. And there were many reasons which greatly favoured this suspicion: For we knew that the *Severn* in particular was extreamly sickly; and this was the more obvious to the rest of the ships, as, in the preceding part of the voyage, her Commander Capt. *Legg* had been remarkable for his exemplary punctuality in keeping his station, till, for the last ten days before his separation, his crew was so diminished and enfeebled, that with his utmost efforts it was not possible for him to maintain his proper position with his wonted exactness. The extraordinary sickness on board him was by many imputed to the ship, which was new, and on that account was believed to be the more unhealthy; but whatever was the cause of it, the *Severn* was by much the most sickly of the squadron: For before her departure from St. *Catherine's* she buried more men than any of them, insomuch that the Commodore was obliged to recruit her with a number of fresh hands; and, the mortality still continuing on board her, she was supplied with men a second time at sea, after our setting sail from St. *Julians*; and notwithstanding these different reinforcements, she was at last reduced to the distressed condition I have already mentioned: So that the Commodore himself was firmly persuaded she was lost; and therefore it was with great joy we received the news of her and the *Pearl's* safety, after the strong persuasion, which had so long prevailed amongst us, of their having both perished.[1] But to proceed with the transactions between Mr. *Anson* and the *Chinese*.

Notwithstanding the favourable disposition of the *Mandarine* Governor of *Janson*, at his leaving Mr. *Anson*, several days were elapsed before he had any advice from him; and Mr. *Anson* was privately informed there were great debates in Council upon his affair; partly perhaps owing to its being so unusual a case, and in part to the influence, as I suppose, of the intrigues of the *French* at *Canton:* For they had a countryman and fast friend residing on the spot, who spoke the language very well, and was not unacquainted with the venality of the Government, nor with the persons of several of the Magistrates, and consequently could not be at a loss for means of traversing the assistance desired by Mr. *Anson*. And this opposition of the *French* was not merely the effect of national prejudice or contrariety of political interests, but was in good measure owing to their vanity, a motive of much more weight with the generality of mankind, than any attachment to the public service of their community: For, the *French* pretending their *India-men* to be Men of War, their officers were apprehensive, that any distinction granted to Mr. *Anson*, on account of his bearing the King's Commission, would render them less considerable in the eyes of the *Chinese*, and would establish a prepossession at *Canton* in favour of ships of war, by which they, as trading vessels, would suffer in their importance: And I wish the affectation of endeavouring to pass for men of war, and the fear of sinking in the estimation of the *Chinese*, if the *Centurion* was treated in a different manner from themselves, had been confined to the officers of the *French* ships only.[1] However, notwithstanding all these obstacles, it should seem, that the representation of the Commodore to the *Mandarines* of the facility with which he could right himself, if justice were denied him, had at last its effect: For, on the 6th of *January*, in the morning, the Governor of *Janson*, the Commodore's Advocate, sent down the Viceroy of *Canton*'s warrant for the refitment of the *Centurion*, and for supplying her people with all they wanted; and, the next day, a number of *Chinese* Smiths and Carpenters went on board, to agree for all the work by the great. They demanded at first, to the amount of a thousand pounds sterling for the necessary repairs of the ship, the boats, and the masts: This the Commodore seemed to think an unreasonable sum, and endeavoured to persuade them to work by the day; but that proposal they would not hearken to; so it was at last agreed, that the Carpenters should have to the amount of about six hundred pounds for their work; and that the Smiths should be paid for their iron-work by weight, allowing them at the rate of three pounds a hundred nearly for the small work, and forty-six shillings for the large.

This being regulated, the Commodore exerted himself to get this most important business compleated; I mean, the heaving down the *Centurion*, and examining the state of her bottom: For this purpose the first Lieutenant was dispatched to *Canton* to hire two country vessels, called in their language junks, one of them being intended to heave down by, and the other to serve as a magazine for the powder and ammunition: At the same time the ground was smoothed on one of the neighbouring Islands, and a large tent was pitched for lodging the lumber and provisions, and near a hundred *Chinese* Caulkers were soon set to work on the decks and sides of the ship. But all these preparations, and the getting ready the careening gear, took up a great deal of time; for the *Chinese* Caulkers, though they worked very well, were far from being expeditious; and it was the 26th of *January* before the junks arrived; and the necessary materials, which were to be purchased at *Canton*, came down very slowly; partly from the distance of the place, and partly from the delays and backwardness of the *Chinese*

Merchants. And in this interval Mr. *Anson* had the additional perplexity to discover, that his fore-mast was broken asunder above the
upper deck partners, and was only kept together by the fishes which
had been formerly clapt upon it.

However, the *Centurion's* people made the most of their time, and
exerted themselves the best they could; and as, by clearing the ship,
the Carpenters were enabled to come at the leak, they took care to
secure that effectually, whilst the other preparations were going forwards. The leak was found to be below the fifteen foot mark, and was
principally occasioned by one of the bolts being wore away and loose
in the joining of the stem where it was scarfed.[1]

At last, all things being prepared, they, on the 22d of *February*, in
the morning, hove out the first course of the *Centurion's* starboard
side, and had the satisfaction to find, that her bottom appeared sound
and good; and, the next day, (having by that time compleated the new
sheathing of the first course) they righted her again, to set up anew
the careening rigging which stretched much. Thus they continued
heaving down, and often righting the ship from a suspicion of their
careening tackle, till the 3d of *March*; when, having compleated the
paying and sheathing the bottom, which proved to be every where
very sound, they, for the last time, righted the ship to their great joy;
for not only the fatigue of careening had been considerable, but they
had been apprehensive of being attacked by the *Spaniards*, whilst the
ship was thus incapacitated for defence. Nor were their fears altogether groundless; for they learnt afterwards, by a *Portuguese* vessel,
that the *Spaniards* at *Manila* had been informed, that the *Centurion*
was in the *Typa*, and intended to careen there;[2] and that thereupon the
Governor had summoned his Council, and had proposed to them to
endeavour to burn her, whilst she was careening, which was an enterprize, which, if properly conducted, might have put them in great
danger: They were farther told, that this scheme was not only proposed, but resolved on; and that a Captain of a vessel had actually
undertaken to perform the business for forty thousand dollars, which
he was not to receive unless he succeeded; but the Governor pretending that there was no treasure in the royal chest, and insisting
that the Merchants should advance the money, and they refusing to
comply with the demand, the affair was dropped: Perhaps the Merchants suspected, that the whole was only a pretext to get forty

thousand dollars from them; and indeed this was affirmed by some who bore the Governor no good will, but with what truth it is difficult to ascertain.

As soon as the *Centurion* was righted, they took in her powder, and gunners stores, and proceeded in getting in their guns as fast as possible, and then used their utmost expedition in repairing the foremast, and in compleating the other articles of her refitment. And being thus employed, they were alarmed, on the 10th of *March*, by a *Chinese* Fisherman, who brought them intelligence that he had been on board a large *Spanish* ship off the grand *Ladrone*, and that there were two more in company with her: He added several particulars to his relation; as that he had brought one of their officers to *Macao*, and that, on this, boats went off early in the morning from *Macao* to them: And the better to establish the belief of his veracity, he said he desired no money, if his information should not prove true. This was presently believed to be the forementioned expedition from *Manila*; and the Commodore immediately fitted his cannon and small arms in the best manner he could for defence; and having then his Pinnace and Cutter in the offing, who had been ordered to examine a *Portuguese* vessel, which was getting under sail, he sent them the advice he had received, and directed them to look out strictly: But no such ships ever appeared, and they were soon satisfied, the whole of the story was a fiction; though it was difficult to conceive what reason could induce the fellow to be at such extraordinary pains to impose on them.

It was the beginning of *April* before they had new-rigged the ship, stowed their provisions and water on board, and had fitted her for the sea; and before this time the *Chinese* grew very uneasy, and extremely desirous that she should be gone; either not knowing, or pretending not to believe, that this was a point the Commodore was as eagerly set on as they could be. On the 3d of *April*, two *Mandarine* boats came on board from *Macao* to urge his departure; and this having been often done before, tho' there had been no pretence to suspect Mr. *Anson* of any affected delays, he at this last message answered them in a determined tone, desiring them to give him no further trouble, for he would go when he thought proper, and not before. On this rebuke the *Chinese* (though it was not in their power to compel him to be gone) immediately prohibited all provisions from being carried on board him, and took such care that their injunctions should be complied with, that from that time forwards nothing could be purchased at any rate whatever.

On the 6th of *April,* the *Centurion* weighed from the *Typa,* and warped[1] to the southward; and, by the 15th, she was got into *Macao* road, compleating her water as she past along, so that there remained now very few articles more to attend to; and her whole business being finished by the 19th, she, at three in the afternoon of that day, weighed and made sail, and stood to sea.

CHAP. VIII.

From *Macao* to Cape *Espiritu Santo:* The taking of the *Manila* galeon, and returning back again.

THE Commodore was now got to sea, with his ship very well refitted, his stores replenished, and an additional stock of provisions on board: His crew too was somewhat reinforced; for he had entered twenty-three men during his stay at *Macao*, the greatest part of which were Lascars or *Indian* sailors, and some few *Dutch*. He gave out at *Macao*, that he was bound to *Batavia*, and thence to *England*; and though the westerly monsoon was now set in, when that passage is considered as impracticable, yet, by the confidence he had expressed in the strength of his ship, and the dexterity of his people, he had persuaded not only his own crew but the people at *Macao* likewise, that he proposed to try this unusual experiment; so that there were many letters put on board him by the inhabitants of *Canton* and *Macao* for their friends at *Batavia*.

But his real design was of a very different nature: For he knew, that instead of one annual ship from *Acapulco* to *Manila*, there would be this year, in all probability, two; since, by being before *Acapulco*, he had prevented one of them from putting to sea the preceding season.[1] He therefore resolved to cruise for these returning vessels off Cape *Espiritu Santo*, on the Island of *Samal*, which is the first land they always make in the *Philippine* Islands. And as *June* is generally the month in which they arrive there, he doubted not but he should get to his intended station time enough to intercept them. It is true, they were said to be stout vessels, mounting forty-four guns apiece, and carrying about five hundred hands, and might be expected to return in company; and he himself had but two hundred and twenty-seven hands on board, of which near thirty were boys: But this disproportion of strength did not deter him, as he knew his ship to be much better fitted for a sea-engagement than theirs, and as he had reason to expect that his men would exert themselves in the most extraordinary manner, when they had in view the immense wealth of these *Manila* galeons.

This project the Commodore had resolved on in his own thoughts, ever since his leaving the coast of *Mexico*. And the greatest mortification which he received, from the various delays he had met with in *China*, was his apprehension, lest he might be thereby so long retarded as to let the galeons escape him. Indeed, at *Macao* it was incumbent on him to keep these views extremely secret; for there being a great intercourse and a mutual connexion of interests between that port and *Manila*, he had reason to fear, that, if his designs were discovered, intelligence would be immediately sent to *Manila*, and measures would be taken to prevent the galeons from falling into his hands: But being now at sea, and entirely clear of the coast, he summoned all his people on the quarter-deck, and informed them of his resolution to cruise for the two *Manila* ships. of whose wealth they were not ignorant. He told them he should chuse a station, where he could not fail of meeting with them; and though they were stout ships, and full manned, yet, if his own people behaved with their accustomed spirit, he was certain he should prove too hard for them both, and that one of them at least could not fail of becoming his prize: He further added, that many ridiculous tales had been propagated about the strength of the sides of these ships, and their being impenetrable to cannon-shot; that these fictions had been principally invented to palliate the cowardice of those who had formerly engaged them; but he hoped there were none of those present weak enough to give credit to so absurd a story: For his own part, he did assure them upon his word, that, whenever he met with them, he would fight them so near, that they should find, his bullets, instead of being stopped by one of their sides, should go through them both.[1]

This speech of the Commodore's was received by his people with great joy: For no sooner had he ended, than they expressed their approbation, according to naval custom, by three strenuous cheers, and all declared their determination to succeed or perish, whenever the opportunity presented itself. And now their hopes, which since their departure from the coast of *Mexico*, had entirely subsided, were again revived; and they all persuaded themselves, that, notwithstanding the various casualties and disappointments they had hitherto met with, they should yet be repaid the price of their fatigues, and should at last return home enriched with the spoils of the enemy: For firmly relying on the assurances of the Commodore, that they should certainly meet with the vessels, they were all of them too sanguine to doubt a moment of mastering them; so that they considered themselves as having them already in their possession. And this confidence was so universally spread through the whole ship's company, that, the Commodore having taken some *Chinese* sheep to sea with them for his own provision, and one day enquiring of his Butcher, why, for some time past, he had seen no mutton at his table, asking him if all the sheep were killed, the Butcher very seriously replied, that there were indeed two sheep left, but that if his Honour would give him leave, he proposed to keep those for the entertainment of the General of the galeons.

When the *Centurion* left the port of *Macao*, she stood for some days to the westward; and, on the first of *May*, they saw part of the Island of *Formosa*; and, standing thence to the southward, they, on the 4th of *May*, were in the latitude of the *Bashee Islands*, as laid down by *Dampier*; but they suspected his account of inaccuracy, as they found that he had been considerably mistaken in the latitude of the South end of *Formosa*: For this reason they kept a good look-out, and about seven in the evening discovered from the mast-head five small Islands, which were judged to be the *Bashees*, and they had afterwards a sight of *Botel Tobago Xima*. By this means they had an opportunity of correcting the position of the *Bashee Islands*, which had been hitherto laid down twenty-five leagues too far to the westward: For by their observations, they esteemed the middle of these Islands to be in 21° : 4′ North, and to bear from *Botel Tobago Xima*, S. S. E. twenty leagues distant, that Island itself being in 21° : 57′ North.

After getting a sight of the *Bashee Islands*, they stood between the S. and S. W for Cape *Espiritu Santo*; and, the 20th of *May* at noon, they first discovered that Cape, which about four o'clock they brought to bear S. S. W, about eleven leagues distant. It appeared to be of a moderate height, with several round hummocks on it; and is exactly represented in the annexed plate. As it was known that there were centinels placed upon this Cape to make signals to the *Acapulco* ship, when she first falls in with the land, the Commodore immediately tacked, and ordered the top-gallant sails to be taken in, to prevent being discovered; and, this being the station in which it was resolved to cruise for the galeons, they kept the Cape between the South and the West, and endeavoured to confine themselves between the latitude of 12° : 50′, and 13° : 5′, the Cape itself lying, by their observations, in 12° : 40′ North, and in 4° of East longitude from *Botel Tobago Xima*.

It was the last of *May*, by the foreign stile, when they arrived off this Cape; and, the month of *June*, by the same stile, being that in which the *Manila* ships are usually expected, the *Centurion's* people were now waiting each hour with the utmost impatience for the happy crisis which was to ballance the account of all their past calamities. As from this time there was but small employment for the crew, the Commodore ordered them almost every day to be exercised in the management of the great guns, and in the use of their small arms. This had been his practice, more or less, at all convenient seasons during the whole course of his voyage; and the advantages which he received from it, in his engagement with the galeon, were an ample recompence for all his care and attention. Indeed, it should seem that there are few particulars of a Commander's duty of more importance than this, how much soever it may have been sometimes overlooked or misunderstood: For it will, I suppose, be confessed, that in two ships of war, equal in the number of their men and guns, the disproportion of strength, arising from a greater or less dexterity in the use of their great guns and small arms, is what can scarcely be ballanced by any other circumstances whatever. For, as these are the weapons with which they are to engage, what greater inequality can there be betwixt two contending parties, than that one side should perfectly understand the use of their weapons, and should have the skill to employ them in the most effectual manner for the annoyance of their enemy, while the other side should, by their awkward management of them, render them rather terrible to themselves, than mischievous to their antagonists? This seems so plain and natural a conclusion, that a person unacquainted with these affairs would suppose the first care of a Commander to be the training his people to the use of their arms.

But human affairs are not always conducted by the plain dictates of common sense. There are many other principles which influence our transactions: And there is one in particular, which, though of a very erroneous complexion, is scarcely ever excluded from our most serious deliberations; I mean custom, or the practice of those who have preceded us. This is usually a power too mighty for reason to grapple with; and is the most terrible to those who oppose it, as it has much of superstition in its nature, and pursues all those who question its authority with unrelenting vehemence. However, in these later ages of the world, some lucky encroachments have been made upon its pre-rogative; and it may reasonably be hoped, that the Gentlemen of the Navy, whose particular profession hath of late been considerably improved by a number of new inventions, will of all others be the readiest to give up those practices, which have nothing to plead but prescription, and will not suppose that every branch of their business hath already received all the perfection of which it is capable. Indeed, it must be owned, that if a dexterity in the use of small arms, for instance, hath been sometimes less attended to on board our ships of war, than might have been wished for, it hath been rather owing to unskilful methods of teaching it, than to negligence: For the common sailors, how strongly soever attached to their own prejudices, are very quick sighted in finding out the defects of others, and have ever shewn a great contempt for the formalities practised in the training of land troops to the use of their arms; but when those who have undertaken to instruct the seamen have contented themselves with inculcating only what was useful, and that in the simplest manner, they have constantly found their people sufficiently docile, and the success hath even exceeded their expectation. Thus on board Mr. *Anson*'s ship, where they were only taught the shortest method of loading with cartridges, and were constantly trained to fire at a mark, which was usually hung at the yard-arm, and where some little reward was given to the most expert, the whole crew, by this management, were rendered extremely skilful, quick in loading, all of them good marksmen, and some of them most extraordinary ones; so that I doubt not but, in the use of small arms, they were more than a match for double their number, who had not been habituated to the same kind of exercise. But to return:

It was the last of *May, N. S.* as hath been already said, when the *Centurion* arrived off Cape *Espiritu Santo*; and consequently the next day began the month in which the galeons were to be expected. The Commodore therefore made all necessary preparations for receiving them, having hoisted out his long boat, and lashed her along side, that the ship might be ready for engaging, if they fell in with the galeons in the night. All this time too he was very solicitous to keep at such a distance from the Cape, as not to be discovered: But it hath been since learnt, that, notwithstanding his care, he was seen from the land; and advice of him was sent to *Manila*, where it was at first disbelieved, but on reiterated intelligence (for it seems he was seen more than once) the Merchants were alarmed, and the Governor was applied to, who undertook (the commerce supplying the necessary sums) to fit out a force consisting of two ships of thirty-two guns, one of twenty guns, and two sloops of ten guns each, to attack the *Centurion* on her station: And some of these vessels did actually weigh with this view; but the principal ship not being ready, and the monsoon being against them, the Commerce and the Governor disagreed, and the enterprize was laid aside.[1] This frequent discovery of the *Centurion* from the shore was somewhat extraordinary; for the pitch of the Cape is not high, and she usually kept from ten to fifteen leagues distant; though once indeed, by an indraught of the tide, as was supposed, they found themselves in the morning within seven leagues of the land.

As the month of *June* advanced, the expectancy and impatience of the Commodore's people each day encreased. And I think no better idea can be given of their great eagerness on this occasion, than by copying a few paragraphs from the journal of an officer, who was then on board; as it will, I presume, be a more natural picture of the full attachment of their thoughts to the business of their cruise, than can be given by any other means. The paragraphs I have selected as they occur in order of time, are as follow:

'*May* 31, Exercising our men at their quarters, in great expectation of meeting with the galeons very soon; this being the eleventh of *June* their stile.'

'*June* 3, Keeping in our stations, and looking out for the galeons.'

'*June* 5, Begin now to be in great expectation, this being the middle of *June* their stile.'

'*June* 11, Begin to grow impatient at not seeing the galeons.'

'*June* 13, The wind having blown fresh easterly for the forty-eight hours past, gives us great expectations of seeing the galeons soon.'

'*June* 15, Cruising on and off, and looking out strictly.'

'*June* 19, This being the last day of *June, N.S.* the galeons, if they arrive at all, must appear soon.'

From these samples it is sufficiently evident, how compleatly the treasure of the galeons had engrossed their imagination, and how anxiously they passed the latter part of their cruise, when the certainty of the arrival of these vessels was dwindled down to probability only, and that probability became each hour more and more doubtful.

However, on the 20th of *June, O. S.* being just a month from their arrival on their station, they were relieved from this state of uncertainty; when, at sun-rise, they discovered a sail from the mast-head, in the S. E. quarter. On this, a general joy spread through the whole ship; for they had no doubt but this was one of the galeons, and they expected soon to see the other. The Commodore instantly stood towards her, and at half an hour after seven they were near enough to see her from the *Centurion's* deck; at which time the galeon fired a gun, and took in her top-gallant sails, which was supposed to be a signal to her consort, to hasten her up,[1] and therefore the *Centurion* fired a gun to leeward, to amuse her. The Commodore was surprized to find, that in all this time the galeon did not change her course, but continued to bear down upon him; for he hardly believed, what afterwards appeared to be the case, that she knew his ship to be the *Centurion*, and resolved to fight him.

About noon the Commodore was little more than a league distant from the galeon, and could fetch her wake, so that she could not now escape; and, no second ship appearing, it was concluded that she had been separated from her consort. Soon after, the galeon haled up her fore-sail, and brought too under top-sails, with her head to the northward, hoisting *Spanish* colours, and having the standard of *Spain* flying at the top-gallant mast-head. Mr. *Anson*, in the mean time, had prepared all things for an engagement on board the *Centurion*, and had taken all possible care, both for the most effectual exertion of his small strength, and for the avoiding the confusion and tumult, too frequent in actions of this kind. He picked out about thirty of his choicest hands and best marksmen, whom he distributed into his tops, and who fully answered his expectation, by the signal services they performed. As he had not hands enough remaining to quarter a sufficient number to each great gun, in the customary manner, he therefore, on his lower tire, fixed only two men to each gun, who were to be solely employed in loading it, whilst the rest of his people were divided into different gangs of ten or twelve men each, which were constantly moving about the decks, to run out and fire such guns as were loaded. By this management he was enabled to make use of all his guns; and instead of firing broad-sides with intervals between them, he kept up a constant fire without intermission, whence he doubted not to procure very signal advantages; for it is common with the *Spaniards* to fall down upon the decks when they see a broadside preparing, and to continue in that posture till it is given; after which they rise again, and, presuming the danger to be for some time over, work their guns and fire with great briskness, till another broad-side is ready: But the firing gun by gun, in the manner directed by the Commodore, rendered this practice of theirs impossible.

The *Centurion* being thus prepared, and nearing the galeon apace, there happened, a little after noon, several squalls of wind and rain, which often obscured the galeon from their sight; but whenever it cleared up, they observed her resolutely lying to; and, towards one o'clock, the *Centurion* hoisted her broad pendant and colours, she being then within gun-shot of the enemy. And the Commodore observing the *Spaniards* to have neglected clearing their ship till that time, as he then saw them throwing over-board cattle and lumber,[1] he gave orders to fire upon them with the chace-guns, to embarass them in their work, and prevent them from compleating it, though his general directions had been not to engage till they were within pistol shot. The galeon returned the fire with two of her stern-chace; and, the *Centurion* getting her sprit-sail-yard fore and aft, that if necessary she might be ready for boarding, the *Spaniards* in a bravado rigged their sprit-sail-yard fore and aft likewise. Soon after, the *Centurion* came abreast of the enemy within pistol-shot, keeping to the leeward with a view of preventing them from putting before the wind, and gaining the port of *Jalapay*, from which they were about seven leagues distant. And now the engagement began in earnest, and, for the first half hour, Mr. *Anson* over-reached the galeon, and lay on her bow; where, by the great wideness of his ports he could traverse almost all his guns upon the enemy, whilst the galeon could only bring a part of hers to bear. Immediately, on the commencement of the action, the mats, with which the galeon had stuffed her netting, took fire, and burnt violently, blazing up half as high as the mizen-top. This accident (supposed to be caused by the *Centurion*'s wads) threw the enemy into great confusion, and at the same time alarmed the Commodore, for he feared least the galeon should be burnt, and least he himself too might suffer by her driving on board him: But the *Spaniards* at last freed themselves from the fire, by cutting away the netting, and tumbling the whole mass which was in flames into the sea. But still the *Centurion* kept her first advantageous position, firing her cannon with great regularity and briskness, whilst at the same time the galeon's decks lay open to her topmen, who, having at their first volley driven the *Spaniards* from their tops, made prodigious havock with their small arms, killing or wounding every officer but one that ever appeared on the quarterdeck, and wounding in particular the General of the galeon himself. And though the *Centurion*, after the first half hour, lost her original situation, and was close along-side the galeon, and the enemy continued to fire briskly for near an hour longer, yet at last the Commodore's grape-shot swept their decks so effectually, and the number of their slain and wounded was so considerable, that they began to fall into great disorder, especially as the General, who was the life of the action, was no longer capable of exerting himself. Their embarasment was visible from on board the Commodore. For the ships were so near, that some of the *Spanish* officers were seen running about with great assiduity, to prevent the desertion of their men from their quarters: But all their endeavours were in vain; for after having, as a last effort, fired five or six guns with more judgment than usual, they gave up the contest; and, the galeon's colours being singed off the ensign staff in the beginning of the engagement, she struck the standard at her main-top-gallant mast-head, the person, who was employed to do it, having been in imminent peril of being killed, had not the Commodore, who perceived what he was about, given express orders to his people to desist from firing.[1]

Thus was the *Centurion* possessed of this rich prize, amounting in value to near a million and half of dollars. She was called the *Nostra Signora de Cabadonga,* and was commanded by the General *Don Jeronimo de Montero,* a *Portuguese* by birth, and the most approved officer for skill and courage of any employed in that service. The galeon was much larger than the *Centurion,*[2] had five hundred and fifty men[3] and thirty-six guns[4] mounted for action, besides twenty-eight pidreroes[5] in her gunwale, quarters and tops, each of which carried a four pound ball. She was very well furnished with small arms, and was particularly provided against boarding, both by her close quarters, and by a strong net-work of two inch rope, which was laced over her waist, and was defended by half pikes. She had sixty-seven killed in the action, and eighty-four wounded,[6] whilst the *Centurion* had only two killed, and a Lieutenant and sixteen wounded, all of whom but one

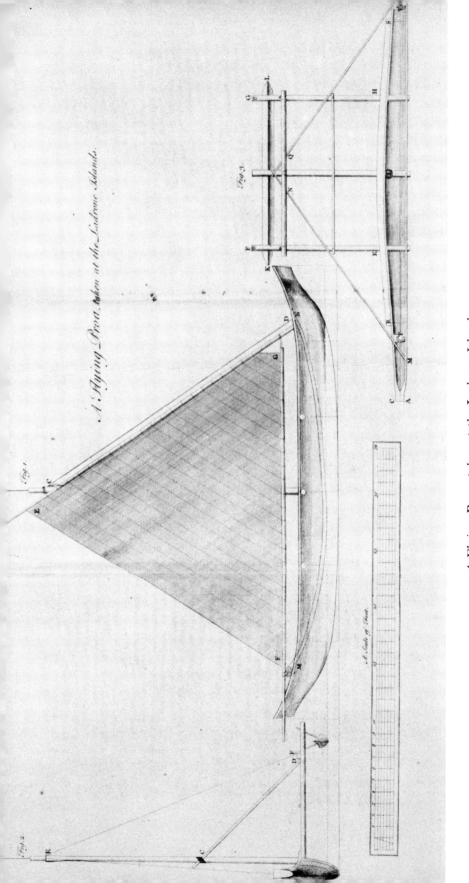

A Flying Proa, taken at the Ladrone Islands

A View of Cape Espiritu Santo on Samal, one
Bearing WSW distant 6 leagues. In the position he
and took the Spanish Galeon call'd Nostra Seignio

e Phillipine Islands, in the latitude of 12:40 *N°*
presented his Majesty's Ship the Centurion engag'd
Cabadonga from Acapulco bound to Manila

Chinese Vessels

recovered: Of so little consequence are the most destructive arms in untutored and unpractised hands.

The treasure thus taken by the *Centurion* having been for at least eighteen months the great object of their hopes, it is impossible to describe the transport on board, when, after all their reiterated disappointments, they at last saw their wishes accomplished. But their joy was near being suddenly damped by a most tremendous incident: For no sooner had the galeon struck, than one of the Lieutenants coming to Mr. *Anson* to congratulate him on his prize, whispered him at the same time, that the *Centurion* was dangerously on fire near the powder-room. The Commodore received this dreadful news without any apparent emotion, and, taking care not to alarm his people, gave the necessary orders for extinguishing it, which was happily done in a short time, though its appearance at first was extremely terrible.[1] It seems some cartridges had been blown up by accident between decks, whereby a quantity of oakum in the after-hatch way, near the after powder-room, was set on fire; and the great smother and smoke of the oakum occasioned the apprehension of a more extended and mischievous fire. At the same instant too, the galeon fell on board the *Centurion* on the starboard quarter, but she was cleared without doing or receiving any considerable damage.

The Commodore made his first Lieutenant, Mr. *Saumarez*, Captain of this prize, appointing her a post-ship in his Majesty's service. Captain *Saumarez*, before night, sent on board the *Centurion* all the *Spanish* prisoners, but such as were thought the most proper to be retained to assist in navigating the galeon. And now the Commodore learnt, from some of these prisoners, that the other ship, which he had kept in the port of *Acapulco* the preceding year, instead of returning in company with the present prize as was expected, had set sail from *Acapulco* alone much sooner than usual, and had, in all probability, got into the port of *Manila* long before the *Centurion* arrived off *Espiritu Santo*; so that Mr. *Anson*, notwithstanding his present success, had great reason to regret his loss of time at *Macao*, which prevented him from taking two rich prizes instead of one.

The Commodore, when the action was ended, resolved to make the best of his way with his prize for the river of *Canton*, being in the mean time fully employed in securing his prisoners, and in removing the treasure from on board the galeon into the *Centurion*. The last of these operations was too important to be postponed; for as the navigation to *Canton* was through seas but little known, and where, from the season of the year, much bad weather might be expected, it was of great consequence that the treasure should be sent on board the *Centurion*, which ship, by the presence of the Commander in Chief, the greater number of her hands, and her other advantages, was doubtless much safer against all the casualties of winds and seas than the galeon: And the securing the prisoners was a matter of still more consequence, as not only the possession of the treasure, but the lives of the captors depended thereon. This was indeed an article which gave the Commodore much trouble and disquietude; for they were above double the number of his own people; and some of them, when they were brought on board the *Centurion*, and had observed how slenderly she was manned, and the large proportion which the striplings bore to the rest, could not help expressing themselves with great indignation to be thus beaten by a handful of boys. The method, which was taken to hinder them from rising, was by placing all but the officers and the wounded in the hold, where, to give them as much air as possible, two hatchways were left open; but then (to avoid all danger, whilst the *Centurion*'s people should be employed upon the deck) there was a square partition of thick planks, made in the shape of a funnel, which enclosed each hatch-way on the lower deck, and reached to that directly over it on the upper deck; these funnels served to communicate the air to the hold better than could have been done without them; and, at the same time, added greatly to the security of the ship; for they being seven or eight feet high, it would have been extremely difficult for the *Spaniards* to have clambered up; and still to augment that difficulty, four swivel guns loaded with musquet-bullets were planted at the mouth of each funnel, and a centinel with lighted match constantly attended, prepared to fire into the hold amongst them, in case of any disturbance. Their officers, which amounted to seventeen or eighteen, were all lodged in the first Lieutenant's cabbin, under a constant guard of six men; and the General, as he was wounded, lay in the Commodore's cabbin with a centinel always with him; and they were all informed, that any violence or disturbance would be punished with instant death. And that the *Centurion*'s people might be at all times prepared, if, notwithstanding these regulations, any tumult should arise, the small arms were constantly kept loaded in a proper place, whilst all the men went armed with cutlasses and pistols; and no officer ever pulled off his cloaths, and when he slept had always his arms lying ready by him.

These measures were obviously necessary, considering the hazards to which the Commodore and his people would have been exposed, had they been less careful. Indeed, the sufferings of the poor prisoners, though impossible to be alleviated, were much to be commiserated; for the weather was extremely hot, the stench of the hold loathsome beyond all conception, and their allowance of water but just sufficient to keep them alive, it not being practicable to spare them more than at the rate of a pint a day for each, the crew themselves having only an allowance of a pint and an half. All this considered, it was wonderful that not a man of them died during their long confinement, except three of the wounded, who died the same night they were taken; though it must be confessed, that the greatest part of them were strangely metamorphised by the heat of the hold; for when they were first taken, they were sightly robust fellows; but when, after above a month's imprisonment, they were discharged in the river of *Canton*, they were reduced to mere skeletons; and their air and looks corresponded much more to the conception formed of ghosts and spectres, than to the figure and appearance of real men.

Thus employed in securing the treasure and the prisoners, the Commodore, as hath been said, stood for the river of *Canton*; and, on the 30th of *June*, at six in the evening, got sight of Cape *Delangano*, which then bore West ten leagues distant; and, the next day, he made the *Bashee Islands*, and the wind being so far to the northward, that it was difficult to weather them, it was resolved to stand through between *Grafton* and *Monmouth Islands*, where the passage seemed to be clear; but in getting through, the sea had a very dangerous aspect, for it ripled and foamed, as if it had been full of breakers, which was still more terrible, as it was then night. But the ships got through very safe, (the prize always keeping a head) and it was found that the appearance which had alarmed them had been occasioned only by a strong tide. I must here observe, that though the *Bashee Islands* are usually reckoned to be no more than five, yet there are many more lying about them to the westward, which, as the channels amongst them are not at all known, makes it adviseable for ships, rather to pass to the northward or southward, than through them; and indeed the

Commodore proposed to have gone to the northward, between them and *Formosa*, had it been possible for him to have weathered them. From hence the *Centurion* steering the proper course for the river of *Canton*, she, on the 8th of *July*, discovered the Island of *Supata*, the westermost of the *Lema* Islands, being the double peaked rock, particularly delineated in the view of the Islands of *Lema*, formerly inserted. This Island of *Supata* they made to be a hundred and thirty-nine leagues distant from *Grafton's* Island, and to bear from it North 82° 37 West: And, on the 11th, having taken on board two *Chinese* Pilots, one for the *Centurion*, and the other for the prize, they came to an anchor off the city of *Macao*.

By this time the particulars of the cargoe of the galeon were well ascertained, and it was found that she had on board 1,313,843 pieces of eight, and 35,682 *oz.* of virgin silver, besides some cochineal, and a few other commodities, which, however, were but of small account, in comparison of the specie.[1] And this being the Commodore's last prize, it hence appears, that all the treasure taken by the *Centurion* was not much short of 400,000 *l.* independent of the ships and merchandise, which she either burnt or destroyed, and which, by the most reasonable estimation, could not amount to so little as 600,000 *l.* more; so that the whole loss of the enemy, by our squadron, did doubtless exceed a million sterling. To which, if there be added the great expence of the Court of *Spain*, in fitting out *Pizarro*, and in paying the additional charges in *America*, incurred on our account, together with the loss of their men of war, the total of all these articles will be a most exorbitant sum, and is the strongest conviction of the utility of this expedition, which, with all its numerous disadvantages, did yet prove so extremely prejudicial to the enemy. I shall only add, that there were taken on board the galeon several draughts and journals, from some of which many of the particulars recited in the 10th chapter of the second book are collected. Among the rest there was found a chart of all the Ocean, between the *Philippines* and the coast of *Mexico*, which was what was made use of by the galeon in her own navigation. A copy of this draught, corrected in some places by our own observation, is here annexed, together with the route of the galeon traced thereon from her own journals, and likewise the route of the *Centurion*, from *Acapulco* through the same Ocean. This is the chart formerly referred to, in the account of the *Manila* trade: And to render it still more compleat, the observed variation of the needle is annexed to several parts both of the *Spanish* and *English* track; which addition is of the greatest consequence, as no observations of this kind in the northern parts of the *Pacific* Ocean have yet to my knowledge been published, and as the quantity of the variation so nearly corresponds to what Dr. *Halley* predicted from his Theory above fifty years ago. And with this digression I shall end this chapter, leaving the *Centurion* with her prize, at anchor off *Macao*, preparing to enter the river of *Canton*.

CHAP. IX.

Transactions in the river of *Canton*.

THE Commodore, having taken Pilots on board, proceeded with his prize for the river of *Canton*; and, on the 14th of *July*, came to an anchor short of the *Bocca Tigris*, which is a narrow passage forming the mouth of that river: This entrance he proposed to stand through the next day, and to run up as far as *Tiger Island*, which is a very safe road, secured from all winds. But whilst the *Centurion* and her prize were thus at anchor, a boat with an officer came off from the *Mandarine*, commanding the forts at *Bocca Tigris* to examine what the ships were, and whence they came. Mr. *Anson* informed the officer, that his ship was a ship of war, belonging to the King of *Great Britain*; and that the other in company with him was a prize he had taken; that he was going into *Canton* river to shelter himself against the hurricanes which were then coming on; and that as soon as the monsoon shifted, he should proceed for *England*. The officer then desired an account of what men, guns, and ammunition were on board, a list of all which he said was to be sent to the Government of *Canton*. But when these articles were repeated to him, particularly when he was told that there were in the *Centurion* four hundred firelocks, and between three and four hundred barrels of powder, he shrugged up his shoulders, and seemed to be terrified with the bare recital, saying, that no ships ever came into *Canton* river armed in that manner; adding, that he durst not set down the whole of this force, least it should too much alarm the Regency. After he had finished his enquiries, and was preparing to depart, he desired to leave two Customhouse officers behind him; on which the Commodore told him, that though as a man of war he was prohibited from trading, and had nothing to do with customs or duties of any kind, yet, for the satisfaction of the *Chinese*, he would permit two of their people to be left on board, who might themselves be witnesses how punctually he should comply with his instructions. The officer seemed amazed when Mr. *Anson* mentioned being exempted from all duties, and told him, that the Emperor's duty must be paid by all ships that came into his ports:

And it is supposed, that on this occasion, private directions were given by him to the *Chinese* Pilot, not to carry the Commodore through the *Bocca Tigris*; which makes it necessary, more particularly, to describe that entrance.

The *Bocca Tigris* is a narrow passage, little more than musquetshot over, formed by two points of land, on each of which there is a fort, that on the starboard-side being a battery on the water's edge, with eighteen embrasures, but where there were no more than twelve iron cannon mounted, seeming to be four or six pounders; the fort on the larboard-side is a large castle, resembling those old buildings which here in *England* we often find distinguished by that name; it is situated on a high rock, and did not appear to be furnished with more than eight or ten cannon, none of which were supposed to exceed six pounders. These are the defences which secure the river of *Canton*; and which the *Chinese* (extremely defective in all military skill) have imagined were sufficient to prevent any enemy from forcing his way through.

But it is obvious, from the description of these forts, that they could have given no obstruction to Mr. *Anson*'s passage, even if they had been well supplied with gunners and stores; and therefore, though the Pilot, after the *Chinese* officer had been on board, refused at first to take charge of the ship, till he had leave from the forts, yet as it was necessary to get through without any delay, for fear of the bad weather which was hourly expected, the Commodore weighed on the 15th, and ordered the Pilot to carry him by the forts, threatening him that, if the ship ran aground, he would instantly hang him up at the yard-arm. The Pilot, awed by these threats, carried the ship through safely, the forts not attempting to dispute the passage. Indeed the poor Pilot did not escape the resentment of his countrymen, for when he came on shore, he was seized and sent to prison, and was rigorously disciplined with the bamboo. However, he found means to get at Mr. *Anson* afterwards, to desire of him some recompence for the chastisement he had undergone, and of which he then carried very significant marks about him; and Mr. *Anson*, in commiseration of his sufferings, gave him such a sum of money, as would at any time have enticed a *Chinese* to have undergone a dozen bastinadings.

Nor was the Pilot the only person that suffered on this occasion;

for the Commodore soon after seeing some royal junks pass by him from *Bocca Tigris* towards *Canton*, he learnt, on enquiry, that the *Mandarine* commanding the forts was a prisoner on board them; that he was already turned out, and was now carrying to *Canton*, where it was expected he would be severely punished for having permitted the ships to pass; and the Commodore urging the unreasonableness of this procedure, from the inability of the forts to have done otherwise, explaining to the *Chinese* the great superiority his ships would have had over the forts, by the number and size of their guns, the *Chinese* seemed to acquiesce in his reasoning, and allowed that their forts could not have stopped him; but they still asserted, that the *Mandarine* would infallibly suffer, for not having done, what all his judges were convinced, was impossible. To such indefensible absurdities are those obliged to submit, who think themselves concerned to support their authority, when the necessary force is wanting. But to return:

On the 16th of *July* the Commodore sent his second Lieutenant to *Canton*, with a letter to the Viceroy, informing him of the reason of the *Centurion*'s putting into that port; and that the Commodore himself soon proposed to repair to *Canton*, to pay a visit to the Viceroy. The Lieutenant was very civilly received, and was promised that an answer should be sent to the Commodore the next day. In the mean time Mr. *Anson* gave leave to several of the officers of the galeon to go to *Canton*, they engaging their parole to return in two days. When these prisoners got to *Canton*, the Regency sent for them, and examined them, enquiring particularly by what means they had fallen into Mr. *Anson*'s power. And on this occasion the prisoners were honest enough to declare, that as the Kings of *Great-Britain* and of *Spain* were at war, they had proposed to themselves the taking of the *Centurion*, and had bore down upon her with that view, but that the event had been contrary to their hopes: However, they acknowledged that they had been treated by the Commodore, much better than they believed they should have treated him, had he fallen into their hands. This confession from an enemy had great weight with the *Chinese*, who till then, though they had revered the Commodore's power, had yet suspected his morals, and had considered him rather as a lawless freebooter, than as one commissioned by the State for the revenge of public injuries. But they now changed their opinion, and regarded him as a more important person; to which perhaps the vast treasure of his prize might not a little, contribute; the acquisition of wealth being a matter greatly adapted to the estimation and reverence of the *Chinese* Nation.

In this examination of the *Spanish* prisoners, though the *Chinese* had no reason in the main to doubt of the account which was given them, yet there were two circumstances which appeared to them so singular, as to deserve a more ample explanation; one of them was the great disproportion of men between the *Centurion* and the galeon; the other was the humanity, with which the people of the galeon were treated after they were taken. The *Mandarines* therefore asked the *Spaniards*, how they came to be overpowered by so inferior a force; and how it happened, since the two nations were at war, that they were not put to death when they came into the hands of the *English*. To the first of these enquiries the *Spaniards* replied, that though they had more hands than the *Centurion*, yet she being intended solely for war had a great superiority in the size of her guns, and in many other articles, over the galeon, which was a vessel fitted out principally for traffic: And as to the second question, they told the *Chinese*, that amongst the nations of *Europe*, it was not customary to put to death those who submitted; though they readily owned, that the Commodore, from the natural bias of his temper, had treated both them and their countrymen, who had formerly been in his power, with very unusual courtesy, much beyond what they could have expected, or than was required by the customs established between nations at war with each other. These replies fully satisfied the *Chinese*, and at the same time wrought very powerfully in the Commodore's favour.

On the 20th of *July*, in the morning, three *Mandarines*, with a great number of boats, and a vast retinue, came on board the *Centurion*, and delivered to the Commodore the Viceroy of *Canton*'s order for a daily supply of provisions, and for Pilots to carry the ships up the river as far as the second bar; and at the same time they delivered him a message from the Viceroy, in answer to the letter sent to *Canton*. The substance of the message was, that the Viceroy desired to be excused from receiving the Commodore's visit, during the then excessive hot weather; because the assembling the *Mandarines* and soldiers, necessary to that ceremony, would prove extremely inconvenient and fatiguing; but that in *September*, when the weather would be more temperate, he should be glad to see both the Commodore himself, and the *English* Captain of the other ship, that was with him. As Mr. *Anson* knew that an express had been dispatched to the Court at *Pekin*, with an account of the *Centurion* and her prize being arrived in the river of *Canton*, he had no doubt, but the principal motive for putting off this visit was, that the Regency at *Canton* might gain time to receive the Emperor's instructions, about their behaviour on this unusual affair.

When the *Mandarines* had delivered their message, they began to talk to the Commodore about the duties to be paid by his ships; but he immediately told them, that he would never submit to any demand of that kind; that as he neither brought any merchandize thither, nor intended to carry any away, he could not be reasonably deemed to be within the meaning of the Emperor's orders, which were doubtless calculated for trading vessels only, adding, that no duties were ever demanded of men of war, by nations accustomed to their reception, and that his Master's orders expressly forbad him from paying any acknowledgement for his ships anchoring in any port whatever.

The *Mandarines* being thus cut short on the subject of the duty, they said they had another matter to mention, which was the only remaining one they had in charge; this was a request to the Commodore, that he would release the prisoners he had taken on board the galeon; for that the Viceroy of *Canton* apprehended the Emperor, his Master, might be displeased, if he should be informed, that persons, who were his allies, and carried on a great commerce with his subjects, were under confinement in his dominions. Mr. *Anson* was himself extremely desirous to get rid of the *Spaniards*, having, on his first arrival, sent about an hundred of them to *Macao*, and those who remained, which were near four hundred more, were, on many accounts, a great incumbrance to him. However, to inhance the favour, he at first raised some difficulties; but permitting himself to be prevailed on, he at last told the *Mandarines*, that to show his readiness to oblige the Viceroy, he would release the prisoners, whenever they, the *Chinese*, would send boats to fetch them off. This matter being thus adjusted, the *Mandarines* departed; and, on the 28th of *July*, two *Chinese* junks were sent from *Canton*, to take on board the prisoners, and to carry them to *Macao*. And the Commodore, agreeable to his promise, dismissed them all, and ordered his Purser to send with them eight days provision for their subsistence, during their sailing down the river; this being dispatched, the *Centurion* and her prize came to her moorings, above the second bar, where they proposed to continue till the monsoon shifted.

Though the ships, in consequence of the Viceroy's permit, found no difficulty in purchasing provisions for their daily consumption, yet it was impossible for the Commodore to proceed to *England*, without laying in a large quantity both of provisions and stores for his use, during the voyage: The procuring this supply was attended with much embarasment; for there were people at *Canton* who had undertaken to furnish him with biscuit, and whatever else he wanted; and his linguist, towards the middle of *September*, had assured him, from day to day, that all was ready, and would be sent on board him immediately. But a fortnight being elapsed, and nothing being brought, the Commodore sent to *Canton* to enquire more particularly into the reasons of this disappointment: And he had soon the vexation to be informed, that the whole was an illusion; that no order had been procured from the Viceroy, to furnish him with his sea-stores, as had been pretended; that there was no biscuit baked, nor any one of the articles in readiness, which had been promised him; nor did it appear, that the Contractors had taken the least step to comply with their agreement. This was most disagreeable news, and made it suspected, that the furnishing the *Centurion* for her return to *Great-Britain* might prove a more troublesome matter than had been hitherto imagined; especially too, as the month of *September* was nearly elapsed, without Mr. *Anson's* having received any message from the Viceroy of *Canton*.

And here perhaps it might be expected that some satisfactory account should be given of the motives of the *Chinese* for this faithless procedure. But as I have already, in a former chapter, made some kind of conjectures about a similar event, I shall not repeat them again in this place, but shall observe, that after all, it may perhaps be impossible for an *European*, ignorant of the customs and manners of that nation, to be fully apprized of the real incitements to this behaviour. Indeed, thus much may undoubtedly be asserted, that in artifice, falshood, and an attachment to all kinds of lucre, many of the *Chinese* are difficult to be paralleled by any other people; but then the combination of these talents, and the manner in which they are applied in particular emergencies, are often beyond the reach of a Foreigner's penetration: So that though it may be safely concluded, that the *Chinese* had some interest in thus amusing the Commodore, yet it may not be easy to assign the individual views by which they were influenced. And that I may not be thought too severe in ascribing to this Nation a fraudulent and selfish turn of temper, so contradictory to the character given of them in the legendary accounts of the *Roman* Missionaries, I shall here mention an extraordinary transaction or two, which I hope will be some kind of confirmation of what I have advanced.

When the Commodore lay first at *Macao,* one of his officers, who had been extremely ill, desired leave of him to go on shore every day on a neighbouring Island, imagining that a walk upon the land would contribute greatly to the restoring of his health: The Commodore would have dissuaded him, suspecting the tricks of the *Chinese,* but the officer continuing importunate, in the end the boat was ordered to carry him. The first day he was put on shore he took his exercise, and returned without receiving any molestation, or even seeing any of the inhabitants; but the second day, he was assaulted, soon after his arrival, by a great number of *Chinese,* who had been hoeing rice in the neighbourhood, and who beat him so violently with the handles of their hoes, that they soon laid him on the ground incapable of resistance; after which they robbed him, taking from him his sword, the hilt of which was silver, his money, his watch, gold-headed cane, snuff-box, sleeve-buttons and hat, with several other trinkets: In the mean time the boat's crew, who were at some little distance, and had no arms of any kind with them, were incapable of giving him any assistance; till at last one of them flew on the fellow who had the sword in his possession, and wresting it out of his hands drew it, and with it was preparing to fall on the *Chinese,* some of whom he could not have failed of killing; but the officer, perceiving what he was about, immediately ordered him to desist, thinking it more prudent to submit to the present violence, than to embroil his Commodore in an inextricable squabble with the *Chinese* Government, by the death of their subjects; which calmness in this Gentleman was the more meritorious, as he was known to be a person of an uncommon spirit, and of a somewhat hasty temper: By this means the *Chinese* recovered the possession of the sword, which they soon perceived was prohibited to be made use of against them, and carried off their whole booty unmolested. No sooner were they gone, than a *Chinese* on horseback, very well dressed, and who had the air and appearance of a Gentleman, came down to the shore, and, as far as could be understood by his signs, seemed to censure the conduct of his countrymen, and to commiserate the officer, being wonderfully officious to assist in getting him on board the boat: But notwithstanding this behaviour, it was shrewdly suspected that he was an accomplice in the theft, and time fully evinced the justice of those suspicions.

When the boat returned on board, and reported what had passed to the Commodore, he immediately complained of it to the *Mandarine*, who attended to see his ship supplied; but the *Mandarine* coolly replied, that the boat ought not to have gone on shore, promising, however, that if the thieves could be found out, they should be punished; though it appeared plain enough, by his manner of answering, that he would never give himself any trouble in searching them out. However, a considerable time afterwards, when some *Chinese* boats were selling provisions to the *Centurion*, the person who had wrested the sword from the *Chinese* came with great eagerness to the Commodore, to assure him that one of the principal thieves was then in a provision-boat along-side the ship; and the officer, who had been robbed, viewing the fellow on this report, and well remembring his face, orders were immediately given to seize him; and he was accordingly secured on board the ship, where strange discoveries were now made.

This thief, on his being first apprehended, expressed so much fright in his countenance, that it was feared he would have died upon the spot; the *Mandarine* too, who attended the ship, had visibly no small share of concern of the occasion. Indeed he had reason enough to be alarmed, since it was soon evinced, that he had been privy to the whole robbery; for the Commodore declaring that he would not deliver up the thief, but would himself order him to be shot, the *Mandarine* immediately put off the magisterial air, with which he had at first pretended to demand him, and begged his release in the most abject manner: And the Commodore appearing inflexible, there came on board, in less than two hours time, five or six of the neighbouring *Mandarines*, who all joined in the same entreaty, and with a view of facilitating their suit, offered a large sum of money for the fellow's liberty. Whilst they were thus solliciting, it was discovered that the

353

Mandarine, who was the most active amongst them, and who seemed to be most interested in the event, was the very Gentleman, who came to the officer, just after the robbery, and who pretended to be so much displeased with the villany of his countrymen. And, on further inquiry it was found, that he was the *Mandarine* of the Island; and that he had, by the authority of his office, ordered the Peasants to commit that infamous action.[1] And it seemed, as far as could be collected from the broken hints which were casually thrown out, that he and his brethren, who were all privy to the transaction, were terrified with the fear of being called before the tribunal at *Canton*, where the first article of their punishment would be the stripping them of all they were worth; though their judges (however fond of inflicting a chastisement so lucrative to themselves) were perhaps of as tainted a complexion as the delinquents. Mr. *Anson* was not displeased to have caught the *Chinese* in this dilemma; and he entertained himself for some time with their perplexity, rejecting their money with scorn, appearing inexorable to their prayers, and giving out that the thief should certainly be shot; but as he then foresaw that he should be forced to take shelter in their ports a second time, when the influence he might hereby acquire over the Magistrates would be of great service to him, he at length permitted himself to be persuaded, and as a favour released his prisoner, but not till the *Mandarine* had collected and returned all that had been stolen from the officer, even to the minutest trifle.

But notwithstanding this instance of the good intelligence between the magistrates and criminals, the strong addiction of the *Chinese* to lucre often prompts them to break through this awful confederacy, and puts them on defrauding the authority that protects them of its proper quota of the pillage. For not long after the above-mentioned transaction, (the former *Mandarine*, attendant on the ship, being, in the mean time, relieved by another) the Commodore lost a top-mast from his stern, which, after the most diligent enquiry, could not be traced: As it was not his own, but had been borrowed at *Macao* to heave down by, and was not to be replaced in that part of the world, he was extremely desirous to recover it, and published a considerable reward to any who would bring it him again. There were suspicions from the first of its being stolen, which made him conclude a reward was the likeliest method of getting it back: Accordingly, soon after, the *Mandarine* told him, that some of his, the *Mandarine*'s, people, had found the top-mast, desiring the Commodore to send his boats to fetch it, which being done, the *Mandarine's* people received the promised reward; but the Commodore told the *Mandarine*, that he would make him a present besides for the care he had taken in directing it to be searched for; and accordingly, Mr. *Anson* gave a sum of money to his Linguist, to be delivered to the *Mandarine*; but the Linguist knowing that the people had been paid, and ignorant that a further present had been promised, kept the money himself: However, the *Mandarine* fully confiding in Mr. *Anson's* word, and suspecting the Linguist, he took occasion, one morning, to admire the size of the *Centurion's* masts, and thence, on a pretended sudden recollection, he made a digression to the top-mast which had been lost, and asked Mr. *Anson* if he had not got it again. Mr. *Anson* presently perceived the bent of this conversation, and enquired of him if he had not received the money from the Linguist, and finding he had not, he offered to pay it him upon the spot. But this the *Mandarine* refused, having now somewhat more in view than the sum which had been detained: For the next day the Linguist was seized, and was doubtless mulcted of all he had gotten in the Commodore's service, which was supposed to be little less than two thousand dollars; he was besides so severely bastinadoed with the bamboo, that it was with difficulty he escaped with his life; and when he was upbraided by the Commodore (to whom he afterwards came begging) with his folly, in risquing all he had suffered for fifty dollars, (the present intended for the *Mandarine*) he had no other excuse to make than the strong bias of his Nation to dishonesty,[1] replying, in his broken jargon, *Chinese man very great rogue truly, but have fashion, no can help.*

It were endless to recount all the artifices, extortions and frauds which were practised on the Commodore and his people, by this interested race. The method of buying all things in *China* being by weight, the tricks made use of by the *Chinese* to encrease the weight of the provision they sold to the *Centurion*, were almost incredible. One time a large quantity of fowls and ducks being bought for the ship's use, the greatest part of them presently died: This alarmed the people on board with the apprehensions that they had been killed by poison; but on examination it appeared, that it was only owing to their being crammed with stones and gravel to encrease their weight, the quantity thus forced into most of the ducks being found to amount to ten ounces in each. The hogs too, which were bought ready killed of the *Chinese* Butchers, had water injected into them for the same purpose: so that a carcass, hung up all night for the water to drain from it, hath lost above a stone of its weight; and when, to avoid this cheat, the hogs were bought alive, it was found that the *Chinese* gave them salt to encrease their thirst, and having by this means excited them to drink great quantities of water, they then took measures to prevent them from discharging it again by urine, and sold the tortured animal in this inflated state. When the Commodore first put to sea from *Macao*, they practised an artifice of another kind; for as the *Chinese* never object to the eating of any food that dies of itself, they took care, by some secret practices, that great part of his live sea-store should die in a short time after it was put on board, hoping to make a second profit of the dead carcasses which they expected would be thrown overboard; and two thirds of the hogs dying before the *Centurion* was out of sight of land, many of the *Chinese* boats followed her, only to pick up the carrion. These instances may serve as a specimen of the manners of this celebrated Nation, which is often recommended to the rest of the world as a pattern of all kinds of laudable qualities. But to return:

The Commodore, towards the end of *September*, having found out (as has been said) that those, who had contracted to supply him with sea-provisions and stores, had deceived him, and that the Viceroy had not sent to him according to his promise, he saw it would be impossible for him to surmount the embarasment he was under, without going himself to *Canton*, and visiting the Viceroy; and therefore, on the 27th of *September*, he sent a message to the *Mandarine*, who attended the *Centurion*, to inform him that he, the Commodore, intended, on the first of *October*, to proceed in his boat to *Canton*; adding, that the day after he got there, he should notify his arrival to the Viceroy, and should desire him to fix a time for his audience; to which the *Mandarine* returned no other answer, than that he would acquaint the Viceroy with the Commodore's intentions. In the mean time all things were prepared for this expedition: And the boat's crew in particular, which Mr. *Anson* proposed to take with him, were cloathed in an uniform dress, resembling that of the Watermen on the *Thames*; they were in number eighteen and a Coxswain; they had scarlet jackets and blue silk waistcoats, the whole trimmed with silver buttons, and with silver badges on their jackets and caps.[1] As it was apprehended, and even asserted, that the payment of the customary duties for the *Centurion* and her prize, would be demanded by the Regency of *Canton*, and would be insisted on previous to the granting a permission for victualling the ship for her future voyage; the Commodore, who was resolved never to establish so dishonourable a precedent, took all possible precaution to prevent the *Chinese* from facilitating the success of their unreasonable pretentions, by having him in their power at *Canton*: And therefore, for the security of his ship, and the great treasure on board her, he appointed his first Lieutenant, Mr. *Brett*, to be Captain of the *Centurion* under him, giving him proper instructions for his conduct; directing him, particularly, if he, the Commodore, should be detained at *Canton* on account of the duties in dispute, to take out the men from the *Centurion's* prize, and to destroy her; and then to proceed down the river through the *Bocca Tigris*, with the *Centurion* alone, and to remain without that entrance, till he received further orders from Mr. *Anson*.

These necessary steps being taken, which were not unknown to the *Chinese*, it should seem as if their deliberations were in some sort embarased thereby. It is reasonable to imagine, that they were in general very desirous of getting the duties to be paid them; not perhaps solely in consideration of the amount of those dues, but to keep up their reputation for address and subtlety, and to avoid the imputation of receding from claims, on which they had already so frequently insisted. However, as they now foresaw that they had no other method of succeeding than by violence, and that even against this the Commodore was prepared, they were at last disposed, I conceive, to let the affair drop, rather than entangle themselves in an hostile measure, which they found would only expose them to the risque of having the whole navigation of their port destroyed, without any certain prospect of gaining their favourite point thereby.

However, though there is reason to imagine that these were their thoughts at that time, yet they could not depart at once from the evasive conduct to which they had hitherto adhered. For when the Commodore, on the morning of the first of *October*, was preparing to set out for *Canton*, his Linguist came to him from the *Mandarine*, who attended his ship, to tell him that a letter had been received from the Viceroy of *Canton*, desiring the Commodore to put off his going thither for two or three days: But in the afternoon of the same day, another Linguist came on board, who, with much seeming fright, told Mr. *Anson*, that the Viceroy had expected him up that day, that the Council was assembled, and the troops had been under arms to receive him; and that the Viceroy was highly offended at the disappointment, and had sent the Commodore's Linguist to prison chained, supposing that the whole had been owing to the Linguist's negligence. This plausible tale gave the Commodore great concern, and made him apprehend that there was some treachery designed him, which he could not yet fathom; and though it afterwards appeared that the whole was a fiction, not one article of it having the least foundation, yet (for reason best known to themselves) this falsehood was so well supported by the artifices of the *Chinese* Merchants at *Canton*, that three days afterwards, the Commodore received a letter signed by all the supercargoes of the *English* ships then at that place, expressing their great uneasiness at what had happened, and intimating their fears that some insult would be offered to his boat, if he came thither before the Viceroy was fully satisfied about the mistake. To this letter Mr. *Anson* replied, that he did not believe there had been any mistake; but was persuaded it was a forgery of the *Chinese* to prevent his visiting the Viceroy; that therefore he would certainly come up to *Canton* on the 13th of *October*, confident that the *Chinese* would not dare to offer him an insult, as well knowing it would be properly returned.

On the 13th of *October*, the Commodore continuing firm to his resolution, all the supercargoes of the *English*, *Danish*, and *Swedish* ships came on board the *Centurion*, to accompany him to *Canton*, for which place he set out in his barge the same day, attended by his own boats, and by those of the trading ships, which on this occasion came to form his retinue; and as he passed by *Wampa*, where the *European* vessels lay, he was saluted by all of them but the *French*, and in the evening he arrived safely at *Canton*. His reception at that city, and the most material transactions from henceforward, till his arrival in *Great-Britain*, shall be the subject of the ensuing chapter.

CHAP. X.

Proceedings at the city of *Canton*, and the return of the *Centurion* to *England*.

WHEN the Commodore arrived at *Canton*, he was visited by the principal *Chinese* Merchants, who affected to appear very much pleased that he had met with no obstruction in getting thither, and who thence pretended to conclude, that the Viceroy was satisfied about the former mistake, the reality of which they still insisted on; they added, that as soon as the Viceroy should be informed that Mr. *Anson* was at *Canton*, (which they promised should be done the next morning) they were persuaded a day would be immediately appointed for the visit, which was the principal business that had brought the Commodore thither.

The next day the Merchants returned to Mr. *Anson*, and told him, that the Viceroy was then so fully employed in preparing his dispatches for *Pekin*, that there was no getting admittance to him for some days; but that they had engaged one of the officers of his Court to give them information, as soon as he should be at leisure, when they proposed to notify Mr. *Anson*'s arrival, and to endeavour to fix the day of audience. The Commodore was by this time too well acquainted with their artifices, not to perceive that this was a falsehood; and had he consulted only his own judgment, he would have applied directly to the Viceroy by other hands: But the *Chinese* Merchants had so far prepossessed the supercargoes of our ships with chimerical fears, that they (the supercargoes) were extremely apprehensive of being embroiled with the Government, and of suffering in their interest, if those measures were taken, which appeared to Mr. *Anson* at that time to be the most prudential: And therefore, least the malice and double dealing of the *Chinese* might have given rise to some sinister incident, which would be afterwards laid at his door, he resolved to continue passive, as long as it should appear that he lost no time, by thus suspending his own opinion. With this view, he promised not to take any immediate step himself for getting admittance to the Viceroy, provided the *Chinese*, with whom he contracted for provisions, would let him see that his bread was baked, his meat salted, and his stores prepared with the utmost dispatch: But if by the time when all was in readiness to be shipped off, (which it was supposed would be in about forty days) the Merchants should not have procured the Viceroy's permission, then the Commodore proposed to apply for it himself. These were the terms Mr. *Anson* thought proper to offer, to quiet the uneasiness of the supercargoes; and notwithstanding the apparent equity of the conditions, many difficulties and objections were urged, nor would the *Chinese* agree to them, till the Commodore had consented to pay for every article he bespoke before it was put in hand. However, at last the contract being past, it was some satisfaction to the Commodore to be certain that his preparations were now going on, and being himself on the spot, he took care to hasten them as much as possible.

During this interval, in which the stores and provisions were getting ready the Merchants continually entertained Mr. *Anson* with accounts of their various endeavours to get a licence from the Viceroy, and their frequent disappointments; which to him was now a matter of amusement, as he was fully satisfied there was not one word of truth in any thing they said. But when all was compleated, and wanted only to be shipped, which was about the 24th of *November*, at which time too the N. E. monsoon was set in, he then resolved to apply himself to the Viceroy to demand an audience, as he was persuaded that, without this ceremony, the procuring a permission to send his stores on board would meet with great difficulty. On the 24th of *November*, therefore, Mr. *Anson* sent one of his officers to the *Mandarine*, who commanded the guard of the principal gate of the city of *Canton*, with a letter directed to the Viceroy. When this letter was delivered to the *Mandarine*, he received the officer who brought it very civilly, and took down the contents of it in *Chinese*, and promised that the Viceroy should be immediately acquainted with it; but told the officer, it was not necessary for him to wait for an answer, because a message would be sent to the Commodore himself.

On this occasion Mr. *Anson* had been under great difficulties about a proper interpreter to send with his officer, as he was well aware that none of the *Chinese*, usually employed as Linguists, could be relied on: But he at last prevailed with Mr. *Flint*, an *English* Gentleman belonging to the factory, who spoke *Chinese* perfectly well, to accompany his officer. This person, who upon this occasion and many others was of singular service to the Commodore, had been left at *Canton* when a youth, by the late Captain *Rigby*. The leaving him there to learn the *Chinese* language was a step taken by that Captain, merely from his own persuasion of the great advantages which the *East-India* Company might one day receive from an *English* interpreter; and though the utility of this measure has greatly exceeded all that was expected from it, yet I have not heard that it has been to this day imitated: But we imprudently choose (except in this single instance) to carry on the vast transactions of the port of *Canton*, either by the ridiculous jargon of broken *English*, which some few of the *Chinese* have learnt, or by the suspected interpretation of the Linguists of other Nations.

Two days after the sending the above-mentioned letter, a fire broke out in the suburbs of *Canton*. On the first alarm, Mr. *Anson* went thither with his officers, and his boat's crew, to assist the *Chinese*. When he came there, he found that it had begun in a sailor's shed, and that by the slightness of the buildings, and the awkwardness of the *Chinese*, it was getting head apace: But he perceived, that by pulling down some of the adjacent sheds it might easily be extinguished; and particularly observing that it was running along a wooden cornish, which would soon communicate it to a great distance, he ordered his people to begin with tearing away that cornish; this was presently attempted, and would have been soon executed; but, in the mean time, he was told, that, as there was no *Mandarine* there to direct what was to be done, the *Chinese* would make him, the Commodore, answerable for whatever should be pulled down by his orders. On this his people desisted; and he sent them to the *English* factory, to assist in securing the Company's treasure and effects, as it was easy to foresee that no distance was a protection against the rage of such a fire, where so little was done to put a stop to it; for all this time the *Chinese* contented themselves with viewing it, and now and then holding one of their idols near it, which they seemed to expect should check its progress: However, at last, a *Mandarine* came out of the city, attended by four or five hundred firemen: These made some feeble efforts to pull down the neighbouring houses; but by this time the fire had greatly extended itself, and was got amongst the Merchants warehouses; and the *Chinese* firemen, wanting both skill and spirit, were incapable of checking its violence; so that its fury encreased upon them, and it was feared the whole city would be destroyed. In this general confusion the Viceroy himself came thither, and the Commodore was sent to, and was entreated to afford his assistance, being told that he might take any measures he should think most prudent in the present emergency. And now he went thither a second time, carrying with him about forty of his people; who, upon this occasion, exerted themselves in such a manner, as in that country was altogether without example: For they were rather animated than deterred by the flames and falling buildings, amongst which they wrought; so that it was not uncommon to see the most forward of them tumble to the ground on the roofs, and amidst the ruins of houses, which their own efforts brought down with them. By their boldness and activity the fire was soon extinguished to the amazement of the *Chinese*; and the buildings being all on one floor, and the materials slight, the seamen, notwithstanding their daring behaviour, happily escaped with no other injuries, than some considerable bruises.

The fire, though at last thus luckily extinguished, did great mischief during the time it continued; for it consumed an hundred shops and eleven streets full of warehouses, so that the damage amounted to an immense sum; and one of the *Chinese* Merchants, well known to the *English*, whose name was *Succoy*, was supposed, for his own share, to have lost near two hundred thousand pound sterling. It raged indeed with unusual violence, for in many of the warehouses, there were large quantities of camphire, which greatly added to its fury, and produced a column of exceeding white flame, which shot up into the air to such a prodigious height, that the flame itself was plainly seen on board the *Centurion*, though she was thirty miles distant.

Whilst the Commodore and his people were labouring at the fire, and the terror of its becoming general still possessed the whole city, several of the most considerable *Chinese* Merchants came to Mr. *Anson*, to desire that he would let each of them have one of his soldiers (for such they stiled his boat's crew from the uniformity of their dress) to guard their warehouses and dwelling houses, which, from the known dishonesty of the populace, they feared would be pillaged in the tumult. Mr. *Anson* granted them this request; and all the men that he thus furnished to the *Chinese* behaved greatly to the satisfaction of their employers, who afterwards highly applauded their great diligence and fidelity.

By this means, the resolution of the *English* at the fire, and their trustiness and punctuality elsewhere, was the general subject of conversation amongst the *Chinese*: And, the next morning, many of the principal inhabitants waited on the Commodore to thank him for his assistance; frankly owning to him, that they could never have extinguished the fire of themselves, and that he had saved their city from being totally consumed. And soon after a message came to the Commodore from the Viceroy, appointing the 30th of *November* for his audience; which sudden resolution of the Viceroy, in a matter that had been so long agitated in vain, was also owing to the signal services performed by Mr. *Anson* and his people at the fire, of which the Viceroy himself had been in some measure an eye-witness.

The fixing this business of the audience, was, on all accounts, a circumstance which Mr. *Anson* was much pleased with; as he was satisfied that the *Chinese* Government would not have determined this point, without having agreed among themselves to give up their pretensions to the duties they claimed, and to grant him all he could reasonably ask; for as they well knew the Commodore's sentiments, it would have been a piece of imprudence, not consistent with the refined cunning of the *Chinese*, to have admitted him to an audience, only to have contested with him. And therefore, being himself perfectly easy about the result of his visit, he made all necessary preparations against the day; and engaged Mr. *Flint*, whom I have mentioned before, to act as interpreter in the conference: Who, in this affair, as in all others, acquitted himself much to the Commodore's satisfaction; repeating with great boldness, and doubtless with exactness, all that was given in charge, a part which no *Chinese* Linguist would ever have performed with any tolerable fidelity.

At ten o'clock in the morning, on the day appointed, a *Mandarine* came to the Commodore, to let him know that the Viceroy was ready to receive him; on which the Commodore and his retinue immediately set out: And as soon as he entered the outer gate of the city, he found a guard of two hundred soldiers drawn up ready to attend him; these conducted him to the great parade before the Emperor's palace, where the Viceroy then resided. In this parade, a body of troops, to the number of ten thousand, were drawn up under arms, and made a very fine appearance, being all of them new cloathed for this ceremony: And Mr. *Anson* and his retinue having passed through the middle of them, he was then conducted to the great hall of audience, where he found the Viceroy seated under a rich canopy in the Emperor's chair of State, with all his Council of *Mandarines* attending: Here there was a vacant seat prepared for the Commodore, in which he was placed on his arrival: He was ranked the third in order from the Viceroy, there being above him only the Head of the Law, and of the Treasury, who in the *Chinese* Government take place of all military officers. When the Commodore was seated, he addressed himself to the Viceroy by his interpreter, and began with reciting the various methods he had formerly taken to get an audience; adding, that he imputed the delays he had met with, to the insincerity of those he had employed, and that he had therefore no other means left, than to send, as he had done, his officer with a letter to the gate. On the mention of this the Viceroy stopped the interpreter, and bid him assure Mr. *Anson*, that the first knowledge they had of his being at *Canton*, was from that letter. Mr. *Anson* then proceeded, and told him, that the subjects of the King of *Great Britain* trading to *China* had complained to him, the Commodore, of the vexatious impositions both of the Merchants and inferior Custom-house officers, to which they were frequently necessitated to submit, by reason of the difficulty of getting access to the *Mandarines*, who alone could grant them redress: That it was his, Mr. *Anson's*, duty, as an officer of the King of *Great-Britain*, to lay before the Viceroy these grievances of the *British* subjects, which he hoped the Viceroy would take into consideration, and would give orders, that for the future there should be no just reason for complaint. Here Mr. *Anson* paused, and waited some time in expectation of an answer; but nothing being said, he asked his interpreter if he was certain the Viceroy understood what he had urged; the interpreter told him, he was certain it was understood, but he believed no reply would be made to it. Mr. *Anson* then represented to the Viceroy the case of the ship *Haslingfield*, which, having been dismasted on the coast of *China*, had arrived in the river of *Canton* but a few days before. The people on board this vessel had been great sufferers by the fire; the Captain in particular had all his goods burnt, and had left besides, in the confusion, a chest of treasure of four thousand five hundred *Tahel*, which was supposed to be stolen by the *Chinese* boat-men. Mr. *Anson* therefore desired that the Captain might have the assistance of the Government, as it was apprehended the money could never be recovered without the interposition of the *Mandarines*. And to this request the

Viceroy made answer, that in settling the Emperor's customs for this ship, some abatement should be made in consideration of her losses.

And now the Commodore having dispatched the business with which the officers of the *East-India* Company had entrusted him, he entered on his own affairs; acquainting the Viceroy, that the proper season was now set in for returning to *Europe*, and that he waited only for a licence to ship off his provisions and stores, which were all ready; and that as soon as this should be granted him, and he should have gotten his necessaries on board, he intended to leave the river of *Canton*, and to make the best of his way for *England*. The Viceroy replied to this, that the licence should be immediately issued, and that every thing should be ordered on board the following day. And finding that Mr. *Anson* had nothing farther to insist on, the Viceroy continued the conversation for some time, acknowledging in very civil terms how much the *Chinese* were obliged to him for his signal services at the fire, and owning that he had saved the city from being destroyed: And then observing that the *Centurion* had been a good while on their coast, he closed his discourse, by wishing the Commodore a good voyage to *Europe*. After which, the Commodore, thanking him for his civility and assistance, took his leave.[1]

As soon as the Commodore was out of the hall of audience, he was much pressed to go into a neighbouring apartment, where there was an entertainment provided; but finding, on enquiry, that the Viceroy himself was not to be present, he declined the invitation, and departed, attended in the same manner as at his arrival; only at his leaving the city he was saluted by three guns, which are as many as in that country are ever fired on any ceremony. Thus the Commodore, to his great joy, at last finished this troublesome affair, which, for the preceding four months, had given him great disquietude. Indeed he was highly pleased with procuring a licence for the shipping of his stores and provisions; for thereby he was enabled to return to *Great-Britain* with the first of the monsoon, and to prevent all intelligence of his being expected: But this, though a very important point, was not the circumstance which gave him the greatest satisfaction; for he was more particularly attentive to the authentic precedent established on this occasion, by which his Majesty's ships of war are for the future exempted from all demands of duty in any of the ports of *China*.[2]

In pursuance of the promises of the Viceroy, the provisions were begun to be sent on board the day after the audience; and, four days after, the Commodore embarked at *Canton* for the *Centurion*; and, on the 7th of *December*, the *Centurion* and her prize unmoored, and stood down the river, passing through the *Bocca Tigris* on the 10th.[1] And on this occasion I must observe, that the *Chinese* had taken care to man the two forts, on each side of that passage, with as many men as they could well contain, the greatest part of them armed with pikes and match-lock musquets. These garrisons affected to shew themselves as much as possible to the ships, and were doubtless intended to induce Mr. *Anson* to think more reverently than he had hitherto done of the *Chinese* military power: For this purpose they were equipped with much parade, having a great number of colours exposed to view; and on the castle in particular there were laid considerable heaps of large stones; and a soldier of unusual size, dressed in very sightly armour, stalkt about on the parapet with a battle-ax in his hand, endeavouring to put on as important and martial an air as possible, though some of the observers on board the *Centurion* shrewdly suspected, from the appearance of his armour, that instead of steel, it was composed only of a particular kind of glittering paper.

The *Centurion* and her prize being now without the river of *Canton*, and consequently upon the point of leaving the *Chinese* jurisdiction, I beg leave, before I quit all mention of the *Chinese* affairs, to subjoin a few remarks on the disposition and genius of that extraordinary people. And though it may be supposed, that observations made at *Canton* only, a place situated in the corner of the Empire, are very imperfect materials on which to found any general conclusions, yet as those who have had opportunities of examining the inner parts of the country, have been evidently influenced by very ridiculous prepossessions, and as the transactions of Mr. *Anson* with the Regency of *Canton* were of an uncommon nature, in which many circumstances occurred, different perhaps from any which have happened before, I hope the following reflections, many of them drawn from these incidents, will not be altogether unacceptable to the reader.

That the *Chinese* are a very ingenious and industrious people, is sufficiently evinced, from the great number of curious manufactures which are established amongst them, and which are eagerly sought for by the most distant nations; but though skill in the handicraft arts seems to be the most important qualification of this people, yet their talents therein are but of a second rate kind; for they are much out-done by the *Japanese* in those manufactures, which are common to both countries; and they are in numerous instances incapable of rivalling the mechanic dexterity of the *Europeans*. Indeed, their principal excellency seems to be imitation; and they accordingly labour under the poverty of genius, which constantly attends all servile imitators. This is most conspicuous in works which require great truth and accuracy; as in clocks, watches, fire-arms, &c. for in all these, though they can copy the different parts, and can form some resemblance of the whole, yet they never could arrive at such a justness in their fabric, as was necessary to produce the desired effect. And if we pass from their manufacturers to artists of a superior class, as painters, statuaries, &c. in these matters they seem to be still more defective, their painters, though very numerous and in great esteem, rarely succeeding in the drawing or colouring of human figures, or in the grouping of large compositions; and though in flowers and birds their performances are much more admired, yet even in these, some part of the merit is rather to be imputed to the native brightness and excellency of the colours, than to the skill of the painter; since it is very unusual to see the light and shade justly and naturally blended, or to find that ease and grace in the drawing, which are to be met with in the works of *European* artists. In short, there is a stiffness and minuteness in most of the *Chinese* productions, which are extremely displeasing: And it may perhaps be asserted with great truth, that these defects in their arts are entirely owing to the peculiar turn of the people, amongst whom nothing great or spirited is to be met with.

If we next examine the *Chinese* literature, (taking our accounts from the writers, who have endeavoured to represent it in the most favourable light) we shall find, that on this head their obstinacy and absurdity are most wonderful: For though, for many ages, they have been surrounded by nations, to whom the use of letters was familiar, yet they, the *Chinese* alone, have hitherto neglected to avail themselves of that almost divine invention, and have continued to adhere to the rude and inartificial method of representing words by arbitrary marks; a method, which necessarily renders the number of their characters too great for human memory to manage, makes writing to be an art that requires prodigious application, and in which no man can be otherwise than partially skilled; whilst all reading, and understanding of what is written, is attended with infinite obscurity and confusion; for the connexion between these marks, and the words they represent, cannot be retained in books, but must be delivered down from age to age by oral tradition: And how uncertain this must prove in such a complicated subject, is sufficiently obvious to those who have attended to the variation which all verbal relations undergo, when they are transmitted through three or four hands only. Hence it is easy to conclude, that the history and inventions of past ages, recorded by these perplexed symbols, must frequently prove unintelligible; and consequently the learning and boasted antiquity of the Nation must, in numerous instances, be extremely problematical.

But we are told by some of the Missionaries, that though the skill of the *Chinese* in science is indeed much inferior to that of the *Europeans*, yet the morality and justice taught and practised by them are most exemplary. And from the description given by some of these good fathers, one should be induced to believe, that the whole Empire was a well-governed affectionate family, where the only contests were, who should exert the most humanity and beneficence: But our preceding relation of the behaviour of the Magistrates, Merchants and Tradesmen at *Canton*, sufficiently refutes these jesuitical fictions. And as to their theories of morality, if we may judge from the specimens exhibited in the works of the Missionaries, we shall find them solely employed in recommending ridiculous attachments to certain immaterial points, instead of discussing the proper criterion of human actions, and regulating the general conduct of mankind to one another, on reasonable and equitable principles. Indeed, the only pretension of the *Chinese* to a more refined morality than their neighbours is founded, not on their integrity or beneficence, but solely on the affected evenness of their demeanor, and their constant attention to suppress all symptoms of passion and violence. But it must be considered, that hypocrisy and fraud are often not less mischievous to the general interests of mankind, than impetuosity and vehemence of temper: Since these, though usually liable to the imputation of imprudence, do not exclude sincerity, benevolence, resolution, nor many other laudable qualities. And perhaps, if this matter was examined to the bottom, it would appear, that the calm and patient turn of the *Chinese*, on which they so much value themselves, and which distinguishes the

Nation from all others, is in reality the source of the most exceptionable part of their character; for it has been often observed by those who have attended to the nature of mankind, that it is difficult to curb the more robust and violent passions, without augmenting, at the same time, the force of the selfish ones: So that the timidity, dissimulation, and dishonesty of the *Chinese*, may, in some sort, be owing to the composure, and external decency, so universally prevailing in that Empire.

Thus much for the general disposition of the people: But I cannot dismiss this subject, without adding a few words about the *Chinese* Government, that too having been the subject of boundless panegyric. And on this head I must observe, that the favourable accounts often given of their prudent regulations for the administration of their domestic affairs, are sufficiently confuted by their transactions with Mr. *Anson*: For we have seen that their Magistrates are corrupt, their people thievish, and their tribunals crafty and venal. Nor is the constitution of the Empire, or the general orders of the State less liable to exception: Since that form of Government, which does not in the first place provide for the security of the public against the enterprizes of foreign powers, is certainly a most defective institution: And yet this populous, this rich and extensive country, so pompously celebrated for its refined wisdom and policy, was conquered about an age since by an handful of *Tartars*; and even now, by the cowardice of the inhabitants, and the want of proper military regulations, it continues exposed not only to the attempts of any potent State, but to the ravages of every petty Invader. I have already observed, on occasion of the Commodore's disputes with the *Chinese*, that the *Centurion* alone was an overmatch for all the naval power of that Empire: This perhaps may appear an extraordinary position; but to render it unquestionable, there is exhibited in the annexed plate[1] the draught of two of the vessels made use of by the *Chinese*. The first of these marked (A), is a junk of about a hundred and twenty tuns burthen, and was what the *Centurion* hove down by; these are most used in the great rivers, though they sometimes serve for small coasting voyages: The other junk marked (B) is about two hundred and eighty tuns burthen, and is of the same form with those in which they trade to *Cochinchina Manila*, *Batavia* and *Japan*, though some of their trading vessels are of a much larger size; its head, which is represented at (C) is perfectly flat; and when the vessel is deep laden, the second or third plank of this flat surface is oft-times under water. The masts, sails, and rigging of these vessels are ruder than their built; for their masts are made of trees, no otherwise fashioned than by barking them, and lopping off their branches. Each mast has only two shrouds made of twisted rattan, which are often both shifted to the weather-side; and the halyard, when the yard is up, serves instead of a third shroud. The sails are made of matt, strengthened every three feet by an horizontal rib of bamboo; they run upon the mast with hoops, as is represented in the figure, and when they are lowered down, they fold upon the deck. These merchantmen carry no cannon; and it appears, from this whole description, that they are utterly incapable of resisting any *European* armed vessel. Nor is the State provided with ships of considerable force, or of a better fabric, to protect them: For at *Canton*, where doubtless their principal naval power is stationed, we saw no more than four men of war junks, of about three hundred tuns burthen, being of the make already described, and mounted only with eight or ten guns, the largest of which did not exceed a four pounder. This may suffice to give an idea of the defenceless state of the *Chinese* Empire. But it is time to return to the Commodore, whom I left with his two ships without the *Bocca Tigris*, and who, on the 12th of *December*, anchored before the town of *Macao*.

Whilst the ships lay here, the Merchants of *Macao* finished their agreement for the galeon, for which they had offered 6000 dollars; this was much short of her value, but the impatience of the Commodore to get to sea, to which the merchants were no strangers, prompted them to insist on so unequal a bargain. Mr. *Anson* had learnt enough from the *English* at *Canton* to conjecture, that the war betwixt *Great-Britain* and *Spain* was still continued; and that probably the *French* might engage in the assistance of *Spain*, before he could arrive in *Great-Britain*; and therefore, knowing that no intelligence could get to *Europe* of the prize he had taken, and the treasure he had on board, till the return of the merchantmen from *Canton*, he was resolved to make all possible expedition in getting back, that he might be himself the first messenger of his own good fortune, and might thereby prevent the enemy from forming any projects to intercept him: For these reasons, he, to avoid all delay, accepted of the sum offered for the galeon; and she being delivered to the Merchants the 15th of *December*

1743, the *Centurion*, the same day, got under sail, on her return to *England*. And, on the 3d of *January*, she came to an anchor at *Prince's Island* in the Streights of *Sunda*, and continued there wooding and watering till the 8th; when she weighed and stood for *The Cape of Good Hope*, where, on the 11th of *March*, she anchored in *Table-bay*.

The Cape of Good Hope is situated in a temperate climate, where the excesses of heat and cold are rarely known; and the *Dutch* inhabitants, who are numerous, and who here retain their native industry, have stock'd it with prodigious plenty of all sort of fruits and provisions; most of which, either from the equality of the seasons, or the peculiarity of the soil, are more delicious in their kind than can be met with elsewhere: So that by these, and by the excellent water which abounds there, this settlement is the best provided of any in the known world, for the refreshment of seamen after long voyages. Here the Commodore continued till the beginning of *April*, highly delighted with the place, which by its extraordinary accommodations, the healthiness of its air, and the picturesque appearance of the country, all enlivened by the addition of a civilized colony, was not disgraced in an imaginary comparison with the vallies of *Juan Fernandes*, and the lawns of *Tinian*. During his stay he entered about forty new men;[1] and having, by the 3d of *April* 1744, compleated his water and provision, he, on that day, weighed and put to sea; and, the 19th of the same month, they saw the Island of *Saint Helena*, which however they did not touch at, but stood on their way; and, on the 10th of *June*, being then in soundings, they spoke with an *English* ship from *Amsterdam* bound for *Philadelphia*, whence they received the first intelligence of a *French* war; the twelfth they got sight of the *Lizard*; and the fifteenth, in the evening, to their infinite joy, they came safe to an anchor at *Spithead*. But that the signal perils which had so often threatened them in the preceding part of the enterprize, might pursue them to the very last, Mr. *Anson*, learnt on his arrival, that there was a *French* fleet of considerable force cruising in the chops of the Channel, which, by the account of their position, he found the *Centurion* had run through, and had been all the time concealed by a fog. Thus was this expedition finished, when it had lasted three years and nine months, after having, by its event, strongly evinced this important truth, That though prudence, intrepidity, and perseverance united, are not exempted from the blows of adverse fortune; yet in a long series of transactions, they usually rise superior to its power, and in the end rarely fail of proving successful.

FINIS.

Explanatory Notes

ABBREVIATIONS

B.M.	British Museum
Falconer	William Falconer, *An Universal Dictionary of the Marine* . . . (1769)
Millechamp	Journal of Lawrence Millechamp, National Maritime Museum, MS. 9354/JOD 36; as printed in *N.R.S.*, pp. 65–82, 111–38, 186–94
N.M.M.	National Maritime Museum
N.R.S.	Glyndwr Williams (ed.), *Documents relating to Anson's Voyage round the World 1740–1744* (Navy Records Society, 1967)
P.R.O.	Public Record Office
Thomas	Pascoe Thomas, *A True and Impartial Journal of a voyage to the South Seas and Round the Globe in His Majesty's Ship the Centurion* . . . (1745)

Page 3. two victories: those over the French off Cape Finisterre—by Anson in May 1747, and by Hawke in October 1747.

Page 10. the ensuing volume: there were thirty-five charts and views, together with seven plates depicting more general scenes.

Page 12. in those seas: Halley's *New and Correct Chart, shewing the Variations of the Compass in the Western and Southern Oceans* was published in 1701.

Page 13. (1) *at the same time:* four survivors from the *Wager* were on board Pizarro's ship, the *Asia*, at the time of Orellana's rising, and the '*English* gentleman' mentioned here was probably Isaac Morris, a midshipman, who later stated that he was 'a Witness to the whole Affair'. See his *Narrative of the Dangers and Difficulties which befell Isaac Morris, a midshipman of the Wager* . . . (1751), p. 71.

(2) *table of Errata:* all have been tacitly corrected in this edition.

Page 14. *commercial information:* the remainder of the Introduction points unmistakably to the scientific Benjamin Robins rather than the ecclesiastical Richard Walter as its author.

Page 15. *South-Seas:* an English translation was published at London in 1717 under the title, *A Voyage to the South-Sea, and along the Coasts of Chili and Peru.*

Page 20. *Sir Charles Wager:* First Lord of the Admiralty, 1733–42.

Page 21. *laid aside:* the private journal of Sir John Norris, Admiral of the Fleet, shows that Wager was invariably present at the discussions between ministers which resulted in Walpole's decision on 5 December 1739 to cancel the proposed expedition to Manila, because 'everybody's thoughts were upon an undertaking in the West Indies as the place where it was thought the Spaniards could be most affected . . .' (B.M. Add. MSS. 28, 132, fo. 87; *N.R.S.*, p. 14).

Page 22. *January 31, 1739:* the date according to the Julian or Old Style, by which the year began on 25 March not 1 January.

Page 23. *have them exchanged:* this may be so, but Norris's journal shows that Wager had been a party to the decision, the previous December, to send invalids with Anson (B.M. Add. MSS. 28, 132, fo. 93; *N.R.S.*, p. 14).

Page 25. *magnified by common report:* the Agents concerned were Hubert Tassell and Henry Hutchinson, whose South Sea Company careers had taken them to Havana, Portobelo, Panama, and Lima. They were brought into the discussions on the projected Cape Horn expedition as early as September 1739, and can in some respects be regarded as originators of the venture. Anson's objection to them was supported by Norris, who wrote: 'It was my opinion that instead of twenty tons of merchandise it might have been better to have carried that quantity of rice or other provisions to prevent the calumny that may arise from the opposers of the Administration, that this expedition is for the advantage of a private trade more than to annoy the enemy' (ibid., p. 17).

Page 26. (1) *permitted to fire:* these were presumably thought fit for active service on the grounds advanced by the Secretary at War in November 1739: 'Newly raised troops are as good on board a man-of-war as disciplined soldiers. In fighting a ship there is no part of the land discipline required but that of loading and firing a musket, and a country fellow from the Plough may be in three days taught to do this' (Cobbett, *Parliamentary History of England*, xi (1812), col. 158).

(2) *in their room:* although the expedition suffered in more than one way from the frustrating delays described here, it is true to say that some of the worst passages around Cape Horn were made in mid-summer (January in the southern hemisphere), when the winds tended to be even stronger than in winter.

Page 29. before he left them: the Spaniards owed this information to the efficiency of the French secret service. The French government wrote to Madrid outlining the strength and destination of Anson's expedition as early as 30 January 1740 (N.S.), only three weeks after these details had been settled by the British government. Further correspondence in the French archives shows that the French government brought considerable pressure to bear on Spain to intercept Anson, and in October a force of five powerful ships under Don José Pizarro left Santander for Madeira, Anson's first port of call (see *N.R.S.*, pp. 52–4).

Page 30. (1) *John Murray:* this should read George Murray.
(2) *Pinks:* the largest of the two-masted vessels.

Page 32. laid down in the charts in 17°: though unemphasized here, this difficulty of calculating longitude in the period before the development of the chronometer was soon to place Anson's ships in deadly peril. See pp. 89–90.

Page 33. Patache: usually a tender or a guard vessel, but here probably meaning a sloop.

Page 47. account of the trade winds: a reference to 'An Historical Account of the Trade Winds . . .', *Philosophical Transactions*, xvi (1686–7), 153–68.

Page 49. ought naturally to have inspired: possibly a reference to the improved system of ventilation by a huge bellows, known as 'the Ship's Lungs', suggested by Dr. Stephen Hales in 1743, and first adopted ten years later. See S. Hales, *Description of Ventilators* (1743); Christopher Lloyd and J. L. S. Coulter, *Medicine and the Navy, iii, 1714–1815* (1961), pp. 72–3. On the passage round Cape Horn, one of Anson's officers later noted, 'The violence of the tempest obliged us to keep the hatches shut, so that we had almost a total stagnation of air. . . . We made the best ventilators our circumstances would admit of, which were broad pieces of thin boards, shaped at one end into a handle. These a certain number of men were employed to wave backwards and forwards, in order to agitate the infected air . . .' (*The Universal Spectator*, 1 Sept. 1744; *N.R.S.*, p. 245).

Page 50. We crossed the equinoctial: Lawrence Millechamp, purser of the

Tryal at this time, noted in his journal that '. . . as is customary, such persons as had not crossed it before were obliged to pay their bottle and pound, or be ducked. The bottle and pound is a bottle of brandy or rum and a pound of sugar, with which forfeitures the seamen make merry. The ducking which is inflicted on those who either through poverty cannot, or being able obstinately refuse, to pay the forfeit, is performed by hoisting the man from deck to the main or fore yard (by lashings and tackle prepared for that purpose), and letting him fall sowse over head and ears in the water. This they repeat five or six times till the offender is as wet as a drowned rat. They then take him in, and as he has contributed so much to their mirth they suffer him to partake of their liquor till he is thoroughly drenched both inside and out' (Millechamp, p. 70).

Page 56. onions and potatoes: Pascoe Thomas's narrative of the voyage flatly contradicted the official account on this subject: 'As for Lemons, Limes, Plantains, Bananaes, Potatoes, and other Roots, Fruits, and Greens, with which those Countries generally abound, which the Authors above-mention'd [Frezier and others] aver to be extremely plentiful here, and which we principally depended on for Sea-Stores, these were so few at the Time of our being there, that I believe we could have consumed all that came to our Knowledge of those things in one Day' (Thomas, p. 12).

Page 57. Frezier and Shelvocke: a reference to Frezier's voyage of 1712–14 and Shelvocke's of 1719–22.

Page 59. Don Jose Sylva de Paz: Brigadier José Silva Pais was governor of Santa Catarina from 1739 to 1749, and had specific instructions to colonize the island with settlers from the Azores in an attempt to strengthen its defences and prevent its use by privateers. See C. R. Boxer, *The Golden Age of Brazil 1695–1750* (1962), pp. 251–3.

Page 63. the present King of Portugal: Dom João V was King of Portugal and Brazil from 1706 to 1750.

Page 64. (1) *woulding:* 'Woolding . . . winding a piece of rope about a mast or yard, to support it in a place where it may have been *fished* or *scarfed*; or when it is composed of several pieces united into one solid.' Falconer.
    (2) *fishes:* 'Fish . . . a long piece of oak, convex on one side and concave on the other. It is used to fasten upon the outside of the lower masts, either as an additional security . . . or to reinforce them after they have received some damage. . . . Thus their form, application and utility are exactly like those of the splinters applied to a broken limb in surgery' (ibid.).

Explanatory Notes

Page 66. preventer shrouds: additional shrouds used to support the normal rigging when severe weather is anticipated.

Page 67. Narborough's account of it: written more than seventy years earlier, during the voyage of 1669–71, and published in *An Account of Several Late Voyages and Discoveries to the South and North, Towards the Streights of Magellan, the South Seas . . . By Sir John Narborough, Captain Jasmen Tasman, Captain John Wood* (1694).

Page 68. (1) *handed:* furled.

(2) *bunted:* took up the 'middle part, or cavity' of the mainsail by the buntlines, 'ropes fastened to the bottoms of the square sails, to draw them up to the yards' (Falconer).

(3) *bilging:* damage to the bottom (usually) or (in this instance) the sides of the vessel.

Page 71. to the southward: or, to quote from Lieutenant Salt's report to the Admiralty: '. . . a lucky accident in our favour happening soon after, by some spawn of fish being upon the surface of the water and much discolouring it, which we had passed through, and they taking it for a shoal bore up for it, by which we forereached on them' (P.R.O. Adm 1/2099, section 3; *N.R.S.*, p. 104).

Page 77. those of Chili: Anson's instructions of January 1740 certainly encouraged him in both Chile and Peru 'to cultivate a good understanding with such Indians as shall be willing to join and assist you in any attempt that you may think proper to make against the Spaniards . . .' (P.R.O. S.P. 42/88, fos. 2–10; *N.R.S.*, p. 35).

Page 80. (1) *purchasing:* raising.

(2) *best bower:* ships in this period carried three main anchors: sheet anchor, best bower, small bower (in order of size and weight), together with a spare.

Page 82. annexed plate: between pp. 84–5.

Page 86. main dead eyes: 'a sort of round, flattish, wooden block . . . pierced with three holes through the flat, in order to receive the rope called a *laniard*, which corresponding with three holes in another dead-eye, creates a purchase employed for various uses, but chiefly to extend the *shrouds* and *stays*, otherwise called the standing rigging' (Falconer).

Page 87. (1) *manning the fore-shrouds:* this refers to the sending of men aloft into the shrouds when it was too dangerous to set any sail. Their bodies gave enough resistance to the wind to carry out limited manoeuvres of the kind described here.

(2) *his irretrievable situation:* this incident led William Cowper, more than fifty years later, to write one of his most moving poems, 'The Castaway'.

Page 88. *puttock-shroud:* also known as futtock shrouds; short shrouds running from the fore, main and mizen shrouds to the topmasts.

Page 89. (1) *gammon:* 'a rope used to bind the inner quarter of the bow-sprit close down to the ship's stem . . . to enable it the better to support the stays of the foremast, and carry sail in the fore part of the vessel' (Falconer).
(2) *haled upon a wind again:* 'to haul the wind . . . to direct the ship's course nearer to that point of the compass from which the wind arises' (Falconer).

Page 90. (1) *half that distance:* this is a dramatic example of the perils which attended the inability of navigators in this period to determine their longitude accurately. There was a 300-mile difference between the ships' supposed and actual positions.
(2) *perished:* the two ships had in fact turned about, reached Rio de Janeiro to refit, and then returned home. There was some criticism of the two captains, Legge and Murray, for their 'desertion', stemming mainly from Pascoe Thomas's entry for the day on which the *Severn* and *Pearl* disappeared: 'We made a very easy Sail all Day and lay by at Night, and fired several Guns as a Signal for them to join us; the Weather being pretty moderate and the Wind fair for them, they might have effected it with Ease. By the Close of the Evening we could but just see them, and from that Time saw them no more' (Thomas, p. 24). Anson does not appear to have shared this viewpoint (see p. 327), and the captains' correspondence shows that their vessels were in a desperate state, with the officers working aloft on the *Pearl*, and the *Severn* reaching Rio with only 144 survivors (and 114 of them sick) out of an original complement of 430 men (see *N.R.S.*, pp. 88–106).

Page 95. *the month of March:* despite the cold, June and July were the best months for the passage because in mid-winter the westerly winds are less regular and violent at the Horn. Anson's ships arrived in March, the worst possible time because of the ferocity of the equinoctial gales.

Page 97. (1) *plenty of fish:* for all the precise detail of Cowley's account, Pepys Island was entirely imaginary.
(2) *in the year 1708:* on his privateering voyage of 1708–11 in the *Duke* and the *Duchess*. Rogers published an account of his voyage at London in 1712 under the title *A Cruising Voyage round the World*.

(3) *so near Cape Horn*: while at the Admiralty Anson strove to put his own recommendation into effect, but a British project in 1749 to establish a base at the Falklands was blocked by strenuous Spanish protests, and the scheme was not revived until the 1760s.

Page 99. annexed plate: see map at end of book.

Page 100. its true quantity: in fact, Cabo Virjenes lies in longitude 68°25′W.

Page 101. much severer usage: these remarks called forth an indignant response from Frezier in a letter printed in *The Gentleman's Magazine*, xx (1750), 63–4.

Page 102. (1) *its true position*: Halley's error was greater than this; he placed the Strait of Magellan seven degrees (approximately 300 miles) too far west.

(2) *chart hereunto annexed*: see map at end of book.

Page 105. affects the human body: the appalling mortality rate from scurvy on Anson's ships, and the continuing failure of the medical profession to reach any agreement on the causes of this age-old scourge of the seas, stimulated James Lind to make a series of experiments and observations from 1747 onwards. In his *Treatise of the Scurvy* (1753) he showed that scurvy was essentially a dietary disease which could be prevented by lemon juice; but even so lemon juice did not become a standard navy issue until the end of the century. See Christopher Lloyd and J. L. S. Coulter, *Medicine and the Navy, iii, 1714–1815* (1961); and Christopher Lloyd (ed.), *The Health of Seamen* (Navy Records Society, 1965).

Page 108. (1) *two streaks to port*: 'Strakes or Streaks, the uniform ranges of planks on the bottom and sides of a ship' (Falconer).

(2) *stirrup our shrouds*: to refit the iron stirrups or straps round the dead-eyes of the shrouds.

(3) *to reeve new lanyards*: 'To reeve, is to pass the end of a rope through any hole, as the channel of a block . . . the principal laniards used in a ship . . . are those employed to extend the shrouds or stays of the masts' (Falconer).

Page 109. upon a meridian: this is another example of how handicapped navigators were in this period by their inability to determine longitude accurately. Anson followed common nautical practice in attempting to find his destination by sailing along the correct line of latitude until he reached it—with the disastrous results described in the next paragraph.

Explanatory Notes

Page 111. (1) *plying:* beating or tacking against the wind.

(2) *wearing the ship:* 'Veering . . . the operation by which a ship, in changing her course from one board to the other, turns her stern to windward. Hence it is used in opposition to *tacking*, wherein the head is turned to the wind, and the stern to leeward' (Falconer).

Page 116. (1) *cackle:* 'Keckling . . . a name given to any old ropes, which are wound about a cable . . . to preserve the surface of the cable from being fretted' (Falconer).

(2) *good rounding:* old ropes used for keckling.

(3) *a clear hawse:* 'A ship is said to ride with a clear hawse, when the cables are directed to their anchors, without lying athwart the stern; or crossing, or being twisted round each other, by the ships winding about, according to the change of the wind, tide, or current' (Falconer).

Page 117. *Our prisoners:* presumably from the *Nuestra Señora del Monte Carmelo,* taken by the *Centurion* in September 1741. See p. 157.

Page 120. (1) *adjoining plate:* opposite p. 85.

(2) *the journal of their voyage:* Selkirk's stay on the island, described in Woodes Rogers's *Cruising Voyage Round the World* (1712), formed of course the basis for Defoe's *Robinson Crusoe.*

Page 123. *annexed plate:* opposite p. 180.

Page 128. *coming to an anchor:* the frustrations of this episode show the difficulties involved in manoeuvring a square-rigged vessel against the wind. As G. S. Laird Clowes pointed out in his edition of *Anson's Voyage Round the World* (1928), p. 121n., the *Centurion's* longboat, with a fore-and-aft rig, was able to sail out to the *Gloucester* and then return to the island without these problems.

Page 130. *no more than thirty hands:* four Spanish men-of-war had cruised off the coast of Chile waiting for Anson, but had given up in the autumn (i.e. March/April) of 1741. See Jorge Juan and Antonio de Ulloa, *Relacion Historica del Viage a la America Meridional* (Madrid, 1758), iii, 260–9, iv, clx–clxi: also pp. 158–60 *supra.*

Page 131. (1) *chain-plates:* 'Chains, strong links or plates of iron, the lower ends of which are bolted through the ship's side to the timbers' (Falconer).

(2) *junk* '. . . any remnants or pieces of old cable' (ibid.).

Page 133. (1) *the partners:* '. . . pieces of plank nailed round the several *scuttles*, or holes, in a ship's deck, wherein are contained the masts and capsterns' (ibid.).

(2) *to pay*: '. . . to daub or anoint the surface of any body, in order to preserve it from the injuries of the water, weather &c.' (ibid.).

(3) *boot-hose tops*: 'Boot-topping is chiefly performed where there is no dock, or other commodious situation for breaming or careening; or when the hurry of a voyage renders it inconvenient to have the whole bottom properly trimmed and cleansed of the filth which gathers to it in the course of a sea-voyage. It is executed by making the ship lean to one side, as much as they can with safety, and then scraping off the grass, slime, shells, or other material, that adheres to the bottom, on the other side, which is elevated above the surface of the water for this purpose, and accordingly daubed with the coat of tallow and sulphur. Having thus finished one side, they make the ship lean to the other side, and perform the same operation, which not only preserves the bottom from the worm, but makes the ship slide smoothly through the water' (ibid.).

Page 136. *the large bay*: this is still shown on modern maps as Bahia Anna Pink.

Page 145. *to confront them*: for reasons which are not altogether clear, but may be connected with a desire to avoid an enquiry into Cheap's pistolling of Cozens, no official charge of mutiny was ever brought against the *Wager* survivors who deserted in the longboat. The court-martial of April 1746 confined itself to the actual shipwreck of the *Wager* on 14 May 1741. On all this see S. W. C. Pack, *The Wager Mutiny* (1964).

Page 146. *the Anna Pink*: this is very doubtful—the *Anna* was anchored a hundred miles or so to the northward.

Page 149. *entirely silent*: Alexander Campbell admitted his change of religion, but in his *Sequel to A Voyage to the South Seas* (1747), strongly denied that he had ever sought employment in the Spanish navy. Some support for his contention came a few years later when Issac Morris, one of the other *Wager* survivors on board the *Asia*, wrote that Pizarro 'endeavoured, though fruitlessly, to persuade them, with great promises of preferment, to enter into the Spanish service' (*A Narrative of the Dangers and Difficulties which befell Isaac Morris, a midshipman of the Wager, and seven more of the crew belonging to the Wager* (1751), p. 84).

Page 152. (1) *knees*: 'knee . . . a crooked piece of timber, having two branches, or arms, and generally used to connect the beams of a ship with her sides or timbers' (Falconer).

(2) *breast-hook*: 'thick pieces of timber . . . used to strengthen the fore-part of the ship' (ibid.).

Explanatory Notes

(3) *water-ways:* '. . . a long piece of timber serving to connect the sides of a ship to her decks, and form a sort of channel to carry off the water from the latter by means of scuppers' (ibid.).

(4) *spirkiting:* '. . . range of planks which lies between the water-ways and the lower edge of the gun-ports' (ibid.).

(5) *wales:* '. . . assemblage of strong planks extending along a ship's side, throughout her whole length, at different heights, and serving to reinforce the decks' (ibid.).

Page 155. *her courses:* 'courses . . . a name by which the principal sails of a ship are usually distinguished, viz. the main-sail, fore-sail, and mizen . . .' (ibid.).

Page 157. *serons:* large panniers or cases.

Page 182. *no other injury:* Pascoe Thomas wrote: '. . . I have had it repeated from several Officers then on Shore, that our Men ran to the Attack and fired in so irregular a manner, that it was, and still Remains a Doubt whether those were not shot by our own People rather than by an Enemy' (Thomas, p. 56).

Page 183. *his own people:* what is evidently a first-hand account of the landing at Paita in the pseudonymous narrative by 'John Philips, Midshipman of the *Centurion*', contains a more credible note on the behaviour of Anson's men: 'As soon as we were Master's of the Town, we began to plunder and play our Tricks. At the Governor's House there was a very large Pier Glas in a fine carved and gilt Frame, of a considerable Value, and having found some Wine and Glasses there, we drank confusion to our Enemies, with Success likewise to our Voyage, and afterwards flung our Glasses at it, and broke it all to Pieces. . . . In the Morning we fell to rummaging for what we could get; some of us were so mad, that if they happened to get a Bag of Dollars, which they could not easily manage, they would give it a rip and hussel them out till they could, never minding what they left behind.' *An Authentic Journal of the late Expedition under the command of Commodore Anson* (1744), p. 82.

Page 188. *annexed plate:* between pp. 180–1.

Page 192. *that prodigious Empire:* writing of his experiences as a prisoner of the Spaniards in Santiago, John Byron, a midshipman on the *Wager*, observed: 'We found many Spaniards here that had been taken by Commodore Anson, and been for some time prisoners on board the *Centurion*. They all spoke in the highest terms of the kind treatment they had received; and it is natural to imagine, that it was chiefly owing to that laudable example of humanity our reception here was so good'. *The Narrative of . . . the Honourable John*

Byron . . . (1768), pp. 233–4. In 1821 Captain Basil Hall, R.N., found during his stay in the area that 'Lord Anson's proceedings, we were surprised to find, are still traditionally known' at Payta; and it furnishes a curious instance of the effect of manners on the opinion of mankind, to observe that the kindness with which that officer invariably treated his Spanish prisoners, is, at the distance of eighty years, better known, and more dwelt upon by the inhabitants of Payta, than the capture and destruction of the town' (*Extracts from a Journal written on the Coasts of Chili, Peru, and Mexico in the Years 1820, 1821, 1822* (1824), ii, 99).

Page 194. *into their hands:* Pascoe Thomas was certainly not satisfied. 'This Action appeared to be very generous; but who were all the fresh Provisions, Sheep, Hogs, Fowls, Pumpkins, Onions, Olives, Sweetmeats, &c. &c. &c, shared among? and to whom did they belong, and who wanted them most?' (Thomas, p. 64).

Page 195. *an immense value:* one of the other accounts adds a description of a dispute not mentioned in the official account, but which in view of the disagreements over prize-money which soured relations in the months ahead may well have been true. 'They likewise informed us, that on the fifteenth, *Payta* bearing then E. by E. five Leagues, they saw a great Smoak to the Leeward of the Town; but this we did not believe, they only saying so to come in for the Plunder; however, the Commodore immediately sent for the Officers Journals, and seal'd them up, and gave strict Orders they should not be open'd upon any Account; and likewise ordered them to keep their Journals from that Time in other Books' ('Philips', *Authentic Journal*, p. 90).

Page 200. *we had the wind large:* i.e. on the beam or quarter.

Page 214. *14th of March, N.S.:* this galleon was the *Pilar*. For a note on dates see note to p. 22.

Page 221. *twelve hundred men on board:* this is a gross over-estimate. The great *Santissima Trinidad*, captured by the British in 1762, and at 2,000 tons one of the largest ships afloat, carried a crew of 384. Passengers of course could swell the numbers. For this, and much else on the galleons, see the authoritative account by W. L. Schurz, *The Manila Galleon* (1939).

Page 231. *her strength:* it was commonly believed that the sides of the galleons were so thick that cannon-balls could not penetrate them. See p. 333. After an unsuccessful attempt to take one of the galleons in 1709 Woodes Rogers wrote: 'we could perceive few of our Shot enter'd her Sides to any purpose . . . tho' we could not place less than 500 Shot (6 Pounders) in her Hull. These large Ships are built at *Manila* with excellent Timber, that will not splinter; they have very thick Sides, much stronger than we build in

Europe'. Woodes Rogers, *A Cruising Voyage round the World* (1928 reprint, ed. G. E. Manwaring), pp. 200, 221. The light calibre of the privateers' guns should be borne in mind here; the *Centurion*, by contrast, carried 24-pounders.

Page 236. the harbour of Chequetan: in 1685, when Dampier reported that 'A Mile and Half from the shore there is a small Key, and within it is a very good Harbour where Ships may careen; there is also a small River of fresh Water, and Wood enough.' William Dampier, *A New Voyage round the World* (1937 reprint, ed. Sir Albert Gray), p. 174.

Page 242. only amounted to sixteen: other journals do not support this version of the incident. Lawrence Millechamp maintained that the Spaniards numbered about a hundred, and were fired upon from the boats immediately they appeared. He added: 'This proceeding was looked on as a little extraordinary, as the Commodore had just before caused advertisements to be posted up in roadways to invite the inhabitants to come and trade with him for the goods he had taken in the South Seas; and in these advertisements he had made a declaration that all hostilities should cease on his part, and that he would immediately leave the coast. I say it was looked on as extraordinary that our people should fire at those Spaniards when they did not know whether or no they were not the very people that were sent to trade with us!' (Millechamp, p. 123). Lieutenant Peircy Brett wrote: 'As they came to a grapnel they discovered a party of Spanish horsemen, to the number of about eight, who made towards the boats, where they had no sooner come within shot, but the boats fired at them, which made them all fly into the bushes' (N.M.M. ADM L/C/83). The official log of the *Centurion*, under Anson's signature, is even more explicit: 'They discovered a party of horsemen upon which my lieutenant ordered his men to give fire and fired several volleys; they did not return one shot but fled to the woods' (N.M.M. ADM L/C/300).

Page 246. the greatest part of her crew: the official account does not mention that there was strenuous opposition to this decision from the officers appointed to the *Tryal Prize*. Millechamp's journal contains copies of the petitions and letters on this subject; see *N.R.S.*, pp. 116–19. It should be said here that Millechamp, in his lively, often critical journal, was concerned to state the case of the officers of the *Gloucester* and *Tryal* in the long wrangle over the distribution of the prize-money from the Acapulco galleon. As purser of the *Tryal*, who moved first to the *Tryal Prize*, then to the *Gloucester*, and finally to the *Centurion*, as one vessel after another was sunk, he had a personal interest in the matter. This was shown when he presented a copy of his journal to Earl Fitzwalter, one of the Lords Commissioners for Appeals in

Prize Cases which in 1747 decided in favour of the officers of the *Centurion*, and thereby reversed a previous decision of the High Court of Admiralty.

Page 247. the South-Seas: printed, for example, in the *London Magazine*, April 1743, pp. 202–3.

Page 253. to assist us: forty-three in all, according to the journal of Lieutenant Saumarez, 6 May 1742.

Page 255. Juan Fernandes: another reference to the privateering voyage of 1708–11 under the command of Woodes Rogers.

Page 264. dictated to them: although the investigations of Antonio de Ulloa and Jorge Juan at this time were revealing the extent of discontent in Spanish America there was little likelihood that outside the Indian peoples, any substantial section of the colonial populace would have welcomed Anson's marauding heretics with open arms. This chapter radiates an easy optimism which does much to justify Horace Walpole's criticism of it in 1748: 'He sets out with telling you that he had no soldiers sent with him but old invalids without legs or arms; and then in the middle of the book there is a whole chapter to tell you, what they would have done if they had set out two months sooner; and that was no less than conquering Peru and Mexico with this disabled army.' (*The Yale Edition of Horace Walpole's Correspondence*, ix (1941), ed. W. S. Lewis, 55).

Page 266. (1) *trussel-trees:* 'Trestle-trees . . . two strong bars of timber fixed horizontally on the opposite sides of the lower mast-head, to support the frame of the top, and the weight of the top-mast' (Falconer).

(2) *hogs and fowls:* but not, apparently, much in the way of fresh fruit and vegetables.

Page 267. fed upon fish: Pascoe Thomas, himself ill with scurvy, compared the lot of the sick on board the *Centurion* unfavourably with those on the *Gloucester*: 'Capt. Mitchell constantly ordered several Boys, who were very dextrous at it, to catch Fish for the Ship's Company, especially the Sick; and those were very justly and regularly divided among them: whereas our Fishermen were left alone to make their Advantage of what they took, and prey on their Fellow Sufferers; and they took Care not to overslip the Opportunity, for the least Fish you could purchase of them would cost you a Bottle of Brandy . . .' (Thomas, pp. 140–1). The fact that Thomas was seriously ill may have coloured his version of events during these weeks.

Page 268. his patients: Thomas has more detail on this: 'Since our passing Cape Horn our surgeon, Henry Ettrick (who was a very good practical surgeon, but in the theory part vain and pragmatical, making science to consist in a flow of words, with little or no meaning) had been very busy in digesting a theory of scurvies; wherein he enumerated many cases very particularly, having been allowed to open and examine as many bodies as were abundantly sufficient for that purpose. His system was principally founded on the observations made on a long passage, in a very cold climate. He took abundant pains to prove, by many instances, that the tone of the blood was broken by this cold nipping air, and rendered so thin as to be unfit for circulation, or any other of the uses of life; and being thus deprived of a proper force and vigour, stagnation and death must necessarily ensue. From this supposition, he had laid it down as an infallible rule, that any food of a glutinous nature, such as salt fish, bread, and several sorts of grains, were alone proper on such voyages. As for liquids, I know not which he had pitched upon as the most salutary on this occasion. But this passage, in a very hot climate, where the symptoms were not only more dreadful, but the mortality much more quick and fatal in proportion to the number of people, put our scheming doctor to a sad nonplus . . .' (ibid., pp. 142–3). After surviving the worst rigours of the voyage Ettrick died during the *Centurion's* stay in the Canton River in September 1743.

Page 269. forecap: 'Cap . . . a strong, thick block of wood, used to confine two masts together, when the one is erected at the head of the other, in order to lengthen it' (Falconer).

Page 270. jury: temporary mast.

Page 271. orlope: '. . . a platform of planks laid over the beams, in the hold of a ship of war, whereon the cables are usually coiled, and the several officers store-rooms contained' (Falconer).

Page 272. a very considerable height: other descriptions of the end of the *Gloucester* are more eloquent than this rather flat passage. Millechamp, for example, wrote: 'She burnt all night, making a most grand, horrid appearance. Her guns, which were all loaded, fired so regularly at about the distance of a minute between each as the fire came to them, that they sounded like mourning guns, such as are fired at the funeral of some great officer. At six o'clock the next morning, the fire having reached her powder room, where was upwards of two hundred barrels of gunpowder, she blew up. That action made an odd appearance, for we first saw a quick streak of smoke fly up with an incredible swiftness, and a prodigious height, and when it had reached a particular region of the air, its velocity ceased, and the top of it grew into a monstrous large cloud, that it seemed for about an hour to be an overgrown column, whose base was fixed to the sea and whose capital supported the clouds. We soon after heard the report, which sounded like a great clap of distant thunder. Thus ended the Gloucester, a ship justly esteemed the beauty of the English navy' (Millechamp, p. 128).

Page 275. expected to founder: the extent of the *Centurion's* plight is shown by the fact that 'her crew was so weak and bad, that her officers were obliged to work at the pumps, and do other work as common seamen, and the Commodore himself sometimes assisted, by pulling or hauling of a rope'—an occurrence of some novelty in the navy of the period. See N.M.M. MS. 9416/ HAR 4.

Page 279. without help: not all the sick were as appreciative of these efforts as the official account suggests. Pascoe Thomas wrote: 'On our being brought on Shore, that is the Sick, it rain'd very hard, so that we were in a manner half drown'd before we could be carry'd up to the Tent; our Bedding was soak'd through, and abundance of it, for want of Help, left washing in the Break of the Sea, where most of it was either spoil'd or lost; nor could those who carry'd us up to the Tent assist us any farther, but left us there half naked on the cold Ground, or a hard Hide, to help ourselves, of which we were utterly uncapable; nor had we for the greatest Part any Person to get us a sour Orange, or a Lime, or one Drop of Water; tho' all these Things abounded within our View, and almost our Reach. In this miserable Condition myself and several other Persons lay unassisted, and, by what we could observe, unpitied . . .' (Thomas, p. 154).

Page 281. Bread Fruit: and not only by Anson's men—Dampier gave a full description of 'The Bread-fruit (as we call it)' after his stay at nearby Guam in 1686 (Dampier, *New Voyage* (ed. Gray), p. 205).

Page 283. view . . . inserted above: opposite p. 181.

Page 285. pooped: that is, swamped by a sea breaking over the stern of the vessel.

Page 286. (1) *on shore:* Millechamp has a quite different version of the incident which led to this decision. 'The affair was as follows. One of the most dextrous of these fellows was sent with the butcher and two more of our own people to kill fresh beef, and happening to meet with a large herd of cattle that were too wild for our people (who were then unacquainted with the manner of taking them) to come within shot of, and having occasion to run round some little way to intercept the herd in a pass they were making for, our butcher imagined the fellow was going to run away with the musket, and really marched off. But the butcher and his crew were too much alarmed at his desertion to stay to look for his arms, being thus frightened out of their wits for fear they should be attacked by those who had at first escaped. They therefore returned and made a most lamentable story of it to the commodore, who immediately ordered all the rest to be confined on board' (Millechamp, p. 131).

(2) *the cut-water*: '. . . the foremost part of a ship's prow' (Falconer).

Page 287. (1) *chincing*: 'To Chinse, is to thrust oakum into a seam or chink with the point of a knife or chissel. This is chiefly used when calking cannot be safely or conveniently performed' (Falconer).

(2) *heaving down*: careening.

(3) *view . . . already inserted*: opposite p. 85.

Page 289. (1) *sheet anchor*: used in deep water, since its cable consisted of two cables spliced together, making a total of 240 fathoms, or 1440 feet.

(2) *to be our last*: the implication here, and on p. 288, is that Walter was among those on the *Centurion* when she was driven out to sea.

Page 294. *the encouragement of his people*: other journals confirm the importance of Anson's example. Millechamp wrote: 'Nor was Mr. Anson himself, Captain Saunders or Mitchell idle upon this occasion, for besides their giving necessary directions they all set themselves hard to work, and would frequently be working with an axe, cross-cut saw, or carrying timber with the meanest seaman we had. This raised an emulation in our common people, and made everyone endeavour to excel, and indeed we soon found that our work went on with great spirit and vigour and was like to succeed far beyond our expectation' (Millechamp, p. 133).

Page 296. *to no purpose*: on this, Thomas reported a rumour which hints once more that the official account sometimes presents a roseate rather than realistic version of crew attitudes. '. . . I have heard, since our being in China, that most of the common People had resolved to desert us in four or five Days more if the Ship had not appear'd in that Time, and to have built themselves Huts in the Woods, and run the Risk of staying on the Island, rather than venture themselves to China in that Bark. I cannot aver the Truth of this; but I believe some of them to be void enough of Reason to have acted after that Manner . . .' (Thomas, p. 159).

Page 299. *the jeers*: '. . . an assemblage of tackles, by which the lower yards of a ship are hoisted up along the mast to their usual station . . .' (Falconer).

Page 307. *annexed plate*: opposite p. 340.

Page 308. *construction or celerity*: in his edition of the *Voyage* Laird Clowes pointed out (p. 322n) the similarity between the outrigger described here and those still used in the early twentieth century in Fiji and Samoa.

Page 309. *the unknown southern Continent:* here the writer was following the common speculation that there existed in the southern hemisphere a vast land-mass (*Terra Australis Incognita*) which might, some of the more extravagant theorists claimed, stretch for 5,000 miles and contain fifty million inhabitants.

Page 313. *capacity of this Nation:* this passage is the first of several critical of the Chinese, but as James Naish (the former East India Company supercargo with long experience of trading at Canton) pointed out in a marginal note in his copy of the 1748 account (B.M. 10025, f. 8) there was another reason for the lack of interest in Anson's ship: 'The Dutch ships which for many years sailed along the coast of China, were larger than the Centurion, though they were Company's ships bound to Japan.'

Page 319. *the Hoppo:* this official was in fact a subordinate officer, not the Hoppo himself, who was the Imperial Commissioner of the Kwantung Customs, and resided at Canton.

Page 320. (1) *on any occasion:* the diary of the East India supercargoes at Canton in 1742 noted—'7 December. We assembled the [Chinese] merchants for the third time to persuade them if possible to prevail with the mandarins to grant Mr. Anson a general chop [permit] for all the necessaries he wants. They told us the mandarins had such strange notion of a ship which went about the world seeking other ships in order to take them, that they could not be brought to hear reason on that head' (India Office Library, Factory Records: China II, 3; *N.R.S.*, p. 145). Millechamp elaborated in his journal: 'These Chinese received us here in an odd manner, for as they had never been accustomed to any ships coming on their coast but such as trade with them, they look on all others as pirates or *Ladrones*. In this manner they received us, calling us always the Grand Ladrone ship, and the mob would frequently insult us in their streets, calling out *Ladrone, Ladrone* and throw stones at us as we passed. Nor was Mr. Anson himself free from these insults. The name he at first went by, even among the mandarins and merchants was the Grand Ladrone captain, or the great captain of the thieves' (Millechamp, p. 137).

(2) *the horror of these dastards:* in a marginal annotation in his copy of the *Voyage* James Naish was sceptical about this: 'there is not the least reason to suppose the Chinese were terrified with the size of the Centurion, and being fitted for war only, for they have often seen larger ships in the river of Canton, from France and Holland, and the Portuguese have had as large ships at Macao . . .' (B.M. 10025, f. 8). He rather attributed the behaviour of the Chinese merchants to the machinations of the French and Dutch supercargoes. In a private letter to Naish from Canton Anson himself wrote: 'the

Chinese merchants and all the Europeans (except the English) were against me for a reason you know, viz. the small Manila ships that arrive here at this season of the year to purchase silks etc. for the great galleon in which they have a principal concern; but my keeping the great ship at Acapulco will probably prevent any coming this year from Manila' (*N.R.S.*, p. 153).

Page 323. the regimentals of the marines: the navy as such had no uniform at this time. See also p. 356.

Page 326. (1) *their European copiers:* 'The Vision of Cathay' which so bedazzled Europeans had been seen primarily through the eyes of the Jesuit missionaries of the seventeenth century. In 1735 perhaps the most comprehensive work on China by a European was published—the Jesuit Du Halde's *Description géographique, historique, etc. de l'empire de la Chine,* translated into English the next year as *The General History of China.* On this subject generally see W. W. Appleton, *A Cycle of Cathay* (1951); Hugh Honour, *Chinoiserie: The Vision of Cathay* (1961).

(2) *embarked with them:* though not without some difficulty. Anson's correspondence with Lieutenant Saumarez, in command on the *Centurion* during the Commodore's visit to Canton, shows that he was adamant that apart from the most senior officers no one was allowed home unless he could find a replacement from the East Indiamen—not even the chaplain. See *N.R.S.*, pp. 148–52.

Page 327. having both perished: in this passage Anson came to the defence of Legge and Murray, who had been criticized by many in England for turning back near Cape Horn (see p. 90 n.2). By the time the official account was published in 1748 Legge was dead, but his brother Henry wrote to Anson thanking him for 'having done honour to my brother . . . the kind, and, I may say, just paragraph (for otherwise I am sure you would never have admitted it) which relates to him, will always have authority enough to protect his memory against coffee-house censurers, and the cavils of those children of ease who sit at home and, without risking themselves, blame every man's conduct they do not and cannot understand' (Sir John Barrow, *The Life of George Lord Anson* (1839), pp. 408–9).

Page 328. the French ships only: a tilt, this, at the officers of the East India Company.

Page 329. (1) *scarfed:* 'Scarf . . . a particular method of uniting two pieces of timber together by the extremities . . . so that the end of one goes over the end of the other, being tapered so that the one may be let into the other, and become even . . .' (Falconer).

(2) *intended to career there:* the Archivo de Indias at Seville contains two anonymous letters from an informant at Canton to the Governor of the Philippines, one dated December 1742, the other later but undated, which gave full details about Anson's activities. They warned: 'And for all the commander's exaggerated remarks about the sad condition of his ship, wanting to take advantage of the remainder of the monsoon to cross to Batavia, and of not being in any state to attack a galleon, but rather to continue his voyage to Europe—it is feared he has other plans. . . . He has incurred many expenses which he would not have had if he had sailed direct to Batavia, where nothing would have been denied him. He has taken so long careening that he is obviously not in any great hurry, although the monsoon season for Batavia is definitely approaching. These circumstances, once perceived by your shrewdness, and the considerable pains Anson has taken to disguise his plans, show beyond doubt that he has designs of the greatest import. I do not think that his intentions go as far as attacking Manila with so few men, though he could easily set fire to any ships he met in the roadstead; but if I am not mistaken he intends to cruise for either the incoming or the outgoing galleon . . .' (*N.R.S.*, pp. 208–9).

Page 331. warped: 'To warp . . . is to change the situation of a ship, by pulling her from one part of a harbour, &c. to some other, by means of warps, which are attached to buoys; to anchors sunk in the bottom; or to certain stations upon the shore, as post, rings, trees, &c. The ship is accordingly drawn forward to those stations, either by pulling on the warps by hand, or by the application of some purchase, as a tackle, windlass, or capstern, upon her deck' (Falconer).

Page 332. the preceding season: the *Pilar*, the galleon held at Acapulco the previous year because of Anson's presence on the coast, had returned to Manila in March 1743; so only one galleon, the *Covadonga*, would be making the crossing at the regular time.

Page 333. should go through them both: Millechamp's journal contains an interesting sidelight on this. 'On the sixteenth [April] we got fairly out of Taipa and anchored in the road in six fathom. We had not been long at an anchor there before a Swedish Indiaman passed us and saluted us. In our returning the salute we observed our guns to make but a small report, and threw the wads but an inconsiderable distance from the ship. This made us something uneasy, fearing the long time we had had it [the powder] on board might have caused it to lose its virtue, and made it too weak to do any execution. And the Acapulco ship's sides had been represented to us of such a monstrous thickness that we were afraid our shot would not penetrate them, especially with such weak powder. However, on trial we found our guns would carry shot a great distance, and that we were only alarmed by some guns that had been long loaded, and the powder had got damp within them' (Millechamp, p. 186).

Page 337. the enterprize was laid aside: it was not the sighting of the **Centurion**, but the letters from Canton describing Anson's actions (see p. 329, n.2) which alarmed the Spaniards at Manila. A council of war decided to send out the *Pilar*, together with some smaller vessels, to escort the *Covadonga* into port; but the expedition's preparations for sea and subsequent movements were painfully slow. A week after the *Covadonga* had been captured by Anson off Cape Espíritu Santo, the relief force was still a hundred miles distant, and the *Pilar* had run aground. See Juan de la Concepción, *Historia General de Philipinas*, xi (Manila, 1791), pp. 132–9.

Page 338. to hasten her up: a signal rather to the escort or supply vessel which the galleon's officers imagined was sailing towards them from the San Bernardino Strait.

Page 339. cattle and lumber: the log of the galleon's second pilot shows that about three weeks before this the crew were 'employed in clearing the ship and knocking down the cabins on the quarter-deck and waist, and there remains nothing but the guns and other warlike stores in sight' (N.M.M. 36 MS. 0827 Log F/7).

Page 340. (1) *desist from firing:* the Spanish accounts give a chilling impression of the effect of the *Centurion*'s cannon and small-arms fire as it swept across the exposed deck of the galleon. They show that Spanish resistance was already weakening when Montero was struck down by a musket-ball in the chest. His second-in-command took over, and remained on deck though hit in the thigh; but as another officer was killed, and the captain of soldiers badly wounded, the crew began to desert their posts. The galleon's steering failed, her guns almost ceased firing, and as the *Centurion* moved across the galleon's bows the Spaniards ignored Montero's final order from the cockpit to blow up the ship, and instead struck their flag.

(2) *larger than the Centurion:* not so; twenty foot shorter on her gun-deck, the *Covadonga*'s tonnage was about 700 tons compared with the 1,005 tons burthen of the *Centurion*.

(3) *five hundred and fifty men:* of the 530 men on board the *Covadonga* only 266 were crew-members, about half of them Filipinos. Apart from a company of forty soldiers, the rest were passengers, servants, and convicts.

(4) *thirty-six guns:* but the heaviest of these were 12-pounders. The rest were 8- or 6-pounders.

(5) *pidreroes:* light swivel guns.

(6) *eighty-four wounded:* and, in Anson's words, 'her masts and rigging were shot to pieces, and 150 shot passed through her hull, many of which were between wind and water, which occasioned her to be very leaky' (P.R.O. S.P.42/88, ff. 87–8).

Page 341. *extremely terrible:* several of the accounts stressed Anson's coolness, now and throughout the action. Thomas wrote; 'This calmness of behaviour caused the whole engagement to be carried on in the same manner; every man knew his duty, and performed it without the least confusion, noise, or disorder; and, exclusive of the continual thunder of our cannon, I have seen or heard six times more confusion, noise, and hurry in hoisting out one small cutter (or small boat) than we had during this whole engagement' (Thomas, p. 283). One of the *Centurion's* officers later recollected: 'As his Honour was upon deck giving his orders, one of our lieutenants came up to him in great hurry and confusion, crying out, "Sir, Sir!" The Commodore went on calmly with what he was saying, and then turning to the lieutenant, "Well, Sir, and what is your pleasure?" The young gentleman had hardly breath or spirits to bring out, "Why Sir, the ship's on fire!"—but received no other answer than the very temperate one, "Well then, Sir, go and put it out!" The ease with which he spoke this, the serenity he preserved in his countenance (for I was just by him) and the regularity with which he still carried on the engagement, were to one admirable, and what I am sure I shall never forget' (*The Universal Spectator*, 25 August 1744).

Page 344. *the specie:* although Millechamp wrote that it was not until the ships' arrival at Whampoa towards the end of July that 'We now began to make a thorough search of the prize, and found a great deal of concealed treasure, some cast into large lumps like cheeses, and so artfully covered in the rind of cheese, that 'twas by the weight only we could discover them. Some parcels of money we found hid between the beams and timbers of the ship, and in all places where there was any possibility of concealment we were sure to find money' (Millechamp, p. 190).

Page 354. *that infamous action:* James Naish sounded a cautionary note here in his copy of the *Voyage.* 'The Portuguese, who were the first Europeans that entered China, comprehend all degrees of the Chinese magistrates and officers, both military and civil, under the word Mandarin; but it must be observed that the most inconsiderable mandarin depends on others, whose powers are greater, and this observation is here made, because I am very sure that every mandarin mentioned in this and the two following pages were in the lowest rank of Custom house officers.'

Page 355. the strong bias of his Nation to dishonesty: this was not an isolated opinion among Anson's crew. Millechamp, for example, wrote that: 'The people are of a low stature and of a yellow complexion, in general ingenious, artful and treacherous. Covetousness seems to be their darling passion, for they will all be guilty of the most infamous crimes to gratify it' (Millechamp, pp. 191–2). On the other hand Naish insisted that 'These instances relate only to the Canalia, or dregs of the people, and such instances as these may be found in every country under the sun, and may not be a reflection upon any nation in general.' That fervent Sinophile, Voltaire, claimed that Anson's experiences at Canton were misleading: 'Je crois qu'il faut plutôt juger d'une puissante nation par ceux qui sont à la tête que par la populace des extrémités d'une province' (*Oeuvres Complètes de Voltaire*, xxviii (1826), 295).

Page 356. jackets and caps: on this occasion, as at Macao the previous December (see p. 323) Anson was improvising a naval uniform. Soon after his appointment to the Board of Admiralty Anson set about the design and selection of a uniform which in April 1748 was made compulsory for officers.

Page 365. (1) *took his leave:* a Chinese account gives a different picture of the confrontation. Anson ('the commander of the red-haired people') is described as being completely intimidated by the Chinese officials, who demanded his Spanish prisoners as tribute. Weeping, grovelling on the floor, and finally crawling into the presence of the Viceroy with his crossbow tucked under his arm, Anson agreed to the Chinese demands, and was then allowed to refit and depart. See Arthur Waley, *Yuan Mei* (1956), pp. 205–9.

(2) *the ports of China:* in fact, the next British man-of-war which entered Whampoa to refit, the *Argo* in 1764, was unable to take advantage of the precedent Anson had set, and was measured by Chinese officials as if she were a merchant ship.

Page 366. on the 10th: Millechamp wrote: 'We were now in a better condition than we had ever before been. We were finely recruited and refreshed in China, where we met with every eatable we could wish. Besides, every man now had lain in a stock of pigs, hens, geese, and Mr. Anson had the decks filled with live cattle and sheep, [so] that we lived nobly for almost all our homeward bound passage' (Millechamp, p. 193).

Page 369. annexed plate: opposite p. 341.

Page 371. *about forty new men:* the *Centurion* arrived home with a crew described by one observer as follows—'. . . besides these English there were men of eighteen other different nations, viz. Dutch, French, Spaniards, Italians, Germans, Swedes, Danes, Muscovites, Portuguese, Lascar Indians, Malays, Persians, Indians of Manila, Timor and Guam, Negroes of Guinea, Creoles of Mexico and Mozambique' (B.M. Add. MSS. 35, 396, fo. 217).

Index

Abrollos (Abrolhos) shoal, 50

Acapulco, 11, 21, 178, 179, 196, 208–53 *passim*, 304, 332, 341, 344; Governor of, 229, 250, 251, 252

Acapulco galleon(s), *see also* Manila galleon(s), *Nuestra Señora de Covadonga*, 227–8, 249, 332, 334

Aguiguan Island, 276, 285, 298

Alexander VI (Pope), 215–16

Alvoredo Island, 52, 55

Anatacan Island, 274, 275

Andes, 94, 107, 171, 174–5

Anson, Commodore George, interest in surveys, 10, 115, 174, 244; knowledge of Spanish America, 12–13; chosen for expedition, 20; his preparations for voyage, 20–9; plans known to enemy, 28–9, 36, 65–6, 329; and provisions, 65, 133, 134, 334; instructions if *Centurion* lost, 67–8, 79–80; and supposed sighting of Juan Fernández, 109; works with crew, 114, 279, 291, 294, 297; treatment of prisoners, 118–19, 157, 169, 180–1, 185–6, 190–2, 253, 342–3; dispute over prize-money, 193–4; plans to take Panama, 195–6; and supposed sighting of galleon, 210; plans to take Acapulco, 233–4; determination to capture galleon, 249, 332–3; experiments with medicines, 268; ill, 287; behaviour at Tinian, 291–2, 297; relations with East India Company, 317; at Macao, 317–31; insistence on arms drill, 335–6; behaviour during engagement with *Covadonga*, 341; in Canton River 346–58; visits Canton, 358–66

Arraucos (Indians), 98, 257–60

Bahía (Salvador), 50, 171

Balchen, Admiral Sir John, 22, 26, 33

Baldivia, *see* Valdivia

Banderas, 224

Barbados, 48

Bashee (Bashi or Batan) Islands, 311, 334, 343–4

Batavia, 320, 321, 332, 369

Bedford, 4th Duke of, 3

Bland, Col. Humphrey, 20, 23, 28

Bocca Tigris, 68, 346, 347, 348, 357, 366, 370

Botel Tobago Xima (Hung-t'on Hsü), 310–11, 334

Brazil, 33, 37, 39, 46, 51, 52, 57, 59–64, 92, 96, 101, 143, 144, 145, 170, 171, 198, 255
bread-fruit, description, 281
Brett, Lieut. Peircy, 17, 117, 168, 175–6, 179–87, 241–2, 252, 296, 306, 357
buccaneers (*see also* privateers), 120, 121, 169, 190, 197, 236, 252
Buenos Aires, 36–43 *passim*, 50, 61, 65, 66, 73–7 *passim*, 130, 149
Byron, Hon. John, 147, 148, 149

Cabite (Cavite), 218, 221, 228
Cadiz, 219, 220
California, 195, 196, 218, 221–6 *passim*
Callao, 130, 154–68 *passim*, 176, 179, 189, 217, 218, 257, 260–2
Campbell, Alexander, 147, 148, 149
Canton, 68, 254, 303, 317, 321, 348, 359–66, 370; Viceroy of, 319–28 *passim*, 348–66 *passim*
Canton (Pearl) River, 315, 317, 341–2, 343, 346, 347, 364
Cape Blanco, 69, 97, 100, 197
Cape Corrientes, 195, 208, 226
Cape Delangano (Engaño), 343
Cape Espíritu Santo, 224, 228, 249, 332, 334, 335, 341
Cape Frio, 50, 51
Cape Horn, 20, 26, 28, 36, 37, 41, 54, 64, 67, 72, 80, 84, 91–6 *passim*, 102, 107, 115, 125, 151, 158, 255, 266
Cape Noir, 90, 103, 141, 326
Cape of Good Hope, 217, 371
Cape St. Bartholomew, 82, 100, 101
Cape St. Thomas, 50
Cape San Diego, 81
Cape San Lucas, 195, 225, 226, 227

Cape Tres Montes, 147
Cape Verde Islands, 33, 34, 47
Cape Virgin Mary (Virgenes), 80–1, 100
Cartagena, 196
Cathcart, Maj.-Gen. Lord Charles, 26, 27, 33
cattle, near Buenos Aires, described, 73–6
Cavendish, Sir Thomas, 218
Charles II (King of England), 99
Cheap, Lieut. (later Capt.) David, 33, 72, 79, 141–9
Chelsea Hospital, 23, 24
Chequetan (Zihuatanejo), 205, 213, 235–50 *passim*
Cheripe, 206
Chile, 13, 21, 40, 77, 98, 110, 115, 117, 133, 151, 165, 256, 259, 263; President of, 13, 41, 258
Chiloé Island, 109, 140, 143, 147, 148, 149
China, 21, 219, 246, 253, 254, 314; Emperor of, 350
Chinese, in Philippines, 219; fishermen, 312–13, 314; general description of, 313, 326, 351–6, 366; pilots, 315, 344, 346, 347; merchants, 319–21, 358, 359, 362; visit *Centurion*, 323–6; repair *Centurion*, 328–9; junks, 369–70
Chonos Islands, 137
Clipperton, John, 180
Cochinchina, 369
Colan, 178
Cocos Island, 197, 208
Concepción, 159
Cornewall, Capt. James, 20
Coromandel, 220
Cowley, Ambrose, 97

Cozens, Henry, 144, 145

Cracherode, Lieut.-Col. Mordaunt, 30, 79, 326

Creoles (Spanish American), 256, 257, 260, 261

Cumberland Bay (Juan Fernández), 115–16

currents, effect on navigation, 51, 69, 81, 84, 89–90, 94–5, 300

Dampier, William, 236, 239, 277

Denis, Lieut. Peter, 168

diamonds, in Brazil, 60–4

dogs, near Buenos Aires, 75; on Juan Fernández, 121–2

Dutch, at Cape of Good Hope, 371

East India Company, ship, 50; in China, 317, 319–20, 321, 326, 358, 359, 361, 364–5

Elliot, William, 147, 148

Falkland Islands, 97, 98

Flint, Mr., 361, 363

Fonchiale (Funchal), 32

Formosa, 303, 310, 311, 312, 334, 344

French, in Pacific, 11, 15; at Canton, 327–8, 358

Frezier, Amedée François, 15, 55, 57, 82, 90, 97, 99–101, 262

Gallan Island (I. San Gallan), 167

Gallo Island, 198

Gerard, Mr., 137, 139–41, 151–3

Goat Island (I. Santa Clara), 115

goats, on Juan Fernández, 120–1, 151

gold, in Brazil, 59–64; in Chile, 98–9, 117

Gordon, Lieut., 297

Gordon, ———, 185

Guam, 227–8, 272, 273, 276–86 *passim*, 300, 303, 304, 308; Governor of, 278, 290–1, 304, 305

Guayaquil, 168, 187, 261

Halley, Dr. Edmund, 12, 47, 97, 100, 101, 102, 345

Hamilton, Lieut., 145, 147, 148, 149

Herriott, Charles, 326

Hoppo, 319, 322

horses, near Buenos Aires, 75–6

Hudson Bay, 171

Hughes, Lieut. John, 162, 189, 235, 248–52

Imperial River, 259

Inchin, 135, 137

'Indians', rebel on board *Asia*, 42–5; character of Spanish American, 76–7, 256–60; of Brazil, 60; near Buenos Aires, 74–5; of Chile, 98, 137–48 *passim*, 251, 258, 263; on Anson's ships, 205, 253, 298; of Mexico, 211–13, 233, 241–8; of California, 255–6; of Peru, 257–8; on Guam, 305; and their proas, 305–8; on Tinian, 277–9, 282–3, 286, 293, 302–4; on Rota, 295, 304

'invalids', *see* pensioners

Jalapay (Palapag), 339

Janson (Jen-shan), Governor of, 322–3, 327, 328

Japan, 309, 369; Japanese, 366

Java, 20

Jesuit(s), 191–2, 217–8, 219, 220, 225–6, 308, 368

Juan Fernández Island, 68, 79, 95, 97, 98, 104, 109–25 *passim*, 141, 144, 146, 150, 157–61 *passim*, 196, 255, 266, 279, 371

Keppel, Hon. Augustus Van, 182
Kidd, Capt. 'Dandy', 30, 32, 70

Ladrone Islands (Marianas), 216, 227, 269, 273, 274, 275, 303–9
lassoo, description of, 74–5
Le Maire Straits, 37, 67, 81–6 *passim*, 91, 93, 100, 103, 105, 109, 111
Leger, Louis, 247–8
Legge, Capt. the Hon. Edward, 30, 79, 174, 326–7
Lema Islands, 314–15, 344
Lezo, Admiral Don Blas de, 13
Lima, 38, 40, 160, 167, 171, 176, 177, 178, 189, 192, 257, 261, 262
Lobos Islands, 175
Lowther, Col., 23
Luconia (Luzon), 20, 217, 218–19

Macao, 68, 208, 290, 291, 303, 310–34 *passim*, 341, 350, 351, 370; Governor of, 317, 318, 319
Madeira, 27–35 *passim*, 51, 158; wines, 32, 225; Governor of, 33
Magellan (Magalhães, Fernão), 216–17, 303
Magellan, Straits of, 72, 73, 76, 80–1, 89, 90, 95, 98–104 *passim*, 143, 145, 216
magnetic variation, 12, 101, 102, 345
Maldonado Bay, 35, 36
Manila, 20–1, 214, 217–37 *passim*, 341, 344, 369
Manila galleon(s), *see also* Acapulco galleon(s), *Nuestra Señora de*

Covadonga, 11, 177, 196, 198, 206, 209–14, 219, 221–7, 229–35 *passim*, 244, 276, 304, 305, 332–44, 349, 370
Manta, 198
'marines', 26, 28, 153
Masa-Fuero (Más Afuera), 132, 150–1
Mendinuetta, Don José, 38, 41, 44, 45
Mexico, 11, 13, 196, 197, 222, 253, 254; Viceroy of, 214, 229, 235, 249
Mexico City, 233
Mitchell, Capt. Matthew, 30, 31, 32, 79, 127, 132, 161, 167, 193, 194, 198, 199, 270–2, 326
Montero, Don Gerónimo, 340, 342
Montevideo, 38, 41, 42
Morena, Mareus, 176
Murray, Capt. the Hon. George, 30, 32, 72, 79

Narborough, Sir John, 67, 71, 73, 76, 77, 98–100, 102
Nasca, 165, 166
Negroes, on Anson's ships, 205, 231, 253, 298
New Guinea, 308
Newcastle, 1st Duke of, 22
Newfoundland fishermen, on *Centurion*, 124, 133
Norris, Admiral Sir John, 22
Norris, Capt. Richard, 30, 32
Nuestra Señora de Socorro (Guamblin I.), 67, 79, 107, 141

Orellana ('Indian' chief), 13, 42–5, 77

Paita, 161, 165, 167, 176–97, 229,

235, 262; Governor of, 176, 181–2, 184

Panama, 21, 28, 165, 175, 178, 179, 185, 195–8, 260–1; Governor of, 256, 260–1

Paraguay, 41

Patagonia, 69, 71, 72–8, 95, 97, 98, 102

Patiño, Don José, 220

Paxaros Island, 274

Paz, Don Jose Sylva de (Pais, Brigadier José Silva), 55–6, 58–9, 65–6, 91–2

pearls, at Quibo I., 203

Pedro Blanco, 312–15 *passim*

Peking, 350, 359

'pensioners', on Anson's ships, 23–4, 28, 153

Pepys Island, 97

Peru, 13, 21, 36, 101, 165, 166, 174, 175, 196, 260; Viceroy of, 13, 40, 158, 159, 161, 164, 256–7, 261

Petaplan, 237, 238, 241, 242, 243, 262

Philippines, 216–17, 222, 304, 344

Pisca, 165

Piura, 177, 178

Pizarro, Admiral Don José, and his squadron in pursuit of Anson, 13, 29, 34, 35–46, 65, 70–1, 72, 80, 81, 130, 149, 153–4, 156, 158–9, 262, 263, 344

Plata Island, 198

Plate, River, 35, 38, 39, 40, 41, 42, 46, 51, 59, 69, 72, 73, 92, 93, 101, 158

Plymouth, 27

Portobelo, 195

Portsmouth, 17, 306

Portuguese, inform Spaniards of

Anson's movements, 36, 59, 65–6, 91–2; smugglers, 42, 59, 63, 66, 92; at Macao, 317–19

Prince's Island (Java), 371

prisoners, Spanish, 11, 13, 117, 118–19, 157–8, 166, 169–70, 177, 180, 185, 190–2, 198, 199, 205, 211, 234, 250–1, 253, 276–7; English, 42, 45; from *Covadonga*, 341–3, 348–51; Negro, 213–14, 229, 278; Indian, 278

privateers (*see also* buccaneers), 120, 121

prize-money, from Spanish American shipping, 157, 163, 168, 173, 194–5, 206, 272; from Paita, 189–90; dispute over, 193–4; from *Covadonga*, 340, 344

proa, description of, 305–8

Quibo Island, 197–208 *passim*

Quicaro Island, 199

Realejo, 178

Rigby, Capt., 361

Rio de Janeiro, 40, 50, 60, 93, 326

Rio de Patas, 39

Rio Grande (Brazil), 65, 145; Governor of, 60, 63

Rogers, Woodes, 97

Rota Island, 227, 282, 295, 304

St. Antonio Island, 55, 56, 57

St. Catherine's Island (Santa Catarina), 25, 33, 36, 39, 47, 51–67 *passim*, 79, 91–3, 100, 158, 172–3, 327; Governor of, 36, 52, 58–9

St. Helena, 50, 371

St. Helens, 19, 22–31 *passim*, 51

St. Jago (San Tiago), 33, 47
St. Julian (San Julián), 67, 71–80
  passim, 102, 158, 327
St. Petersburg, 172–3
Salt, Lieut. Sampson, 70
San Ignatio de Agand (Agana,
  Guam), 304
Santa Fé, Viceroy of, 13
Santiago, 40, 149; President of, 256
Saumarez, Lieut. Philip, 72, 156–7,
  165, 170, 289, 341
Saunders, Lieut. (later Captain)
  Charles, 72, 113, 133, 162, 163,
  164, 165, 166, 170, 231, 326
Saypan (Saipan) Island, 276, 285,
  303, 304
Schouten, Willem Cornelisz, 309
scurvy (*see also* sickness), 105–7,
  108, 112, 113, 114–15, 118,
  133, 153, 223, 224, 244, 255,
  266–8, 273, 275, 279, 281, 287
Sebaco Island, 199, 200
sea lion, description of, 122–4, 133,
  151
Seguataneio, *see* Chequetan
Selkirk, Alexander, 120, 124
Serigan Island, 274
Shelvocke, George, 57, 199
Ships:
  Anna, 48, 50, 64, 68, 72, 79, 84,
    89, 129, 133–4, 135–41, 146,
    151–3, 159, 161, 164
  Argyle, 21
  Arranzazu (*Nuestra Señora del
    Arranzazú*), see *Tryal Prize*
  Asia, 34–41 *passim*, 149
  Centurion, 20, 27, 30, 36, 51, 54,
    66, 70, 79, 80, 105, 106, 107,
    132, 153, 155, 162, 165, 167,
    168, 170, 174, 183, 189, 198,
    199, 230, 231, 248, 250, 253,

  265, 269, 272, 285, 288–301
    passim, 317–31, 334, 338–51,
    366, 369, 371
  Dragon, 27, 31
  Duchess, 97, 120, 255
  Duke, 97, 120, 255
  Esperanza, 35, 37, 38, 41, 46
  Gloucester, 22, 30, 32, 50, 68, 70,
    80, 81, 87, 88, 126–9, 131–2,
    153, 159, 161, 162, 165, 175,
    193–5, 197, 198, 199, 206, 209,
    210, 230, 231, 236, 246, 248,
    250, 253, 266, 268–73
  Guipúscoa, 35, 37, 38–40, 46
  Haeslingfield, 364
  Hermiona, 35, 37, 40, 46
  Industry, 48
  Jesús Nazareno, 206
  Lark, 30
  Nuestra Señora de Carmin, 176–7,
    189, 209, 231, 235, 236, 246,
    248
  Nuestra Señora de Covadonga, 338–
    44, 346, 349, 357, 366
  Nuestra Señora del Monte Carmelo,
    156–61, 162, 163, 167, 189,
    196, 209, 210, 230, 231, 235,
    236, 246, 248
  Pearl, 21, 29, 30, 31, 32, 36, 68,
    72, 83, 90, 141, 158, 326–7
  Prince Frederick, 27
  Rye, 31
  St. *Albans*, 27, 31
  Salisbury, 23
  San Estévan, 35, 38, 41, 46
  Santa Teresa de Jesús, 168–9, 189,
    191, 197
  Severn, 21, 30, 70, 90, 141, 174,
    326–7
  Solidad, 189, 197
  South-Sea Castle, 31

Tryal, 21, 30, 32, 50, 64–5, 66, 68, 71, 72, 79, 80, 83, 87, 88, 113, 125, 126, 132, 133, 134, 150, 153, 155, 159, 160, 161, 162–5, 166

Tryal Prize, 162–3, 164, 165, 189, 210, 230, 231, 236, 246, 248

Wager, 21, 25, 30, 32, 50, 71, 72, 84, 88, 89, 100, 141–9, 155

Winchester, 27, 30, 31

sickness (*see also* scurvy), 37–9, 49, 51–2, 54, 57, 66, 105–10 *passim*, 111, 112, 114–15, 128–9, 153, 327

silver (*see also* prize-money), 59, 60, 163, 220, 226–7, 344

Sonsonate, 177, 178

South Sea Company, 24, 28

Spaniards, their colonies on outbreak of war, 20–1, 218, 259–62; criticism of their seamanship, 36, 219, 223; their treatment of Indians, 42, 282–3, 305; their treatment of prisoners, 42, 44, 248, 291; inaccuracy of their accounts, 138–9; their attitude towards Anson, 190–2

Spithead, 26, 32, 37

Staten Land, 38, 82, 84, 98

Sunda, Strait of, 371

Tassell, Hubert, 326

Terra del Fuego, 81–2, 89, 90, 91, 94, 95, 98, 100, 103, 107

Tinian, 276–310, 371

trade winds, 47–8, 51, 209, 217–18, 223, 265, 269

Tres Marias Islands, 208

Truxillo (Trujillo), 180

turtles, description of, 204–5

Typa (Taipa), 318, 329, 331

Urrunaga, Bartolomé, 168

Valdivia, 79, 91, 99, 109, 141, 143, 255, 259, 263

Valencia, 220

Valero, Marquis de, 225

Valparaiso, 155, 157, 161–7 *passim*

Vanderas, *see* Banderas

Vernon, Vice-Admiral Edward, 195

Wager, Sir Charles, 20, 21–2, 23

Wager's Island (Isla Wager), 146, 147

Walter, Revd. Richard, 3; first-person references in text, 109, 243, 278, 288, 326

Wampa (Whampoa), 358

'Ward's pill', 268

Williams, John, 176

Wood, John, 102

Zamorra, Manuel, 157

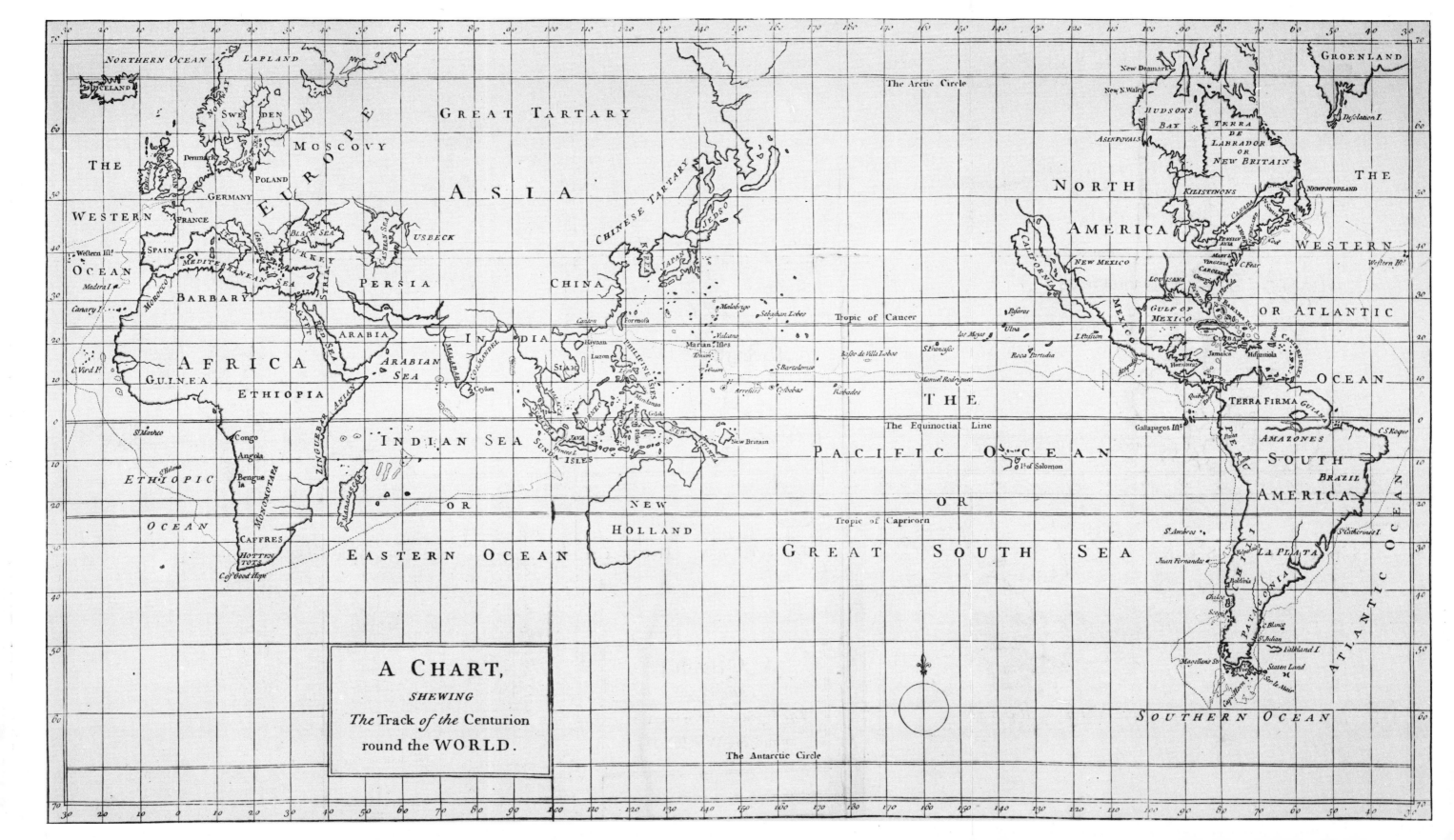

NORTHERN OCEAN   LAPLAND

GROENLAND

GREAT TARTARY

The Arctic Circle

New Denmark

New N. Wales

Desolation I.

SWEDEN   MOSCOVY

HUDSONS BAY   TERRA DE LABRADOR OR NEW BRITAIN

ASINIPOVALS

ASIA

Denmark

POLAND

GERMANY   EUROPE

NORTH   AMERICA

KILISTINONS

Newfoundland

THE   WESTERN   OCEAN

FRANCE

BLACK SEA   CASPIAN SEA   USBECK

CHINESE TARTARY

JEDSO   KOREA   JAPAN

PENSYLVANIA

THE   WESTERN

SPAIN   TURKEY   SYRIA

MEDITERRANEAN SEA

PERSIA

CHINA

CALIFORNIA   NEW MEXICO

MARYL.   VIRGINIA   CAROLE.   C. Fear

Western Ifs.

Madera I.

BARBARY

ARABIA

Canton   Formosa

Malabrigo   Sebastian Lobes

Tropic of Cancer

los Myrtes   Ulva

Roca Partida

LOUISIANA

GULF OF MEXICO

OR ATLANTIC

Canary I.

C. Verd I.

MOROCCO

RED SEA   ARABIAN SEA

INDIA

Hainan   Luzon

MALABAR   COROMANDEL

Vilduno

Marian Ifles

Tonam   Guam   S. Francesco

Bajos de Villa Lobos

Pisares

L. Passion

CUBA   Hispaniola

Jamaica

AFRICA   GUINEA   ETHIOPIA

SIAM

Ceylon

S. Bartolomeo

Manuel Rodriguez

Honduras

OCEAN

CARIBEE ISLES

St. Matheo

Arrecifes   Cesoobas   Kobados

THE

Quibo

TERRA FIRMA   GUIANA

Congo

INDIAN SEA

MALACCA   MOLUCCAS   NEW GUINEA

The Equinoctial Line

Gallapagos Ifls.

Puna

AMAZONES

Angola

SUNDA ISLES   JAVA   Francois I.   Goloh

New Britain

PACIFIC OCEAN

Ifl. of Solomon

PERU   SOUTH

BRAZIL

S. Helena

Bengue la

MONOMOTAPA

MADAGASCAR

OR

NEW

OR

AMERICA

ETHIOPIC   OCEAN

ZINGUEBER   ANJAN

CAFFRES

HOLLAND

Tropic of Capricorn

S. Ambros

LA PLATA

S. Catherine I.

HOTTENTOTS

EASTERN OCEAN

GREAT   SOUTH   SEA

Juan Fernandez

CHILI

Baldivia

C. of Good Hope

Valparaiso

Chiloe

Seco

S. Julian

Falkland I.

ATLANTIC OCEAN

PATAGONIA

C. Blanco

Magellans Str.

Staten Land

Str. le Mair

SOUTHERN OCEAN

A CHART,

SHEWING

The Track of the Centurion
round the WORLD.

The Antarctic Circle